Gestalt der Bewegung

Annett Zinsmeister (Hg.)

AF411640

jovis

Content

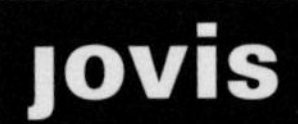

Figure of Motion
Annett Zinsmeister (Ed.)

edition weissenhof

Inhalt

Annett Zinsmeister has been a professor of visual arts and experimental **design at the State Academy of Fine Arts Stuttgart** since 2007, and direc**tor of the Weißenhof Institute** since 2009. From 2003–07 she was a profes**sor at the Kunsthochschule Berlin and the Bergische University Wuppertal;** **among others, she also taught at the Bauhaus University Weimar.** Specialist **subjects: art, architecture, cultural and media science.** Publications **include:** *update! 90 years of bauhaus – what now?* (ed., 2010), *Jour Fixe.* *Zeitgenössische Positionen in Architektur, Design, Kunst* (co-ed. with **T. Wallisser, 2010),** *City + War. A Trip to Sarajevo* (2008), *welt[stadt]raum.* *Mediale Inszenierungen* (ed., 2007), *constructing utopia. Konstruktionen* *künstlicher Welten* (ed., 2005), *Plattenbau oder die Kunst, Utopie im Bau-* *kasten zu warten* (ed., 2002).

Annett Zinsmeister
Gestalt der Bewegung

Annett Zinsmeister ist seit 2007 Professorin für Gestaltung und Experimen-
telles Entwerfen an der Staatlichen Akademie der Bildenden Künste Stuttgart
und seit 2009 Leiterin des Weißenhof-Instituts. 2003–07 war sie Professorin
an der Kunsthochschule Berlin und der Bergischen Universität Wuppertal,
zuvor u. a. Lehre an der Bauhaus-Universität Weimar. Tätigkeitsschwer-
punkte: Kunst, Architektur, Kultur- und Medienwissenschaft. Publikationen
u. a.: *update! 90 years of bauhaus – what now?* (Hg., 2010), *Jour Fixe. Zeitgenössische Positionen in Architektur, Kunst, Design* (Hg. mit T. Wallisser 2010),
City + war. A trip to Sarajevo (2008), *welt[stadt]raum. Mediale Inszenierungen* (Hg., 2007), *constructing utopia. Konstruktionen künstlicher Welten* (Hg.,
2005), *Plattenbau oder die Kunst Utopie im Baukasten zu warten* (Hg., 2002).

Motion is both elementary and fleeting; it is the fundamental precondition to our survival and our civilisation. Motion is the functional basis to our discovery, measurement and exploration of the world that we live in. Elucidating and calculating motion are central issues within our culture, which is based on a history of dynamics and acceleration. The idea of a cosmic constellation and changes in our image of the world, for example, result from observation and explanation of the planets and stars and calculation of their motions.[1] Aristotle, the founder of physics and other sciences, understood motion as the diversity of changing forms; he distinguished four types of motion and triggers indicating the complex, wide-ranging possibilities of observing motion and showing the widely differing branches of science and discourse which it can be handled.[2] In order to restrict the topic of *motion,* this volume will focus on just one of the four types of motion according to Aristotle, on motion *in space.* The following essays, therefore, will elaborate on the observation, presentation, and design of motion in space from very different perspectives and disciplines. In this context, it is neither possible nor our intention to present the complete subject, *The Figure of Motion,* on the basis of our occidental cultural history. Far more, this publication represents an attempt to highlight lines of development and points of intersection between different disciplines and introduce these into the wider thematic spectrum with reference to their historic roots. The design of motion is preceded by perception of motion and an ability to grasp and depict it. In this introduction, therefore, I will also take a look at developments in depiction and design methods from the mechanical to the digital, as it is here that new foundations are presently being constructed for a creative investigation into forms of motion.[3]

"Things that are in motion were set into motion by something else, the mover."
– Aristotles

The renaissance of antiquity meant that the fifteenth and sixteenth centuries provided many fresh insights concerning the scientific investigation of motion. Thanks to the invention of the printing press and typesetting with movable letters, the texts of antiquity were distributed more widely, creating the foundation for new explanatory models: the first systematic representation of ancient mathematical astronomy, which developed key importance in the mediaeval period in particular, went into print in 1496. It had been written in the second century A.D. by Claudius Ptolemy. Ptolemy had developed a mathematical-geometrical model of the planetary motions in his *Megalè syntaxis mathematiké* and in his later thesis *Hypotheses planetarum* he attempted to derive mechanics and physics of the heavens from them. The so-called *Copernican Change* in 1514 meant that the earth finally lost its place at the dynamic centre of the universe, forcing scientists to undertake fresh observations and formulate a new understanding of the cosmos. At this time Leonardo da Vinci, more than

Bewegung ist elementar und flüchtig zugleich, sie ist grundlegende Voraussetzung für unser Überleben und unsere Zivilisation. Bewegung ist die funktionale Basis der Entdeckung, Vermessung und Erschließung unserer Lebenswelt. Bewegung zu erklären und zu berechnen sind zentrale Fragestellungen unserer Kultur, der eine Geschichte der Dynamik und Beschleunigung zugrunde liegt. Die Vorstellung eines kosmischen Gefüges und der Wandel unseres Weltbildes sind zum Beispiel der Beobachtung, Erklärung und Berechnung der Organisation von Bewegungen von Himmelskörpern geschuldet.[1] Aristoteles, der Begründer der Physik und anderer Wissenschaften, verstand Bewegung als eine Formenvielfalt von Veränderungen und unterschied vier Arten von Bewegung und Ursachen, die Hinweise geben, wie komplex und breit gefächert das Thema der Bewegung betrachtet und in welch unterschiedlichen Wissenschaftszweigen und Diskursfeldern es verhandelt werden kann.[2] Um das Thema einzugrenzen, wird der vorliegende Band lediglich eine der vier Bewegungsarten nach Aristoteles fokussieren: die *örtliche* Bewegung. Demnach werden die folgenden Beiträge die Beobachtung, die Darstellung und die Gestaltung von Bewegung im Raum aus sehr unterschiedlichen Blickwinkeln und Disziplinen heraus erörtern. Es ist in diesem Kontext weder möglich noch beabsichtigt, das Thema *Gestalt der Bewegung* anhand unserer abendländischen Kulturgeschichte umfassend zu erörtern. Der vorliegende Band ist vielmehr ein Versuch, Entwicklungslinien und Kreuzungspunkte zwischen unterschiedlichen Disziplinen aufzuzeigen und mit dem Verweis auf historische Wurzeln in die breitgefächerte Thematik einzuführen. Der Gestaltung von Bewegung geht die Wahrnehmung von Bewegung und die Fähigkeit, Bewegung zu erfassen und darzustellen voraus. In der Einführung werde ich demzufolge auch Entwicklungen von mechanischen zu digitalen Darstellungsmöglichkeiten und Gestaltungstechniken in den Blick nehmen, da sich hier aktuell neue Grundlagen für die kreative Auseinandersetzung mit Bewegungsformen bilden.[3]

„Alles was sich bewegt, wird von einem Beweger bewegt." – Aristoteles

Das 15. und 16. Jahrhundert gebar mit der Wiedergeburt der Antike eine Vielzahl an neuen Erkenntnissen hinsichtlich der wissenschaftlichen Beschäftigung mit Bewegung. Dank der Erfindung der Druckerpresse und des Schriftsatzes mit beweglichen Lettern fanden die antiken Schriften Verbreitung und schufen die Grundlagen zu neuen Erklärungsmodellen: 1496 ging die erste systematische Darstellung der antiken mathematischen Astronomie, die insbesondere im Mittelalter an Bedeutung gewann, in Druck. Sie war von Claudius Ptolemaeus im zweiten Jahrhundert n. Chr. verfasst worden. Ptolemaeus hatte in seiner *Megalè syntaxis mathematiké* ein mathematisch-geometrisches Modell der Bewegungen der Himmelskörper entwickelt und in der späteren Schrift *Hypotheses planetarum* versucht, daraus eine Himmelsmechanik und -physik zu entwerfen. Mit der sogenannten *Kopernikanischen Wende* 1514 wurde schließlich die Erde aus dem

any other artist, was concerned with depicting and conveying motion: numerous studies on the motion of water and cloud formations evidence his search for forms of portrayal (*1* p. 16). And his invention of mechanical devices—whether hydraulic water pumps, martial equipment for warmongering or flying apparatus–provide evidence of an extremely diverse, heterogeneous interest in motion and its scientific, economic, and creative potentials. In 1590, Galileo Galilei developed the *laws of free fall* following experiments dropping balls from the Leaning Tower of Pisa. Meanwhile theologian, mathematician, and astronomer Johannes Kepler set about not only observing, describing, and predicting planetary motions, but also calculating their paths and researching into the reasons behind them.[4] Isaac Newton combined Galilei's and Kepler's theories of motion into a unified theory of gravitation and published the *three principles of motion* in his *Philosophiae Naturalis Principia Mathematica* in 1687. This text represented the foundation of mechanics up to and even into the twentieth century.[5] Numerous branches of physics developed from investigations of this kind and their explanations of motion; for instance *mechanics* and its branch *kinematics,* the geometrical description of motion in space; *dynamics,* which can be divided into subcategories such as *kinetics* and *statics;* and also *aerodynamics, thermodynamics,* etc. Physics has provided us with formalised explanatory models to calculate and depict motion and consequently, with a large number of technical achievements that, over the past 300 years, have radically transformed the world in which we live and work.

SYSTEMS FOR THE NOTATION OF MOTION—Artistic practice (in fine, applied, or performing art) is shaped by differing techniques that make use of specific instruments. The history of the techniques of representation, like those in architecture and dance, for example, could be described as the search for a universal aesthetic programme: unexpected parallels and reciprocal interplay are revealed in a genealogical observation of architecture as a notational system of construction and planning elements on the one hand, and choreography as a notational system of motion on the other; as programmes, architecture, and choreography appear to have experienced media-technical fulfilment with the development of the computer.[6] Programmes do not automatically profit aesthetics, but they have always been aesthetic tools— as the theory of, or the search for principles and derivative laws about construction and composition, in the sense of beauty and harmony. Rules of proportion and dimensions help us to apply an objectifiable mathematical principle of order to our practical design of the world. This types of theoretical rules, which shape our occidental design practice, already existed in ancient Egypt, and we are aware of corresponding writings dating from antiquity. They played a part in the aesthetic construction and representation of ideal and real architecture, as well as the concept of an ideal man. The Canon of Polyclitus, conceived as a theory of proportion for artists, divides for example, the human body into aspect and

dynamischen Zentrum des Universums gerissen und zwang zu einer neuen Betrachtung und einem neuen Verständnis des Kosmos. Leonardo da Vinci setzte sich zu dieser Zeit wie wohl kaum ein anderer Künstler mit der Darstellung und Übertragung von Bewegung auseinander: Zahlreiche Studien zur Bewegung von Wasser und Wolkenformationen belegen seine Suche nach Darstellungsformen. (1 S. 16) Und seine Erfindungen mechanischer Apparaturen – seien es hydraulische Wasserpumpen, martialisches Kriegsgerät oder Flugapparaturen – geben Zeugnis von einer überaus vielseitigen und komplexen Beschäftigung mit Bewegung und ihrem wissenschaftlichen, ökonomischen sowie gestalterischen Potenzial. 1590 entwickelte Galileo Galilei aus seinen Experimenten mit fallenden Kugeln vom schiefen Turm in Pisa die *Gesetze des freien Falls*. Der Theologe, Mathematiker und Astronom Johannes Kepler machte es sich unterdessen zur Aufgabe, die Bewegung der Himmelskörper nicht nur zu beobachten, zu beschreiben und vorauszusagen, sondern sie darüber hinaus zu berechnen und nach ihrer Ursache zu forschen.[4] Isaac Newton vereinte die Bewegungstheorien Galileis und Keplers in einer einheitlichen Theorie zur Gravitation und veröffentlichte 1687 die *drei Grundgesetze der Bewegung* in seiner *Philosophiae Naturalis Principia Mathematica,* die eine Grundlage der Mechanik bis ins 20. Jahrhundert bildet.[5] Aus derlei Untersuchungen und Erklärungen von Bewegung entwickelten sich zahlreiche Teilgebiete der Physik; beispielsweise die *Mechanik* mit dem Bereich der *Kinematik* als geometrische Beschreibung von Bewegung im Raum, die *Dynamik,* die sich wiederum in Subkategorien wie *Kinetik* und *Statik* unterteilen lässt, außerdem die *Aerodynamik, Thermodynamik,* etc. Der Physik verdanken wir formalisierte Erklärungsmodelle zur Berechnung und Darstellung von Bewegung und in der Folge eine Vielzahl an technischen Errungenschaften, welche unsere Arbeits- und Lebenswelt in den vergangenen 300 Jahren radikal veränderten.

AUFSCHREIBESYSTEME VON BEWEGUNG—Auch die künstlerische Praxis (ob in der bildenden, der angewandten oder der darstellenden Kunst) ist von unterschiedlichen Techniken geprägt, die sich spezifischer Instrumente bedienen. Die Geschichte der Darstellungstechniken, wie zum Beispiel in der Architektur und im Tanz, könnte als eine Suche nach einem universalen ästhetischen Programm beschrieben werden: In einer genealogischen Betrachtung von Architektur als Aufschreibesystem von Konstruktions- und Planungselementen einerseits, und Choreografie als Aufschreibesystem von Bewegung andererseits, zeigen sich unerwartete Parallelen und Wechselwirkungen; Architektur und Choreografie als Programm haben mit der Entwicklung des Computers scheinbar ihre medientechnische Erfüllung gefunden.[6] Programme dienen nicht zwangsläufig ästhetischen Überlegungen, sind aber seit jeher Werkzeuge der Ästhetik als einer Lehre von oder Suche nach Grundlagen und abgeleiteten Gesetzmäßigkeiten zur Konstruktion und Komposition im Sinne von Schönheit und Harmonie. Proportions- und

distance ratios as an aesthetic, simultaneously universal system of reference. The division of a whole into units—*modulus*—gained significance when measuring spaces and bodies in search of ideal proportions, as in the anthropometry of antiquity and the Renaissance, for instance. As a term for a unit of measurement, the word module points to its origins in mathematics. The conceivable division and recombination of modular systems has had a lasting influence on the design of space and motion, as will be seen later on.

An extremely diverse spectrum of new, precise techniques of reproduction and translation emerged in the Renaissance; the production and use of drawings as a medium to represent, record, and pass on the design of space and information about space acquired far-reaching importance for the first time. In order to study and reconstruct the cultural heritage of antiquity, not only ancient architectural monuments were fixed in writing, images, and numbers from the middle of the fifteenth century, but also traditional social dances. These collections of data served the purposes of recording and transmitting, teaching, and deeper studies of proportion, composition, and motion. Revolutionary technical innovations in methods of portrayal and reproduction prompted the production of many tracts and pattern sheets, which were quickly disseminated. Only since this period have architecture and the art of motion in dance been communicated by means of pictorial illustration.[7]

In 1700, the first consistent programme of visualisation in the history of choreography became widely known with the appearance of the *Beauchamp-Feuillet notation,* which Pierre Beauchamp developed in the sixteen-eighties and Raoul-Roger Feuillet set down in writing: the *Beauchamp-Feuillet notation*[8] stands for a record of motion using specially devised symbols, which—as in the grammar of the German language—comprise morphemes, that is, the smallest of semantic units. When combined, they project meandering paths or complex outlines in an imaginary space (*2* p. 16). The invention of a code, i.e., an abstract and thus international language of dance, means that the art of motion can be taught and learnt independent of time and space, and independent of an author. Indeed, it can be practised and performed all over the world. I will come back to this in the section *Motion Space.*

***THE MOVING IMAGE — MOTION IN THE IMAGE*—The displacement of classical mechanics and the breakthrough of modern physics in the first half of the nineteenth century led to the conception of new theories of light, e.g., by Augustin Jean Fresnel. This French physicist and engineer noted that light consists of transversal oscillations and on the basis of his research into visual effects such as after-images and the stroboscopic effect, he demonstrated that a rapid sequence of sensory impressions may produce the effect of overlapping due to the slowness of the eye. Only four years later, in 1825, the English doctor and lexicographer Peter Mark Roget pointed out that our view of the spokes of train wheels through the slats of a garden fence creates the illusion that the wheels are**

Maßregeln dienen der Anwendung eines objektivierbaren mathematischen Ordnungsprinzips auf ein praktisches Gestalten von Welt. Derlei theoretische Regeln, die unsere abendländische gestalterische Praxis prägen, gab es bereits im alten Ägypten, und schon seit der Antike sind entsprechende Schriften bekannt. Sie fanden Eingang in die ästhetische Konstruktion und Darstellung von idealer und realer Architektur sowie in die Konstruktion eines idealen Menschentypus. Der Kanon des Polyklet, als Proportionslehre für Künstler konzipiert, zergliederte beispielsweise den menschlichen Körper als ästhetisches und zugleich universales Bezugssystem in Längen- und Abstandsverhältnisse. Die Unterteilung eines Ganzen in Einheiten – *Modulus* – gewann bei Vermessungen von Räumen und Körpern auf der Suche nach idealen Proportionen, wie zum Beispiel in der Anthropometrie, in der Antike und erneut in der Renaissance an Bedeutung und verwies als Begriff für eine Maßeinheit auf seine Herkunft aus der Mathematik. Die mögliche Zerteilung und Re-Kombination von modularen Systemen hatte einen nachhaltigen Einfluss auf die Gestaltung von Raum und Bewegung, wie sich später noch zeigen wird.

Mit der Renaissance entstand ein überaus vielgestaltiges Spektrum an neuen und präzisen Techniken von Abbild- und Übertragungsverfahren; die Produktion und Verwendung von Zeichnungen als Medium zur Darstellung, Speicherung und Überlieferung von Raumgestalt und Rauminformation gewann erstmalig an weitreichender Bedeutung. Um das Kulturerbe des Altertums studieren und rekonstruieren zu können, wurden ab Mitte des 15. **Jahrhunderts nicht nur antike Baudenkmäler in Schrift, Bild und Zahl fixiert, sondern auch tradierte Gesellschaftstänze. Diese Datensammlungen dienten der Speicherung und Überlieferung, der Lehre und weiterführenden Proportions-, Kompositions- und Bewegungsstudien. Die technischen Innovationen in der Darstellungs- und Reproduktionstechnik förderten die Entstehung zahlreicher Traktate und Musterblätter, die schnell Verbreitung fanden. Erst seit dieser Zeit werden Architektur und die Kunst der Bewegung im Tanz mittels bildhafter Darstellung kommuniziert.**[7]

1700 fand mit dem Erscheinen der *Beauchamp-Feuillet Notation*[8] das erste konsequente Visualisierungsprogramm in der Geschichte der Choreografie Verbreitung; sie steht für eine Bewegungsschrift mit eigens entwickelten Zeichen, die sich wie die Grammatik der deutschen Sprache aus Morphemen, das heißt kleinsten semantischen Einheiten, zusammensetzt und die in der Aneinanderreihung verschlungene Pfade bzw. komplexe Grundrisse in einen imaginären Raum projiziert. (2 S. 16). Mit der Erfindung eines Codes, also einer abstrakten und somit internationalen Sprache für den Tanz, wird die Kunst der Bewegung unabhängig von Zeit und Raum lehr- und lernbar und kann, unabhängig von einem Autor oder Urheber, überall in der Welt zur Aus- und Aufführung gebracht werden. Daran werde ich im Abschnitt *Bewegung Raum* nochmals anschließen.

standing still or even turning backwards. Such personal observations and analyses of industrial forms of motion led to the idea of creating illusions of motion with the help of a grid. Belgian physicist Joseph Antoine Ferdinand Plateau, who also investigated after-images in experiments and ultimately lost his sight by looking directly at the sun, summed up his insights in the *Theory of the persistence of the visual impression* (1829): "If several objects, progressively different in form and position, are presented to the eye for very short intervals and sufficiently close together, the impressions they make upon the retina will join together without being confused, and one will believe he is seeing a single object gradually changing form and position." From this insight, Plateau began to develop an optical illusion: the so-called *phenakistoscope,* a disk subdivided into sixteen alternating slits and images, which could be purchased in London from 1833 (*3* p. 16). Such an apparatus was regarded as a popular means of entertainment and was used privately or at public fairs, for example. It is not terribly surprising, therefore, that Austrian mathematician Simon Stampfer invented the stroboscope only one year later, and that a large number of other technical devices appeared as well. In the course of the century, they taught images to walk, as prerequisites to the development of the *zoopraxiscope* and *cinematography.* However, it was not until the invention of perforated celluloid film reels that an almost smooth, continuous running of the film strip was possible during recording and projecting. The human eye was deceived optically by the rhythm of sequences comprising separate images (twenty-four images per second). Patterns of motion previously assembled from single images, and therefore jerky, became more fluid and seemed to reconstruct a real situation perfectly. One anecdote still told today, although unconfirmed by research evidence, describes the Parisian audience's reaction to one of the first film projections by the Lumière brothers in 1895: *L'Arrivée du train a la Ciotat,* a black and white film lasting about one minute, showed the arrival of a steam engine in a station, and according to legend, prompted the audience to flee from the scene in panic. Today, due to our familiarisation with increasingly perfect illusionary techniques, it is no longer possible to imagine such an audience reaction.

Interestingly, images were first set in motion before it became possible to reproduce motion without blurring using the medium of photography. Until the introduction of highly-sensitive dry plates in the eighteen-seventies, long exposure times compelled photographers to choose static subjects like architectural or landscape motifs, or alternatively condemned human subjects to seemingly endless, immobile waiting; in the very early days of photography they had to keep still for up to one hour. It was only over the decades that exposure times could be shortened to a few seconds.[9] Until then, animals could only appear as motifs either asleep or dead, as even the slightest motion would have led inevitably to unwanted blurring.

BILD IN BEWEGUNG – BEWEGUNG IM BILD—Mit der Ablösung der klassischen Mechanik und dem Durchbruch der modernen Physik in der ersten Hälfte des 19. Jahrhunderts entstanden neue Lichttheorien, beispielsweise von Augustin Jean Fresnel. Der französische Physiker und Ingenieur erkannte, dass Licht aus transversalen Schwingungen besteht und belegte anhand seiner Untersuchungen zu visuellen Effekten wie der Nachbildforschung und des Stroboskopeffektes, dass aufgrund der Trägheit des Auges eine rasche Aufeinanderfolge von Sinneseindrücken Überblendungen bewirken kann. Nur vier Jahre später, 1825, wies der englische Arzt und Lexikograf Peter Mark Roget darauf hin, dass der Blick auf die Speichen von Eisenbahnrädern durch die Latten eines Gartenzaunes die Illusion stillstehender bzw. rückwärtsdrehender Räder erzeugt. Aus derlei Selbstbeobachtungen und Analysen industrieller Bewegungsformen entstand erstmals die Idee der Erzeugung von Bewegungsillusionen mithilfe eines Rasters. Der belgische Physiker Joseph Antoine Ferdinand Plateau, der sich ebenfalls mit Nachbildexperimenten beschäftigte und durch den Blick in die Sonne schlussendlich sein Augenlicht verlor, brachte seine Erkenntnisse in seiner *Theorie von der Beharrlichkeit des Seheindrucks* (1829) auf den Punkt: „Wenn dem Auge rasch nacheinander mehrere Gegenstände von stufenweise sich verändernder Form und Position dargeboten werden, verschmelzen die hervorgerufenen Eindrücke zu einem unverworrenen Bild, vorausgesetzt, die Gegenstände befinden sich nah genug beisammen. Es entsteht dann der Anschein, ein einziger Gegenstand verändere nach und nach seine Form und Position." Diese Erkenntnis nahm Plateau zum Anlass, ein Gerät zur Augentäuschung zu entwickeln: das sog. *Phenakistoskop,* eine 16-fach in Schlitz und Bild unterteilte Scheibe, die ab 1833 in London käuflich zu erwerben war. (*3* S. 16) Derlei Apparaturen galten als publikumswirksame Unterhaltungsmedien und kamen im Privaten oder in der Öffentlichkeit von Jahrmärkten zum Einsatz. So ist es nicht verwunderlich, dass nur ein Jahr später der österreichische Mathematiker Simon Stampfer das Stroboskop erfand, außerdem eine Vielzahl weiterer technischer Gerätschaften auftauchten, die im Laufe des Jahrhunderts Bildern das Laufen lehrten und Voraussetzung waren für die Entwicklung des *Zoopraxiskops* und der *Kinematografie.* Allerdings wurde erst durch die Erfindung perforierter Zelluloidfilmrollen ein nahezu reibungsloser und kontinuierlicher Lauf des Filmstreifens bei der Aufnahme und der Vorführung möglich. Mit der Taktung von Einzelbildfolgen (24 Bilder pro Sekunde) wurde das menschliche Auge optisch getäuscht. Die zuvor aus einzelnen Bildern zusammen montierten, ruckartigen Bewegungsabläufe wurden fließender und schienen eine reale Situation perfekt wiederzugeben. Eine bis heute kursierende, jedoch in der Forschung bis dato unbelegte Anekdote beschreibt die Zuschauerreaktion auf eine der ersten Filmvorführungen der Gebrüder Lumière 1895 in Paris: Der ca. einminütige Schwarzweißfilm *L'Arrivée du train à la Ciotat,* der das Einfahren einer Dampflok in einen Bahnhof wiedergab, ließ das Publikum – so die Legende – in Panik aus dem Veranstaltungsraum flüchten. Aus heutiger Sicht,

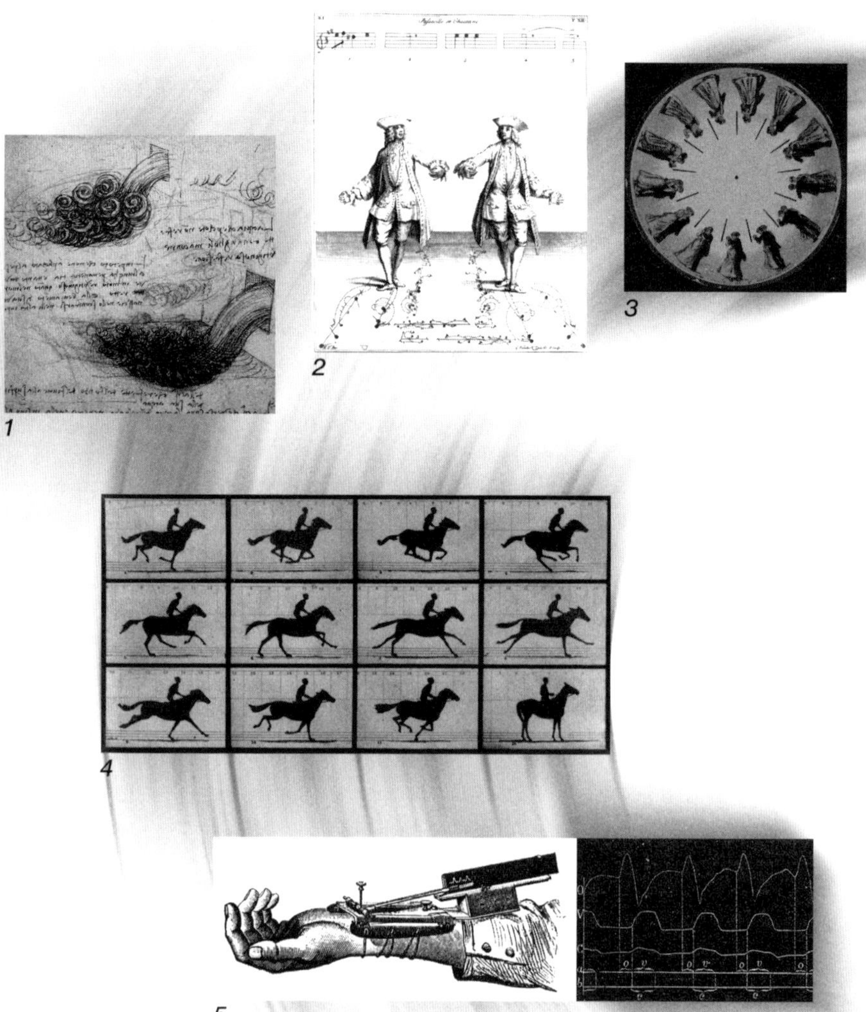

1 Leonardo da Vinci: *Sheet with water studies*, detail, around 1508–10 — 2 John Weaver: *A Collection of Ball Dances*, 1706/1985 — 3 Eadweard Muybridge: *Phenakistiscope — A Couple Waltzing No. 35*, 1893 — 4 Eadweard Muybridge: *The Horse in Motion*, Palo Alto racing course, 1878 — 5 Étienne-Jules Marey: *left Sphygmograph*, directly fixed to the wrist for recording artery pulse waves, around 1860; *right Pulse waves*, recorded intracardiac-sphygmographically with chronological reference, 1861–1863 — 6 Étienne-Jules Marey: *left Runner, with device for measuring different pace rates*, from *Animal Mechanism*, 1874; *middle Air panthograph*, from *La Méthode Graphique*, 1878; *right Sequenced drawing of a seagull's wingbeat from all perspectives*, 1887 — 7 Étienne-Jules Marey: *Chronophotographic Gun*, woodcarving, 1882 — 8 Étienne-Jules Marey: *Flight of a Seagull*, 1886

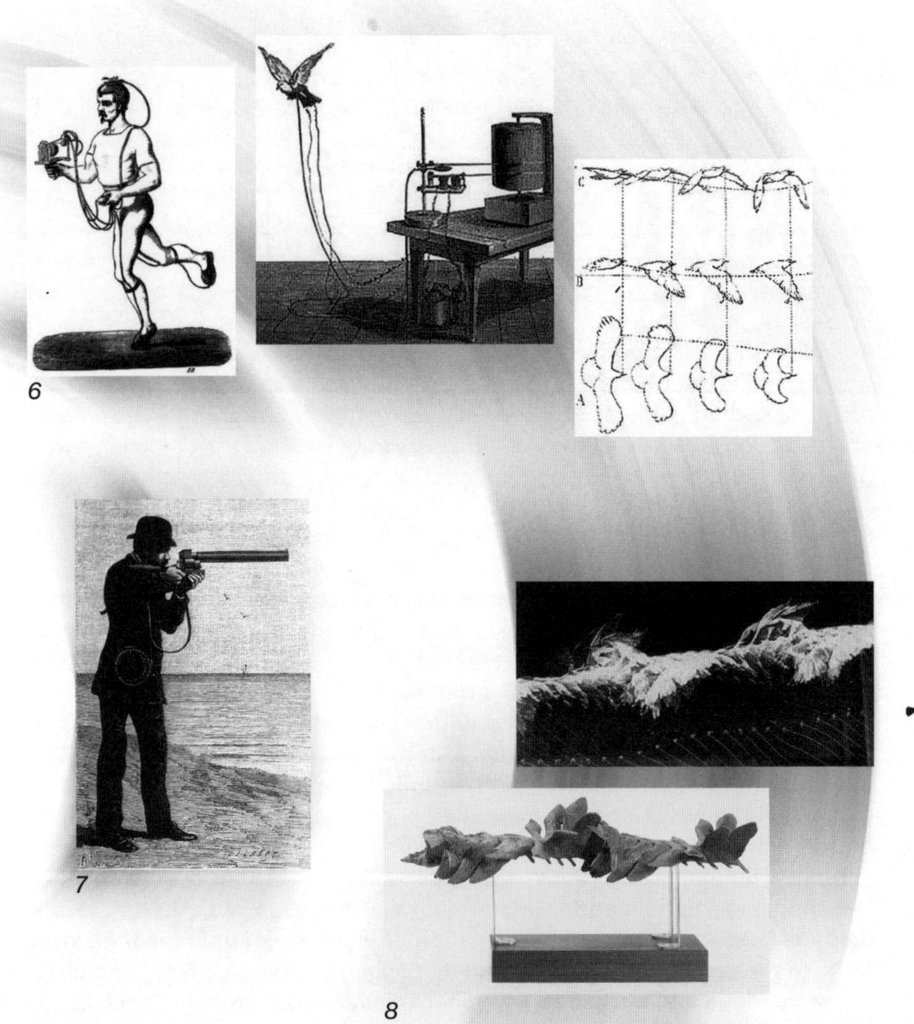

1 Leonardo da Vinci: *Blatt mit Wasserstudien,* Ausschnitt, um 1508–10 — *2* John Weaver: *Eine Sammlung von Balltänzen,* 1706/1985 — *3* Eadweard Muybridge: *Phenakistiskop – Ein Paar im Walzertakt No. 35,* 1893 — *4* Eadweard Muybridge: *Ein galoppierendes Pferd,* Rennbahn Palo Alto, 1878 — *5* Étienne-Jules Marey: *links* Sphygmograf zur direkten arteriellen Pulskurvenschreibung am Handgelenk, um 1860; *rechts* Pulsdruckkurven mit chronologischer Zuordnung der Herzaktionsphasen, 1861–1863 — *6* Étienne-Jules Marey: *links* Läufer mit Gerät zur Messung unterschiedlicher Geschwindigkeiten aus: *La Méthode Graphique,* 1878; *Mitte* Air panthograph, aus: *La Méthode Graphique,* 1878; *rechts* Étienne-Jules Marey: *Zeichnung der Flügelbewegung einer Möwe,* 1887 — *7* Étienne-Jules Marey: *Fotografisches Gewehr,* Holzschnitt, 1882 — *8* Étienne-Jules Marey: *Flug einer Seemöwe,* 1886

So it is no wonder that Eadweard Muybridge, who celebrated his ninth birthday in photography's "year of birth" in 1839 and was later regarded as one of the best landscape photographers in California, did not move on to animal photography until 1872.[10] He was commissioned by Leland Stanford, former governor of California and railway tycoon, to document the correct positions of a horse's legs at a fast trot and when galloping. Muybridge conceived a linear set of twelve cameras (later twenty-four and then thirty-six) along the racetrack in Palo Alto and set up contact wires to trigger these cameras as the horse galloped past. With the help of accelerated replay, using the *zoopraxiscope* he had developed, it was then possible not only to record but also to replay in sharp, detailed images a pattern of motion that was so fast. This apparatus was a disk-shaped stroboscope, which projected the individual images onto a wall one after another with the help of a light source.[11] From then onwards, this innovative reproductive process enabled people to create visual documentation of the patterns of motion made by animals and people, cutting them into sequences and so creating the optical basis for more precise observations. His visual studies and so-called *chronophotographs* appeared in 1887 in the publication *Animal locomotion,* as well as in a revised edition entitled *The Human Figure in Motion* in 1901. This pioneering picture atlas comprised 781 series of images based on circa 20,000 negatives, and documents not only the latest state of contemporary technology in photography and printing processes, but also the interaction of artistic and scientific observation and the analysis of motion (*4* p. 16).

In 1878, French physiologist Étienne-Jules Marey discovered Muybridge's *Series of Extraordinary Photographs* in the magazine *La Nature* and was filled with enthusiasm. Marey had already been working on notations of motion in medicine since the mid-nineteenth century. He developed a number of technical devices for the measurement and notation of blood pressure, heartbeats, pulse frequencies, etc., such as a further development of the sphygmograph invented by Karl von Vierordt (*5* p. 16). Another of his fields of research was the investigation of motion. *Animal Mechanism: A treatise on terrestrial and aerial locomotions* appeared in 1874: it includes many drawings and describes a graphic apparatus developed especially for the purpose, which could reproduce Marey's notations and investigations creating patterns of motion by animals and people (*6* p. 16). Inspired by Muybridge, Marey devoted himself to chronophotography, and in 1887 he constructed a so-called chronophotographic gun (*7* p. 17), which made it possible to fix several stages of motion in only one image using a single recording device[12] (*8* p. 17). In this device, Marey had developed a precursor to the cinematographic camera or a technique of single-image photography that could not only document but also reconstruct patterns of motion. In 1894, he also invented the first *slow-motion camera,* which was capable of chopping up complex patterns of motion into detailed single images, at a rate of 700 images per second.

und gemäß unserer Gewöhnung an die Darstellung von Bewegung mit Hilfe einer immer perfekteren Illusionstechnik, kann man sich eine solche Zuschauerreaktion kaum noch vorstellen.

Interessant ist, dass zuerst Bilder in Bewegung gerieten, bevor man Bewegung im Medium der Fotografie ohne Unschärfen abbilden konnte. Lange Belichtungszeiten erzwangen bis zur Einführung hochempfindlicher Trockenplatten in den 70er Jahren des 19. Jahrhunderts statische Sujets, wie zum Beispiel Architektur- oder Landschaftsmotive, oder aber ein scheinbar endlos andauerndes, unbewegliches Ausharren von Personen, die in den Anfängen der Fotografie bis zu einer Stunde stillhalten mussten. Erst im Laufe der Jahrzehnte sollte sich die Belichtungszeit bis auf wenige Sekunden verkürzen.[9] Tiere als Motiv konnten bis dahin nur schlafend oder leblos in Erscheinung treten, jegliche Form von geringster Bewegung hatte zwangsläufig ungewollte Unschärfen zur Folge.

So nimmt es nicht Wunder, dass Eadweard Muybridge, der im „Geburtsjahr" der Fotografie 1839 neun Jahre alt wurde und später als einer der besten Landschaftsfotografen Kaliforniens galt, sich erst 1872 an die Tierfotografie wagte.[10] Er war von Leland Stanford, einem ehemaligen kalifornischen Gouverneur und Eisenbahn-Tycoon beauftragt worden, die tatsächliche Beinstellung eines Pferdes im schnellen Trab und Galopp zu dokumentieren. Muybridge installierte entlang der Rennbahn in Palo Alto ein lineares Set von zwölf Kameras (später 24 und dann 36) und spannte Kontaktdrähte, durch die das vorbeigaloppierende Pferd die Kameras auslöste. 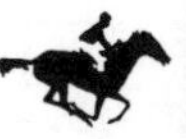 Mithilfe einer beschleunigten Wiedergabe durch das von ihm entwickelte *Zoopraxiskop* konnte dann eine derart rasante Bewegungsfolge scharf und en détail nicht nur erstmalig abgebildet, sondern auch wiedergegeben werden. Dabei handelte es sich um ein scheibenförmiges Stroboskop, das mit Hilfe einer Lichtquelle die Einzelaufnahmen nacheinander auf eine Wand projizierte.[11] Dieses innovative Abbildverfahren erlaubte von nun an, Bewegungsabläufe von Tieren und Menschen visuell zu dokumentieren, in Sequenzen zu zerlegen und damit optische Grundlagen für eine genauere Beobachtung zu schaffen. Muybridges visuelle Studien und sogenannte *Chronofotografien* wurden 1887 unter dem Titel *Animal Locomotion* veröffentlicht und 1901 in *The Human Figure in Motion* neu aufgelegt. Der bahnbrechende Bildatlas umfasste 781 Bildserien, basierend auf ca. 20.000 Negativen, und dokumentiert nicht nur den damals neuesten Stand der Technik in Fotografie und im Druckverfahren, sondern auch das Zusammenwirken künstlerischer und wissenschaftlicher Betrachtung und Analyse von Bewegung. (4 S. 16)

1878 entdeckte der französische Physiologe Étienne-Jules Marey in der Zeitschrift *La Nature* Muybridges *Serie außergewöhnlicher Fotografien* und war begeistert. Marey beschäftigte sich bereits seit Mitte des 19. Jahrhunderts mit Bewegungsaufzeichnungen in der Medizin. Er entwickelte zahlreiche technische Geräte zur Messung und Aufzeichnung von Blutdruck, Herzschlag, Pulsfrequenzen etc., wie zum Beispiel die Weiterentwicklung des Sphygmographen von Karl von Vierordt. (5 S. 16)

It is striking that Marey, as a scientist, and Muybridge, as a photographer and artist, each handled chronophotography and the resulting picture material in differing ways. Marey's interest was in scientifically precise, quantifiable studies that sought to represent motions within one image. Using linear constructs along the human body, he succeeded in combining the photographic image and graphic notation in a way that enabled him to visualise temporality. Marey made the camera into a scientific instrument—quite in contrast to Muybridge, who continued to understand the camera as an artistic medium and did not view records of motion as pure study material, but also as material for compositions that could be arranged according to aesthetic viewpoints (this was possible using his technique of the image series).[13] It is no wonder, therefore, that the investigative work of Muybridge and Marey inspired many other scientists and artists from a wide range of disciplines, stimulating them to make their own studies of motion patterns and devise new ways of portraying and designing motion.[14]

MOTION IN ART—A direct translation can be followed with particular clarity in the work of Marcel Duchamp, who made a painterly response to the sequence of images *Woman Walking Downstairs* by Eadweard Muybridge in *The Human Figure in motion* (1901), with his famous painting *Nu descendant un escalier no. 2* (*Nude Descending a Staircase No. 2*) (9 p. 26). He made the following comment on this in his essay *The Creative Act* from 1957: "This final version of the *Nude Descending a Staircase,* painted in January 1912, was the convergence in my mind of various interests among which [were] the cinema, still in its infancy, and the separation of the static positions in the photochronographs of Marey in France, Eakins and Muybridge in America. Painted, as it is, in severe wood colors, the anatomical nude does not exist, or at least cannot be seen, since I discarded completely the naturalistic appearance of a nude, keeping only the abstract lines of some twenty different static positions in the successive action of descending."[15]

In painting at the end of the ninetheenth century, artists were already beginning to cut up external reality into separate pictorial elements. Impressionism, which derived new techniques for painting from subjective perception, and Pointilism, which studied the constitution of image and perception on a more rational level, made use of physiological insights and so employed painting to visualise many things that were invisible. Cubism took this type of fragmentation further, beyond the division of object and space via painterly technique towards more sculptural segmentation. Comparing Duchamp and Muybridge, it becomes clear how Cubism—by overlapping different views of an object or different stages of motion—introduced temporality into painting as a fourth dimension and so discovered an innovative pictorial language.

Ein weiteres Forschungsgebiet war die Untersuchung von Bewegung.
1874 erschien *Animal Mechanism: A treatise on terrestrial and aerial*
***locomotions,* mit zahlreichen Abbildungen eigens entwickelter Apparatu-**
ren, die Mareys Aufzeichnungen und Untersuchungen an Bewegungsab-
läufen von Tier und Mensch grafisch wiedergeben konnten. (*6* S. 17) Ins-
piriert von Muybridge widmete sich Marey der Chronofotografie und
konstruierte 1887 die sogenannte *chronofotografische Flinte* (*7* S. 17), die
es ermöglichte, mit einem einzigen Aufzeichnungsgerät mehrere Bewe-
gungszustände in nur einem Bild zu fixieren.[12] (*8* S. 17) Marey entwickelte
damit einen Vorläufer der kinematografischen Kamera bzw. eine Tech-
nik der Einzelbildfotografie, die Bewegungsabläufe nicht nur zu doku-
mentieren, sondern auch zu rekonstruieren verstand. Mit seiner Erfin-
dung der ersten *Slow-Motion-Kamera* 1894 gelang es mit 700 Bildern
pro Sekunde auch komplexe Bewegungsabläufe detailliert in Einzelbilder
zu zerlegen.

Bemerkenswert ist der unterschiedliche Umgang mit der Chronofotografie
von Marey, dem Wissenschaftler, und Muybridge, dem Fotografen und
Künstler: Mareys Interesse galt wissenschaftlich exakten und quantifizierba-
ren Studien, die Bewegungen innerhalb eines Bildes darzustellen suchten.
Mit linearen Konstruktionen am menschlichen Körper gelang ihm die Kombi-
nation von fotografischem Abbild und grafischer Aufzeichnung zur Visualisie-
rung von Zeitlichkeit. Marey machte die Kamera zu einem wissenschaftlichen
Instrument – ganz im Gegensatz zu Muybridge, der die Kamera nach wie vor 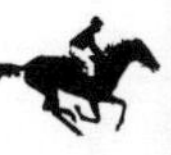
als künstlerisches Medium verstand und Bewegungsaufzeichnungen nicht als
reines Studien-, sondern auch als kompositorisches Material, das nach ästhe-
tischen Gesichtspunkten arrangiert werden konnte.[13] Demnach verwundert
es nicht, dass die investigative Arbeit von Muybridge und Marey zahlreiche
Wissenschaftler und Künstler aus unterschiedlichsten Disziplinen inspirierte
und zum Studium von Bewegungsabläufen und neuen Darstellungs- und
Gestaltungsformen von Bewegung anregte.[14]

BEWEGUNG IN DER KUNST—Eine unmittelbare Übersetzung der chronofotografischen Studien in die Kunst ist besonders deutlich bei Marcel Duchamp nach-
zuvollziehen, der mit seinem berühmten Gemälde *Nu descendant un escalier no. 2*
(Akt die Treppe herabsteigend Nr. 2) eine malerische Antwort gibt zu der sequenziellen Bildfolge *Woman walking downstairs* von Eadweard Muybridge aus *The
human figure in motion* von 1901. (*9* S. 26) Er äußerte sich dazu 1957 in seinem
Essay *The Creative Act* folgendermaßen: „Diese Endfassung des Aktes, eine
Treppe herabsteigend, im Januar 1912 gemalt, ergab sich aus der Konvergenz
verschiedener Interessen in meinem Geist, darunter der noch in den Kinderschu-
hen steckende Film und die Separation der statischen Positionen in den Chronofotografien von Marey in Frankreich, von Eakins und Muybridge in Amerika. In stren-
gen Holzfarben gemalt, existiert er nicht als anatomischer Akt oder kann zumindest
nicht als solcher gesehen werden, denn ich verzichtete völlig auf die naturalistische

At the beginning of the twentieth century, industrialisation and motorisation literally set the acceleration of production processes and locomotion into motion. This had far-reaching effects, not only on spatial contextsand social ideas and values. Carl Benz' invention of a vehicle driven by a combustion engine in 1886 revolutionised the mobility of the individual and thus personal transport in the first half of the twenthieth century. The increasing spread of the railways beginning in the eighteen-thirties had already had a lasting impact on the national and international figure of space; after the first successful flights made by the Wright brothers, from 1903 onwards, there seemed to be almost no limit to mobilisation in the air, either. These technical achievements changed working conditions, everyday life, and the understanding of society and the individual.[16] And so it is no wonder that motion and acceleration, in particular automobility, were themes also expressed in art: "We affirm that the world's magnificence has been enriched by a new beauty: the beauty of speed. A racing car whose hood is adorned by great pipes, like serpents of explosive breath (…), a roaring car that seems to ride on grapeshot is more beautiful than the Victory of Samothrace. We want to hymn the man at the wheel, who hurls the lance of his spirit across the Earth, along the circle of its orbit…," Italian lawyer and poet Filippo Tommaso Marinetti wrote in the *First Futurist Manifesto,* which was published in the French newspaper *Le Figaro* in 1909. In their manifestos the Futurists referred unashamedly to the power of technology and acceleration, even to the fascination behind the destructive power of war and weapons technology, which was also developing faster and faster. By contrast to those documentary experiments carried out by Marey, Muybridge, and in painting, the Futurists were not concerned with reproducing motion in an analytical way, but with the occurrence itself and with individual experience, for which they sought an expression. In visual abstraction, they found two- and three-dimensional means of expression to lend shape to the figure of motion and its patterns.[17] Giacomo Balla's painting *Street Light* from 1909 is regarded as the first futurist painting, although the artist had not yet joined the Futurists at the time of his work. Balla was very enthusiastic about racing cars and attempted to find a form to represent their speed in abstraction. From 1912 his motifs and style of painting changed as he attempted to portray the simultaneity of several phases of motion in one image and to create a visual expression for acoustic experience.[18] Examples of this are his works *Speed of a Car* (1913) or *Plastic Construction of Noise and Speed* (1914/15). It is impossible to overlook the analogy to works by Marey and Muybridge (*12* p. 27).
Motions are events in space and time. Motions are fleeting, impossible to grasp and hold onto, and difficult to portray. The visualisation of motion highlights the limitations of portrayal and the necessity for abstraction, which is fundamental to both artistic and scientific deliberations and processes.

Erscheinung eines nackten Körpers und behielt nur diese etwa zwanzig
verschiedenen statischen Positionen im sukzessiven Akt des Herabstei-
gens."[15] Bereits Ende des 19. Jahrhunderts gab es in der Malerei
Ansätze, eine äußere Wirklichkeit in einzelne Bildelemente zu zerlegen.
Der Impressionismus, der aus einer subjektiven Wahrnehmung neue
Techniken für die Malerei ableitete und der Pointilismus, der sich vielmehr auf rationaler Ebene mit der Konstituierung von Bild und Wahrnehmung auseinandersetzte, machten sich physiologische Erkenntnisse
zunutze und brachten mit dem Medium der Malerei Unsichtbarkeiten zur
Ansicht. Der Kubismus führte diese Art der Fragmentierung weiter, fort
von einer maltechnischen und hin zu einer bildnerischen Zerlegung von
Objekt und Raum. In der Gegenüberstellung von Duchamp und Muybridge
wird deutlich, wie der Kubismus in der Überlagerung verschiedener
Ansichten eines Objektes oder unterschiedlicher Bewegungsstadien Zeitlichkeit als vierte Dimension in die Malerei einführte und so zu einer neuen
Bildsprache fand.

Die Industrialisierung und die Motorisierung setzten zu Beginn des 20. Jahrhunderts eine Beschleunigung der Produktionsprozesse und der Fortbewegung buchstäblich in Gang. Dies hatte weitreichende Auswirkungen nicht
nur auf räumliche Zusammenhänge und gesellschaftliche Vorstellungen und
Bewertungen. Mit der Erfindung eines mit Verbrennungsmotor betriebenen
Gefährts von Carl Benz 1886 wurde die Mobilität des Einzelnen und somit der 
Individualverkehr in der ersten Hälfte des 20. Jahrhunderts revolutioniert.
Bereits die zunehmende Verbreitung der Eisenbahn seit den 30er Jahren des
19. Jahrhunderts veränderte nationale und internationale Raumgefüge nach-
haltig; mit den ersten erfolgreichen Flügen der Gebrüder Wright ab 1903
schien auch einer Mobilisierung in den Lüften kaum noch Grenzen gesetzt.
Diese technischen Errungenschaften veränderten die Arbeitsbedingungen,
den Lebensalltag sowie das Verständnis von Gesellschaft und Individuum.[16]
Und so nimmt es nicht Wunder, dass das Thema der Bewegung und Beschleunigung, insbesondere der Automobilität, auch in der Kunst Niederschlag fand:
„Wir erklären, dass sich die Herrlichkeit der Welt um eine neue Schönheit bereichert hat: die Schönheit der Geschwindigkeit. Ein Rennwagen, dessen Karosserie große Rohre schmücken, die Schlangen mit explosivem Atem gleichen (...),
ein aufheulendes Auto, das auf Kartätschen zu laufen scheint, ist schöner als die
Nike von Samothrake. Wir wollen den Mann besingen, der das Steuer hält, dessen Idealachse die Erde durchquert, die selbst auf ihrer Bahn dahinjagt ... ",
schrieb der italienische Jurist und Dichter Filippo Tommaso Marinetti im *Ersten
futuristischen Manifest,* das 1909 in der französischen Zeitung *Le Figaro* veröffentlicht wurde. In ihren Manifesten beriefen sich die Futuristen unverhohlen auf die
Kraft der Technik und Beschleunigung, sogar auf die Faszination der Zerstörungs-
kraft einer sich immer schneller entwickelnden Kriegs- und Waffentechnologie. Im
Gegensatz zu den dokumentarischen Experimenten von Marey, Muybridge und der

MOTION IN THE SCIENCES—The interplay of space, time and motion was considered in a quite different context during this era, as well as being translated into images and objects: in 1913, Frederick Winslow Taylor laid the foundations for the optimised organisation of industry, in economic terms, with his *principles of scientific management.* On the basis of a strictly hierarchical organisational structure, the worker was synchronised with the production process by automising patterns of human motion. Scientist couple Frank and Lillian Gilbreth devoted themselves to precise observation of motion patterns in different professional fields. They developed photographic studies of motion, as well as models as a basis for *scientific management,* which sought to analyse and optimise motions in working processes. Similar to chrono-photographic presentations, their models were underlain with a grid structure, enabling them to work out comparable, measurable patterns of motion in space and time on the basis of a diagrammatic system of reference (*13* p. 27). First of all, Gilbreth documented the erection of reinforced concrete constructions using these spatial-temporal studies in 1908. A year later, he was already hoping to accelerate the whole of the building industry many times over. Specific *motion studies* helped to optimise the pattern of motions involved, for example in building walls so that a resultant reduction of the radius of motion and physical relief provided by an adjustable scaffold led to an increase in processing from 120 to 350 bricks per hour: a bricklayer's daily performance could thus be increased threefold. Taylor and the Gilbreths created the basis for the division of labour and optimising of the workforce with this *scientific management* and efficient choreography of motion in working processes. Division of labour in production processes (Adam Smith) was split up into standardised elements and sequences of motions; motor repetition of actions in a particular order took the place of specified skills.[19] Flowing motions, as continuous series, were divided into visual sequences, abstracted, and transposed into a modular system of momentary images and units of motion. The resulting flexible (re-)construction principle also plays a part in performing art, in particular in the constitution and portrayal of motion patterns in dance.[20]

MOTION IN SPACE—At the beginning of the twentieth century, criticism of the world's increasing mechanisation gave way to a belief in the salvation of mankind via the machine. "The belief that its rational construction and perfect achievements made the machine a moral force, even the moral force, setting fresh standards for man—this belief made it easier to equate the new technology, even in its ugliest manifestations, with human progress. The sinner no longer failed to measure up to human possibilities, he failed to utilise the machine to a maximum."[21] The architecture of modernism propagated an understanding of space and design shaped by technology, capable of confronting rational dimensions and production conditions, and facing up to comparison with technical apparatus. Le Corbusier's concept of the *living machine* is only one**

Malerei ging es den Futuristen nicht um ein analytisches Abbilden von Bewegung, sondern um das Ereignis und das individuelle Erleben, für welches ein Ausdruck gefunden werden sollte. In der visuellen Abstraktion fanden sie das ideale Darstellungsmittel im Zwei- und Dreidimensionalen, um der Bewegung und Bewegungsabläufen Gestalt zu verleihen.[17] Giacomo Ballas Gemälde *Straßenlaterne* von 1909 gilt als das erste futuristische Bild, obwohl der Künstler sich zu diesem Zeitpunkt noch nicht den Futuristen angeschlossen hatte. Balla begeisterte sich für Rennwagen und versuchte in der Abstraktion eine Form und Darstellung für deren Geschwindigkeit zu finden. Ab 1912 veränderten sich dann die Motive und sein Malstil, als auch er versuchte, die Gleichzeitigkeit von Bewegung in mehreren Phasen ins Bild zu setzen und zudem einen visuellen Ausdruck für das akustische Erleben zu schaffen.[18] Beispiele dafür sind seine Werke *Geschwindigkeit eines Autos* (1913) oder *Plastische Konstruktion von Geräuschen und Geschwindigkeiten* (1914/15). Eine Analogie zu den Arbeiten von Marey und Muybridge ist unverkennbar. (*12* S. 27)
Bewegungen sind Ereignisse in Raum und Zeit. Bewegungen sind flüchtig, nicht greifbar, unhaltbar und schwer darstellbar. Die Visualisierung von Bewegung verweist auf die Grenzen der Darstellung und die Notwendigkeit von Abstraktionen, die grundlegend sind für künstlerische, aber auch für wissenschaftliche Überlegungen und Prozesse.

BEWEGUNG IN DER WISSENSCHAFT—Überlegungen im Zusammenhang von Raum, Zeit und Bewegung wurden zu dieser Zeit auch in ganz anderem Kontext angestellt und in Bild und Objekt übersetzt: Frederick Winslow Taylor legte 1913 mit seinen *Grundsätzen wissenschaftlicher Betriebsführung* das Fundament für ökonomisch optimierte Betriebsorganisationen. Auf der Basis einer streng hierarchischen Organisationsstruktur wurde der Arbeiter mittels Automatisierung menschlicher Bewegungsfolgen in den Produktionsablauf eingetaktet. Das Wissenschaftlerpaar Frank und Lillian Gilbreth widmete sich der präzisen Beobachtung von Bewegungsabläufen in unterschiedlichen Berufssparten und entwickelte als Grundlage für die Arbeitswissenschaft *(scientific management)* fotografische Bewegungsstudien und Modelle, um Bewegungen in Arbeitsprozessen zu analysieren und zu optimieren. Ihre Modelle waren, ähnlich wie die chronofotografischen Arrangements, mit einer Rasterstruktur hinterlegt, um anhand eines diagrammatischen Bezugssystems vergleichbare und messbare Bewegungsabläufe in Raum und Zeit zu ermitteln. (*13* S. 27) Mit diesen Raum-Zeit-Studien dokumentierte Gilbreth 1908 zunächst die Ausführung von Eisenbetonkonstruktionen. Ein Jahr später beabsichtigte er bereits, das gesamte Bauhandwerk um ein Vielfaches zu beschleunigen. Die spezifischen *motion studies* halfen dabei, die Bewegungsabläufe beispielsweise beim Mauern so zu optimieren, dass dank der daraus resultierende Verkleinerung der Bewegungsradien und der körperlichen Entlastung mit Hilfe eines verstellbaren Gerüstes die Verarbeitung von 120 auf 350 Ziegeln pro Stunde gesteigert und somit die Tagesleistung

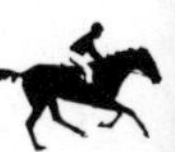

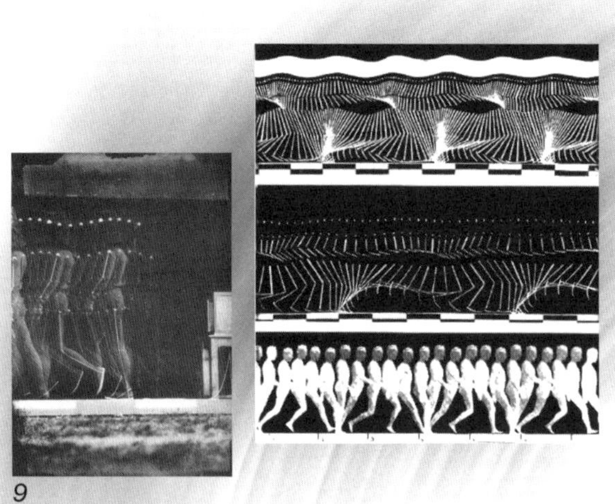

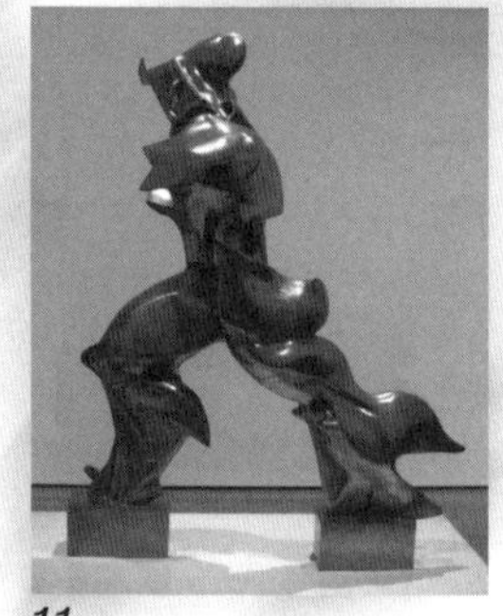

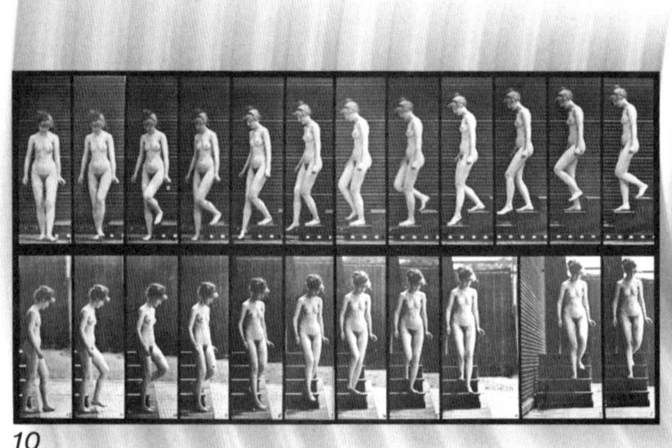

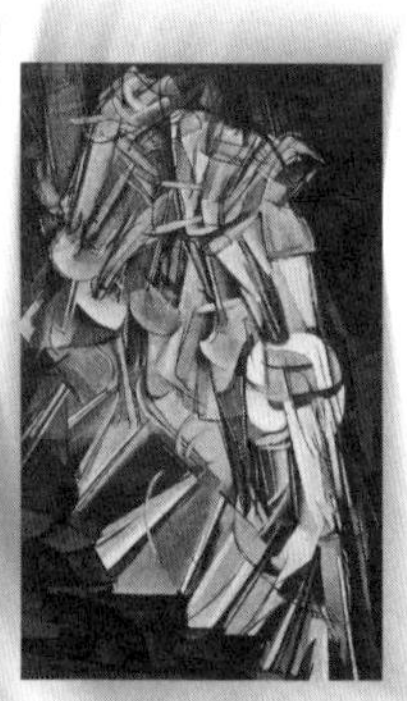

9 Étienne-Jules Marey: *Chronophotographic Study of the Human Locomotion*, 1886 — *10 left* Eadweard Muybridge: *Woman Walking Downstairs*, 1887; *right* Marcel Duchamp: *Nu descendant un escalier no. 2*, 1912 — *11* Umberto Boccioni: *Archetypes of Movement in Space*, 1913 — *12* Giacomo Balla: *top Flight of the Swallows*, 1913; *middle Plastic Construction of Noise and Speed*, 1914/15, reconstruction 1968; *bottom Speed of a Car*, 1913 — *13* Frank Bunker Gilbreth: *top Cyclographic Recordings of a Surgeon's Gestures*, 1914; *bottom Standard wire models*, 1918 — *14* Guy Debord: *The Naked City*, 1957

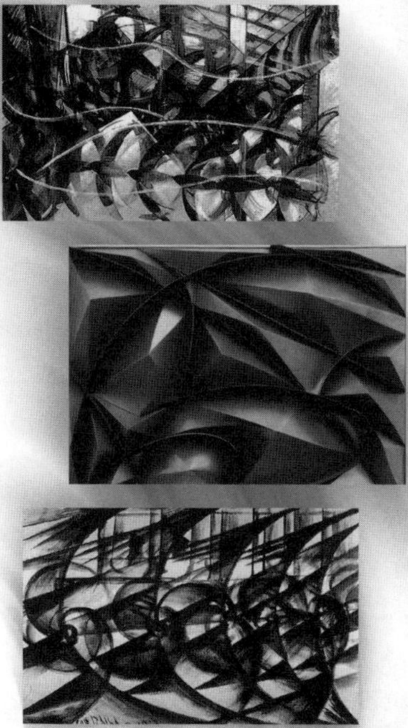

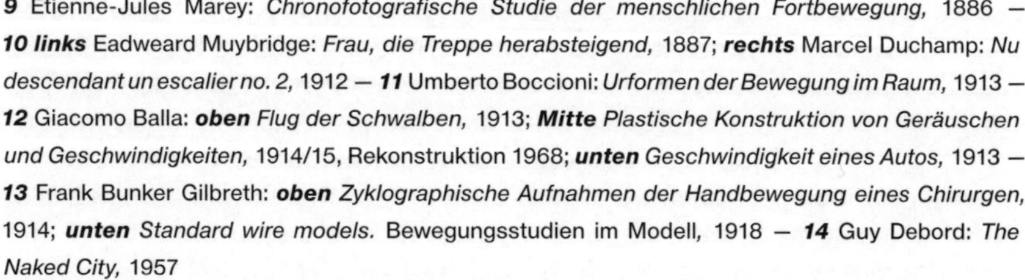

9 Étienne-Jules Marey: *Chronofotografische Studie der menschlichen Fortbewegung*, 1886 — 10 *links* Eadweard Muybridge: *Frau, die Treppe herabsteigend*, 1887; *rechts* Marcel Duchamp: *Nu descendant un escalier no. 2*, 1912 — 11 Umberto Boccioni: *Urformen der Bewegung im Raum*, 1913 — 12 Giacomo Balla: *oben Flug der Schwalben*, 1913; *Mitte* Plastische Konstruktion von Geräuschen und Geschwindigkeiten, 1914/15, Rekonstruktion 1968; *unten* Geschwindigkeit eines Autos, 1913 — 13 Frank Bunker Gilbreth: *oben* Zyklographische Aufnahmen der Handbewegung eines Chirurgen, 1914; *unten* Standard wire models. Bewegungsstudien im Modell, 1918 — 14 Guy Debord: *The Naked City*, 1957

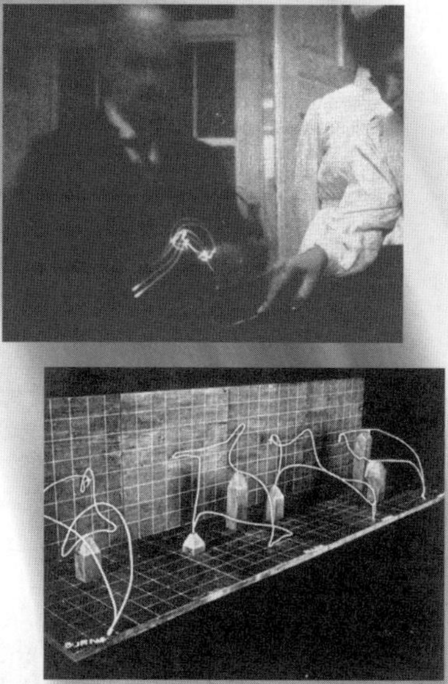

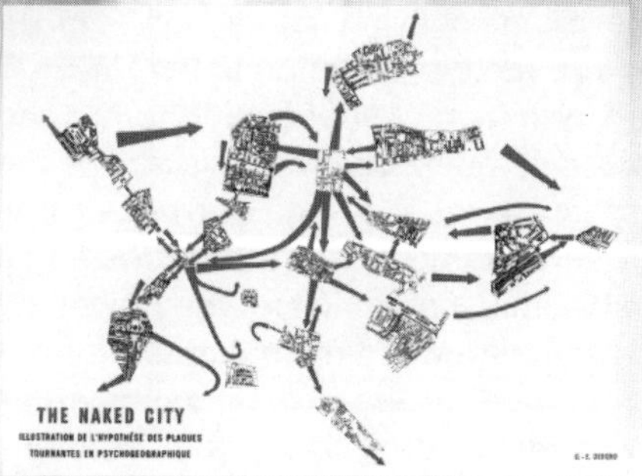

example of this, as there were also architectural designs intended less as a meta-phor and more as mechanical constructions, which could even be set in motion in various ways. The idea of mobile spatial elements has a surprisingly long history: the Roman emperor Nero was said to have had a rotating dining room built in the *Domus Aurea,* the so-called *Golden House,* in Rome. Spanish filmmaker Segundo de Chomón gave us the first technical vision of a fully automated hotel of the future: in his film *Hotel Eléctrico* dating from 1905, all the functional objects can be moved mechanically; the cutlery, comb, and wardrobe function at the press of a button, and even in the bathroom a self-cleaning process can be set in motion. One of the most impressive realisations of a moving house is surely *Villa Girasole,* which was built on a hill around Marcellise by the Italian engineer Angelo Invernizzi in 1935. The whole L-shaped structure set on a multistorey, cylindrical pedestal can be turned a full 360 degrees with the help of a motor and so directed towards the sun.[22]

Rapid technical development spurred visions of new technologies, new appa-rates, miracle weapons and spatial constructions. Cars, planes, and rockets were no longer technical fiction but became real products to revolutionise our handling of the constructed world. The dissolution of spaces, a shifting of spa-tial boundaries, effects of doubling, etc., were phenomena that played a role in architecture parallel to the early days of film. Dissolving architectural volumes using new steel and glass constructions, transparency, dematerialisation, and colourfulness formed the basis for a vision of crystalline architecture and in-spired for example visions of flying habitations.[23] In 1922 Marinetti described a city that seemed to melt into motion in his futuristic novel *Gli Indomabili.* The constant transformation of spaces and forms caused by changing light conditions and fleeting, indefinable materials anticipates the urban-develop-mental visions of Stanislaw Lem—e.g., in *Transfer* from 1961. A liquid chaos evolves to replace three-dimensional structures and clearly defined spaces, exploding our spatial imagination. Here, the power of the technical—motion itself—becomes a space-generating material.[24]

Meanwhile, the members of the artists' association *Lettrist International* experimented with *disorientation* (spatial chaos) as a critical strategy against modernity's rational urban planning. *Dérive* described this drifting without significance or planning—following intuition alone, or rather the emotional impact of urban architecture. The rather rigid official definition published in the specially released *Revue internationale situationniste* read as follows: "Experimental behaviour or the technique of accelerated passage through different types of environment linked to the conditions of urban society." Such roaming led to the development of *psychogeogra-phy,* "research into the precise effects of the geographical environment, which directly influences the emotional behaviour of the individual— whether consciously planned or not. Effects that the immediate impact of one's geographical environment triggers in one's emotional life," and was visualised in maps characterised by mood (*14* p. 27). The idea of

eines Maurers verdreifacht werden konnte. Taylor und das Ehepaar Gilbreth schufen mit dem *scientific management* und einer effizienten Choreografie von Bewegung in Arbeitsprozessen die Basis für die Zerlegung und Optimierung des Arbeiterkörpers. Die arbeitsteiligen Produktionsprozesse (Adam Smith) wurden in standardisierte Bewegungselemente und -abfolgen zerlegt, sodass an die Stelle von fachspezifischem Wissen die motorische Wiederholung von Handgriffen in bestimmten Reihenfolgen trat.[19] Die fließende Bewegung als eine kontinuierliche Abfolge wird in visuelle Sequenzen zerlegt, abstrahiert und in ein modulares System von Momentaufnahmen und Bewegungseinheiten überführt. Dieses nun flexible (Re-)Konstruktionsprinzip spielt auch in der darstellenden Kunst eine Rolle, insbesondere in der Konstituierung und Darstellung von Bewegungsabläufen beim Tanz.[20]

BEWEGUNG IM RAUM—Die Kritik an einer zunehmenden Mechanisierung der Lebenswelt wich zu Beginn des 20. Jahrhunderts dem Glauben an eine Erlösung des Menschen durch die Maschine. „Die Auffassung, wonach die Maschine auf Grund ihrer rationellen Konstruktion und der Vollkommenheit ihrer Leistung nun eine moralische Kraft war, ja die moralische Kraft *par excellence,* die dem Menschen neue Maßstäbe setzte – diese Auffassung erleichterte es, die neue Technologie, auch in ihren hässlichsten Erscheinungsformen, mit menschlichem Fortschritt gleichzusetzen. 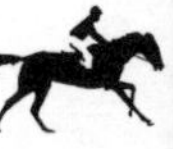 Sünde bedeutete nun nicht mehr, unter dem Maß menschlicher Möglichkeiten, sondern unter dem Maß der maximalen Nutzung der Maschine zu bleiben."[21] Die Architektur der Moderne propagierte ein technisch geprägtes Raum- und Gestaltungsverständnis, das rationalen Maßstäben und Produktionsbedingungen und dem Vergleich mit technischen Apparaturen standhalten sollte. Le Corbusiers Begriff der *Wohnmaschine* ist dafür nur ein Beispiel, denn es gab auch Architekturentwürfe, die sich weniger als Metapher, sondern tatsächlich als mechanische Konstruktionen verstanden und vielgestaltig in Bewegung setzen konnten. Die Idee beweglicher Raumteile hat eine überraschend weit zurückreichende Geschichte: Bereits der römische Kaiser Nero soll in der *Domus Aurea,* dem sogenannten *goldenen Haus* in Rom, ein rotierendes Esszimmer eingerichtet haben. Der spanische Filmemacher Segundo de Chomón lieferte die erste technische Vision eines vollautomatischen Hotels der Zukunft: In seinem Film *Hotel Eléctrico* von 1905 sind alle funktionalen Gegenstände mechanisch beweglich; das Besteck, der Kamm, der Kleiderschrank funktionieren auf Knopfdruck, sogar im Badezimmer lässt sich eine Selbstreinigung in Gang setzen. Eines der eindrücklichsten Beispiele für die Realisierung eines sich bewegenden Hauses ist sicher die *Villa Girasole,* die 1935 von dem italienischen Ingenieur Angelo Invernizzi auf dem Hügel um Marcellise erbaut wurde. Der gesamte L-förmige Baukörper, der auf einem mehrgeschossigen, zylindrischen Sockel aufsitzt, kann mit Hilfe eines Motorenantriebs um 360 Grad gedreht und nach der Sonne ausgerichtet werden.[22]

unitary urbanism saw emotionally based town maps as a foundation to the construction of new utopian environments as well as *situations.* Chance, passion, and unpredictability were seen as counter strategies to research into space and motion, whereby rejecting lasting cultural and artistic production left few starting points for design, apart from spatial models by Constant Anton Nieuwenhuys.[25] The artist developed *New Babylon*—an urban model as a conceptual living space for a creative *homo ludens.* Transformation and the nomadic lifestyle were keywords backing the flexible and the temporary, the playful and the event-based against rigidity and immovability. These approaches, which revert decisively to Henri Lefèbvre among others, became legible in a wide range of manifestations in many alternative urban models during the following decades. Interestingly, the object of criticism (immobility) and the counter model (flexibility) entered into a surprising symbiosis: place-less megastructures with newly developed, exchangeable living modules aimed to do justice to the citizen's freedom and provide individual spaces for self-realisation. The *Groupe d'Architecture mobile* (GEAM), founded in Paris in 1957, was devoted to the study of mobile architecture and attempted, among other things, to test the flexibility of such concepts. The group *Archigram* took the concept of mobility quite literally and taught the cities of the future to walk.[26]

Every space is a place of motion, a place of change, a place of permanent transformation. Consequently, motion is inscribed into the space or is choreographed by the space—by means of topographies, systems of paths, cubature, and sequences of rooms. But architectural planning may unfold its own dramaturgy of motion in the design, going far beyond access defined by usage or a system of escape routes. One need only think of English landscape gardens, which lead the walker along meandering paths through a supposedly natural park, offering constantly new and unexpected views wherever paths and viewing axes cross and architectural elements are placed systematically. There is also the concept of fluid space, which architect Zaha Hadid, for example, translates into architecture in constantly original ways, inasmuch as users and visitors are guided through the dynamically constructed architectural volume by means of ramps and ingeniously arranged paths (*15* p. 36). In direct contrast, there is the urban grid of many cities, necessitating the layout of orthogonal paths and viewing axes and, with its structural homogenisation, achieving a dramaturgy of spatial experience only by means of concentration and differentiated spatial programmes. Architecture, therefore, choreographs the flow of motion in space.

THE ART OF MOTION—At the beginning of the twentieth century the question of space in architecture and dance was raised again, in a new way. While non-site-specific programmes had previously shaped the choreography of motion within a more or less abstracted space, now experiments were taking place with spatially oriented concepts of motion.

Die rasante technische Entwicklung beflügelte Visionen von neuen Technologien, neuen Apparaten, Wunderwaffen und räumlichen Konstruktionen. Automobile, Flugzeuge und Raketen waren nicht mehr technische Fiktionen, sondern Produkte, die den Umgang mit der gebauten Umwelt revolutionieren sollten. Die Auflösung von Räumen, das Fließen von Raumgrenzen, Effekte der Verdopplung usw. waren Phänomene, die parallel zu den Anfängen im Film auch in der Architektur eine Rolle spielten. Die Auflösung der baulichen Massen durch neue Stahl- und Glaskonstruktionen, Transparenz, Entstofflichung und Farbigkeit begründeten die Vision einer kristallinen Architektur und beflügelten beispielsweise Visionen von fliegenden Siedlungen.[23] Marinetti beschrieb 1922 in seinem futuristischen Roman *Gli Indomabili* eine Stadt, die sich in der Bewegung aufzulösen scheint. Mit dem stetigen Wandel von Räumen und Formen durch die Transformation von Licht und flüchtigen, unbestimmbaren Materialien nimmt er die stadträumlichen Visionen von Stanislaw Lem – zum Beispiel in *Transfer* von 1961 – vorweg. Anstelle von dimensionalen Strukturen und klar definierten Orten tritt ein liquides Chaos, das die räumliche Vorstellungskraft sprengt. Die Kraft des Technischen, die Bewegung selbst, wird zur raumbildenden Materie.[24]

Die Mitglieder der künstlerischen Vereinigung *Lettristische Internationale* erprobten indes die *Desorientierung* (räumliches Chaos) als kritische Strategie gegen die rationalen Stadtplanungen der Moderne. *Dérive* bezeichnet das sich sinn- und planlos Treibenlassen – nur der Intuition folgend oder besser gesagt der emotionalen Wirkung städtischer Architektur. „Mit den Bedingungen der städtischen Gesellschaft verbundene experimentelle Verhaltensweise oder Technik des beschleunigten Durchgangs durch verschiedenartige Umgebungen", lautete Jahre später etwas hölzern die offizielle Definition, die in der eigens herausgegebenen *Revue internationale situationniste* veröffentlicht wurde. Im Umherschweifen entwickelte sich die Psychogeografie, die „Forschung nach den genauen Wirkungen der das Gefühlsverhalten der Individuen unmittelbar beeinflussenden geografischen Umwelt – bewusst eingerichtet oder nicht. Das, was die unmittelbare Wirkung der geografischen Umwelt auf das Gefühlsleben zur Erscheinung bringt" und in stimmungsgeprägten Karten zur Gestalt wurde. (*14* S. 27) Mit der Idee eines *Unitären Urbanismus* sollten emotional begründete Stadtpläne die Grundlage bilden für Konstruktionen neuer utopischer Umgebungen sowie von *Situationen.* Zufall, Leidenschaft, Unberechenbarkeit galten als Gegenstrategien zu der Erkundung und Gestaltung von Raum und Bewegung, die in der Ablehnung nachhaltiger kultureller und künstlerischer Produktion bis auf die Raummodelle von Constant nur wenige gestalterische Ansätze hinterließ. Der Künstler Constant Anton Nieuwenhuys entwickelte *Neu Babylon* – ein städtisches Modell als konzeptionellen Lebensraum für einen kreativen *homo ludens.*[25] Transformation und Nomadentum waren Schlagwörter, die das Wandelbare und Temporäre, das Spielerische und Ereignishafte der Starrheit und Fixierung entgegensetzten. Diese Ansätze, die unter anderem maßgeblich auf Henri

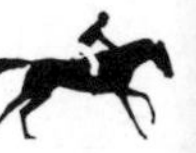

Around the turn of the century, Swiss composer Émile Jaques-Dalcroze designed a theory of motion and training, which he set out methodically in his texts from 1898 to 1919: space, time and motion were conceived within rhythmic, i.e., temporally restricted conditions. At the *Bildungsanstalt für angewandten Rhythmus (Educational Institute for Applied Rhythm)* in Hellerau, his idea of *plastic motion* was applied experimentally against the backdrop of specially developed stage architecture by Swiss architect and stage designer Adolphe Appia. Appia's concept of *rhythmic spaces* (1911–14) is probably the most striking example of a choreography of motion that employs modular spatial elements in varying compositions (*15* p. 36). The stage area was divided into dynamic zones, making it possible to derive constantly new combinations of forms and dynamics of motion from the sculpturally designed, variable spatial structures. Subsequently, these could be joined in a similar way to the spatial elements to create choreographic compositions. Appia's modular stage architecture broke with the tradition of the illusionary stage, being representative of modernist approaches and conceptual features, particularly with respect to the handling of space and architecture.[27]

As early as 1910, Walter Gropius propagated the modular construction kit system as an efficient architectural concept for the future; the foundation of the Bauhaus in 1919 introduced the development of this architectonic programme not only into artistic training, but also into industrial production. In this way, it was applied extensively in everyday design. A construction kit contains an assortment of standardised elements that are combinable, i.e., connectable via a specific system because of their standardisation. Any complex construction constituted in this way is only one of a range of possible combinations; in theory, it can always be dismantled and reassembled or repeated in practice.

In 1936—when Konrad Zuse constructed the first computer in Berlin and Alan Turing was developing the model of the universal, discrete machine—a book about architecture appeared on the market *Bauentwurfslehre (Building Design Theory)* by architect Ernst Neufert is a manual of architectural planning, which is still commonly used today. Neufert studied at the State Bauhaus in Weimar and worked as an assistant in Walter Gropius's private architectural studio; his manual propagates comprehensive standardisation and digitalisation of space and the architectonic object world using a visual grammar. This programme typifies and calculates not only room sizes and construction components as combinable elements, but every object located within the space: everything that is found in the constructed environment, from a single brick to a human being, from a play-pen to an airfield—whether standing, walking, driving or flying—is measured, set into a unifying spatial grid, and consequently oriented using a *snap to grid* system. Today, such numerical or encoded compilation of virtual object libraries forms the basis of *computer-aided design* programmes and computer games, among other things.[28]

While Ernst Neufert was compiling the principles for his *Bauentwurfslehre,* Rudolph von Laban was developing choreographic studies and

Lefèbvre zurückgehen, werden in unterschiedlichsten Ausprägungen in zahlreichen alternativen Stadtmodellen der folgenden Jahrzehnte ablesbar. Interessanterweise gehen hierbei der Gegenstand der Kritik (Unbeweglichkeit) und das Gegenmodell (Flexibilität) eine überraschende Symbiose ein: Ortlose Megastrukturen mit neu entwickelten, austauschbaren Wohnmodulen sollten der Freiheit des Bürgers Rechnung tragen und individuelle Verwirklichungsräume bieten. Die 1957 in Paris gegründete *Groupe d'Architecture mobile* (GEAM) widmete sich dem Studium mobiler Architektur und versuchte unter anderem die Flexibilität dieser Konzepte auszuloten. Die Gruppe *Archigram* nahm den Begriff der Mobilität wörtlich und ließ die Städte der Zukunft gleich das Laufen lernen.[26]

Jeder Raum ist ein Ort der Bewegung, ein Ort der Veränderung, ein Ort permanenter Transformationen. Bewegung ist folglich dem Raum eingeschrieben bzw. wird durch den Raum choreografiert, mittels Topografien, Wegesystemen, Kubaturen, räumlicher Folgen. Die architektonische Planung kann aber jenseits einer nutzungsbedingten Erschließung und von Fluchtwegsystemen eine ganz eigene Dramaturgie von Bewegungsräumen im Entwurf entfalten. Man denke an die englischen Landschaftsgärten, die den Spaziergänger auf geschlungenen Pfaden durch einen vermeintlich natürlichen Park leiten und in der Verschneidung von Wegen und Sichtachsen und mit gezielt gesetzten Architekturen immer neue und unerwartete Ausblicke offerieren. Oder das Konzept des fließenden Raumes, das zum Beispiel die Architektin Zaha Hadid immer wieder neu in Architektur übersetzt, indem die Nutzer und Besucher mittels Rampen und virtuos angelegter Wege durch die dynamisch geformten Baukörper geleitet werden. (*15* S. 36) Ganz im Gegensatz dazu steht das urbane Raster zahlreicher Stadtgründungen, das orthogonale Wege- und Sichtachsen erzwingt und in einer strukturellen Homogenisierung eine Dramaturgie räumlichen Erlebens nur durch Dichte und differenzierte Raumprogramme erreichen kann. Architektur choreografiert folglich unablässig und zwangsläufig Bewegungsströme im Raum.

KUNST DER BEWEGUNG—Zu Beginn des 20. Jahrhunderts wurde die Frage nach der Bedeutung und Funktion von Raum in der Architektur und im Tanz mehrfach neu gestellt. Prägten bis dato ortsunabhängige Programme die Choreografie von Bewegung in einem mehr oder weniger abstrahierten Raum, so wurden nun räumlich orientierte Bewegungskonzepte erprobt. Der Schweizer Komponist Émile Jaques-Dalcroze entwarf um die Jahrhundertwende eine rhythmische Bewegungs- und Erziehungslehre, die er in seinen Schriften von 1898 bis 1919 methodisch darlegte: Raum, Zeit und Bewegung wurden in rhythmischen, das heißt zeitlich begrenzten Relationen gedacht. An der *Bildungsanstalt für angewandten Rhythmus* in Hellerau erfuhr seine Idee der *plastischen Bewegung* experimentelle Anwendung an einer eigens entwickelten Bühnenarchitektur des Schweizer Architekten und Bühnenbildners Adolphe Appia. Appias Konzept der *Rhythmischen Räume* (1911–14) ist wohl das prägnanteste Beispiel für eine Choreografie

wrote, among other things, the first texts on his developed notation *Labanotation*.[29] The dancer and choreographer began his unusual studies of motion on *Monte Vérita* in Ascona during the First World War; by dividing up and adding rhythm to gardening work, for example, Laban combined studies of trivial and effective patterns of motion with his ideas on the art of motion, the question of individual expression, composition, and artistic gesture. He published his theories on *kinetography* or *Labanotation* in *Schrifttanz (Script-Dance)* in 1928, only a few years before the appearance of the *Bauentwurfslehre.* Laban was also interested in the theory of harmony as well as abstracted, mathematical referential systems of body and space. He developed a catalogue of choreographic symbols, aiming to facilitate a description and reconstruction of the body's repertoire of motion (*16* p. 37). In the meantime, diverse computer programmes for *Labanotation* are available, containing all the necessary components for *computer-aided* choreography as a modular programme package.[30]

Here, it is important to state that there have always been other concepts in the development of dance, choreography and architecture; concepts seeking to avoid a specified canon of motion and design, and their calculability. Only a few decades after Appia, and concurrent with the Situationist experiments mentioned above, Merce Cunningham developed his approach to dance and space, understanding space as an undefined area—independent of location—for undefined, abstract, and above all non-site-related motion and improvisation. Cunningham saw motion as limited only by "physical ability, but within these limitations our possibilities are infinite." He abandoned defined frameworks of reference, i.e., all the design parameters of a traditional theory of harmony like symmetries, diagonals, parallels, even spatial points of reference between which one could draw invisible lines of composition. This de-limitation of space and motion, beyond all calculable patterns of motion, meant that dance seemed to "lose control," becoming an unpredictable and unique event. Only the development of new media, especially of film technology, made it possible to record and store dance performances in real time.

In his exploration of the "humanly possible" Cunningham made use of new technologies and their possibilities very early on; the camera became a choreographic element in and completely new arrangements could be produced, like the *Mixed-Media Ballet.* Initially, this work on motion may appear to have a counter effect to the comprehensibility and repeatability of programmes, but Merce Cunningham actually began to include the computer in his choreographies very early on. Digital programmes not only trigger calculable strategies of aesthetic action, but also offer the possibility of employing chance in a creative way. Unplanned occurrences in dance can be recorded by means of new computer technologies such as *motion capturing,* but they can also be described in detail and reconstructed. In turn, it is possible in this way to develop independent programmes of training and motion, like the *improvisation technologies* of dancer and choreographer William Forsythe, or the Internet project

von Bewegung mittels variierender Kompositionen modularer Raumelemente. (*16* S. 36) Der Bühnenraum wurde dynamisch zoniert und ermöglichte aus diesen skulptural gebildeten, variablen Raumkompositionen immer neu kombinierbare Bewegungsformen und -dynamiken abzuleiten, die dann ähnlich den Raumelementen zu choreografischen Kompositionen zusammengesetzt werden konnten. Appias modulare Bühnenarchitektur brach mit der Tradition der Illusionsbühne und repräsentierte zugleich Ansätze der Moderne und ihrer konzeptionellen Ausprägungen, insbesondere im Umgang mit Raum und Architektur.[27]

Bereits 1910 propagierte Walter Gropius das modulare Baukastensystem als effizientes Architekturkonzept der Zukunft; mit der Gründung des Bauhauses 1919 fand die Entwicklung dieses architektonischen Programms nicht nur Eingang in die künstlerische Lehre, sondern auch in die industrielle Warenproduktion und somit umfassend Anwendung in der Gestaltung unserer Lebenswelt. Ein Bausatz beinhaltet ein Sortiment an genormten Elementen, die aufgrund der Vereinheitlichung nach einem spezifischen Organisationssystem kombinierbar, das heißt anschlussfähig werden. Ein so konstituiertes komplexes Gefüge ist eine Konstruktion aus einer Vielfalt möglicher Kombinationen, die theoretisch immer zerlegbar und praktisch immer wiederholbar ist.

1936, als Konrad Zuse in Berlin den ersten Computer baute und Alan Turing das mathematische Modell einer universalen, diskreten Maschine entwickelte, erschien das wohl meistverkaufte Architekturbuch der Geschichte: In seiner *Bauentwurfslehre,* dem bis heute gängigen Lehrbuch zur architektonischen Planungsanweisung, propagierte der Architekt Ernst Neufert, der am Staatlichen Bauhaus in Weimar studierte und Mitarbeiter im privaten Bauatelier von Walter Gropius war, mit Hilfe einer visuellen Grammatik die umfassende Normierung und Digitalisierung des Raumes und der gesamten architektonischen Objektwelt. Mit diesem Programm werden nicht nur Raumgrößen und Bauteile typisiert und als kombinierbare Einheiten arithmetisiert, sondern auch sämtliche im Raum lozierten Objekte: Alles, was sich im gebauten Umraum befindet, vom Ziegel bis zum Menschen, vom Laufstall bis zum Flugplatz – ob stehend, gehend, fahrend oder fliegend – jedes Objekt wurde einer Messung unterzogen, in ein vereinheitlichendes räumliches Raster eingefügt und mittels *snap to grid* daran ausgerichtet. Diese numerische bzw. codierte Zusammenstellung von virtuellen Objektbibliotheken bildet heute auch die Grundlage von *Computer-Aided-Design*-Programmen und Computerspielen.[28]

Während Ernst Neufert die Grundlagen für sein Programm der *Bauentwurfslehre* zusammentrug, entwickelte Rudolph von Laban seine choreografischen Studien und verfasste unter anderem die ersten Schriften zu der eigens entwickelten *Labanotation.*[29] Der Tänzer und Choreograf begann zur Zeit des Ersten Weltkrieges mit seinen ungewöhnlichen Bewegungsstudien auf dem *Monte Vérita* in Ascona; in der Zerlegung und Rythmisierung beispielsweise von Gartenarbeiten verquickte Laban Studien von trivialen und effektiven Bewegungsabläufen mit

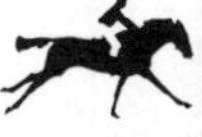

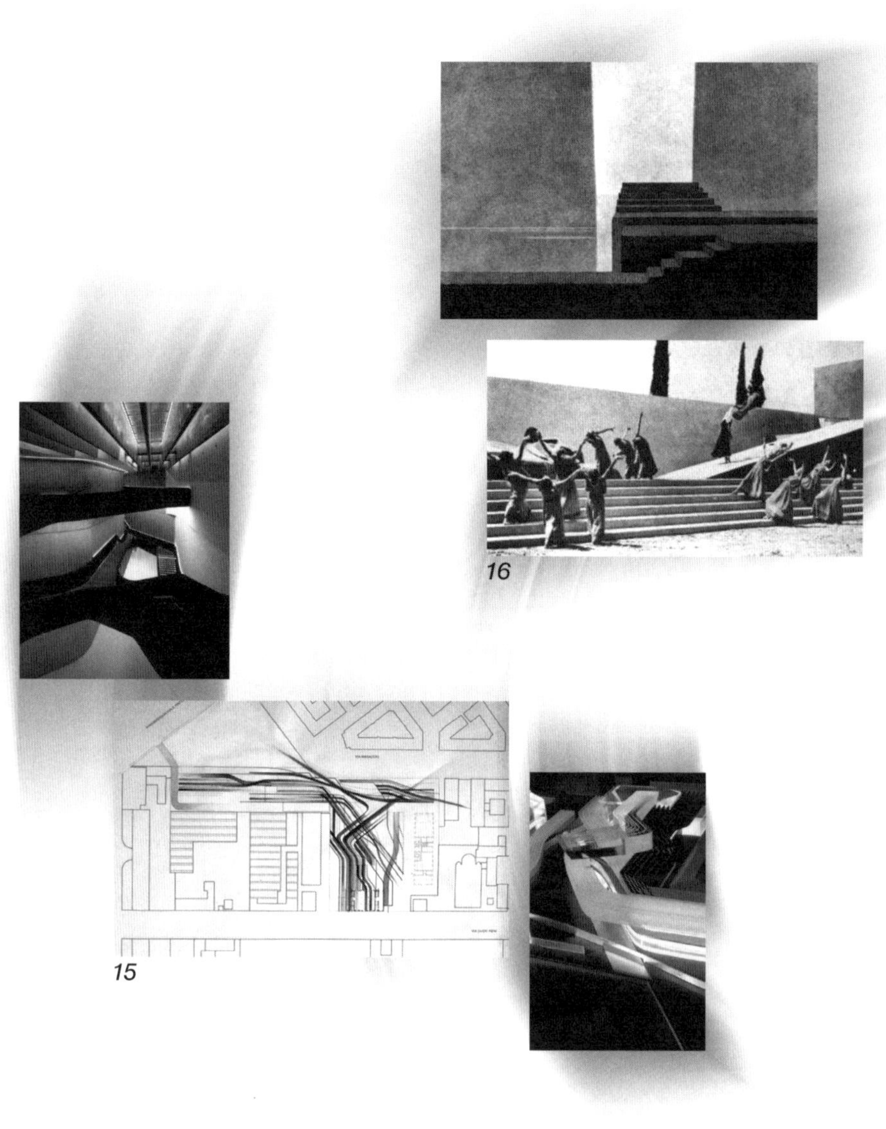

15 Zaha Hadid: *MAXXI* National Museum of XXI Century Arts, Rome, 2009 — 16 Adolphe Appia: *top Rhythmic Space, Stairs,* drawing, 1909; *bottom Cenário para coreografia de E. J. Dalcroze para As Traquínias, com alunas de sua Escola de Euritmia,* 1933 — 17 Rudolf von Laban: *top left Choreology* – motion in an icosahedron space; *bottom left* Notation system for the recording of motion; *right Laban space,* 1928 — 18 William Forsythe: *Improvisation Technologies. A Tool for the Analytical Dance Eye,* 2003

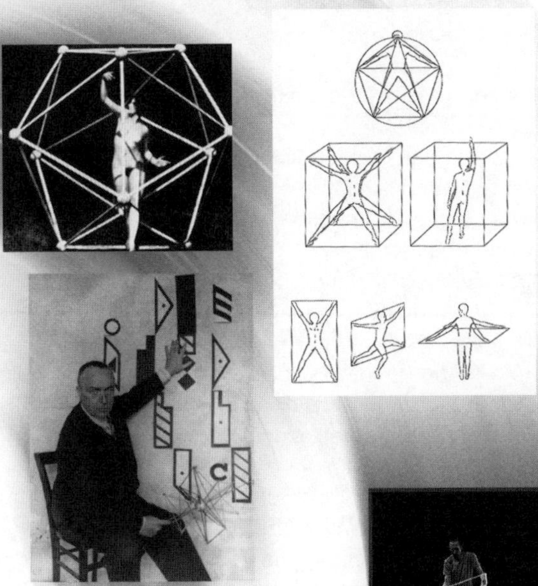

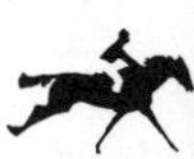

15 Zaha Hadid: *MAXXI* Nationalmuseum für Kunst des 21. Jahrhunderts in Rom, 2009 — **16** Adolphe Appia: **oben** *Rhythmischer Raum, Treppe,* Zeichnung, 1909; **unten** *Cenário para coreografia de E. J. Dalcroze para As Traquínias, com alunas de sua Escola de Euritmia,* 1933 — **17** Rudolf von Laban: **oben links** *Choreologie* – Bewegung im Raum eines Ikosaeders; **unten links** Notationssystem zur Bewegungsaufnahme; **rechts** *Labanraum,* 1928 — **18** William Forsythe: *Improvisation Technologies. A Tool for the Analytical Dance Eye,* 2003

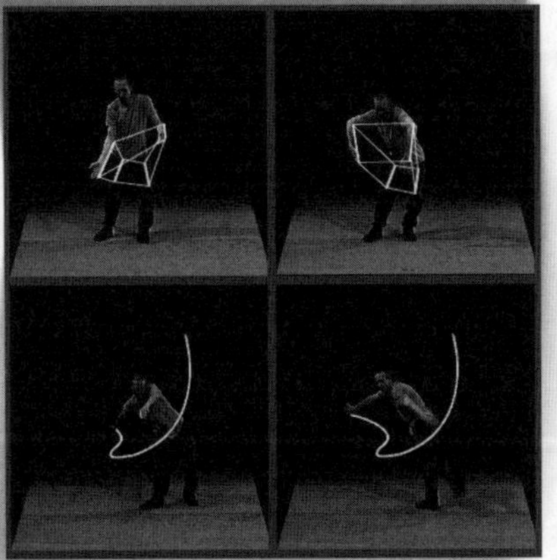

Synchronous Objects.[31] The limitation and de-limitation of motion and space led subsequently to many diverse conceptions of space and motion, not only in dance, but also in art, architecture, and literature.

EPILOGUE—In everyday life, meanwhile, we delegate our physical motion to vehicles–letting ourselves be moved rather than moving ourselves. We move images in faster and faster sequences, and one of the quickest growing fields today, the computer game industry, has dedicated itself to the simulation of motion for profit while dictating its own canon of motion in functional gestures.[32] This shift from the analogue to the digital world of experience is a continuing process in which we participate more or less consciously. It is a process that calls for close observation, as—in face of the continual development of new technologies, which have a much longer structural pre-history than one might generally suppose— we need to ask about the role of the design of space and motion, particularly when aesthetic concepts are being distanced from their authors by the programmes described. Does this distance merely signify the independence of an artwork, which unfolds an uncontrollable dialogue with the viewer, dancer or recipient face-to-face, in spatial deployment, in physical experience? Or do programmes cause a disconnection between the work and the individual, inasmuch as their modular system of (in-)finite units and calculable operations means they can even be realised by a machine? Currently, the complexity of design processes is generating an increasingly porous boundary between individual and mechanical creativity; although the computer is capable of mastering and calculating mathematical operations and geometries of immense complexity, it is tied to fixed programmes and chains of orders, which must be inscribed into it first so that it can make formatted choices. In the run-up, therefore, a mechanical-aesthetic choice must be based on a predefined decision and calculable logics, meaning that even today this kind of apparatus-based *creativity* continues to involve more restrictions than freedoms. Meanwhile, research is aiming at a wider spectrum of possibilities, and there is still much to be discovered, investigated and developed with respect to the transformation and spatialisation of motion. As a result, observing the artistic processes that accompany developments of this kind continues to be extremely interesting.

How can a compendium of essays based in different disciplines be distilled from the far-reaching, diverse significance of motion, from a range of themes that is apparently limitless? This collection of interdisciplinary texts examines the diversity of the figure of motion and motion's significance for design from different perspectives. Contributions from the fields of performing and fine art, architecture, design, landscape architecture, media and cultural studies, etc. illustrate the importance and depiction of motion in art, architecture, and design on the basis of historical developments and border-crossing contexts, and discuss current and future trends.

Überlegungen zu einer Kunst der Bewegung, der Frage nach individuellem Ausdruck, Komposition und künstlerischem Gestus. Seine Überlegungen zur *Kinetografie* oder *Labanotation* veröffentlichte er 1928, also wenige Jahre vor dem Erscheinen der *Bauentwurfslehre,* in der Publikation *Schrifttanz.* Auch Laban beschäftigte sich mit der Harmonielehre sowie abstrahierten und mathematisierten Bezugssystemen von Körper und Raum. Er entwickelte einen Katalog von choreografischen Zeichen, die das körperliche Bewegungsrepertoire umfassend beschreibbar und rekonstruierbar machen sollten. (*17* S. 37) Mittlerweile gibt es diverse Computerprogramme zur *Labanotation,* die als modulares Programmpaket alle notwendigen Komponenten für eine computer-gestützte-Choreografie beinhalten soll.[30]

Wichtig zu erwähnen ist, dass es auch in der Entwicklung des Tanzes, der Choreografie und der Architektur andere Konzepte gab und gibt, die sich von einem spezifischen Bewegungs- und Gestaltungskanon und dessen Berechenbarkeit zu befreien suchen. Merce Cunningham entwickelte nur wenige Jahrzehnte nach Appia und gleichzeitig zu den erwähnten situationistischen Experimenten einen ganz eigenen Umgang mit Tanz und Raum, indem er Raum als undefinierte und ortsungebundene Fläche für eine undefinierte, abstrahierte und vor allem ortsungebundene Bewegung und Improvisation verstand. Cunningham sah die Grenzen von Bewegung ausschließlich „im körperlichen Können, aber innerhalb dieser Grenzen sind unsere Möglichkeiten unendlich." Er verabschiedete sich von definierten Bezugsrahmen, das heißt von sämtlichen Gestaltungsparametern einer tradierten Harmonielehre wie zum Beispiel von Symmetrien, Diagonalen, Parallelen, sogar von räumlichen Bezugspunkten, zwischen denen unsichtbare Kompositionslinien hätten aufgespannt werden können. Mit dieser Entgrenzung von Raum und Bewegung geriet der Tanz jenseits kalkulierbarer Bewegungsarrangements scheinbar „außer Kontrolle" und wurde zu einem unberechenbaren und einmaligen Ereignis. Erst die Entwicklung neuer Medien, insbesondere der Filmtechnik, ermöglichte es, diese Ereignisse in Echtzeit aufzuzeichnen und zu speichern. In der Erforschung des „Menschenmöglichen" machte Cunningham sich sehr früh die Möglichkeiten neuer Techniken zunutze; die Kamera wurde zum choreografischen Element und es entstanden neue Arrangements wie beispielsweise das *Mixed-Media-Ballett.* Scheint sich diese Bewegungsarbeit zur Überschaubarkeit und Wiederholbarkeit von Programmen zunächst gegenläufig zu verhalten, begann Merce Cunningham doch sehr früh den Computer in seine Choreografien miteinzubeziehen.

Digitale Programme provozieren eben nicht nur kalkulierbare Strategien ästhetischen Handelns, sondern auch die Möglichkeit eines kreativen Umgangs mit dem Zufall. Und auch unvorhersehbare Tanzereignisse sind durch neue Computertechnologien wie *Motion Capturing* nicht nur zu speichern, sondern auch detailliert zu beschreiben und zu rekonstruieren. Somit können wiederum eigenständige Lehr- und Bewegungsprogramme entwickelt werden, wie beispielsweise die

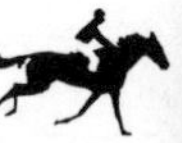

The texts are based on a symposium of the same name organised by the Weißen-hof-Institute at the State Academy of Fine Arts in Stuttgart, which regards itself as an interdisciplinary platform and aims to promote dialogue between different subject fields, as well as between theory, teaching, and practice. Typically, the authors are qualified at the periphery of each of their disciplines or even in several disciplines, or they connect design practice with theoretical investigation. To ensure that there is a thread running through this publication despite its far reaching themes, the essays have been carefully combined to highlight reciprocal thematic overlaps and/or links. The purpose of this compilation of texts, therefore, is to provide the interested reader with multifaceted insights and, I sincerely hope, with inspiration.

NOTES—[1] Apparatuses such as the gnomon and the hemicyclum, both precursors to the sundial, could also be found among the Babylonians ca. 3000 B.C. Cf. also: Pichot, André: *Die Geburt der Wissenschaft. Von den Babyloniern zu den frühen Griechen.* Frankfurt/Main 1995, 103f.— [2] Aristotle: *Physics.* Volume 8. Leipzig 1829, 191ff: Four Types of Motion: 1. Motion as becoming and decaying, 2. Motion as qualitative change, 3. Motion as quantitative change (increase and decrease) and 4. Motion as change in space.—[3] For an introduction to these themes, see also the essay: *Mobile and Stabile* by Margitta Buchert, 48–70—[4] Kepler's work: *Astronomia Nova* (The New Astronomy) appeared in 1609; among other things, it described the two primary laws of the planets: 1. The planets orbit the sun on elliptical paths. 2. The radius vector (connecting line sun – planet) always takes the same time to pass the same area.—[5] The *principle of velocity (lex prima):* "Every body remains in a state of constant velocity unless acted upon by an external unbalanced force." The *principle of action (lex secunda):* "A body of masse m subject to a net force F undergoes an acceleration a that has the same direction as the force and a magnitude that is directly proportional to the force and inversely proportional to the mass." The *principle of reaction (lex tertia):* actio – reactio— [6] The following passages include extracts from an essay that was published in 2010: Zinsmeister, Annett: "Modularisierung von Raum und Bewegung als ästhetisches Programm". In: Brandstetter, Gabriele/Wiens, Birgit: *Theater ohne Fluchtpunkt.* Berlin 2010, 76–104.—[7] In the mediaeval mason's lodges, as a rule instructions for design were passed on orally (from generation to generation, as well) and usually only fixed in writing as the basis of a contract or in schematic drawings.—[8] The *Beauchamp-Feuillet Notation* was developed by Pierre Beauchamp in the sixteen-eighties and then set out in writing by Raoul-Roger Feuillet.—[9] At the end of the eighteen-seventies and beginning of the eighteen-eighties, exposure times were shortened successfully again by means of the collodion process, and later using bromide silver gelatine.—[10] In 1839, the new technology was demonstrated in public by a number of protagonists in different countries: William Henry Fox Talbot read his memorial thesis, *The Art of Photogenic Drawing,* at the Royal Society in London on 31.1.1839, private researcher Hippolyte Bayard showed photographs he had made using a camera obscura for the first time in an exhibition on 24.6.1839, and on 19.8.1839 the daguerreotype process was first presented to the public in the Institut de France by Louis-Jaques-Mandé Daguerre. Cf. also: Frizot, Michel: *Neue Geschichte der Fotografie.* Cologne 1998—[11] The first moving projection using a laterna magica was presented to his cadets by field marshal lieutenant Franz von Uchatius in 1845. Using a

Improvisation Technologies **des Tänzers und Choreografen William For-sythe, oder auch das Internetprojekt** *Synchronous Objects*[31]**. Durch Begrenzung und Entgrenzung von Bewegung und Raum entstanden folglich sehr unterschiedliche Raum- und Bewegungskonzeptionen nicht nur im Tanz, sondern auch in der Kunst, Architektur und Literatur.**

EPILOG—**Im Alltag delegieren wir seit der Motorisierung unserer Lebenswelt im 20.Jahrhundert unsere körperliche Bewegung zunehmend an Vehikel: Wir lassen uns bewegen, anstatt uns selbst zu bewegen. Wir bewegen Bilder in immer schnelleren Frequenzen, und eine der wachstumsstärksten Branchen, die Computerspielbranche, die sich gewinnbringend der Simulation von Bewegung verschrieben hat diktiert zugleich einen Bewegungskanon funktionaler Gesten.[32] Diese Verschiebung von analoger zu digitaler Erfahrungswelt ist ein fortwährender Prozess, an dem wir mehr oder weniger bewusst teilhaben und den es zu beobachten gilt. Denn angesichts der fortwährenden Entwicklung neuer Technologien, die strukturell schon eine viel längere Vorgeschichte haben, als man gemeinhin annehmen könnte, stellt sich die Frage nach der Rolle der Gestaltung von Raum und Bewegung immer wieder neu, insbesondere dann, wenn sich durch jene beschriebenen Programme ästhetische Konzepte vermeintlich von ihren Verfassern distanzieren. Bedeutet diese Distanz lediglich die Unabhängigkeit eines Kunstwerkes, das in der Gegenüberstellung, in der räumlichen Nutzung und leiblichen Erfahrung einen unkontrollierbaren Dialog mit dem**  **Betrachter, Tänzer, Rezipienten entfaltet? Oder schaffen Programme eine Entkopplung von Werk und Individuum, indem sie durch ihr modulares System (un-)endlicher Einheiten und berechenbarer Operationen auch von einer Maschine ausgeführt werden könnten? Die Komplexität von Gestaltungsprozessen markiert derzeit eine vielleicht zunehmend poröse Grenze zwischen individueller und maschineller Kreativität; denn obgleich der Computer Rechenoperationen und Geometrien von ungeheurer Komplexität zu bewältigen und zu berechnen weiß, so ist er doch an fixierte Programme und Befehlsketten gebunden, die zunächst einmal geschrieben werden müssen, um formatierte Entscheidungen treffen zu können. Einer maschinell-ästhetischen Entscheidung muss also bereits im Vorfeld eine definierte Entscheidung und berechenbare Logik zugrunde liegen, die dieser Art maschineller** *Kreativität* **heute nach wie vor mehr Grenzen als Freiheiten bietet. Die Forschung zielt indes auf ein erweitertes Spektrum an Möglichkeiten ab, und auch bezüglich der Transformation und Verräumlichung von Bewegung gibt es noch viel zu entdecken, zu erforschen und zu entwickeln. Umso interessanter bleibt die Beobachtung, welche künstlerischen Prozesse derlei Entwicklungen begleiten.**
Wie also kann man aus dieser weitreichenden und vielgestaltigen Bedeutsamkeit von Bewegung und einem demnach scheinbar grenzenlosen Themenfeld ein Kompendium mit Beiträgen aus verschiedenen Disziplinen destillieren? Die vorliegende Textsammlung erörtert die Vielseitigkeit der Gestalt von Bewegung und die Bedeutung

combination of stroboscopic effect and Plateau's wheel of life, he succeeded in projecting the flight of missiles he drew on the wall of the lecture room and thus creating the illusion of moving images (phenakistiscope).— [12] Based on the invention of the astronomical revolver by French astronomer Pierre Jules César Janssen in 1874, which was developed in the same year in Japan to record the crossing of Venus before the sun.—[13] More detail on Etienne Jules Marey: Braun, Marta: *Picturing Time: The Work of Etienne Jules Marey 1830-1904.* Chicago 1992. On Eadweard Muybridge and the development of the instantaneous photograph: Prodger, Phillip: *Time stands still. Muybridge and the instantaneous photography motion.* New York 2003—[14] ...or even led to correction of one's own work: Meissonier, for example, who was a subscriber to *Animal locomotion* was said to have corrected the foot positions of horses in two of his paintings after reading it. On this, cf.: Frizot, Michel: *E.J. Muybridge: Animal Locomotion* In: ibid.: *Neue Geschichte der Fotografie.* Cologne 1998—[15] Duchamp, Marcel: *Der kreative Akt,* first published in: *Art News,* No. 4. New York 1957, 28-29—[16] On the topic "Mobilität und gesellschaftlicher Wandel heute" see the essay: *The Reinvention of Mobility. The Politcs of Mobility as World Design* by Stephan Rammler. 160-176—[17] On the treatment of motion in fine art, from the futurist theory of dynamismo by Umberto Boccioni to contemporary positions, see the essay: *Dynamismo of Post-Industry* by Söke Dinkla, 74-90—[18] On the design of automobiles and the significance of emotionality in car design, see the interview with Chris Bangle: *Strategise Emotions. Considering Car Design.* 212-226—[19] Studies of this kind led to the timing and standardisation of patterns of motion, but also to investigation of peripheral and binocular vision and the measurement and quantification of optical phenomena and forms—according to Jonathan Crary this meant a standardisation of vision or a disciplining of the viewer, via the adaptation of the eye, to rationalised forms of motion, on this, cf.: Crary, Jonathan: *Techniques of the Observer. Vision and Modernity in the Nineteenth Century.* Massachusetts 1990. In this way, the human body becomes part of an apparatus-based combination of media.—[20] On changing and habitualising body techniques through rhythms in many areas of modern life, see the essay: *The Form of Movement and Life. Modern Ergonomics and Rhythmicising life* by Inge Baxmann 114-128—[21] Mumford, Lewis: *Mythos der Maschine. Kultur, Technik und Macht. Die umfassende Darstellung der Entdeckung und Entwicklung der Technik* (The Myth of the Machine 1966). Munich 1984, 571.—[22] On design using mobile elements in architecture today, see the interview with Michael Schumacher: *The Poetry of Motion in Architecture,* 198-210—[23] Like the flying city designs by Wenzel Hablik circa 1903.—[24] Zinsmeister, Annett : *Constructing Utopia. Konstruktionen künstlicher Welten.* Zurich, Berlin 2005—[25] Nieuwenhuys, Constant Anton: *New Babylon,* 1957–74. A utopian urban project manifest in models, drawings, collages, writing, etc. Constant was a member of the Situationist International from 1957–1960.—[26] The vision of setting entire cities in motion was already conceived centuries before by Cyrano de Bergerac in his fictive novel *Journey to the Moon States* from 1642, in which he described a lunar state with wandering houses and walls on wheels, which could move with the help of sails. The way in which entirely real gigantic landscape masses can be set in motion today and adopt fresh shape as new artificial constructions is described in the essay: *Landscape in Motion* by Christophe Girot, 178-194—[27] A comprehensive work on Adolphe Appia appeared in 1994: Beacham, Richard C.: *Adolphe Appia: Artist and Visionary of the Modern Theatre,* Chur: Harwood Press.—[28] See more details on: Zinsmeister, Annett: *Analogien im Digitalen. Architektur zwischen Messen und Zählen* in Warnke, Coy, Tohlen: *Hyperkult II. Zur Ortsbestimmung analoger und digitaler Medien.* Bielefeld 2005, 95-109.—[29] Rudolph von Laban: *Kinetografie. Labanotation: Einführung in die Grundbegriffe der Bewegungs- und Tanzschrift.* Claude Perrottet (ed.), Noetzel 1995, *Choreutik:*

von Bewegung für die Gestaltung aus unterschiedlichen Perspektiven. Die Beiträge aus der darstellenden und bildenden Kunst, aus Architektur, Design, Landschaftsarchitektur, Medien- und Kulturwissenschaft, Soziologie etc. illustrieren die Bedeutung und Darstellung von Bewegung in Kunst, Architektur und Design anhand historischer Entwicklungen, grenzüberschreitender Zusammenhänge und diskutieren aktuelle sowie zukünftige Tendenzen.

Die Texte basieren auf dem gleichnamigen Symposium des Weißenhof-Instituts an der Staatlichen Akademie der Bildenden Künste in Stuttgart, das sich als interdisziplinäre Plattform versteht und den Dialog zwischen unterschiedlichen Disziplinen, zwischen Theorie, Lehre und Praxis befördert. Die Autoren zeichnet aus, dass sie auch an den Rändern ihrer jeweiligen Disziplin, oder in mehreren Disziplinen qualifiziert sind, oder gestalterische Praxis mit theoretischen Untersuchungen verbinden. Um trotz der weitreichenden Thematik einen roten Faden aufzeigen zu können, ist die Zusammenstellung der Beiträge entsprechend sorgfältig aufgebaut, sodass sie untereinander thematische Schnittmengen bzw. Anknüpfungen bieten und den geneigten Lesern in ihrer Zusammenstellung facettenreiche Einsichten und hoffentlich auch Inspirationen bieten können.

ANMERKUNGEN—1 Gerätschaften wie der Gnomon und das Hemicyclum, beides Vorläufer der Sonnenuhr, finden sich bereits bei den Babyloniern um ca. 3000 vor unserer Zeitrechnung. Siehe auch: Pichot, André: *Die Geburt der Wissenschaft. Von den Babyloniern zu den frühen Griechen,* Frankfurt/Main 1995, 103f.—**2** Aristoteles: *Physik,* 8. Buch. Leipzig 1829, 191ff: Vier Arten der Bewegung: 1. Bewegung als Entstehen und Vergehen, 2. Bewegung als qualitative Veränderung, 3. Bewegung als quantitative Veränderung (Zu- und Abnahme) und 4. Bewegung als örtliche Veränderung.—**3** Zur Einführung in die Thematik siehe auch den Beitrag: *Mobile und Stabile* von Margitta Buchert, 49-73—**4** 1609 erschien Keplers Werk: *Astronomia Nova* (Die neue Astronomie), in der unter anderem die beiden ersten Planetengesetze beschrieben werden: 1. Die Bahnen der Planeten sind Ellipsen, in deren Brennpunkt die Sonne steht. 2. Der Radiusvektor (Verbindungslinie Sonne – Planet) überstreicht in gleichen Zeiten gleiche Flächen.—**5** Das *Trägheitsprinzip (lex prima):* „Ein Körper verharrt im Zustand der Ruhe oder der gleichförmigen Translation, sofern er nicht durch einwirkende Kräfte zur Änderung seines Zustands gezwungen wird." Das *Aktionsprinzip (lex secunda):* „Die Änderung der Bewegung einer Masse ist der Einwirkung der bewegenden Kraft proportional und geschieht nach der Richtung derjenigen geraden Linie, nach welcher jene Kraft wirkt." Das *Reaktionsprinzip (lex tertia):* actio – reactio—**6** Folgende Passagen enthalten u.a. Auszüge aus einem Beitrag, der 2010 erschienen ist: Zinsmeister, Annett: „Modularisierung von Raum und Bewegung als ästhetisches Programm". In: Brandstetter, Gabriele/Wiens, Birgit: *Theater ohne Fluchtpunkt,* Berlin 2010, 76-104.—**7** In den Bauhütten des Mittelalters wurden Gestaltungsanweisungen in der Regel mündlich überliefert (auch von Generation zu Generation) und meist nur als Vertragsgrundlage schriftlich oder auch in schematischen Zeichnungen fixiert.—**8** Die *Beauchamp-Feuillet Notation* wurde von Pierre Beauchamp in den 1680er Jahren entwickelt und daraufhin von Raoul-Roger Feuillet schriftlich fixiert,—**9** Ende der 1870er und Anfang der 1880er Jahre gelang es zudem

Grundlagen der Raumharmonielehre des Tanzes, Noetzel 1991. —[30] E.g. *DanceForms 1.0/EW Notator18,* and *LED&LINTEL,* a Windows Editor and Interpreter for *Labanotation.* Others are being developed, e.g. *Limelight,* a modular program package that is said to contain all the necessary components for computer-aided choreography. *Labanpad* is a program design for interactive comprehension of *Labanotation,* as well as notation and protocols during performances. Cf. also: Christian Griesbeck: *Computer Choreographie/Choreologie Projekt,* University of Frankfurt/Main 1996: http://user.unifrankfurt.de/~griesbec/CHOREO.HTML examples and interactive websites: http://www.dance.ohio-state.edu/labanlab/—[31] William Forsythe: *Improvisation Technologies. A Tool for the Analytical Dance Eye.* Zentrum für Kunst und Medientechnologie, Deutsches Tanzarchiv Köln, Stiftung Kultur, 2003. For more details on *Synchronious Objects,* cf. the essay: *Traces and Artefacts of Physical Intelligence* by Scott de Lahunta. 94-108 —[32] On the figure of motion in the functional gestures of everyday electronics, see the essay: *The Legibility of Movement* by Claus Pias. 130-158

durch das Kollodiumverfahren und später mittels Bromsilbergelatine, die Belichtungszeiten zu verkürzen.—**10** Im Jahr 1839 wurde die neue Technik von unterschiedlichsten Protagonisten in unterschiedlichen Ländern öffentlich vorgestellt: William Henry Fox Talbot verlas am 31.1.1839 in der Royal Society in London seine Denkschrift zur „Kunst der photogenischen Zeichnung", der Privatforscher Hippolyte Bayard zeigte am 24.6.1839 erstmals Fotografien in einer Ausstellung, die er mit einer Camera Obscura gemacht hatte, und am 19.8.1839 wurde im Institut de France erstmalig das Verfahren der Daguerrotypie von Louis-Jaques-Mandé Daguerre der Öffentlichkeit präsentiert. Siehe auch: Frizot, Michel: *Neue Geschichte der Fotografie,* Köln: Könemann 1998—**11** Die erste bewegte Projektion mit einer Laterna Magica inszenierte der Feldmarschallleutnant Franz von Uchatiu 1845 vor seinen Kadetten. Mit der Kombination aus Stroboskopeffekt und Plateau'schem Lebensrad gelang es ihm, den Flug selbst gezeichneter Geschosse an die Wand des Hörsaales zu projizieren und somit die Illusion bewegter Bilder zu erzeugen (Phenakistioskop).—**12** Basierend auf der Erfindung des astronomischen Revolvers des französischen Astronomen Pierre Jules César Janssen im Jahr 1874, der zur Aufzeichnung des Venusdurchgangs vor der Sonne in Japan im selben Jahr entwickelt wurde.—**13** Ausführlich zu Etienne Jules Marey: Braun, Marta: *Picturing Time: The Work of Etienne Jules Marey 1830-1904.* Chicago 1992. Und zu Eadweard Muybridge und der Entwicklung der Momentaufnahme: Prodger, Phillip: *Time stands still. Muybridge and the instantaneous ohotography movement,* New York 2003—**14** ...oder sogar zu Korrekturen im eigenen Werk verleitete: Meissonier, der u.a. auch zu den Subskribenten von *Animal locomotion* zählte, soll z.B. nach der Lektüre die Fußstellung der Pferde in zwei seiner Gemälde korrigiert haben. Vgl. hierzu: Frizot, Michel: *E.J. Muybridge: Animal Locomotion* In: Ders.: *Neue Geschichte der Fotografie.* Köln 1998—
15 Duchamp, Marcel: *Der kreative Akt,* Erstveröffentlichung in: *Art News,* Nr. 4. New York 1957, 28-29.—**16** Zum Thema „Mobilität und gesellschaftlicher Wandel heute" siehe den Beitrag: *Die Neuerfindung der Mobilität. Mobilitätspolitik als Weltdesign* von Stephan Rammler, 161-177—**17** Über den Umgang mit Bewegung in der bildnerischen Kunst, ausgehend von der futuristischen Theorie des Dynamismo von Umberto Boccioni bis zu zeitgenössischen Positionen siehe den Beitrag: *Dynamismo der Postindustrie* von Söke Dinkla, 75-93—**18** Zur Gestaltung von Automobilen und der Bedeutung von Emotionalität im Autodesign siehe das Interview mit Chris Bangle: *Strategize Emotions. Considerations about cardesign.* 213-231—**19** Derlei Studien führten zu einer Taktung und Normierung von Bewegungsabläufen; aber auch die Erforschung des peripheren und binokularen Sehens und der Messung und Quantifizierung optischer Phänomene und Formen hatten laut Jonathan Crary eine Normierung des Sehens bzw. eine Disziplinierung des Betrachters durch die Anpassung des Auges an rationalisierte Bewegungsformen zur Folge, vgl. hierzu: Crary, Jonathan: *Techniques of the Observer. Vision and Modernity in the Nineteenth Century.* Massachusetts 1990. Der menschliche Körper wird damit zu einem Teil eines apparativen Medienverbundes.—**20** Zur Veränderung und Habitualisierung von Körpertechniken in unterschiedlichsten Lebensbereichen in der Moderne durch maschinelle Rhythmen siehe den Beitrag: *Bewegungsform und Lebensform. Moderne Arbeitswissenschaft und die Rhythmisierung des Lebens* von Inge Baxmann, 115-129—**21** Mumford, Lewis: *Mythos der Maschine. Kultur, Technik und Macht. Die umfassende Darstellung der Entdeckung und Entwicklung der Technik* (The Myth of the Machine 1966). München 1984, 571.—**22** Zum gestalterischen Umgang mit beweglichen Elementen in der Architektur heute siehe das Interview mit Michael Schumacher: *Die Poesie der Bewegung,* 199-211—**23** Wie zum Beispiel die fliegenden Standtentwürfe von Wenzel Hablik um 1903—**24** Zinsmeister, Annett: *Constructing Utopia. Konstruktionen künstlicher Welten,* Zürich, Berlin 2005—**25** Nieuwenhuys, Constant Anton: *New Babylon,*

1957–74. Utopisches Stadtprojekt, das sich in Modellen, Zeichnungen, Collagen, Schriften etc. manifestierte. Constant war von 1957–1960 Mitglied der Situationistischen Internationale.—26 Die Vision, ganze Städte in Bewegung zu setzen, ersann übrigens bereits Jahrhunderte zuvor Cyrano de Bergerac in seinem fiktiven Roman *Mondstaaten* von 1642, in dem er wandernde Häuser und Mauern auf Rädern in einem lunaren Staat beschrieb, die sich mit Hilfe von Segeln fortbewegen konnten. Wie heute aber überaus real gigantische Landschaftsmassen in Bewegung gesetzt werden können und als neue artifizielle Konstruktionen Gestalt annehmen können, beschreibt der Beitrag: *Landschaft in Bewegung* von Christophe Girot, 179-197—27 2006 ist ein umfassendes Werk über Adolphe Appia auch in deutscher Übersetzung erschienen: Beacham, Richard C.: *Adolphe Appia: Künstler und Visionär des Modernen Theaters,* Berlin: Alexanderverlag 2006 Über das aktuelle Erbe Appias ist zu empfehlen: Brandstetter, Gabriele/Wiens, Birgit: *Theater ohne Fluchtpunkt.* Berlin 2010.—28 Hierzu ausführlich: Zinsmeister, Annett: *Analogien im Digitalen. Architektur zwischen Messen und Zählen* in Warnke, Coy , Tohlen: *Hyperkult II. Zur Ortsbestimmung analoger und digitaler Medien.* Bielefeld 2005, 95-109.—29 Rudolph von Laban: *Kinetografie. Labanotation: Einführung in die Grundbegriffe der Bewegungs- und Tanzschrift.* Claude Perrottet (Hg.), Noetzel 1995, *Choreutik: Grundlagen der Raumharmonielehre des Tanzes,* Noetzel 1991.—30 zum Beispiel *DanceForms 1.0/EW Notator18,* sowie *LED&LINTEL,* ein Windows Editor und Interpreter für *Labanotation,* oder sind in der Entwicklung, zum Beispiel *Limelight,* ein modulares Programmpaket, das alle notwendigen Komponenten für eine Computer-Aided-Choreografie beinhalten soll. *Labanpad* ist ein Programmentwurf zur interaktiven Erfassung von *Labanotation,* zur Aufzeichnung und für Mitschriften bei Aufführungen. Siehe auch: Christian Griesbeck: *Computer Choreographie/Choreologie Projekt,* Universität Frankfurt/Main 1996: http://user.unifrankfurt.de/~griesbec/CHOREO.HTML Beispiele und interaktive Webseiten: http://www.dance.ohio-state.edu/labanlab/—31 William Forsythe: *Improvisation Technologies. A Tool fort he Analytical Dance Eye.* Zentrum für Kunst und Medientechnologie, Deutsches Tanzarchiv Köln, Stiftung Kultur, 2003. Siehe ausführlich zur Arbeit von William Forsythe und *Synchronious Objects* den Beitrag: *Spuren und Artefakte physischer Intelligenz* von Scott deLahunta 95-113—32 Zur Gestalt der Bewegung in der funktionalen Gestik von Alltagselektronik siehe den Beitrag: *Die Lesbarkeit der Bewegung* von Claus Pias, 131-159

Margitta Buchert
Mobile and Stabile

Margitta Buchert has been **Professor for Architecture and Art in 20./21.Centuries at IGT, Faculty of Architecture and Landscape Sciences,** Leibniz Universität Hannover since 2000. Main topics of research: Reflexive Design, Urban Architecture, Aesthetics and Contextuality of Architecture, Art, City and Nature. Publications include: „Relations. Design and Research in Architecture" in: *Eklat,* 76-86 (ed.: Ute Frank, 2011), „Actuating. Koolhaas' urban aesthetics" in: *Mimarlikta Estetik Düsünce,* 223-231 (ed.: Jale Erzen, 2010), *In Bewegung... Architektur und Kunst* (ed. with Carl Zillich, 2008), *Über Architektur. Bernard Tschumis Parc de la Villette in Paris* (1995).

Margitta Buchert
Mobile und Stabile

Margitta Buchert ist seit 2000 Professorin für Architektur und Kunst im 20./21. Jahrhundert am Institut für Geschichte und Theorie der Architektur, Fakultät für Architektur und Landschaft, Leibniz Universität Hannover. Forschungsschwerpunkte: Reflexives Entwerfen, Urbane Architekturen sowie Ästhetik und Kontextualität von Architektur, Kunst, Stadt und Natur. Publikationen u. a.: „Formen der Relation. Entwerfen und Forschen in der Architektur" in: *Eklat,* 76-86 (Hg.: Ute Frank, 2011), „Actuating. Koolhaas' urban aesthetics" in: *Mimarlikta Estetik Düsünce,* 223-231 (Hg.: Jale Erzen, 2010), *In Bewegung... Architektur und Kunst* (Hg. mit Carl Zillich, 2008), *Über Architektur. Bernard Tschumis Parc de la Villette in Paris* (1995).

THE SHAPE OF MOVEMENT?—The question of the shape of movement possesses a dynamising force of its own. Shape is often equated with external form, with a figure or outline—with something's external appearance and condition. In some modern scientific concepts, the ideas of conciseness or integrity already easily associated with these terms are more strongly linked to moments of stabilisation. As an epistemological concept in perceptual psychology or robotics, for example, shape is described as a tendency to order one's environment into meaningful units. It is also associated with invariables that are constituted from sensory data or information streams by means of simplification.[1] In contrast to the stable, which the concept of shape thus implies, the significant field of movement refers to a broad area of alterable relations.

The existentially fundamental significance of movement in man's basic orientation and reference to his environment,[2] as well as the otherness of the phenomenological field of movement by contrast to such simplified tangibility explains the enduring power of its fascination—for centuries—in many disciplines of research and creativity like mathematics, physics and astronomy, or philosophy and the arts. In contrast to rationally determined, objective registration and logical integration—dominant in the development and use of technical instruments and apparatuses, for example, as well as in measuring and measurable procedures as opposed to attempts to fix, manipulate, and test motion in definable systems—the intention of architectural and artistic design beyond this is to sensitise man's aesthetic awareness and his capacity for differentiation.[3] This helps to avoid one-sided approaches and to open up qualitative spaces for cultural balance. The creation of variations is one of the principal motors of aesthetic design; the creative, inventive process itself is characterised by its dynamic nature.[4] The question of the shape of movement includes the ambiguity between more or less fixed shaping and the processual quality of motion, between permanence and change, between the static and the dynamic—mobile and stabile. Interestingly, relations of these conditional states also offer the potential to characterise contemporary cultural conditions.

GLOBAL FLOW—Globally, a high level has been reached not only of mechanised movement by means of vehicles, but also of increasing movement by human beings due to migration and multilocation, as well as the movement of information, money, goods, ideas, knowledge, and practices; as a consequence, motion plays a decisive part in shaping contemporary cultures.[5] Current macrostructurally integrative diagnostic discourse selects interpretative models in which flowing movement, the mobile, and the resting, the stabile, appear as central aspects.[6] Thus, for example, a sphere of trends towards contemporary information-technological and economic globalisation is compared and contrasted to a sphere of familiar orders.[7] In another interpretation developed via historical comparison, the past phase of modernity is now regarded as a stable point from which it is possible to distinguish today's contemporary, fleeting, flowing

GESTALT DER BEWEGUNG?—Die Frage nach der Gestalt der Bewegung birgt eine dynamisierende Kraft. Oftmals wird Gestalt mit äußerer Form, mit Figur und Umriss oder auch mit Erscheinung und Beschaffenheit gleichgesetzt. Die bereits mit diesen Begriffen assoziierbaren Vorstellungen einer Prägnanz oder Ganzheit werden in einigen modernen wissenschaftlichen Konzepten noch stärker mit Stabilisierungsmomenten verknüpft. Gestalt als erkenntnistheoretisches Konzept der Wahrnehmungspsychologie oder Robotik beispielsweise wird beschrieben als eine Tendenz zur Ordnung der Umwelt in sinnvolle Einheiten. Sie wird auch verbunden mit Invarianten, die aus Sinnesdaten oder Informationsströmen durch Vereinfachung konstituiert werden.[1] Im Unterschied zu einem Stabilen, das der Begriff damit anzeigt, weist das Bedeutungsfeld von Bewegung auf ein weites Feld veränderlicher Relationen.

Die existenziell grundlegende Bedeutung von Bewegung in der Grundorientierung und im Umweltbezug des Menschen[2] sowie das Anderssein des Phänomenfelds der Bewegung gegenüber jeder vereinfachten Fassbarkeit begründet ihre Faszinationskraft für viele forschende und schöpferische Disziplinen wie beispielsweise für die Mathematik, Physik und Astronomie oder die Philosophie und die Künste seit Jahrhunderten. Gegenüber einer rationalistisch geprägten objektiven Erfassung und logischen Integration, wie sie beispielsweise in der Entwicklung und Anwendung technischer Instrumente und Apparate sowie in mess- und bemessbaren Verfahren vorherrscht, gegenüber den Versuchen, Bewegung in definierbaren Systemen zu fixieren, zu manipulieren und zu kontrollieren, intendiert architektonische und künstlerische Gestaltung darüber hinaus eine Sensibilisierung des ästhetischen Bewusstseins der Menschen und ihrer Differenzierungsfähigkeit.[3] Dies trägt dazu bei, Vereinseitigungen zu vermeiden und qualitative Freiräume für eine kulturelle Balance zu öffnen. Variantenbildung ist einer der grundlegenden Motoren ästhetischer Gestaltung, der kreativ schöpferische Prozess selbst durch einen dynamischen Charater geprägt.[4] Die Frage nach der Gestalt der Bewegung enthält die Ambiguität zwischen dem mehr oder weniger fixierten Gestalthaften und einer Prozessualität von Bewegung, zwischen Permanenz und Veränderung, zwischen Statischem und Dynamischem – Mobile und Stabile. Interessanterweise bieten Relationen dieser Zustandsformen auch das Potenzial, zeitgenössische kulturelle Konditionen zu charakterisieren.

GLOBALES FLIESSEN—Nicht nur die technisierte Fortbewegung mit Fahrzeugen, auch die zunehmende Bewegung von Menschen durch Migration und Multilokalität, die Bewegung von Informationen, Finanzen, Gütern, Ideen, Wissen und Praktiken hat global ein hohes Ausmaß erreicht und prägt die zeitgenössischen Kulturen wesentlich mit.[5] Makrostrukturell übergreifende, gegenwartsdiagnostische Diskurse wählen Interpretationsmodelle, in denen das fließend Bewegte, Mobile ebenso wie das eher Ruhende, Stabile als zentrale Aspekte auftreten.[6] So wird beispielsweise einem Raum der Ströme der zeitgenössischen informationstechnologischen und

modernity,[8] in which the shape of life is linked to a concept of mobility and flexibility as well as concepts of the constantly moving, ultra-flexible human being. Various current experiences of everyday life also point to characteristics of movement, as accentuated in observations of contemporary sociocultural conditions.[9] The conditions—described and conveyed by the media—of mobility, velocity, change, being on the move, flexibility, transformation, and restlessness on the one hand, and the complementary states of deceleration, slowness, endurance, and stability on the other centre on qualitative characteristics in the significant fields of movement.

In contemporary architecture and art, movement as a thematic focus is often linked to a specific understanding of universal spatiotemporal conditions. Time is not only described as a continuous sequence and space not merely as something that can be defined by physical borders. Familiar orders and orientations are imagined and interpreted in a qualitatively different way by means of alterable, more complex structures.[10] Something very similar emerged as early as the beginning of the twentieth century due to industrialisation and the development of new technical media like film, and with reference to natural scientific models like Albert Einstein's four-dimensional space-time. Associated with this were fragmentation, overlapping, and the permeation of spatiotemporal perceptions: qualities for which corresponding creative methods were sought in all fields of art.[11] Here, the described creative intentions of succession and simultaneity as they appeared in Cubism and Futurism, for example, or the architectural spatial concepts of flowing space, or the *promenade architecturale* of classical modernism, including associations with movement, all point to this close connection between space and time. The question of how relations between mobile and immobile conditional states are characterised here still remains open.

RELATIVE MOTION—One distinction made in human experiences of movement is extremely relevant to expressions of design in architecture and art, and helps to outline these aspects rather more clearly. Two large work groups by American artist Alexander Calder are suited ideally to showing up a first level of differentiation (*1, 2* p. 56). When, in Paris in 1931, Marcel Duchamp suggested the term *mobile* for his colleague's works in view of their mobility, he was referring to a group of abstract sculptures, most of which were hung from the ceiling, made from light metal plates cut into shape, steel tubes, wire, and wood; their components were set in motion by wind, water, electronic motors, or simply by hand.[12] The inherent mobility of these artistic works is linked to their forms' irregular striving in different directions, a dynamic quality with which art theorist and psychologist Rudolf Arnheim, for example, characterised representations of movement in paintings and statues more comprehensively.[13]

Calder's mobiles, which were stimulated by two-dimensional, non-representational painting and accentuated by largely monochrome colouration, are examples in which the application of external energy causes a

wirtschaftlichen Globalisierung der Raum der Orte der vertrauten Ordnungen gegenübergestellt.[7] In einer anderen, über den historischen Vergleich entwickelten Interpretation wird die vergangene Phase der Moderne nun als stabil betrachtet, von der sich die zeitgenössische flüchtige, fließende Moderne unterscheide,[8] in der sich Lebensgestaltung mit einem Konzept von Mobilität und Flexibilität verbinde sowie mit Vorstellungen des ständig bewegten und ultraflexiblen Menschen. Auf Bewegungseigenschaften verweisen ebenfalls verschiedene der gegenwärtigen Alltagserfahrungen, wie sie in Beobachtungen zeitgenössischer soziokultureller Konditionen hervorgehoben werden.[9] Die beschriebenen und medial kommunizierten Zustände von Mobilität, Geschwindigkeit, Veränderung, Unterwegssein, Flexibilität, Wandel und Rastlosigkeit einerseits und die komplementären Zustandsformen der Entschleunigung, der Langsamkeit, der Dauer und des Stabilen andererseits kreisen um qualitative Eigenschaften in den Bedeutungsfeldern von Bewegung.

In der zeitgenössischen Architektur und Kunst ist die Thematisierung von Bewegung oftmals verbunden mit einer spezifischen Auffassung raum-zeitlicher Weltverhältnisse. Zeit wird nicht nur als kontinuierliche Abfolge beschrieben und Raum nicht allein als über physische Grenzen definierbar. Vertraute Ordnungen und Orientierungen werden durch veränderliche, komplexere Gefüge qualitativ anders vorgestellt und interpretiert.[10] Durchaus Ähnliches zeichnete sich infolge der Industrialisierung und der Entwicklung neuer technischer Medien wie beispielsweise des Films sowie im Bezug auf naturwissenschaftliche Modelle wie Albert Einsteins vierdimensionale Raumzeit bereits zu Beginn des letzten Jahrhunderts ab. Fragmentierung, Überlagerung und Durchdringung von Raum-Zeit-Wahrnehmungen wurden damit verbunden, Eigenschaften, zu denen in allen künstlerischen Bereichen entsprechende Gestaltungsweisen gesucht wurden.[11] Dabei verweisen die beschriebenen gestalterischen Intentionen von Sukzession und Simultaneität, wie sie beispielsweise im Kubismus und Futurismus auftraten, oder die Bewegungsassoziationen einschließenden architektonischen Raumkonzepte des *fließenden Raumes* oder der *promenade architecturale* der klassischen Moderne auf diese enge Verbindung von Raum und Zeit. Offen bleibt die Frage, wie damit immer auch Relationen zwischen bewegten und unbewegten Zustandsformen charakterisiert werden.

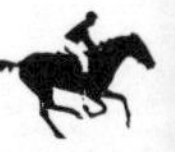

RELATIVE BEWEGUNG—Eine Unterscheidung menschlicher Bewegungserfahrungen, die für gestalterische Artikulationen in Architektur und Kunst von hoher Relevanz ist, kann diese Aspekte etwas deutlicher umreißen. Die beiden großen Werkgruppen des amerikanischen Künstlers Alexander Calder eignen sich hervorragend, um eine erste Differenzierungsebene aufzuzeigen (*1, 2* S. 56). Als Marcel Duchamp 1931 in Paris für die Werke seines Künstlerkollegen im Blick auf deren Beweglichkeit die Bezeichnung *Mobile* vorschlug, bezog er sich auf eine Gruppe abstrakter, meist an der Decke aufgehängter Skulpturen, die aus leichten, in Formen

dynamic structure to develop[14]; a process that can also be found—without necessarily being connected to any artistic intention—in architecture, e.g., in the factual physical movement of shade or ventilation elements on façades and windows. In contrast to aspects of movement that can be grasped using technical logic, Calder's artistic works—with their playful, weightless alternation between mobility and multistability—point to the intangible dimensions of the phenomenon of movement in our experience of the world. Above all, the mobile creations mentioned above share the ability to motivate active movement of our eyes; their visual perception takes place from a relatively stable position.

However, the fact that something moves and is thus perceived visually is only one possible relation and type of perception. The human body in motion reveals an additional level. In the case of a later group of works by Calder—which also owe their name *stabiles* to an artist colleague, this time to Hans Arp—concrete physical movement on the part of the viewer is incorporated into the conception of the monumental sculptural works as an intended aspect of perception.[15] They are not manifest as mass formations in the sense of self-contained formal volumes, but were constructed from heavy triangular and arc-shaped, monochrome metal plates leaning against each other. The parts of the sculptural composition are immobile. Nonetheless, a three-dimensional formation as well as kinetic potential is suggested by the flat, angular, and rounded elements pointing in various directions. In addition, their size and the open spaces between them prompt the viewer's physical movement around and even through the work. In a comparable way to the perception of architecture, the experience of this sculpture highlights the specific significance of our own physical movement in the perception of the three-dimensional environment.

An endless repertoire of potential possibilities opens up when the focus shifts to the representation of the human body in motion. Let us take a look, for example, at some sculptures made by Alberto Giacometti after 1945. In sculptures like *Falling Man* or *Walking Man* movements are merely suggested by means of reduced gestures (*3* p. 57).[16] Volume in the extremely thin human figures has been retracted to a minimum, the proportions are altered, and the rough qualities of the material blur the contours. In space-generating interim states, which seem to contain not only what went before but what will come in the future, the figures do not embody or represent any actual course of motion. What is conveyed is a meaningful, succinct section of the movement, but in an immobile state. The mobile and the stabile work together to help us understand these sculptures, inasmuch as the characteristic section of movement refers to our own experience of physical movement.

Knowledge of such patterns of movement is stored in the human consciousness, as neuroscientific research has indicated. Basic types are remembered—acquired and stored as a result of one's own practice and the observation of other movements.[17] The content of perception is a combination of those memories and what is perceived in the artwork,

geschnittenen Metallplatten, Stahlrohr, Draht und Holz gemacht waren und deren Bestandteile durch Wind, Wasser, Elektromotoren oder mittels der Hand in Bewegung versetzt wurden.[12] Die inhärente Beweglichkeit dieser künstlerischen Werke ist mit einem ungleichmäßigen Streben der Formen nach verschiedenen Richtungen verbunden, eine dynamische Eigenschaft, mit der beispielsweise der Kunsttheoretiker und Psychologe Rudolf Arnheim Bewegungsrepräsentationen in Gemälden und Statuen auch übergreifender charakterisierte.[13]

Bei den durch die flächige, nicht-gegenständliche Malerei angeregten und durch wenige monochrome Farbigkeit betonten Mobiles von Calder handelt es sich um Beispiele, bei denen externe Energiezufuhr eine dynamische Struktur entstehen lässt,[14] ein Verfahren, das auch, ohne in jedem Fall mit einer künstlerischen Intention verbunden zu sein, in der Architektur zu finden ist, beispielsweise bei der faktischen physikalischen Bewegung von Verschattungs- oder Belüftungselementen an Fassaden und Fenstern. Im Unterschied zu den mit technischer Logik begreifbaren Bewegungsaspekten weisen die künstlerischen Werke Calders in ihrer spielerischen, schwerelosen Vielfalt zwischen Mobilität und Multistabilität auf die unfassbaren Dimensionen des Bewegungsphänomens in der lebensweltlichen Erfahrung. Gemeinsam ist den genannten beweglichen Gestaltungen, dass sie vor allem die Bewegungstätigkeit der Augen motivieren und die visuelle Wahrnehmung, die von einem relativ stabilen Standort erfolgt.

Doch: Dass sich etwas bewegt und visuell wahrgenommen wird, ist nur eine der möglichen Relationen und Wahrnehmungsarten. Der menschliche Körper  in Bewegung zeigt eine weitere Ebene an. Bei einer späteren Werkgruppe Calders, die ihre Bezeichnung *Stabile* wiederum einem Künstlerkollegen, diesmal Hans Arp verdankt, ist konkrete körperliche Bewegung des Menschen als intendierter Wahrnehmungsanteil in die Konzeption der monumentalen skulpturalen Werke einbezogen.[15] Sie erscheinen nicht als Massenbildungen im Sinne geschlossener Körperformen, sondern wurden aus schweren, aneinandergelehnten dreieckigen und bogenförmigen Metallplatten in monochromer Farbigkeit konstruiert. Die Teile der skulpturalen Komposition sind immobil. Durch die in verschiedene Richtungen weisenden winkeligen und gerundeten Flächenelemente suggeriert die dreidimensionale Formation gleichwohl kinetisches Potenzial. Zudem evozieren ihre Größe und ihre offenen Zwischenräume die physische Bewegung der Betrachtenden um das Werk herum und durch es hindurch. Vergleichbar einer Architekturwahrnehmung weist das Erleben dieser Skulptur auf die spezifische Bedeutung der eigenen körperlichen Bewegung in der Wahrnehmung dreidimensionaler Umwelt hin.

Ein unendliches Repertoire potenzieller Möglichkeiten öffnet sich, wenn die Repräsentation des menschlichen Körpers in Bewegung in den Fokus tritt. Beispielhaft seien einige nach 1945 entstandene Skulpturen Alberto Giacomettis in den Blick genommen. In Skulpturen wie *Taumelnder Mann* oder *Schreitender Mann* werden durch reduzierte Gesten Bewegungen nur angedeutet.[16] (3 S. 57) In den überschmalen

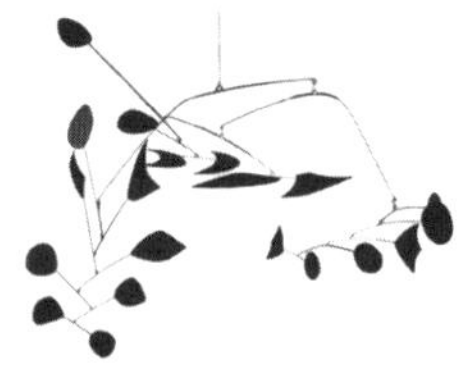

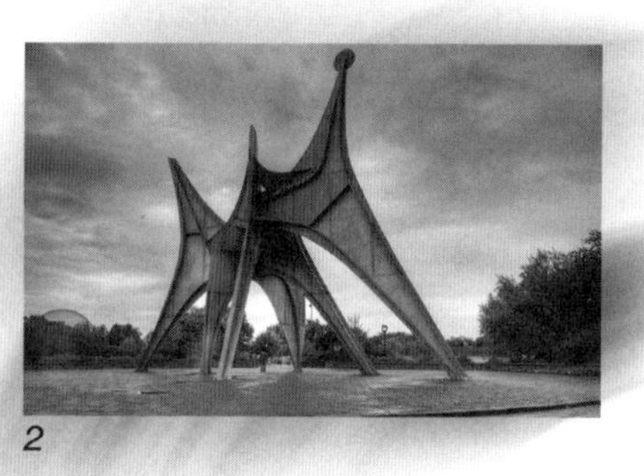

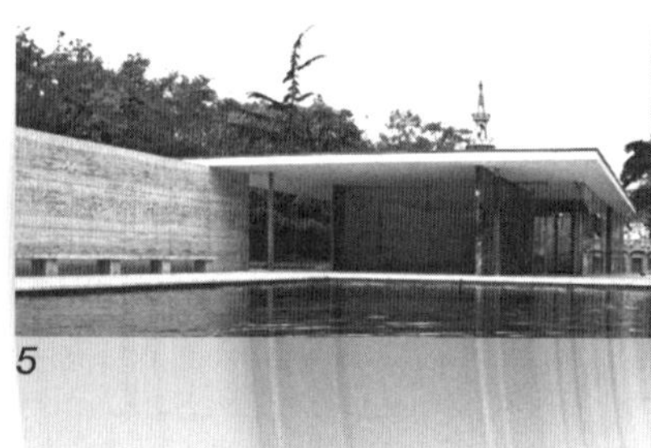

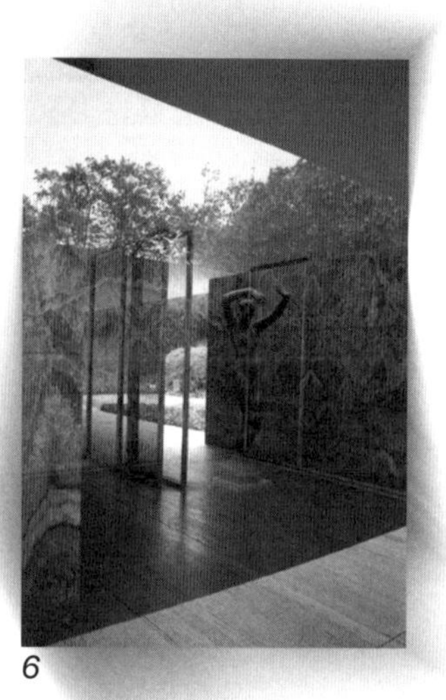

1 Alexander Calder: *The Y,* 1960 — *2* Alexander Calder: *Man* (Stabile), Expo Montreal, 1967 — *3* Alberto Giacometti: *Falling Man,* 1950, bronze — *4* Naum Gabo: *Linear Construction,* 1957–58 or 1969 — *5* Mies van der Rohe: Barcelona Pavilion, 1929, exterior (reconstruction 1986) — *6* Mies van der Rohe: Barcelona Pavilion, 1929, view of inner courtyard (reconstruction 1986) — *7* Le Corbusier: Maison La Roche-Jeanneret, 1923–25, north façade — *8* Le Corbusier: Maison La Roche-Jeanneret, 1923–25, interior view

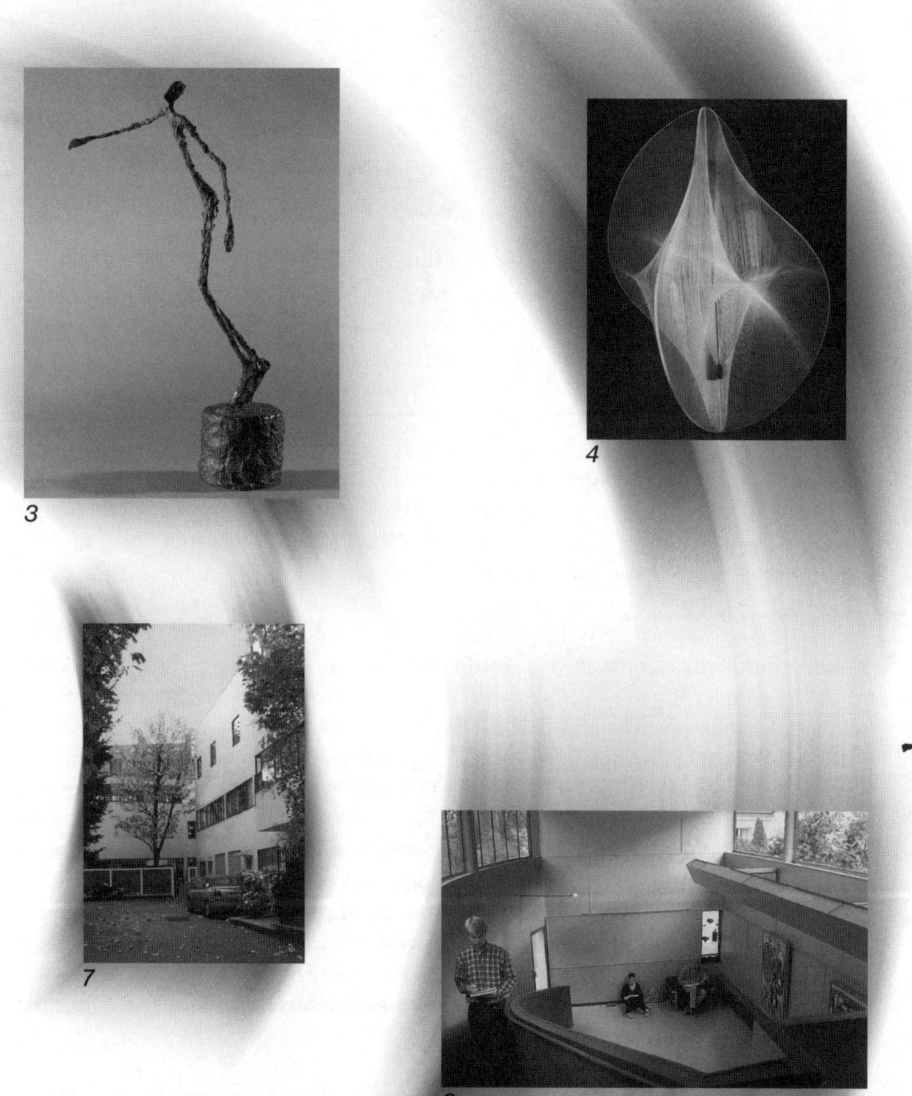

1 Alexander Calder: *The Y,* 1960 — **2** Alexander Calder: *Man* (Stabile), Expo Montreal, 1967 —
3 Alberto Giacometti: *Taumelnder Mann,* 1950, Bronze — **4** Naum Gabo: *Lineare Konstruktion,*
1957—58 oder 1969 — **5** Mies van der Rohe: Barcelona Pavillon, 1929, Außen (Rekonstruktion 1986) —
6 Mies van der Rohe: Barcelona Pavillon, 1929, Ansicht vom Innenhof (Rekonstruktion 1986) —
7 Le Corbusier: Maison La Roche-Jeanneret, 1923–25, Nordfassade — **8** Le Corbusier: Maison La
Roche-Jeanneret, 1923–25, Innenansicht

and this is supplemented and completed into shapes of movement. Although the aforementioned works by Giacometti disclose a number of meaningful dimensions, astonishment at the suggestion of movement is a significant part of their impact. The alienated artistic expression draws more attention to the interrelations and diversity of our perception of reality, also directing us towards quality constellations and the qualitative transformation of states, which is fundamental to our experience and creations of movement. An analytical breakdown of the artistic concept into elements and structures shortens the impact caused by the manifestation, but can also contribute to an outlining—by a first approach—of more stable moments in the progress of movement. The line stands out because of the tall bodies' extreme narrowness. Within the reduced expression, this vertical orientation—in conjunction with the formations of body parts pointing in different directions, slightly curved or angular—acts as a trigger suggesting movement. The fact that actual movement is not a precondition to kinetic perception and that the experience of movement can develop via an imaginary play of forces is illustrated in a different way by Naum Gabo's sculptural constructions inspired by natural scientific models (*4* p. 57).[18] The work group entitled *Linear Construction,* produced in approximately twenty versions from the nineteen-fifties, comprises sculptural objects constructed from interpenetrating, related concave and convex segments made of wire, translucent plastic, and stretched nylon threads. They are characterised by irregular outlines and almost weightless, open volumes. The eye is led from one section to the next. As a result of different light qualities, meaning that translucence and transparency become components incorporated into the design, the effect of overlapping and layering is heightened in a varied, sequential process of perception. The interwoven phenomena of light effects, two-dimensional structure, and geometric formation give the impression of a composition in slight motion, perhaps comparable to vibration.[19] Within the spectrum of typical basic elements of design—structures directly linkable to the evocation of an experience of movement and possessing a degree of transferability—there is also overlapping and layering, as well as lighting and transparent or translucent material qualities.

CHOREOGRAPHIES—In architecture, the way in which parameters and their structural coincidence with modes of functioning engage in a multivalent linkage becomes very apparent. For instance, the dissolution of self-contained voluminosity presented in the artworks above also characterises Mies van der Rohe's Barcelona Pavilion, which was completed in 1929 and rebuilt in 1986 (*5, 6* p. 56). The façade, or rather the wall as a principle terminating space, was replaced by open structures. Permanent extension of the spatial experience is generated not only through the real link between inside and out, however, which is produced as an aspect of perception. Dynamic experiential moments are accentuated by means of free-standing, asymmetrically placed wall segments and by

menschlichen Figuren ist das Volumen auf ein Minimum zurückgedrängt, sind Proportionen verändert und verwischen raue Materialqualitäten die Konturen. In raumschaffenden Zwischenzuständen, die das Vorhergehende und das Zukünftige zu enthalten scheinen, verkörpern und repräsentieren die Figuren keinen tatsächlichen Bewegungsverlauf. Vermittelt wird ein bedeutender, prägnanter Ausschnitt der Bewegung in einem immobilen Zustand. Mobile und Stabile wirken im Verstehen dieser Skulpturen zusammen, indem der charakteristische Bewegungsausschnitt auf die eigene körperliche Bewegungserfahrung verweist.

Im Bewusstsein der Menschen ist, wie neurowissenschaftliche Forschungen zeigen, die Kenntnis solcher Bewegungsmuster gespeichert. Durch die eigene Praxis und durch die Beobachtung von Bewegungen anderer erworbene und gespeicherte Grundtypen werden erinnert.[17] Im Wahrnehmungsinhalt verknüpfen sich das Erinnerte und das im künstlerischen Werk Wahrgenommene und werden zu Bewegungsgestalten ergänzt und vervollständigt. Auch wenn die genannten künstlerischen Werke Giacomettis verschiedenste Bedeutungsdimensionen darbieten, bildet das Staunen über die Bewegungssuggestion einen bedeutenden Anteil ihrer Wirksamkeit. Durch die verfremdende künstlerische Artikulation wird die Aufmerksamkeit für die Relationen und die Vielfalt von Wirklichkeitswahrnehmung erhöht und hierbei auch auf Eigenschaftsgefüge und den qualitativen Wandel von Zuständen gelenkt, der für Bewegungserfahrungen und -gestaltungen grundlegend ist. Eine analytische Auflösung der künstlerischen Gestaltung in Elemente und Strukturen verkürzt das durch die Erscheinung Wirksame, kann aber dazu beitragen, eher stabile Momente von Bewegungsverläufen näherungsweise zu umreißen. Mit der extremen Schmalheit der hoch aufgeschossenen Körper tritt die Linie hervor. In der reduzierten Gestik wirkt diese vertikale Orientiertheit zusammen mit den in unterschiedliche Richtungen weisenden, leicht geschwungenen bzw. gewinkelten Formationen der Körperteile als Auslöser für Bewegungssuggestionen.

Dass kinetische Wahrnehmung keine tatsächlichen Bewegungen voraussetzen und Bewegungserfahrung durch ein imaginäres Kräftespiel entstehen kann, verdeutlichen die durch naturwissenschaftliche Modelle angeregten skulpturalen Konstruktionen Naum Gabos in einer noch anderen Weise.[18] (4 S. 57) Bei der ab den 1950er Jahren in ca. 20 Versionen entstandenen Werkgruppe mit dem Titel *Lineare Konstruktion* handelt es sich um skulpturale Objekte, die aus sich durchdringenden, konkav und konvex zueinander gestellten Flächensegmenten aus Draht, lichtdurchlässigem Kunststoff und verspannten Nylonfäden konstruiert wurden. Sie sind charakterisiert durch irreguläre Umrisse und nahezu schwerelose offene Volumina. Der Blick wird von einem Ausschnitt zum nächsten gelenkt. Durch unterschiedliche Lichtqualitäten, mit denen Transluzenz und Transparenz als gestalterische Komponenten einbezogen sind, verstärkt sich die Wirkung von Überlagerung und Schichtung in einem vielfältig sequenziellen Wahrnehmungsprozess. In der Verflechtung der Erscheinungen von Lichtwirkung, Flächenstruktur und

deliberately leading the eye in diagonals and long axes, by using reflecting, transparent and translucent materials, and the evocation of kinaesthetic activity. Experiences of movement are created through visual, multimodal physical movement within the spatial constellations, whereby walking and remaining still in one place are reciprocal and complementary.

Architecture is the design of experience whenever it is viewed as more than a set framework, neutral background, or indifferent container for activity or usages. Architectonic spaces that form and enclose—in contrast to artworks—the everyday reality of people's lives, provide multisensory stimulation, whereby movement and the surrounding conditions function in unison.[20] Analogies to creative choreography can be found not only in the case of architectonic designs that explicitly intend an experience of movement. In circa 1700 at the latest, the term choreography became associated with a written and/or graphic recording of sequences of dance movements. Since the middle of the twentieth century, its meaning has been changing into an understanding of choreography as the creation of a dance composition in the sense of an artistic organisation of movement.[21] Architecture discloses options for movements; indeed, it is almost inconceivable without them.[22] Stairways or enfilades, for example, are sources of the experience of climbing movement or linear access; an experience that is intersubjective. The approach to buildings from a distance, the transition from outside to inside, access, staying within and assimilation are guided and shaped by the organisation of guiding "route areas" and centralised "place areas," and the transitions between them. The way in which architectonic elements and geometries are arranged—as straight, bent or curving forms, as sequential or rhythmic—the way in which the light or our attention is directed, and in which material qualities are interpreted: all this has an effect on our sequence of movements and our individual, specific experience of movement and architecture.[23]

"This goes so far," architect Le Corbusier expressed in his letters to students, "that architectures can be separated into the dead and the living, depending on whether walking through them is disregarded or, by contrast, is brilliantly regarded."[24] In his designs for the Maison la Roche-Jeanneret in Paris or the Villa Savoye dating from the nineteen-twenties, he had already created architectonic choreographies using the self-explanatory terminology *promenade architecturale* (7, 8 p. 57). Le Corbusier anticipated paths through his architecture and designed sequential structures within the cubic architectural volume using ramps, steps, corridors, and galleries with viewing points along the way. Those paths directed the user's gaze along the building's horizontal and vertical planes and into its depths, and even into the surrounding landscape as well as the outside areas, and thus guided his movements.[25] In this way, the experience of architecture is shaped by moving and standing still within the context of a stable physical-material and constructive structure; it becomes a kinaesthetic sensory experience constituted via memory, current experience,

geometrischer Formation entsteht der Eindruck, als sei die Komposition in leichter Bewegung einer Vibration vergleichbar.[19] Im Spektrum typischer gestalterischer Grundelemente und Strukturen, die mit der Evokation von Bewegungserfahrung in besonderer Weise verbunden werden können und über einen gewissen Grad an Übertragbarkeit verfügen, befinden sich ebenfalls Überlagerung und Schichtung sowie Lichtführung und transparente bzw. transluzente Materialqualitäten.

CHOREOGRAFIEN—Wie Parameter und ihre strukturelle Fügung mit Wirkungsweisen in einer mehrwertigen Verknüpfung ineinandergreifen, zeigt sich in der Architektur in besonderer Weise. Die Auflösung abgeschlossener Körperhaftigkeit, wie sie sich in der Erscheinung der künstlerischen Werke darbot, charakterisiert beispielsweise Mies van der Rohes 1986 rekonstruierten Barcelona-Pavillon von 1929 (*5, 6* S. 56). Die Fassade bzw. die Wand als raumabschließendes Prinzip wurde durch offene Strukturen ersetzt. Eine kontinuierliche Ausdehnung der Raumerfahrung wird aber nicht nur durch die realiter und als Wahrnehmungsinhalt hervorgerufene Verbindung von Innen und Außen bewirkt. Durch frei und asymmetrisch eingestellte Wandsegmente und gezielte Blickführungen in Diagonalen und langen Achsen, durch spiegelnde, transparente und transluzente Materialien verstärken sich dynamische Erfahrungsmomente und evozieren eine kinästhetische Aktivität. Bewegungserfahrungen bilden sich über die visuelle und die multimodale körperliche Bewegung in den räumlichen Konstellationen, wobei sich Gehen und Verweilen wechselweise ergänzen.

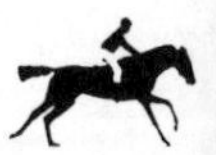

Architektur ist dort, wo sie nicht nur als fixierter Rahmen, neutraler Hintergrund oder indifferenter Behälter von Handlungen bzw. Nutzungen betrachtet wird, Erfahrungsgestaltung. Architektonische Räume, die im Unterschied zu künstlerischen Werken die alltägliche Lebensrealität der Menschen bilden und umgeben, bieten eine multisensorische Stimulation, bei der Bewegung und Umgebungsbedingungen zusammenspielen.[20] Analogien zu choreografischer Gestaltung finden sich nicht nur bei architektonischen Entwürfen, die Bewegungserfahrung explizit intendieren. Spätestens um 1700 wurde der Begriff Choreografie mit der schriftlichen und grafischen Fixierung von tänzerischen Bewegungsabläufen verbunden. Seine Bedeutung wandelte sich seit Mitte des 20. Jahrhunderts zu einem Verständnis von Choreografie als Kreation einer Tanzkomposition im Sinne einer gestalterischen Bewegungsorganisation.[21] Architektur öffnet Bewegungsoptionen, ist ohne sie nahezu nicht denkbar.[22] Treppen beispielsweise oder Enfiladen sind Quellen für Bewegungserfahrungen des Auf- und Absteigens oder der linearen Erschließung, die intersubjektiv teilbar sind. Die Annäherung an Gebäude aus der Ferne, der Übergang von Außen nach Innen, Erschließung, Aufenthalt und Aneignung werden geleitet und geprägt durch eine Organisation gerichteter Wegräume und zentralisierender Orträume und ihrer Übergänge. Wie architektonische Elemente und Geometrien gerade, geknickt oder gebogen gestaltet und sequenziell und rhythmisierend geordnet sind, wie Licht-

and expectation, as well as through differences and links between the *mobile* and *stabile.* This multimodal, sensory-perceptual condition is an essential aspect of the experience of architecture. In contemporary architectural designs, it prompts the formation of architectonic spaces also taking into account the phenomenology of movement. New evocative contexts are added, as reference is made to currently dominant architectural and cultural conditions, in particular to the use of advanced CAAD-programmes or digital communication media. Similar influences providing impulses for multivalued interpretations of architectural-spatial forms are contemporary, natural, scientific, and philosophical interpretations of the world—like chaos and complexity theories or the theory of the rhizome, presented by philosophers Gilles Deleuze and Felix Guattari.

The aim to enable experiences of navigation through architectonic space, for example, is a leading theme in designs by the Dutch architectural office UNStudio. For many years, the strong fascination of motion phenomena prompted Ben van Berkel to research manifestations of motion and its diagrammatic, model representations in the fields of architecture, art, music, dance, and the natural sciences. He discovered many expressive notations of movement, as well as models and patterns of movement referring to dynamic organisational structures. The resulting design archive comprises collections of sketches and transformed diagrams.[26] Mathematical models containing ideas of infinite motion have become stimuli for designs. The design of the Möbius House, built near Amsterdam in 1999, was developed by linking the model of a Möbius strip, which is characterised by a multiplicity defying orientation, with the anticipation of potential uses (*9, 10* p. 64).[27] The glass and concrete walls of the horizontally oriented construction made up of angled, partially interlocking volumes were structured and textured in the same way and using the same material surfaces—on both ceilings and floors—in the internal and external areas. When viewing the house, one is struck not by individual components so much as transitions and connections. In actions related to use and movement, the rooms evoke permanently discontinuous areas of experience in the sense of a dynamic suggestion of motion, although their assimilation is not necessarily associated with concrete physical forms of movement.

It was also the intention of the architects designing the Mercedes Benz Museum, which was built in Stuttgart in 2002–2006 and developed with the aid of digital design programmes[28] (*11, 12* p. 65), to enable a fresh experience of spatiality and of the complexity of motional modalities. In the outside area, the curving form of the structural volume of this eightstorey, concrete and glass building, with minimally ascending floor and ceiling panels on individual floors, appears to be a dynamic configuration. Although in some areas this impression is accentuated by bands of glass at various angles to each other and by slightly overhanging or receding elements, when walking around the building an impression of solidity is paired with familiar expressive architectonic forms. This changes inside, where directly contrasting impulses are interwoven: apparently interlocking

und Blickführungen erfolgen und Materialqualitäten interpretiert werden, hat Auswirkungen auf die Bewegungsfolge und die individuell spezifische Bewegungs- und Architekturerfahrung.[23]

„Das geht so weit", hatte der Architekt Le Corbusier in seinen Briefen an die Studenten geäußert, „daß die Architekturen sich in tote und lebendige einteilen lassen, je nachdem, ob das Durchwandern nicht oder ob es im Gegenteil glänzend befolgt wurde."[24] Bereits in seinen Entwürfen der 1920er Jahre für die Maison la Roche-Jeanneret in Paris oder die Villa Savoye wurden mit der selbsterklärenden Terminologie der *promenade architecturale* bezeichnete architektonische Choreografien geschaffen (*7, 8* S. 57). Le Corbusier antizipierte Wege durch die Architektur und gestaltete innerhalb der kubischen Baukörper sequenzielle Strukturen aus Rampen, Treppen, Korridoren und Galerien mit Aussichtspunkten an diesen Wegen, die in der Horizontalen, Vertikalen und in der Tiefe ausgedehnte Blicke innerhalb des Gebäudes und in die umgebende Landschaft sowie die Außenräume führen und Bewegungen leiten.[25] Die Architekturerfahrung wird in dieser Weise geprägt durch Bewegen und Verweilen im Kontext einer stabilen physisch-materiellen und konstruktiven Struktur, wird zu einer kinästhetischen Sinneserfahrung, die über Erinnerung, aktuelle Erfahrung und Erwartung sowie über Differenzen und Verbindungen von *Mobile* und *Stabile* konstituiert werden.

Diese multimodale sinnliche Wahrnehmungskondition als ein wesentliches Moment der Architekturerfahrung bildet auch in zeitgenössischen Architekturentwürfen Anlass, architektonische Räume in Verbindung mit Bewegungsphänomenalität zu denken. Die Bezugsetzung zu aktuell vorherrschenden architektonischen und kulturellen Konditionen, insbesondere zur Anwendung avancierter CAAD-Programme oder zur Nutzung digitaler Kommunikationsmedien, treten als evokative Kontexte hinzu. Ebenso wirken zeitgenössische naturwissenschaftliche und philosophische Weltinterpretationen beispielsweise der Chaos- und Komplexitätstheorie oder des Rhizoms, das von den Philosophen Gilles Deleuze und Félix Guattari vorgestellt wurde, als impulsgebend für mehrwertige Interpretationen baulich-räumlicher Formationen.

Die Intention, Erfahrungen des Navigierens durch architektonische Räume zu ermöglichen, bildet beispielsweise ein Leitthema der Entwürfe des niederländischen Architekturbüros UNStudio. Die Faszinationskraft von Bewegungsphänomenen veranlasste Ben van Berkel über Jahre hinweg zur forschenden Suche nach ihren Erscheinungen sowie diagrammatischen und modellhaften Darstellungen in den Bereichen Architektur, Kunst, Musik, Tanz oder Naturwissenschaften. Er entdeckte zahlreiche gestische Bewegungsnotationen sowie auf dynamische Organisationsstrukturen Bezug nehmende Modelle und Bewegungsmuster, die in Skizzensammlungen und in transformierten Diagrammen zu einem Entwurfsarchiv wurden.[26] Mathematische Modelle, in denen Vorstellungen von Endlosbewegungen enthalten sind, wurden zu Entwurfsimpulsen. Der Entwurf des 1999 in der Nähe von Amsterdam gebauten Möbiushauses wurde entwickelt aus der Verknüpfung

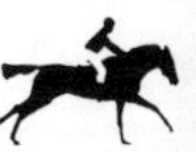

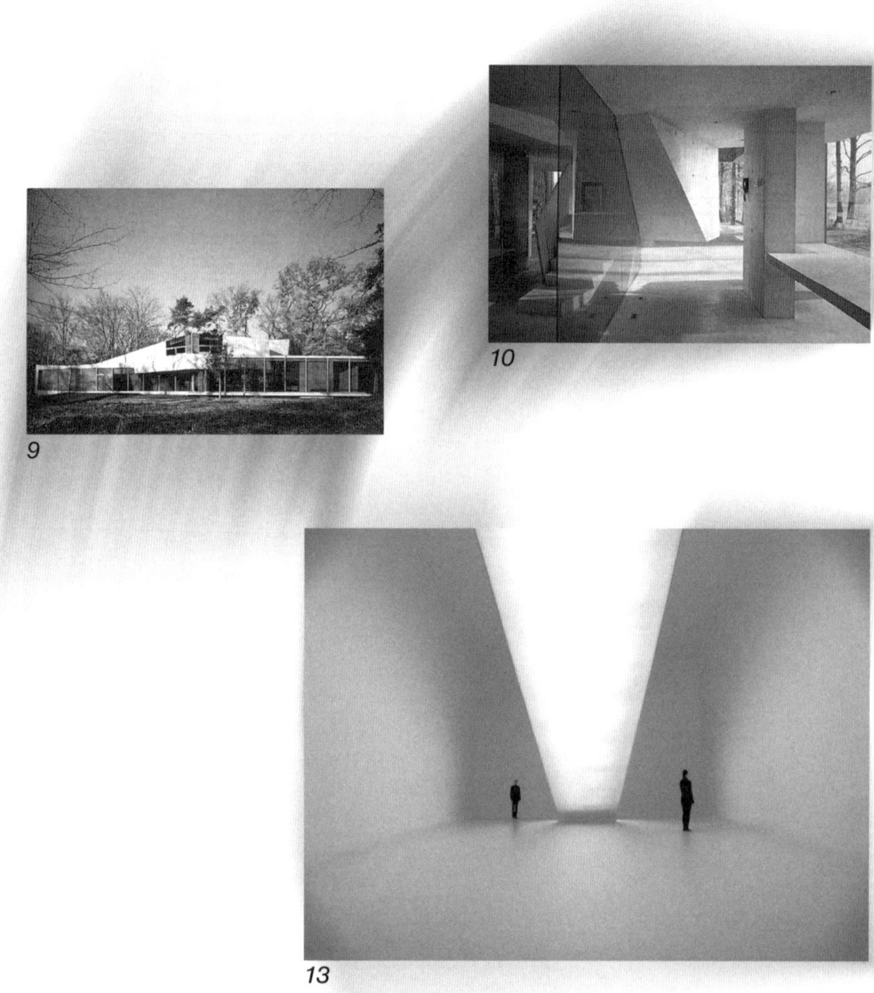

9 UNStudio/Ben van Berkel and Caroline Bos: Möbius House, 'T Gooi near Amsterdam, 1999, exterior view — 10 UNStudio/Ben van Berkel and Caroline Bos: Möbius House, 'T Gooi near Amsterdam, 1999, interior view — 11 UNStudio/Ben van Berkel and Caroline Bos: Mercedes Benz Museum Stuttgart, 2006, diagram — 12 UNStudio/Ben van Berkel and Caroline Bos: Mercedes Benz Museum Stuttgart, 2006, exterior view — 13 James Turrell: *Wolfsburg Project,* 2009, Kunstmuseum Wolfsburg — 14 SANAA Rolex Learning Center of the Ècole Polytechnique Fédérale de Lausanne, Lausanne 2010, north façade

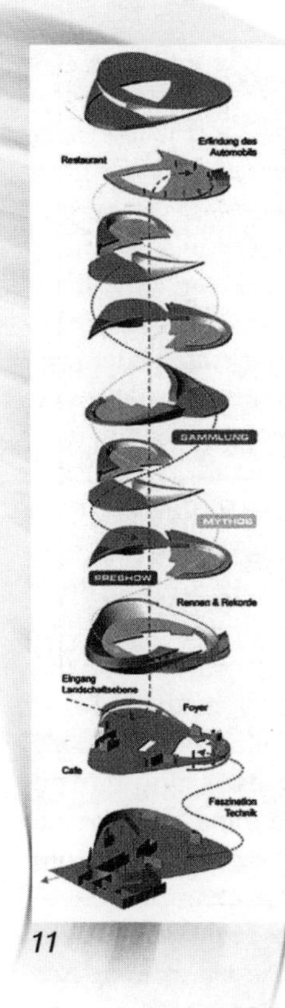

11

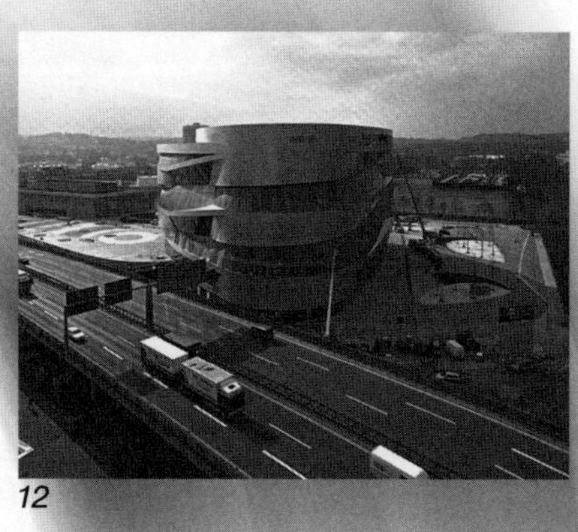

12

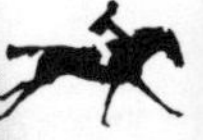

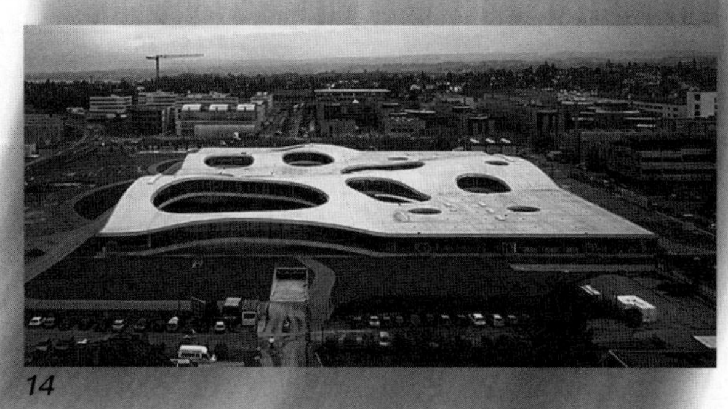

14

9 UNStudio/Ben van Berkel und Caroline Bos: Möbiushaus, 'T Gool bei Amsterdam, 1999, Außenansicht — 10 UNStudio/Ben van Berkel und Caroline Bos: Möbiushaus, 'T Gool bei Amsterdam, 1999, Innenansicht — 11 UNStudio/Ben van Berkel und Caroline Bos: Mercedes Benz Museum Stuttgart, 2006, Diagramm — 12 UNStudio/Ben van Berkel und Caroline Bos: Mercedes Benz Museum Stuttgart, 2006, Außenansicht — 13 James Turrell: *Wolfsburg Project,* 2009, Kunstmuseum Wolfsburg — 14 SANAA Rolex Learning Center der Ècole Polytechnique Fédérale de Lausanne, Lausanne 2010, Nordfassade

spirals and route systems, curving flat surfaces and platforms with alternating, graduated radii wind around a large empty space the height of the building, making orientation extremely difficult. The impression of dynamic diversity and linkage is increased via a sequential experience of movement using ramps and platforms as well as a large number of possible vantages and spatial perspectives. The complicated recombination of familiar components, elements and structures of spatial perception and the experience of motion, which include spiral-shaped formations and geometric distortions, for example, lead to unfamiliar and irritating experiences of architecture. What may appear to be a visually complex labyrinth suggesting potentials of movement develops perceptual stability in the building's tectonic qualities. Aspects of the unstable and of transition are interwoven with tectonic stability in the building's overall impact.

Works by contemporary artist James Turrell, which also motivate the viewer's active physical movement in space, relate to comparable qualities in the phenomenal field of movement but are articulated differently, using few creative means.[29] The *Wolfsburg Project* created in the central museum hall of Wolfsburg Art Museum in 2009 is an accessible, two-part, space-within-a-space installation filled by gradual modulations of changing coloured light (*13* p. 64).[30] In a large rectangular space entered via a ramp, his perception of the slowly changing colour atmospheres prevents the visitor from constituting a fixed experience, and this failure is multiplied still further by the movement of his own body. Misty zones of coloured light appear, almost impossible to pin down, and linear contours are transformed of the ramp, for example, develops convex and concave formations. A second space can be entered through a cut-out section of the wall. Looking back from this second space, the previous area of coloured light now appears to be framed by the opening—as a plane of colour or shadows, or a more extensive area of colour. Now, the dominant visual perception from a fixed point causes the larger room to appear just as changeable in its coloration, but accentuates the experience of stabilisation. Such artworks can be interpreted as choreography of perception and experience incorporating movement in different qualitative states. Linking different conditions of perception and phenomenal qualities not only makes it possible to perceive the perceptions in themselves, but also discloses the only vaguely familiar qualities of intangible phenomena and transitions.

To an increasing extent, experiential qualities of continuum and transition shape people's perceptual spectrum in our contemporary world, which is particularly defined by the information and communication media. To grant specific qualities of expression to this in architecture and simultaneously open up potentials for movement and assimilation is one aim of the Japanese architectural office SANAA.[31] In their latest project, the Rolex Learning Centre der École Polytechnique Fédérale de Lausanne built in 2010, the intention was to organise the overall spatial programme as well as individual spatial units as zones slipping one into the next, and to

des Modells eines Möbiusbandes, das durch eine nicht orientierbare
Mannigfaltigkeit geprägt ist, mit der Antizipation der potenziellen Nutzungen.[27] (*9, 10* S. 64). Die Glas- und Betonwände des aus gewinkelten
und in Teilen ineinander greifenden Volumenbildungen konstruierten,
horizontal lagernden Gebäudes wurden im Innen- und Außenraum sowie
in ihren Materialoberflächen, auch an Decken und Böden, in gleicher
Weise strukturiert und texturiert. In der Wahrnehmung treten weniger
einzelne Komponenten als vielmehr Übergänge und Verbindungen hervor. In der nutzungsbezogenen Aktion und in der Bewegung können die
Räume als kontinuierlich diskontinuierliche Erfahrungsräume wirken im
Sinne einer dynamischen Bewegungssuggestion, ohne dass ihre Aneignung dadurch zwangsläufig mit konkreten körperlichen Bewegungsfor-
mationen verbunden ist.

Räumlichkeit und die Komplexität von Bewegungsmodalitäten auf neue
Weise erfahrbar zu machen, war auch die Intention der Architekten beim
Entwurf des Mercedes-Benz-Museums, das 2002–2006 in Stuttgart ent-
stand und mithilfe digitaler Entwurfsprogramme entwickelt wurde.[28] (*11, 12*
S. 65). Im Außenraum erscheint die geschwungene Baukörperbildung des in
Beton und Glas erbauten achtgeschossigen Gebäudes mit leicht ansteigen-
den Boden- und Deckenplatten einzelner Geschosse in einer dynamischen
Konfiguration. Auch wenn diese in einigen Bereichen durch gewinkelt zueinander geneigte Glasbänder sowie partiell leicht ausgreifende und zurücktre-
tende Formelemente noch verstärkt wird, verbindet sich der Eindruck des
Soliden im Umwandern des Gebäudes mit vertrauten expressiven architektonischen Formbildungen. Dies verändert sich im Inneren. Dort verflechten sich
unmittelbar unterschiedliche Impulse. Scheinbar ineinander verkeilte Raum-
spiralen und Wegesysteme, gekrümmte Flächen und in wechselnden Radien
versetzte Plattformen, die sich um einen großen gebäudehohen Luftraum win-
den, erschweren die Orientierung. Der Eindruck dynamischer Vielfalt und Verbindung wird durch sequenzielle Bewegungserfahrung über Rampen und Plattformen sowie eine Vielzahl möglicher Blicke und Raumperspektiven verstärkt.
Die erschwerte Rekombination bekannter Bestandteile, Elemente und Strukturen räumlicher Wahrnehmung und Bewegungserfahrung, die hier beispielsweise
spiralförmige Formationen und geometrische Verzerrungen einschließen, führen
zu unvertrauten und auch irritierenden Architekturerfahrungen. Was der visuellen
Anschauung wie ein mannigfaltiges, Bewegungspotenziale suggerierendes Labyrinth erscheinen mag, gewinnt Wahrnehmungsstabilität in den tektonischen
Eigenschaften des Gebäudes. Aspekte des Nicht-Stabilen und der Übergänge
verflechten sich in der Wirkung des Gebäudes mit tektonischer Stabilität.
In Arbeiten des zeitgenössischen Künstlers James Turrell, die ebenfalls die aktive
körperliche Bewegung der Betrachtenden im Raum motivieren, werden vergleichbare Eigenschaften im Phänomenfeld von Bewegung berührt, jedoch in einer
davon unterschiedenen Weise mit wenigen gestalterischen Mitteln anders artiku-
liert.[29] Das 2009 in der zentralen Museumshalle des Wolfsburger Kunstmuseums

design the architecture as a laboratory of aesthetic experience (*14* p. 65).[32] Far removed from traditional typologies, the low, one-storey, rectangular volume with an irregularly curving floor raised from the ground in some places and ceiling panels in shiny exposed concrete appears as a wave-like formation. Almost complete glazing of the outer walls, and atriums created with rounded forms heighten the perception of specific mobility by means of differing emergent viewing axes between the inside and outside, the nearby and the distant. Together with one's own physical movement, slight modulation causes one's impressions to change. The structure of space—comprising gently and irregularly rising and falling floor formations and non-hierarchical connecting spaces—not only motivates movement through the seemingly fully open sequences of the interior spaces, but also suggests flexible locations through assimilation. Free courses of movement are facilitated, yet one is oriented and guided via emphasis of the structure's horizontal extension and the slight slopes. The architectonic choreography is open to active interpretation and transformation and to activity in everyday usage. In this context, the linking quality of the wave and its slight deformations characterises not so much a difference between place area and transitional space as their relations and interconnections, which can be permanently actualised in an open sequence and linkage of mobile and stabilising assimilation.

SHAPES OF MOVEMENT—Having outlined the question of the *Shape of Movement* from various aspects, the hidden diversity and explicative inaccessibility of the issue has been revealed. The focal point seems to be the sensory-physical definition of perceptual possibilities through visual, kinaesthetic, and imaginative components. One may assume the generic combination of movement's diversity and effects into qualitatively differing shapes due to interlacing immediate impressions, evocative memories, and mental imagination. Thus, such shapes are not explicable or creatable merely from elements and structural qualities that may appear stronger here or weaker there. Horizons of perception and interpretation are variable according to history and culture as well, emerging with constantly altered transformations and interpretations. Ultimately, the only thing that appears stable is our recognition of the inexhaustible, unassailable nature and phenomenology of movement.

NOTES—[1] Cf. for example Glotzbach, Ulrich: *Technikstil und Gestalt. Zur Ethik gestaltenden Handelns,* Hamburg 2006, 96–108.—[2] Cf. Pachoud, Bernard: "The Teleological Dimension", in: ders./Petitot, Jean/Roy, Jean-Michel/Varela, Francisco J. (Hg.): *Naturalizing Phenomenology: Issues in Contemporary Phenomenology and Cognitive Science,* Stanford 1999, 206–210.—[3] Bill, Max: "Der Einfluß der zweiten industriellen Revolution auf die Kultur", in: ders.: *Funktion und Funktionalismus. Schriften: 1945–1988,* hrsg. v. Jakob Bill, Bern 2008, 116–122.—[4] Cf. Heisenberg, Werner: *Ordnungen der Wirklichkeit,* München 1989, 146–150. Cf. Lenk, Hans: *Kre-*

enstandene *Wolfsburg Project* ist gebildet als begehbare, zweigliedrige Raum-in-Raum-Installation, die von langsam sich ändernden Farblicht-modulationen erfüllt ist.[30] (*13* S. 64) In einem über eine Rampe zu betre-tenden großen rechteckigen Raumbereich entzieht sich die Wahrneh-mung der sich langsam verändernden Farbraumatmosphären jeder fixierenden Erfahrungskonstitution und wird in Verbindung mit der eigen-körperlichen Bewegung noch vervielfältigt. Nebelartige, nahezu nicht lokalisierbare Farblichtzonen zeigen sich ebenso wie Transformationen linearer Konturen, beispielsweise der Rampe, zu konvexen und konkaven Formationen. Über einen Wandausschnitt kann ein zweiter Raum betreten werden. Blickt man von diesem aus zurück, erscheint der vorhergehende Farblichtraum durch die Öffnung nun gerahmt als Farb- oder Schattenflä-che oder tiefer ausgedehnter Farbbereich. Die hier vorrangig visuelle Wahrnehmung von einem festen Standpunkt lässt den größeren Raum in der Farbtönung zwar ebenfalls veränderlich erscheinen, verstärkt aber die stabilisierende Erfahrung. Solche künstlerischen Arbeiten können als Cho-reografien der Wahrnehmung und Erfahrung interpretiert werden, die Bewe-gung in unterschiedlichen qualitativen Zustandsformen einbezieht. Die Ver-knüpfung unterschiedlicher Wahrnehmungskonditionen und phänomenaler Erscheinungsqualitäten macht nicht nur Wahrnehmungen selbst wahrnehm-bar, sondern auch die nur vage vertrauten Eigenschaften ungreifbarer Phä-nomene und Übergänge.

Erfahrungsqualitäten von Kontinuen und Übergängen prägen in der zeitge-nössischen Lebenswelt in einem zunehmenden Umfang, insbesondere bedingt durch die Informations- und Kommunikationsmedien, das Wahrneh-mungsspektrum der Menschen. Diesen in der Architektur eigene Ausdrucks-qualitäten zu verleihen und gleichzeitig in besonderer Weise Bewegungs- und Aneignungspotenziale zu öffnen, ist ein Anliegen des japanischen Architektur-büros SANAA.[31] Bei ihrem jüngsten Projekt, dem Rolex Learning Center der École Polytechnique Fédérale de Lausanne von 2010, intendierten sie das Raumprogramm ebenso wie einzelne räumliche Einheiten als ineinander glei-tende Raumzonen zu organisieren und die Architektur wie ein Labor ästheti-scher Erfahrung zu gestalten.[32] (*14* S. 65) Von traditionellen Typologien gelöst, erscheint der flach gelagerte und teilweise vom Boden gelöste eingeschossige Rechteckkörper mit unregelmäßig geschwungenen Boden- und Deckenplatten aus glänzendem Sichtbeton wie eine wellenartige Raumkörperbildung. Eine nahezu vollständige Verglasung der Außenwände und in gerundeten Formationen gebildete Lichthöfe verstärken durch die unterschiedlich eröffneten Blickachsen zwischen Innen und Außen, Nähe und Ferne die Wahrnehmung einer spezifi-schen Beweglichkeit. In Verbindung mit der eigenen körperlichen Bewegung ver-ändern sich die Eindrücke in leichten Modulationen. Die Raumstruktur aus sich sanft und unregelmäßig hebenden und senkenden Bodenformationen und eine hierarchielose Verbindung der verschiedenen Raumbereiche motivieren nicht nur Bewegungen durch die scheinbar überall offenen Raumfolgen, sondern auch die

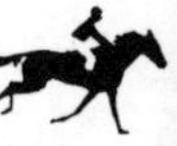

ative Aufstiege. Zur Philosophie und Psychologie der Kreativität, Frankfurt/Main 2000, 296–300.— [5] Cf. Appadurai, Arjun: *Modernity at large. Cultural dimensions of globalization,* Minneapolis 1997, 33–47.— [6] Cf. Buchert, Margitta: "Fließende Räume", in: /Zillich, Carl (Hg.): *In Bewegung… Architektur und Kunst,* Berlin 2008, 103–104.— [7] Castells, Manuel: *The Rise of the Network Society. The Information Age: Economy, Society and Culture,* Bd. 1, Cambridge, Mass. 1996, 476–477.— [8] Bauman, Zygmunt: *Liquid Modernity,* Cambridge 2000, 2.— [9] For example Rosa, Hartmut: *Beschleunigung. Die Veränderungen der Zeitstrukturen in der Moderne,* Frankfurt/Main 2005, 237–239.— [10] Grosz, Elisabeth: *Architecture from the Outside: Essays on Virtual and Real Space.* Cambridge, Mass. 2001, 116.; Hensel, Michael/Menges, Achim: "The Heterogeneous Space of Morpho-Ecologies", in: dies./ Hight, Christopher: *Space Reader. Heterogenous Space in Architecture,* Chichester 2009, 195.— [11] Cf. Jormakka, Kari: *Genius locomotionis,* Wien 2005.— [12] Arnason, H. Harvard/Calder, Alexander: „Interview", in: dies./Mulas, Ugo (Hg.): *Calder,* Paris 1971, 69–73.— [13] Arnheim, Rudolf: *Kunst und Sehen,* Berlin 1964, 358.— [14] Trier, Eduard: *Bildhauertheorien im 20. Jahrhundert,* Berlin 1992, 113.— [15] Upjohn, Judith F.: "The Calderian Experience", in: Rower, Alexander S.C. (Hg.): *Calder. Sculptor of Air,* Mailand 2009, 39–43.— [16] Küster, Ulf: "Giacometti. Überlegungen zur Ausstellung in der Fondation Beyeler", in: Beyeler Museum AG (Hg.): *Giacometti,* Ostfildern 2009, 17.— [17] Rizzolatti, Giacomo/ Sinigaglia, Corrado: *Empathie und Spiegelneurone. Die biologische Basis des Mitgefühls,* Frankfurt am Main 2008, 131–132.— [18] Nash, Steven A.: "Naum Gabo: Die Transparenz der konstruktiven Form", in: ders./Merkert, Jörn (Hg.): *Naum Gabo. Sechzig Jahre Konstrutivismus,* München 1986, 136.— [19] Hopsch, Lena: *Rytmens estetik, formens kraft,* Göteborg 2008, 148–149.— [20] Cf. Ingarden, Roman: *Untersuchungen zur Ontologie der Kunst,* Tübingen 1962, 273–275.— [21] Wortelkamp, Isa: „Choreografien der Landschaft", in: Avanession, Armen /Hofmann, Franck (Hg.): *Raum in den Künsten. Konstruktion-Bewegung-Politik,* München 2010, 129–131.— [22] Meisenheimer, Wolfgang: *Der Rand der Kreativität. Planen und Entwerfen,* Wien 2010, 34.— [23] Meisenheimer, Wolfgang: *Choreografie des architektonischen Raumes. Das Verschwinden des Raums in der Zeit,* Munbal-li 2007.— [24] Le Corbusier: *An die Studenten,* Reinbek b. Hamburg 1962, 30.— [25] Cf. Joedicke, Jürgen: "Die Rampe als architektonische Promenade im Werk Le Corbusiers", in: *Daidalos 12* (1984), 104–108.— [26] Cf. Berkel, Ben van/Bos, Caroline: *Move, Vol. 1–3,* Amsterdam 1999, Vol 2: 21–23. — [27] Cf. ibid., Vol. 3: 18–20.— [28] Berkel, Ben van/Bos, Caroline: "After image", in: Stiftung Städelschule für Baukunst/Luise King (Hg.): *Architektur & Theorie – Produktion und Reflexion,* Hamburg 2009, 153 and 159.— [29] Cf. Torres, Ana Maria: *James Turrell,* Valencia IVAM 2004, 333–334.— [30] Cf. Brüderlin, Markus/Kirschner, Esther B. (Hg.): *James Turrell. The Wolfsburg Project,* Ostfildern 2009.— [31] Cf. Cortés, Juan Antonio/ Nishizawa, Ryue/Sejima, Kazuyo: "Conversation", in: Cecilia, Fernando Marquez /Levene, Richard (Hg.): *SANAA. Kazuyo Sejima. Ryue Nishizawa 2004–2008* (El Croquis 139), Madrid 2007, 19–31.— [32] Cf. Redecke, Sebastian: "Campus mit Teppichlandschaft", in: *Bauwelt 101,* 2010/13, 14–23.

flexible Verortung durch Aneignung. Bewegungsabläufe sind in einer freien Organisation ermöglicht und doch auch orientiert und gelenkt durch die Betonung der horizontalen Ausdehnung und die leichten Schrägen. Die architektonische Choreografie ist offen für interpretierende und transformierende Aktionen und Handlungen in den alltäglichen Nutzungsprozessen. Die Verknüpfungseigenschaft der Welle mit ihren leichten Verformungen charakterisiert dabei weniger eine Differenz zwischen Ortraum und Wegraum als vielmehr ihre Relationen und Verflechtungen, die in einer offenen Folge und Verbindung von mobiler und stabilisierender Aneignung aktualisiert werden können.

GESTALTEN DER BEWEGUNG—Bereits das skizzenhafte Umkreisen der Frage nach der *Gestalt der Bewegung* lässt die darin verborgene Vielfalt und explikative Unerreichbarkeit erkennen. Zentral erscheint die sinnlich-körperliche Bedingtheit der Wahrnehmungsmöglichkeiten durch visuelle, kinästhetische und imaginative Konstituenten. In der Verflechtung von unmittelbarem Eindruck, evokativer Erinnerung und mentaler Imagination ist die generische Zusammenführung der Mannigfaltigkeiten von Bewegungswirkungen zu qualitativ unterschiedlichen Gestalten zu vermuten. Daher sind sie nicht allein aus Elementen und den mal stärker, mal schwächer hervortretenden strukturellen Eigenschaften erklär- oder gestaltbar. Wahrnehmungs- und Interpretationshorizonte sind zudem historisch und kulturell variant, sie zeigen sich in immer wieder anderen Transformationen und Interpretationen. Stabil scheint letztlich nur die Erkenntnis der Unerschöpflichkeit und uneinholbaren Phänomenalität von Bewegung.

ANMERKUNGEN—[1] Vgl. zum Beispiel Glotzbach, Ulrich: *Technikstil und Gestalt. Zur Ethik gestaltenden Handelns,* Hamburg 2006, 96–108.—[2] Vgl. Pachoud, Bernard: „The Teleological Dimension", in: ders./Petitot, Jean/Roy, Jean-Michel/Varela, Francisco J. (Hg.): *Naturalizing Phenomenology: Issues in Contemporary Phenomenology and Cognitive Science,* Stanford 1999, 206–210.—[3] Vgl. Bill, Max: „Der Einfluß der zweiten industriellen Revolution auf die Kultur", in: ders.: *Funktion und Funktionalismus. Schriften: 1945–1988,* hrsg. v. Jakob Bill, Bern 2008, 116–122.—[4] Vgl. Heisenberg, Werner: *Ordnungen der Wirklichkeit,* München 1989, 146–150. Und vgl. Lenk, Hans: *Kreative Aufstiege. Zur Philosophie und Psychologie der Kreativität,* Frankfurt/Main 2000, 296–300—[5] Vgl. Appadurai, Arjun: *Modernity at large. Cultural dimensions of globalization,* Minneapolis 1997, 33–47.—[6] Vgl. Buchert, Margitta: „Fließende Räume", in: dies./Zillich, Carl (Hg.): *In Bewegung ... Architektur und Kunst,* Berlin 2008, 103–104.—[7] Castells, Manuel: *The Rise of the Network Society. The Information Age: Economy, Society and Culture,* Bd. 1, Cambridge, Mass. 1996, 476–477.—[8] Bauman, Zygmunt: *Liquid Modernity,* Cambridge 2000, 2.—[9] Zum Beispiel Rosa, Hartmut: *Beschleunigung. Die Veränderungen der Zeitstrukturen in der Moderne,* Frankfurt/Main 2005, 237–239.—[10] Zum Beispiel Grosz, Elisabeth: *Architecture from the Outside: Essays on Virtual and Real Space.* Cambridge, Mass. 2001, 116.; Hensel, Michael/Menges, Achim: „The Heterogeneous

Space of Morpho-Ecologies", in: dies./Hight, Christopher: *Space Reader. Heterogenous Space in Architecture,* Chichester 2009, 195.—[11] Vgl. Jormakka, Kari: *Genius locomotionis,* Wien 2005.— [12] Arnason, H. Harvard/Calder, Alexander: „Interview", in: dies./Mulas, Ugo (Hg.): *Calder,* Paris 1971, 69–73.—[13] Arnheim, Rudolf: *Kunst und Sehen,* Berlin 1964, 358.—[14] Trier, Eduard: *Bildhauertheorien im 20. Jahrhundert,* Berlin 1992, 113.—[15] Upjohn, Judith F.: „The Calderian Experience", in: Rower, Alexander S.C. (Hg.): *Calder. Sculptor of Air,* Mailand 2009, 39–43.—[16] Küster, Ulf: „Giacometti. Überlegungen zur Ausstellung in der Fondation Beyeler", in: Beyeler Museum AG (Hg.): *Giacometti,* Ostfildern 2009, 17.—[17] Rizzolatti, Giacomo/Sinigaglia, Corrado: *Empathie und Spiegelneurone. Die biologische Basis des Mitgefühls,* Frankfurt am Main 2008, 131–132.—[18] Nash, Steven A.: „Naum Gabo: Die Transparenz der konstruktiven Form", in: ders./Merkert, Jörn (Hg.): *Naum Gabo. Sechzig Jahre Konstrutivismus,* München 1986, 136.—[19] Hopsch, Lena: *Rytmens estetik, formens kraft,* Göteborg 2008, 148–149.—[20] Ingarden, Roman: *Untersuchungen zur Ontologie der Kunst,* Tübingen 1962, 273–275.—[21] Wortelkamp, Isa: „Choreografien der Landschaft", in: Avanession, Armen /Hofmann, Franck (Hg.): *Raum in den Künsten. Konstruktion-Bewegung-Politik,* München 2010, 129–131.—[22] Meisenheimer, Wolfgang: *Der Rand der Kreativität. Planen und Entwerfen,* Wien 2010, 34.—[23] Meisenheimer, Wolfgang: *Choreografie des architektonischen Raumes. Das Verschwinden des Raums in der Zeit,* Munbal-li 2007.—[24] Le Corbusier: *An die Studenten,* Reinbek b. Hamburg 1962, 30.—[25] Vgl. Joedicke, Jürgen: „Die Rampe als architektonische Promenade im Werk Le Corbusiers", in: *Daidalos 12* (1984), 104–108.—[26] Vgl. Berkel, Ben van/Bos, Caroline: *Move, Vol. 1–3,* Amsterdam 1999, Vol 2: 21–23.—[27] Vgl. ebd., Vol. 3: 18–20.—[28] Berkel, Ben van/Bos, Caroline: „After image", in: Stiftung Städelschule für Baukunst/Luise King (Hg.): Architektur & Theorie – Produktion und Reflexion, Hamburg 2009, 153 und 159.—[29] Vgl. Torres, Ana Maria: *James Turrell,* Valencia IVAM 2004, 333–334.—[30] Vgl. Brüderlin, Markus/Kirschner, Esther B. (Hg.): *James Turrell. The Wolfsburg Project,* Ostfildern 2009.—[31] Vgl. Cortés, Juan Antonio/Nishizawa, Ryue/Sejima, Kazuyo: „Conversation", in: Cecilia, Fernando Marquez /Levene, Richard (Hg.): *SANAA. Kazuyo Sejima. Ryue Nishizawa 2004–2008* (El Croquis 139), Madrid 2007, 19–31.—[32] Vgl. Redecke, Sebastian: „Campus mit Teppichlandschaft", in: *Bauwelt 101,* 2010/13, 14–23.

Söke Dinkla
Dynamismo of Post-Industry

Söke Dinkla is director of art in public space for the city of Duisburg. From
**2005–2010 she was artistic director of the Cultural Capital Office RUHR.2010
in Duisburg. As an art historian, her doctorate was on the aesthetics of interactive media art. She works as a curator and critic in the fields of contemporary art, art in public space, and new media. Lecturing and jury activities
incl. work for Ars Electronica, the Transmediale, and ISEA** (International Sym-
posium of Electronic Arts). Publications include: *Ruhrlights: Twilight Zone*
(ed., 2011), *PubliCity: Constructing the Truth. Kunst im öffentlichen Raum*
(ed., 2006), *Jenny Holzer: Die Macht des Wortes/The Power of Words* (2006),
Paradoxien des Öffentlichen (ed., 2008).

Söke Dinkla
Dynamismo der Postindustrie

Söke Dinkla ist künstlerische Leiterin für Kunst im öffentlichen Raum bei der Stadt Duisburg. Von 2005 bis 2011 arbeitete sie als künstlerische Leiterin des Kulturhauptstadtbüros RUHR.2010 Duisburg. Die Kunsthistorikerin promovierte über die Ästhetik interaktiver Medienkunst und arbeitet als Kuratorin für zeitgenössische Kunst, Kunst im öffentlichen Raum und Elektronische Medien. Vorträge und Jurytätigkeit u. a. bei Ars Electronica, Transmediale und ISEA (International Symposium of Electronic Arts). Publikationen u. a.: *Ruhrlights: Twilight Zone* (Hg., 2011), *PubliCity: Constructing the Truth. Kunst im öffentlichen Raum* (Hg., 2006), *Jenny Holzer. Die Macht des Wortes / The Power of Words* (2006), *Paradoxien des Öffentlichen* (Hg., 2008).

Today, movement as a fundamental requisite to life is the subject of a wide range of scientific disciplines and lines of research. The cultural sciences have been concerned with the metaphor of "movement" since the nineteenth century. As a force generating shape, various forms of movement have played a part in the art of all periods. In the main, the impression of movement has been used to express or evoke a specific feeling, a state of mind or a mood. In the twentieth century, the field of research began to widen as physical movement itself became artistic material, particularly in fine art. As an instrument of art criticism, the pathos formula by Aby Warburg is useful when tracking the significance of movement and impressions of movement in art. Especially in contemporary art in public space—outside the separate, extraordinary space of the White Cube—movement has become a constitutive element of the work: today, it presupposes a basic mental and physical ability to migrate on the part of the former viewer.

In the painting of the quattrocento Aby Warburg discovered "disquiet," a feature he regarded as spectacular dynamics, a heightened mobility of bodies and robes. He saw the symbolic expression of "passionate stimulation" in the mobile fashioning of robes and hair, coining the term "pathos formula" for this.[1] Warburg regarded the history of culture as a history of human passions. He was interested in their essential elements: the "will to possess," the "will to give," the "will to die," and the "will to kill." In other words, he grasps movement as primarily emotional with his pathos formula. Energetic symbols of action and the expression of physical movement are among the most effective pathos formulae; they are expressive means with universal validity.

The Warburg pathos formula provides a set of instruments in art criticism that can be used to describe different qualities of emphasis in movement, as not every form of movement is capable of becoming a pathos formula. Only in situations where it is "charged with energy" and polarising is movement an "explosive material" with a liberating force. Inasmuch as it attempts to identify the specific quality of the emphasis of movement and the energy of an artwork, the pathos formula may prove a suitable method of analysing movement and impressions of movement in works of fine art.

It is no coincidence, surely, that Warburg devised his pathos formula at a time when motion was being introduced to our pictorial world by film.[2] The image was no longer an expression of movement; it was being set in motion itself. The moving image was the most suitable medium for an accelerated age: movement produced by machines freed man more than ever before from his embeddedness in a time continuum, the measures of which he prescribed with his own physical potentials. The comprehensive industrialisation of working and everyday life changed our perception definitively. A highly influential, genre-spanning artistic trend in literature, fine art, and architecture, Futurism celebrated movement as emblematic of a new age.[3]

Bewegung als fundamentale Voraussetzung des Lebens ist heute Gegenstand unterschiedlichster Wissenschaftsdisziplinen und Forschungsrichtungen. Die Kulturwissenschaften beschäftigen sich seit dem 19. Jahrhundert mit der Metapher „Bewegung". Als formgebende Kraft hat sie in der Kunst zu allen Zeiten in verschiedenen Formen eine Rolle gespielt. Meist diente der Bewegungseindruck dazu, ein bestimmtes Gefühl, eine Gemütslage zum Ausdruck zu bringen bzw. hervorzurufen. Im 20. Jahrhundert begann sich das Forschungsfeld zu erweitern, denn gerade in der bildenden Kunst wurde die physische Bewegung selbst zum künstlerischen Material. Die Pathosformel von Aby Warburg kann uns als Instrument der Kunstkritik dabei helfen, der Bedeutung von Bewegung und Bewegungseindrücken in der Kunst nachzugehen. Gerade in der aktuellen Kunst im öffentlichen Raum – außerhalb des abgesonderten, extraordinären Raums des White Cube – wird Bewegung zu einem konstituierenden Element des Werkes: Es setzt heute eine grundlegende mentale und körperliche Migrationsfähigkeit des ehemaligen Betrachters voraus.

In der Malerei des Quattrocento hat Aby Warburg eine „Unruhe" entdeckt, eine für ihn aufsehenerregende Dynamik, eine gesteigerte Beweglichkeit des Körpers und der Gewandung. In dem bewegten Beiwerk der Gewänder und Haare sieht er den symbolischen Ausdruck „leidenschaftlicher Erregung", für die er den Begriff der „Pathosformel" prägte.[1] Die Geschichte der Kultur ist für Warburg eine Geschichte der menschlichen Leidenschaften. Er  beschäftigt sich mit den wesentlichen Elementen: dem „Habenwollen", dem „Gebenwollen", dem „Sterbenwollen" und dem „Tötenwollen". Das heißt, er fasst in seiner Pathosformel Bewegung vor allem emotional auf. Energiesymbole der Aktion und der Ausdruck physischer Bewegung gehören zu den wirkungsstärksten Pathosformeln, sie sind Ausdrucksmittel mit universaler Gültigkeit.

Die Warburgsche Pathosformel stellt uns ein kunstkritisches Instrumentarium zur Verfügung, mit dem wir unterschiedliche Qualitäten von Bewegungsemphase beschreiben können. Denn nicht jede Form der Bewegung kann zur Pathosformel werden. Ein „Sprengmittel" mit befreiender Kraft ist sie nur da, wo sie „energiegeladen" und „polarisierend" wirkt. Indem die Pathosformel gerade die spezifische Qualität der Bewegungsemphase und Energie eines Kunstwerks zu fassen versucht, kann sie sich als geeignete Methode zur Analyse von Bewegung und Bewegungseindrücken in Werken der bildenden Kunst erweisen.

Es ist sicher kein Zufall, dass Warburg seine Pathosformel zu einer Zeit formulierte, in der sich mit dem Film unsere Bildwelt zu mobilisieren begann.[2] Das Bild war nicht länger nur Ausdruck von Bewegung, sondern geriet selbst in Bewegung. Das bewegte Bild war das adäquate Medium einer beschleunigten Zeit: Durch Maschinen produzierte Bewegung löste den Menschen stärker als zuvor aus seinem Eingebundensein in ein Zeitkontinuum, dessen Maßstäbe vor allem er selbst mit seinen körperlichen Potenzialen vorgab. Die umfassende Industrialisierung des Arbeits- und Alltagslebens veränderte unsere Wahrnehmung maßgeblich. Der Futurismus als einflussreiche, gattungsübergreifende Kunstrichtung in Literatur,

Umberto Boccioni formulated the theory of "dynamismo" in consequence: as he saw it, movement was an aesthetic force that triggered very specific states of mind and mood—in a similar way to Warburg's thinking (*1* p. 84).

Marinetti and Umberto Boccioni created a theoretical basis that enabled movement to move on from being merely the subject of the pathos formula to being the actual pathos formula in itself. Movement and speed became the epitome of progress and a radical break with tradition. The first kinetic works in the first and second decades of the twentieth century were no longer concerned with imagined movement extending into mental movement and emphasis; movement became their central aesthetic aspect, as in Marcel Duchamp's *Roue de bicyclette* (1913), for example, and the *Kinetic Construction* (1920) by Naum Gabo. Like these early examples, others—in retrospect—were equally groundbreaking, including the *Light-Space-Modulator* by Moholy-Nagy and Man Ray's *Spiral* from 1919. In their own time, however, they remained isolated exceptions (*2* p. 84).

Contrary to appearances, there was no unbroken continuity from these early examples to the kinetic forms of the nineteen-fifties and nineteen-sixties. There was a great desire for a new beginning after the Second World War, and a suitable metaphor of this new beginning seemed to be the moving artwork, which lent shape to the necessity for change and flexibility. In the emerging, almost incomprehensible range of possible ways to mobilise the artwork, movement does not always develop into a pathos formula. It becomes so only when movement is more than a motif of technicity. It becomes so when art involves a utopian power that gives form to social change. One example of this is Jean Tinguely's oeuvre: he constructed his movable machines as a conscious counterweight to perfected, invisible technology. His painting machines enable the user to produce abstract artworks in a mechanical way. The *Méta-Matics* demonstrate that the artwork possesses creative powers in itself and cannot be regarded as something final and complete. They are also an affront to *art informel,* indeed to painting in general. After the exhibition of *Méta-Matics* in Galerie Iris Clert in 1959, Tristan Tzara said that this represented the end of painting; the successful climax to forty years of Dada.[4] (*3* p. 85)

The works of Jean Tinguely paved the way for two significant issues in early twenty-first-century art: it seemed that his painting machines were an ironic wink at his own role as an artist, throwing it into question. He took painting as a creative act to the point of absurdity by delegating it to a machine. At the same time, he created monumental machines that exploded the museum context and thus found a way into urban public space until into the ninteen-nineties.

Art in public space—initially art in architecture—had developed as an increasingly separate trend during the post-war period with its extensive public building programmes. The sculptures, fountains, and moving façade designs of artists in the group ZERO around Düsseldorf artists

bildender Kunst und Architektur feierte die Bewegung als Insignium einer neuen Zeit.[3]

Daran anknüpfend formulierte Umberto Boccioni die Theorie des „Dynamismo": Für ihn ist Bewegung eine ästhetische Kraft, die ähnlich wie bei Warburg ganz bestimmte Gemütszustände auslöst. (*1* S. 84)

Marinetti und auch Umberto Boccioni schufen die theoretische Grundlage dafür, dass Bewegung nicht länger nur Gegenstand der Pathosformel war, sondern selbst zur Pathosformel wurde. Bewegung und Geschwindigkeit wurden zum Inbegriff des Fortschritts und des radikalen Bruchs mit Traditionen. In den ersten kinetischen Werken der 1910er und 1920er Jahre ging es nicht länger nur um imaginierte Bewegung, die sich in mentale Bewegung und Emphase verlängert, sondern Bewegung wurde zum zentralen ästhetischen Moment, wie zum Beispiel in Marcel Duchamps *Roue de bicyclette* (1913) und in der *Kinetischen Konstruktion* (1920) von Naum Gabo. Ebenso wie diese frühen Beispiele bekommen auch andere, wie der *Licht-Raum-Modulator* von Moholy-Nagy und Man Rays Spirale von 1919 rückblickend die Funktion von Vorläufern, blieben in ihrer Zeit aber zunächst vereinzelt. (*2* S. 84)

Auch wenn es so scheint, hat es keine ungebrochene Kontinuität von diesen frühen Beispielen bis zu den Formen der Kinetik der 1950er und 1960er Jahre gegeben. Nach dem Zweiten Weltkrieg war die Sehnsucht nach einem Neuanfang groß, eine geeignete Metapher für diesen Neuanfang schien das Kunstwerk in Bewegung zu sein, das der Notwendigkeit zur Veränderung und zur Flexibilität eine Form gab. In der jetzt entstehenden, fast schon unübersichtlichen Vielfalt an Möglichkeiten, das Kunstwerk zu mobilisieren, wird Bewegung nicht in jedem Fall zur Pathosformel. Sie wird es nur da, wo Bewegung mehr ist als ein technizistisches Motiv. Sie wird es da, wo Kunst eine utopische Kraft besitzt, die gesellschaftlichen Veränderungen eine Form gibt.  Ein Beispiel dafür sind die Werke von Jean Tinguely: Er konstruierte seine beweglichen Maschinen als bewusstes Gegengewicht zur perfektionierten unsichtbaren Technik. Mit Hilfe seiner Malmaschinen kann der Nutzer auf mechanische Weise abstrakte Kunstwerke herstellen. Die *Méta-Matics* zeigen, dass das Kunstwerk selbst schöpferische Kräfte besitzt und nicht als etwas endgültig Vollendetes angesehen werden kann. Sie sind ebenso ein Affront gegen die Kunst des Informel wie gegen die Malerei ganz generell. Nach der Ausstellung der *Méta-Matics* in der Galerie Iris Clert 1959 sagte Tristan Tzara, dass dies das Ende der Malerei sei, das erfolgreiche Ende von 40 Jahren Dada.[4] (*3* S. 85)

Die Arbeiten Jean Tinguelys haben zwei Wege bereitet, die für die Kunst des beginnenden 21. Jahrhunderts bedeutend sind: Mit seinen Malmaschinen hat er seine eigene Rolle als Künstler augenzwinkernd in Frage gestellt. Er hat das Malen als künstlerischen Akt ad absurdum geführt, indem er diese Tätigkeit an eine Maschine delegierte. Zugleich schuf er monumentale Maschinen, die jeden musealen Rahmen sprengten und so bis in die 1990er Jahre hinein ihren Weg in den öffentlichen Raum der Städte fanden.

Otto Piene, Günther Uecker, and Heinz Mack embodied political determination for a fresh start in an exemplary way; legitimised by commissions, committees, and juries, they stood for change in the public sphere.

In the following years, such abstract sculpture represented art's freedom from political utilisation of any kind. Its intended new task was to lend form to the values of freedom laid out in the constitution: "To date, the abstract monumental sculpture represented the last attempt to stage public space in the name of unity. But the majority of the population rejected this art, meaning that it had failed in its task," Monika Wagner concludes.[5] Many of the works being produced failed to meet with consensus because they refused to tell a story and convey a clear message. Another thing that made them incapable of consensus, however, was that they did not convincingly embody the democratic principles for which they stood.

In the meantime, much had been set in motion—not only the artwork itself, but also some of its essential characteristics. Digital media were so successful because they presupposed and helped to advance the democratising and activation of the former viewer.[6] This development brings a dilemma for art: does the unique work create an exceptional situation, capable of lending form to human passions and so having a didactic impact, as Warburg and Schiller[7] before him assumed and demanded? Or does the increasing rapprochement between art and life mean that the artwork, once so elite, simply merges into the everyday? Every work of art in public space sets out to walk this thin line. It steps down, so to speak, from its pedestal of superiority and makes itself the same as other urban furnishings, events or visual offers. In this way, it undergoes a change in its claim to authority: the role of the artist as a genius, as knowledgeable, as someone superior to the viewer, may be celebrated by the art market as much as ever today, but this claim appears less and less convincing to the public.[8]

Emphasis of movement is an artistic strategy used to maintain the balance between apparently irreconcilable poles. Jenny Holzer borrows the media of spectacle for her projection works in public space. Using powerful xenon searchlights, she sets monumental illuminated words in motion. Her "Truisms" promise unshakeable truths, but the fleeting, mobile medium of light means they also evade us, never taking on a lasting form. The outlines of the objects dissolve in the movement of light and immaterialise the carrying medium.[9] (*4* p. 85)

Movement becomes a pathos formula—an explosive means with liberating force—in those works that cause the former viewer to rise above his role as an observer and adopt a constitutive part in the work. Migrating works develop at the interface between art, architecture, and performative staging, co-produced by the now enabled participant. They employ their creative energy to impact on their urban surroundings. The *Cake Monument* produced by the group raumlaborberlin for the project "PubliCity" in Duisburg, 2006 is this kind of urban generator.[10] (*5* p. 84)

In der Nachkriegszeit hat sich mit den umfassenden öffentlichen Bauprogrammen die Kunst im öffentlichen Raum – zunächst als Kunst am Bau – als zunehmend eigenständige Richtung entwickelt. Die Skulpturen, Brunnen und bewegten Fassadengestaltungen der Künstler der Gruppe ZERO (Null) um die Düsseldorfer Künstler Otto Piene, Günther Uecker und Heinz Mack verkörperten beispielhaft den politischen Willen zum Neuanfang; legitimiert durch Kunstkommissionen, Beiräte und Jurys standen sie für eine veränderte Öffentlichkeit.

In den folgenden Jahren stand die abstrakte Skulptur für die Befreiung der Kunst von jeder politischen Inanspruchnahme. Ihre neue Aufgabe sollte es sein, den freiheitlichen Werten der Verfassung eine Form zu geben: „Die abstrakte Monumentalskulptur war der bisher letzte Versuch, den öffentlichen Raum im Namen einer Einheit zu bespielen. Doch ein großer Teil der Bevölkerung lehnte diese Kunst ab. Daher verfehlte sie ihre Aufgabe", schlussfolgert Monika Wagner.[5] Viele der entstehenden Werke waren nicht konsensfähig, weil sie sich weigerten, eine Geschichte zu erzählen und eine klare Botschaft zu vermitteln. Sie waren aber auch deshalb nicht konsensfähig, weil sie die demokratischen Prinzipien, für die sie standen, nicht glaubwürdig verkörperten.

Vieles war inzwischen in Bewegung geraten, nicht nur das Kunstwerk selbst, sondern einige seiner wesentlichen Eigenheiten. Die digitalen Medien wurden deshalb so erfolgreich, weil sie die Demokratisierung und Aktivierung des ehemaligen Betrachters mit vorantrieben und voraussetzten.[6] Mit dieser 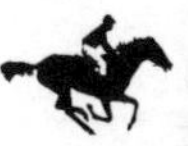 Entwicklung gerät das Kunstwerk in ein Dilemma: Ist es das einzigartige Werk, das einen Ausnahmezustand schafft und in besonderer Weise in der Lage ist, den menschlichen Leidenschaften eine Form zu geben und damit erzieherisch zu wirken, wie es Warburg und vor ihm auch Schiller[7] annahmen und forderten? Oder geht das ehemals elitäre Werk in der zunehmenden Annäherung von Kunst und Leben im Alltag auf? Auf diese Gratwanderung begeben sich alle Kunstwerke im öffentlichen Raum. Sie treten gewissermaßen vom Sockel ihrer Superiorität hinab und machen sich gleich mit anderem städtischen Inventar, Ereignissen und visuellen Angeboten. Sie vollziehen damit einen Wandel in ihrem Autoritätsanspruch: Die Rolle des Künstlers als Genius, als Wissender, der dem Betrachter überlegen ist, wird zwar heute nach wie vor gerade vom Kunstmarkt zelebriert, erscheint dem Publikum aber zunehmend unglaubwürdig.[8]

Bewegungsemphase ist eine künstlerische Strategie, um die unvereinbar scheinenden Pole in Balance zu halten. Jenny Holzer entwendet für ihre Projektionsarbeiten im öffentlichen Raum die Medien des Spektakels. Mit lichtstarken Xenon-Scheinwerfern setzt sie monumentale Lichtwörter in Bewegung. Ihre „Truismen" (Binsenweisheiten) versprechen unumstößliche Wahrheiten. Zugleich entziehen sie sich unserem Zugriff und der dauerhaften Bewahrung im flüchtigen, bewegten Medium des Lichts. In der Bewegung des Lichts lösen sich Objektgrenzen auf und immaterialisieren das Trägermedium.[9] (4 S. 85)

A cool zinc box occupies hostile places in the city. In the darkness, a semitransparent package unfolds from it as if from another world. Lit brightly from within, it fills "non-places" under a motorway bridge, in a neglected inner-city avenue of plane trees or in a playground, becoming a place to share cooking, eating, drinking, playing music, reciting poetry, and dancing. It changes its location every evening and provides space to new users. raumlaborberlin tracks down places with urban and communicative potentials that have been wasted previously. In Duisburg, the residents cook for each other; in Mülheim, when the monument moves on, people dance in the transformed "Ballroom Ruhrperle," in Hamburg they picnic, in Liverpool and Berlin the emerging spaces are used for discussion. A "gentle guerrilla-architecture"[11] develops with the pneumatic monument, a space that subversively penetrates the existing architecture, a space that incorporates a wide range of utopias: it promises temporary healing in the twenty-first-century city. It creates a sphere apart from the everyday, a seemingly private inner space that merges with the public urban exterior and works as a catalyst for temporary communities.

But how is it possible to go on conveying content in this new situation in which the former viewer becomes a participant? Yves Netzhammer asks what images still can be employed today to make a relevant statement about the world. In works like *Stores of Abstraction,* he tracks down the reality of moving and still images in a constantly tense state between representation and abstraction. He provides a walk-in, labyrinthine arrangement in which computer animations in small houses suggestive of stables, silhouettes of deer, and various other installative elements invite visitors on a "voyage to discover the viewer's role"[12] (*6* p. 84).

Moving through the labyrinth opens up numerous perspectives, standpoints and angles of viewing. Developed for the Palazzo Strozzi in Florence, Netzhammer's *Stores of Abstraction* examines the central perspective and sets the pictorial methods of the Renaissance alongside contemporary possibilities. Movement and changes of perspective help the viewer to understand the work.

Netzhammer consistently chops the linear, continuous narrative space into fragments, the *Space Fragments* of the title, in his work for the Observatory in Bochum. Short narrative sequences on the dome-shaped shell blend into monochrome states of sudden brightness suggesting lightning, which lead in turn to psychedelic abstract patterns, so catapulting us right out of the narrative sphere (7 p. 85).

Different artistic means—drawing, animation, narrative, abstract colour movement, monochrome light states—enter into competition with each other. They create proximities and unexpected references, repeatedly leading us to create new combinations of meanings. Despite the range of possible meanings, Netzhammer centers on recurrent themes in his works, as if wishing to make certain that he has not missed any conceivable aspect. The people in Netzhammer's pictorial worlds are both

Bewegung wird in den Werken zur Pathosformel – zu einem Sprengmittel mit befreiender Kraft –, in denen der ehemalige Betrachter seiner Rolle als Betrachter entwächst, um eine konstitutive Rolle im Werk einzunehmen. An der Schnittstelle zwischen Kunst, Architektur und performativer Inszenierung entstehen migrierende Werke, die von dem nun ermächtigten Teilnehmer mit geschaffen werden. Ihre schöpferische Energie verwenden sie, um auf ihr urbanes Umfeld einzuwirken. Das *Küchenmonument* der Gruppe raumlaborberlin, das sie 2006 für das Projekt „PubliCity" in Duisburg produzierten, ist ein solcher urbaner Generator.[10] **(5 S. 84)**
Eine kühle Zinkbox bezieht unwirtliche Orte in der Stadt. Bei Dunkelheit entfaltet sich aus ihr eine semitransparente Hülle wie aus einer anderen Welt. Von innen hell erleuchtet, füllt sie „Unorte" unter einer Autobahnbrücke, in einer missachteten Platanenallee der Innenstadt, auf einem Spielplatz und wird dort zu einem gemeinsamen Ort des Kochens, Essens, Trinkens, Musizierens, Rezitierens und Tanzens. Jeden Abend wechselt sie ihren Ort und bietet Raum für neue Nutzer. raumlaborberlin spürt Orte auf, die bislang brach liegende urbane und kommunikative Potenziale besitzen. In Duisburg kochen die Bewohner füreinander, in Mülheim, wohin das Monument im Anschluss zieht, tanzen die Menschen im verwandelten „Ballsaal Ruhrperle", in Hamburg picknicken sie, in Liverpool und Berlin entstehen Räume für Diskussionen. Mit dem pneumatischen Monument entsteht eine „sanfte Guerilla-Architektur"[11]**, ein Raum, der sich subversiv in die existierende Architektur hineinschiebt, ein Raum, der vielfältige Utopien in sich trägt: In der Stadt des 21. Jahrhunderts verspricht er temporäre Heilung. Er schafft eine Sphäre abseits des Alltäglichen, einen privat anmutenden Innenraum, der sich mit dem öffentlichen Außen der Stadt verbindet und als Katalysator für temporäre Gemeinschaften wirkt.**

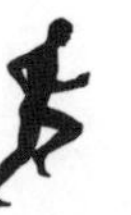

Wie lassen sich aber in dieser neuen Situation, in der der ehemalige Betrachter zum Teilnehmer wird, noch Inhalte vermitteln? Yves Netzhammer fragt danach, mit welchen Bildern sich heute noch etwas Relevantes über die Welt aussagen lässt. In Arbeiten wie *Abstraktionsvorräte* spürt er dem Wirklichkeitsstatus des bewegten und unbewegten Bildes nach, die sich in einer ständigen Spannung zwischen Gegenständlichkeit und Abstraktion befinden. Er stellt eine begehbare, labyrinthische Anordnung bereit, in der Computeranimationen in kleinen, stallartigen Häuschen, Silhouetten von Damwild und unterschiedliche installative Elemente zu einer „Entdeckungsreise zur Rolle des Betrachters" einladen.[12] (*6* S. 84)

In der Bewegung durch das Labyrinth ergibt sich eine Vielzahl von Perspektiven, Standpunkten und Blickwinkeln. Entstanden für den Palazzo Strozzi in Florenz, beschäftigen sich Netzhammers *Abstraktionsvorräte* mit der Zentralperspektive und stellen der Bildtechnik der Renaissance zeitgenössische Möglichkeiten an die Seite. Der Betrachter erschließt sich das Werk durch Bewegung und Perspektivwechsel.

In seiner Arbeit für die Sternwarte Bochum zerlegt Netzhammer den linearen, kontinuierlichen Erzählraum konsequent in Fragmente, in *Raumscherben,* so der Titel. Auf der kuppelförmigen Hülle gehen kurze narrative Sequenzen über in monochrome, teils

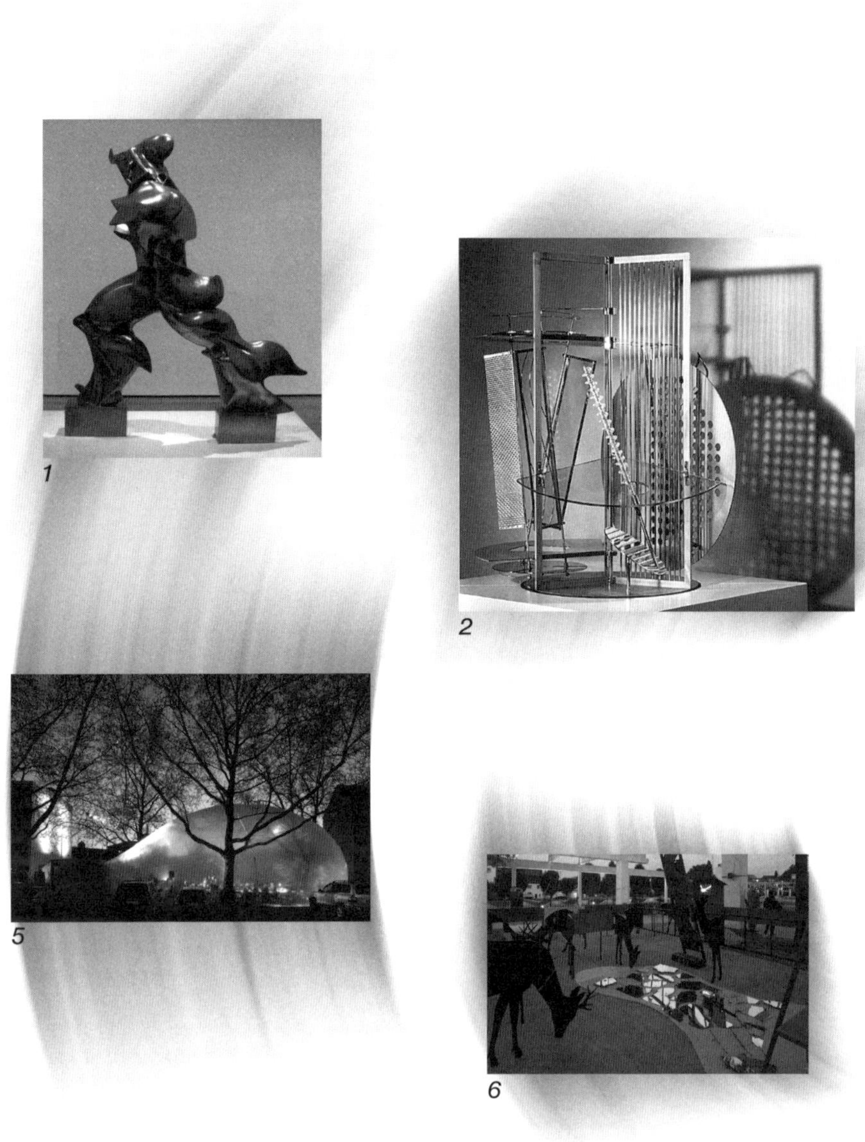

1 Umberto Boccioni: *Unique Forms of Continuity in Space,* 1913 — 2 László Moholy-Nagy: *Light-Space Modulator,* light prop for an electric stage, 1922–1930 — 3 Jean Tinguely: *Méta-Matic No. 6,* 1959 — 4 Jenny Holzer: *Xenon for Duisburg,* 2004 — 5 raumlaborberlin: *Kitchen Monument,* pneumatic sculpture, Duisburg and different locations 2006 — 6 Yves Netzhammer: *Stores of Abstraction,* 2009/2010 — 7 Yves Netzhammer: *Space Fragments,* Bochum 2010 — 8 Heike Mutter & Ulrich Genth: *Tiger & Turtle Magic Mountain* (simulation), Duisburg 2010 (in construction) — 9 Jochen Gerz: *2–3 Streets. An exhibition in the streets of the Ruhrgebiet,* 2006-2010

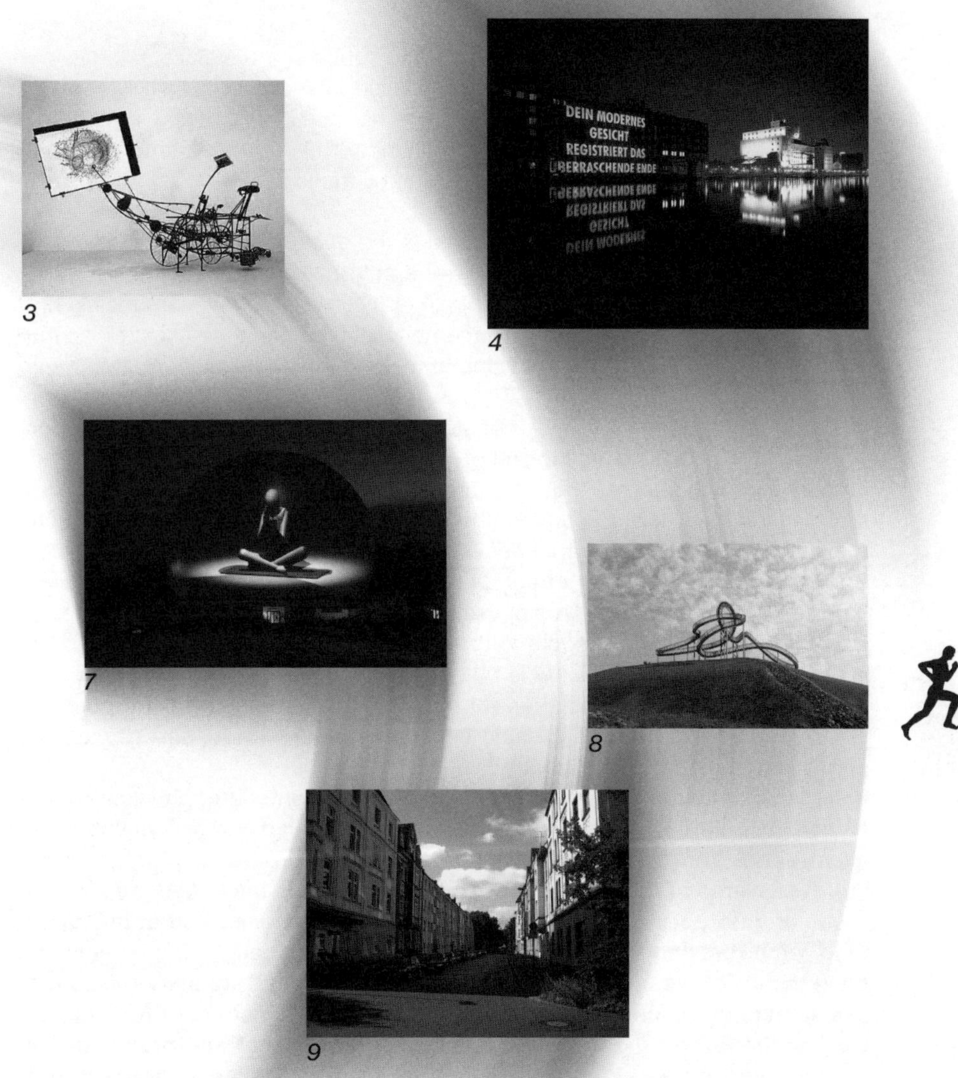

1 Umberto Boccioni: *Einzigartige Formen der Kontinuität im Raum,* 1913 — *2* László Moholy-Nagy: *Licht-Raum-Modulator,* Lichtrequisit einer elektrischen Bühne, 1922–1930 — *3* Jean Tinguely: *Méta-Matic No. 6,* 1959 — *4* Jenny Holzer: *Xenon für Duisburg,* 2004 — *5* raumlaborberlin: *Küchenmonument,* pneumatische Skulptur, Duisburg und an unterschiedlichen Orten, 2006 — *6* Yves Netzhammer: *Abstraktionsvorräte,* 2009/2010 — *7* Yves Netzhammer: *Raumscherben,* Bochum 2010 — *8* Heike Mutter & Ulrich Genth: *Tiger & Turtle Magic Mountain* (Simulation), Duisburg 2010 (im Bau) — *9* Jochen Gerz: *2–3 Straßen. Eine Ausstellung in Städten des Ruhrgebiets,* 2006-2010

helpless and cruel; they move through an environment that continually takes on a life of its own and so evades their control. Here, human sovereignty is broken in many respects and embedded in a world ruled by technology that we cannot grasp rationally, only intuitively. The work is not completed until we follow the sounds into the inside of the dome. The sounds circle us, move through space, meeting obstructions and swirling around after-images in our visual memory to measure out the unfamiliar space.

In works of contemporary art, movement is the decisive aspect that creates a state of inner emphasis, both mentally and physically. Ulrich Genth and Heike Mutter use archetypes of the recent past in their works, which are mainly produced for public space. Even more than previous works, their latest piece currently being made for Heinrich-Hildebrand-Höhe in south Duisburg is the epitome of movement and velocity. *Tiger & Turtle / Magic Mountain* is a walk-on sculpture in the form of a roller-coaster. The twenty-metre-high construction with its curving tracks cites the archetype of the leisure industry.[13] (*8* p. 85)

Its gentle irony highlights the Ruhr inhabitants' obsession with escaping grey reality in the many leisure parks of the region. As an image, it seduces us from a distance and promises rapid acceleration—the exceptional physical state— but not without a sobering effect as we come closer, for it is strenuous climbing up the path on foot. This physical movement opposes the metaphor of movement with all its associations and levels of meaning as schooled on avant-garde art. *Tiger & Turtle* is both a sculpture and a mobilising "apparatus": it is intended to be admired for its grace and creates a raised position where people—while moving—see the "landscape" with its severity, urban sprawl, and post-industrial beauty.

In all the examples cited, movement is linked to mental and physical participation. Its different current manifestations emerge in a complex debate with avant-garde principles of order. The optimism of progress, which shaped the dynamismo of the avant-garde, no longer stands unchallenged; a wide range of different counterparts accompany its emphasis. And at the same time, what remained theory in the avant-garde is actually being implemented in the art of the early twenty-firts-century: Jochen Gerz modernises the assignment of the political artist. He has designed the concept for a public work in the Ruhr region, which draws together many of the threads of his past works. In a work with the succinct title *2–3 Streets,* he risks the utmost: in other words, he puts himself on the line (*9* p. 85).

Rather than fulfilling the widespread desire for revitalisation through visual alterations, Jochen Gerz promises the region characterised by structural change something it cannot achieve with its own strength and numerous urban renewal projects: creative individuals who move there. In the European Cultural Capital Year, people from all over the world were invited to live rent-free in Duisburg, Mülheim, and Dortmund for a year. In October 2009, a total of seventy-eight people moved into fifty-

blitzartig aufleuchtende Zustände, die wiederum überleiten zu psychedelisch abstrakten Mustern und uns vollends aus dem Raum der Erzählung hinauskatapultieren. (7 S. 85)
**Die unterschiedlichen bildnerischen Mittel – Zeichnung, Animation,
Erzählung, abstrakte Farbbewegung, monochrome Lichtzustände – treten miteinander in Wettstreit. Sie kreieren Nachbarschaften und unerwartete Bezüge, die uns dazu bringen, immer wieder neue Kombinationen von
Bedeutungen zu bilden. Trotz der Vielfalt an möglichen Bedeutungen
umkreist Netzhammer in seinen Werken wiederkehrende Themen, als
würde er sicherstellen wollen, dass ihm keiner der möglichen Aspekte entgangen ist. Die Menschen in Netzhammers Bildwelten sind hilflos und grausam zugleich, sie bewegen sich durch eine Umgebung, die sich immer wieder verselbstständigt und ihrer Kontrolle entzieht. Menschliche Souveränität
ist hier vielfach gebrochen und eingebunden in eine technologisierte Welt,
zu der wir keinen rationalen, sondern nur einen intuitiven Zugang haben. Das
Werk vervollständigt sich erst dann, wenn wir den Klängen ins Innere der
Kuppel folgen. Die Klänge umkreisen uns, bewegen sich durch den Raum,
treffen auf Widerstände und umspielen die Nachbilder in unserem visuellen
Gedächtnis, um einen nicht gekannten Raum zu vermessen.**
Bewegung ist in den Arbeiten der aktuellen Kunst das entscheidende
Moment, das uns mental wie auch körperlich in innere Emphase versetzt.
Ulrich Genth und Heike Mutter arbeiten in ihren Werken, die größtenteils für
den öffentlichen Raum entstehen, mit Archetypen der jüngsten Vergangenheit.
Wie keine ihrer Arbeiten zuvor ist das jüngste Werk, das gerade für die Heinrich-Hildebrand-Höhe im Duisburger Süden entsteht, der Inbegriff von Bewegung und Geschwindigkeit. *Tiger & Turtle / Magic Mountain* ist eine begehbare
Skulptur in Form einer Achterbahn. Das 20 Meter hohe Bauwerk zitiert mit seinen geschwungenen Wegen den Archetypus der Freizeitindustrie.[13] (*8* S. 85)
Mit leiser Ironie verweist es auf die Obsession der Menschen im Ruhrgebiet, in
den zahlreichen Freizeitparks der grauen Realität zu entfliehen. Es verführt als
Bild aus der Ferne und verspricht rasante Beschleunigung – den physischen
Ausnahmezustand –, nicht ohne uns bei zunehmender Annäherung zu ernüchtern, denn es ist anstrengend, die Wege zu Fuß zu ersteigen. Die Metapher
Bewegung mit ihren Assoziationen und all den an der Kunst der Avantgarde
geschulten Bedeutungsebenen läuft der physischen Bewegung entgegen. *Tiger
& Turtle* ist sowohl Skulptur als auch „Gerät" der Mobilisierung: Es möchte in seiner Anmut bewundert werden und bietet einen erhabenen Ort, an dem die Menschen in ihrer Bewegung die „Landschaft" in ihrer Härte, Zersiedelung und postindustriellen Schönheit sehen.
In all den genannten Beispielen hat Bewegung mit mentaler und körperlicher Teilhabe zu tun. Ihre unterschiedlichen aktuellen Manifestationen entstehen in komplexer Auseinandersetzung mit den Ordnungsprinzipien der Avantgarde. Der Fortschrittsoptimismus, der den Dynamismo der Avantgarde prägte, steht jetzt nicht
mehr unwidersprochen im Raum, seine Emphase wird begleitet von verschiedensten

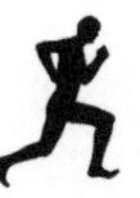

seven apartments in the three cities. Their "basic wage" was the rent-free apartment; in return they wrote daily on a text that was to be published in a book at the end of the year.[14]

In *2–3 Streets,* Gerz plays with different forms of behaviour that characterise our culture today: he refers to the dominant event culture with its helpless attempts to turn the public space of the city into a stage and resuscitate outdated forms of representation. He initiates an "anti-event" with *2–3 Streets,* which has nonetheless mastered the repertoire of event culture. It does not gather a mass audience in a specific place where something extraordinary is taking place at a specific time. It backs slowness and the long term as opposed to short-term effects. It rejects huge images and creates a great number of images in the mind. At the same time, *2–3 Streets* is a media spectacle: which of us would not like to live somewhere for a year without paying rent? But who would declare himself willing to move to the Ruhr region for a year—a region that is struggling with massive shrinking processes and high unemployment? How do the new residents experience the environment of the former workers' estates in which the proportion of people who came here as migrants seeking work in the nineteen-sixties and nineteen-seventies is well above average, nearing forty per cent? Do the "old" tenants see injustice when they are paying more for apartments that are not even renovated than those who have moved in? What social tensions develop as a result? All of these questions create instabilities. *2–3 Streets* intervenes in a fragile balance and adds to the level of fragility. Like the artists of the avant-garde, Jochen Gerz is anxious to promote the development of something new. But he knows that it can only develop from society itself, and that is why he wishes *2–3 Streets* to be "more of a cultural development" and "less realised by one author or an individual invention," but also "a minimal change in the same, which can only be registered by the contemporary consciousness."[15]

In a society where the principles of democracy have become a matter of course after fifty years, today we need to initiate work arrangements that lead us a step away from the sometimes very pleasant immobility into which we have settled as consumers. The emphasis of Warburg's "desire to possess" is set into a fragile balance with the "desire to give" in works like *2–3 Streets.* In the post-industrial era, movement (in the singular) becomes movements (in the plural). They follow innumerable different directions, which may also change in the short term. Their calculated ambiguities, paradoxes, and contradictions make them into the expression of a pluralist, multicultural society, which is getting ready to deal with the unreasonable demands of constant change in a globalised world.

Counterparts. Und zugleich wird in der Kunst des beginnenden 21. Jahrhunderts auch das umgesetzt, was in der Avantgarde bloße Theorie blieb: Jochen Gerz aktualisiert die Aufgaben des politischen Künstlers. Er entwirft ein Konzept für ein öffentliches Werk im Ruhrgebiet, in dem viele der Fäden seiner vorangegangenen Arbeiten zusammenlaufen. Unter dem lapidaren Titel *2–3 Straßen* setzt er alles aufs Spiel, was ein Werk aufs Spiel setzen kann: nämlich sich selbst. (*9* S. 85)

Anstatt dem weitverbreiteten Wunsch nach Revitalisierung durch visuelle Veränderung zu entsprechen, stellt Jochen Gerz der vom Strukturwandel gekennzeichneten Region das in Aussicht, was sie durch eigene Kraft und mit den Mitteln zahlreicher Stadterneuerungsprojekte nicht bewirken kann: den Zuzug von Kreativen. Im Kulturhauptstadtjahr sind Menschen aus allen Gegenden der Welt eingeladen, für ein Jahr mietfrei in Duisburg, Mülheim und Dortmund zu wohnen. Im Oktober 2009 ziehen insgesamt 78 Menschen in 57 Wohnungen in Duisburg, Mülheim und Dortmund. Ihr „Grundgehalt" ist die mietfreie Wohnung, ihre Gegenleistung das tägliche Schreiben an einem Text, der am Ende des Jahres in einem Buch veröffentlicht wird.[14]

In *2–3 Straßen* spielt Gerz mit unterschiedlichen Verhaltensformen, die unsere heutige Kultur kennzeichnen: Er bezieht sich auf die vorherrschende Eventkultur mit ihren hilflosen Versuchen, den öffentlichen Raum der Stadt zur Bühne zu machen und überholte Formen der Repräsentation lebendig zu halten. Gerz initiiert mit *2–3 Straßen* ein „Anti-Event", das zugleich das 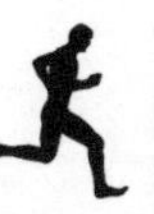 Repertoire der Eventkultur beherrscht. Es versammelt kein massenhaftes Publikum zu einer bestimmten Zeit an einem bestimmten Ort, an dem etwas Außerordentliches passiert. Es setzt auf Langsamkeit und Langfristigkeit anstatt auf kurzfristige Effekte. Es verzichtet auf große Bilder und kreiert eine Vielzahl von imaginären Bildern. Zugleich ist *2–3 Straßen* ein Medienspektakel: Ein Jahr lang mietfrei wohnen, wer möchte das nicht? Dennoch: Welche Menschen erklären sich bereit, für ein Jahr ins Ruhrgebiet zu ziehen, das mit massiven Schrumpfungsprozessen und hoher Arbeitslosigkeit zu kämpfen hat? Wie erleben die neuen Bewohner die Umgebung in den ehemaligen Arbeitervierteln, in denen der Anteil der Menschen, die in den 1960er und 1970er Jahren als Arbeitsmigranten gekommen sind, mit bis zu 40 Prozent überdurchschnittlich hoch ist? Empfinden es die „alten" Mieter als Ungerechtigkeit, dass sie für Wohnungen, die nicht renoviert sind, mehr zahlen als die Zugezogenen? Welche sozialen Spannungen entstehen daraus? All diese Fragen kreieren Instabilitäten. *2–3 Straßen* greift in ein fragiles Gleichgewicht ein und erhöht die Fragilität. Auch Jochen Gerz geht es wie den Künstlern der Avantgarde darum, Neues entstehen zu lassen. Doch er weiß, dass sich dieses nur aus der Gesellschaft selbst entwickeln kann, deshalb wünscht er sich, dass es sich bei *2–3 Straßen* eher „um eine kulturelle Entwicklung" handelt und „weniger um die Realisierung eines Autors oder um eine individuelle Erfindung", sondern „um eine minimale Veränderung im Gleichen, die sich nur vom zeitgenössischen Bewusstsein registrieren lässt".[15]

NOTES—[1] Cf. Warnke, Martin/Syamken, Georg/Hofmann, Werner: *Die Menschenrechte des Auges. Über Aby Warburg,* Frankfurt/Main 1980, 62. In both my lecture and this written version, I refer on occasion to my text "Kinetische Kunst – ein mentales Übungsfeld für den mobilisierten Betrachter (Kinetic Art – A Field of Mental Exercise for the Mobilised Beholder)," in: Peter Pakesch (ed.): *Beweg-liche Teile. Formen des Kinetischen (Moving Parts. Forms of the Kinetic),* Cologne 2005, 94–110.—[2] Cf. the essay of Margitta Buchert *Mobile and Stabile,* 48–70—[3] In the First Futurist Manifesto, Filippo Tommaso Marinetti writes: "We intend to exalt aggressive action, a feverish insomnia, the racer's stride, the mortal leap, the punch and the slap. We affirm that the world's magnificence has been enriched by a new beauty: the beauty of speed." Marinetti, Filippo Tommaso: "El Manifes-to Futurista, Le Figaro, 20. Februar 1909," In: Umbro Appollonio (ed.): *Der Futurismus. Manifeste und Dokumente einer künstlerischen Revolution,* Cologne 1972, Cf. also http://www.kunstzitate.de/bildendekunst/manifeste/futurismus.htm. (last visit: 15.04.11)—[4] Hulten, Pontus: *Jean Tinguely. A Magic Stronger than Death,* New York 1987, 55.—[5] Here Monika Wagner refers among other things to the sculpture *Large Two Forms* by Henry Moore, which was erected in front of what was then the Chancellor's Office in Bonn in 1979. Wagner, Monika: "Die Parzellierung des Öffentlichen – oder Kunst als sozialer Kitt?" In: Söke Dinkla/Karl Janssen (eds.): *Paradoxien des Öffentlichen,* Nurem-berg 2007, 24–33.—[6] On this, cf. in more detail Dinkla, Söke: *Pioniere Interaktiver Kunst,* Ostfildern 1995.—[7] "Art alone succeeds in creating political and social freedom," Schiller wrote in 1795 in his letters *On the Aesthetic Education of Man,* which was tellingly reprinted in 1965 (Schiller, Friedrich: *Über die ästhetische Erziehung des Menschen in einer Reihe von Briefen,* Stuttgart 1965).—[8] On this, see also the analysis by Wolfgang Ullrich, who shows how art today has largely lost its funda-mental opposition to reality. Ullrich, Wolfgang: *Tiefer hängen,* Berlin 2003. See also Jochen Gerz in an interview with Joachim Kreibohm: "Der Betrachter ist im Nachteil, er hat keine Chance ge-genüber der Summe der vorweggenommenen Entmündigungen." In: Jochen Gerz: *Gegenwart der Kunst, Interviews (1970–1995),* Regensburg 1995, 216.—[9] This occurs in a programmatic manner in the works of Peter Kogler. Like few other artists, Kogler has presented a complete declination of the figure of the net. Here, he not only refers to social networks but also to the new forms of perception introduced by the computer, which he already began to use in the 1980s. In his most space-con-suming projection work to date, *Untitled (2010),* he covered the waterside promenade of the future Eurogate by Norman Foster in Duisburg with illuminated net data, which move over the steps with varying speed. As darkness progresses their presence begins to dissolve: they are no longer spa tially or temporally fixed due to their mobilisation, their dynamism. On this, cf. Dinkla, Söke/Janssen, Karl et al. (eds.): *Ruhrlights. Twilight Zone.* Ostfildern 2010, 44–49.—[10] Cf. Dinkla, Söke (ed.): *Publi City. Constructing the Truth.* Nuremberg 2006, 43–53. In 2010, the Cake Monument will be present-ed at the architecture biennial in Venice.—[11] Maak, Niklas: "*Küchenmonument,* raumlaborberlin," in: Söke Dinkla (ed.): *PubliCity. Constructing the Truth.* Nuremberg 2006, 44.—[12] For more detail on this, cf. Draganovic, Julia: "Yves Netzhammer. Abstraktionsvorräte," in: Söke Dinkla/Karl Janssen et al. (eds.): *Ruhrlights. Twilight Zone.* Ostfildern 2010, 51–55.—[13] Cf. Dinkla, Söke/Janssen, Karl (eds.): *Tiger & Turtle / Magic Mountain. Eine Landmarke für Duisburg,* Ostfildern 2011.—[14] Gerz, Jochen: *2–3 Straßen TEXT.* Cologne 2011. The book is appearing in a slip case together with *2–3 Straßen MAKING OF.* Cologne 2011, See also www.2–3strassen.eu and www.du2010.de.—[15] Jochen Gerz in his concept for *2–3 Streets.* Gerz, Jochen: *2–3 Straßen MAKING OF. Eine Ausstellung in Städten des Ruhrgebiets,* Cologne 2011, 10–19, here: 19.

In einer Gesellschaft, in der die Prinzipien der Demokratie nach mehr als 50 Jahren selbstverständlich geworden sind, geht es heute darum, Werkanordnungen zu initiieren, die uns dazu verführen, aus der manchmal angenehmen Immobilität herauszutreten, in der wir uns als Konsumenten eingerichtet haben. Die Emphase des Warburgschen „Habenwollens" wird in Werken wie *2–3 Straßen* mit dem „Gebenwollen" in eine fragile Balance gebracht. Aus der Bewegung (im Singular) werden in der Zeit der Postindustrie die Bewegungen (im Plural). Sie folgen unterschiedlichsten, auch kurzfristig wechselnden Richtungen. Mit kalkulierten Mehrdeutigkeiten, Paradoxien und Widersprüchen sind sie Ausdruck einer pluralistischen, multikulturellen Gesellschaft, die sich darauf einstellt, mit den Zumutungen der ständigen Veränderung in einer globalisierten Welt zurechtzukommen.

ANMERKUNGEN—[1] Vgl. Warnke, Martin/Syamken, Georg/Hofmann, Werner: *Die Menschenrechte des Auges. Über Aby Warburg,* Frankfurt/Main 1980, 62. In meinem Vortrag und dieser Verschriftlichung beziehe mich in Teilen auf meinen Text „Kinetische Kunst – ein mentales Übungsfeld für den mobilisierten Betrachter (Kinetic Art – A Field of Mental Exercise for the Mobilised Beholder)", in: Pakesch, Peter (Hg.): *Bewegliche Teile. Formen des Kinetischen (Moving Parts. Forms of the Kinetic),* Köln 2005, 94–110.—[2] Vgl. den Beitrag von Margitta Buchert *Mobile und Stabile,* 49–73—[3] Im ersten futuristischen Manifest schreibt Filippo Tommaso Marinetti: „Wir wollen preisen die angriffslustige Bewegung, die fiebrige Schlaflosigkeit, den Laufschritt, den Salto Mortale, die Ohrfeige, den Faustschlag. Wir erklären, daß sich die Herrlichkeit der Welt um eine neue Schönheit bereichert hat: die Schönheit der Geschwindigkeit." Marinetti, Filippo Tommaso: „El Manifesto Futurista, Le Figaro, 20. Februar 1909", Umbro Appollonio (Hg.): *Der Futurismus. Manifeste und Dokumente einer künstlerischen Revolution,* Köln 1972, Vgl. auch http://www.kunstzitate.de/bildendekunst/manifeste/futurismus.htm. (Letzter Zugriff 30. April 2011).—[4] Hulten, Pontus: *Jean Tinguely. A Magic Stronger than Death,* New York 1987, 55.—[5] Monika Wagner bezieht sich hier unter anderem auf die Skulptur *Large Two Forms* von Henry Moore, die 1979 vor dem damaligen Bundeskanzleramt in Bonn aufgestellt wurde. Wagner, Monika: „Die Parzellierung des Öffentlichen – oder Kunst als sozialer Kitt?", in: Dinkla, Söke/ Janssen, Karl (Hg.): *Paradoxien des Öffentlichen,* Nürnberg 2007, 24–33.—[6] Vgl. dazu ausführlicher Dinkla, Söke: *Pioniere Interaktiver Kunst,* Ostfildern 1995.—[7] „Erst mit Hilfe der Kunst würde es gelingen, politische und gesellschaftliche Freiheit zu schaffen", schrieb Schiller 1795 in seinen Schriften *Über die ästhetische Erziehung des Menschen,* die bezeichnenderweise 1965 wieder aufgelegt wurden (Schiller, Friedrich: *Über die ästhetische Erziehung des Menschen in einer Reihe von Briefen,* Stuttgart 1965).—[8] Siehe dazu auch die Analyse von Wolfgang Ullrich, der zeigt, wie die Kunst ihre Fundamentalopposition zur Wirklichkeit heute in weiten Teilen verloren hat. Ullrich, Wolfgang: *Tiefer hängen,* Berlin 2003. Siehe auch Jochen Gerz im Interview mit Joachim Kreibohm: „Der Betrachter ist im Nachteil, er hat keine Chance gegenüber der Summe der vorweggenommenen Entmündigungen.", in: Gerz, Jochen: *Gegenwart der Kunst, Interviews (1970–1995),* Regensburg 1995, 216.—[9] Programmatisch geschieht dies in den Arbeiten von Peter Kogler. Wie kaum ein anderer Künstler hat Kogler die Figur des Netzes in all seinen Formen durchdekliniert. Er bezieht sich damit nicht

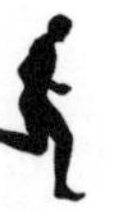

nur auf die sozialen Netze, sondern auch auf die neuen Wahrnehmungsformen, die der Computer einführt, den er schon in den 1980er Jahren verwendete. In seiner bislang raumgreifendsten Projektionsarbeit *Ohne Titel (2010)* hat er die Uferpromenade des zukünftigen Eurogate von Norman Foster in Duisburg mit leuchtenden Netzformationen überzogen, die sich in wechselnden Geschwindigkeiten über die Stufen bewegen. Mit fortschreitender Dunkelheit beginnt sie sich in ihrer Präsenz aufzulösen. In seiner Mobilisierung, seinem Dynamismus, ist er nicht mehr räumlich oder zeitlich fixiert. Vgl. dazu Dinkla, Söke/Janssen, Karl u.a. (Hg.): *Ruhrlights. Twilight Zone.* Ostfildern 2010, 44–49—[10] Vgl. Dinkla, Söke (Hg.): *PubliCity. Constructing the Truth.* Nürnberg 2006, 43–53. Im Jahr 2010 wird das *Küchenmonument* auf der Architektur Biennale in Venedig präsentiert.—[11] Maak, Niklas: „Küchenmonument, raumlaborberlin", in: Söke Dinkla (Hg.): *PubliCity. Constructing the Truth.* Nürnberg 2006, 44.—[12] Vgl. ausführlicher dazu Draganovic, Julia: „Yves Netzhammer. Abstraktionsvorräte", in: Dinla, Söke Dinkla/Karl Janssen u.a. (Hg.): *Ruhrlights. Twilight Zone.* Ostfildern 2010, 51–55.—[13] Vgl. Dinkla, Söke/Janssen, Karl (Hg.): *Tiger & Turtle / Magic Mountain. Eine Landmarke für Duisburg,* Ostfildern 2011.—[14] Gerz, Jochen: *2–3 Straßen TEXT.* Köln 2011. Das Buch erscheint gemeinsam in einem Schuber mit *2–3 Straßen. MAKING OF.* Köln 2011. Siehe auch www.2–3strassen.eu und www.du2010.de.—[15] Jochen Gerz im Konzept zu *„2–3 Straßen".* Gerz, Jochen: *2–3 Straßen. MAKING OF.* Eine Ausstellung in Städten des Ruhrgebiets, Köln 2011, 10–19.

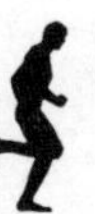

Scott deLahunta
Traces and Artefacts of Physical Intelligence

Scott deLahunta is an author, researcher, and manager of international performing arts projects focusing on the combination of choreography and other disciplines. He is currently Senior Research Fellow Coventry University and R-Research Director for Wayne McGregor|Random Dance and is Project Leader of Motion Bank realised by The Forsythe Company. Publications include contributions to: *Knowledge in Motion: Perspectives of Artistic and Scientific Research in Dance* (ed.: Gehm, Husemann, von Wilcke, 2007), *SwanQuake: the User Manual* (ed., 2007).

Scott deLahunta
Spuren und Artefakte physischer Intelligenz

Scott deLahunta ist Autor, Forscher und Manager von internationalen Projekten der Darstellenden Künste mit dem Fokus auf die Verbindung von Choreografie mit anderen Disziplinen. Derzeit ist er leitender Wissenschaftler an der Coventry University, Forschungsdirektor bei Wayne McGregor|Random Dance und Projektleiter des Projektes Motion Bank von The Forsythe Company. Publikationen u. a. : *Knowledge in Motion: Perspectives of Artistic and Scientific Research in Dance* (Hg.: Gehm, Husemann, von Wilcke, 2007). *SwanQuake: the user manual* (Hg., 2007).

In sport and dance, speed and precision combined with fluidity and ease in the execution of certain movement sequences is often said to demonstrate "physical intelligence." The problem is that for practices so firmly rooted in the physical, this intelligence tends to be equated with an unconscious intuition, a level of special expertise that "thinking" can only get in the way of.[1] This misconception contributes to the persistent view that mind and body are separate modes of engaging with and making sense of the world. This misconception contributes to the undervaluing of embodied practices in a society that assumes abstract knowledge making to be the highest forms of cultural production, and associates language, reasoning, and rational thought with this knowledge. A growing number of scholars and scientists are working to change this misconception, drawing on new interdisciplinary research connections and bringing fundamental assumptions about the constitution of our intelligent thinking selves into question. This involves, for example, the empirical study of how forms of abstract knowledge are the result of direct sensory motor engagement with the world and theorising how knowledge is constituted from the interaction of the many parts of one's experience.[2]

What could dance (as a body-based practice) and dancers (as experience "experts") offer as an alternative way of approaching the question of physical intelligence? Could methods of documentation, movement analysis, and notation be improved so as to capture and make underlying patterns of choreographic thinking accessible? Could choreographic ideas and processes be rendered tangible, revealing hidden aspects of creativity or visualising the finished dance's latent structure? These are the kinds of questions interdisciplinary research groups working in collaboration with a small but increasing number of contemporary choreographers have been addressing. The result is a growing collection of choreographic resources, which are helping to build a unique context for the discovery, materialisation, and subsequent study of traces and artefacts of physical intelligence.

The first step in understanding how these projects connect to questions about physical intelligence is to acknowledge the extent to which choreographers and dancers make use of the page as a site for creative work, specifically focusing on the drawn or written score.[3] In *A Choreographer's Handbook,* choreographer Jonathan Burrows describes two main approaches to the idea of a score. The first kind of score is like a classical music score "written as a representation of the piece itself. (...) In the other kind of score, what is written or thought is a tool for information, image, and inspiration, which acts as a source for what you will see, but whose shape may be very different from the final realisation."[4]

1 is a relatively well-known diagram drawn by American choreographer Trisha Brown and is one of several choreographic systems Brown invented (*1* p. 104). This one, titled Locus (1975), is a twenty-seven-point cube in which a different number is assigned to each point. The choreography involved generating a score by translating a written autobiographical

Wenn im Sport und beim Tanz komplexe Bewegungskombinationen mit höchster Geschwindigkeit und Präzision und gleichzeitig fließend und mühelos ausgeführt werden, gilt dies oft als Beleg für das Vorhandensein einer „physischen Intelligenz". Das Problem besteht aber darin, dass bei einer Bewegungspraxis, die so fest im Körperlichen verwurzelt ist, diese Intelligenz mit unbewusstem Empfinden bzw. Intuition gleichgesetzt wird, mit einem spezifischen Wissen, bei dem rationales Bewusstsein nur hinderlich sein kann.[1] Diese irrige Vorstellung trägt dazu bei, dass sich die Auffassung von Intellekt und Körperlichkeit als separate Modi unserer Interaktion mit der Welt und unserer Weltsicht hartnäckig hält. Die Folge ist nicht zuletzt, dass in einer Gesellschaft, die geistiges Wissen in Verbindung mit Sprache, Argumentationskraft und rationalem Denken als höchste kulturelle und zivilisatorische Leistung ansieht, jede praktische, körperliche Tätigkeit unterbewertet wird. Immer mehr Wissenschaftler unterschiedlicher Disziplinen arbeiten heute daran, diesen Irrtum zu korrigieren. Sie beziehen sich dabei auf neue interdisziplinäre Forschungsansätze, um bislang geltende Grundannahmen hinsichtlich Struktur und Funktion des Gehirns als Sitz unserer Intelligenz infrage zu stellen. Das geschieht zum Beispiel durch empirische Untersuchungen zu der Frage, ob und inwieweit bestimmte Formen abstrakten Wissens das direkte Ergebnis physischer, das heißt sensorischer und motorischer Abläufe sind, und wie menschliches Wissen sich aus den Wechselwirkungen zwischen körperlichen, emotionalen und intellektuellen Erfahrungen konstituiert.[2]

Welche alternativen Lösungswege könnte der Tanz – als Körper-Praxis – und könnten Tänzer – als Experten dieser Praxis – uns bieten? Wird es uns gelingen, bestimmte Formen von choreografischer Dokumentation, kinetischen Studien und „Notationen" zu optimieren, um die Strukturen choreografischen Denkens zu erklären? Könnten choreografische Ideen und Prozesse so plausibel dargestellt werden, dass unsichtbare schöpferische Aspekte oder die einem Tanzstück zugrunde liegenden Strukturen sichtbar werden?

Mit derlei Fragen beschäftigen sich verschiedene Gruppen von Wissenschaftlern unterschiedlicher Disziplinen seit einiger Zeit in Zusammenarbeit mit einer kleinen, aber wachsenden Zahl von Choreografen. Aus ihren Forschungen sind eine Reihe von choreografischen Erkenntnissen und Methoden hervorgegangen, die eine nie dagewesene Grundlage zur Ermittlung, Realisierung und Erforschung von Spuren und Artefakten physischer Intelligenz schaffen.

Um zu verstehen, was diese Projekte mit Fragen der physischen Intelligenz zu tun haben, muss in einem ersten Schritt erläutert werden, in welchem Umfang Choreografen und Tänzer das Blatt Papier als kreatives Arbeitsmittel nutzen – vor allem, um Zeichnungen und schriftliche Tanzpartituren zu Papier zu bringen.[3] In seinem Handbuch für Choreografen beschreibt Jonathan Burrows die zwei Hauptaspekte des Prinzips der Tanzpartitur. Die erste Form ähnelt der klassischen musikalischen Partitur, die das „Musikstück darstellt oder abbildet. (...) Bei der zweiten Form ist das Geschriebene oder auch nur Gedachte zugleich

statement into numbers, which were then transposed to points on the cube by the dancer who could "move through, touch, look at, jump over, or do something about each point in the series, either one point at a time or clustered."[5]

Trisha Brown is one of a small number of choreographers who have developed a distinctive way of moving. Hers is often referred to as "release technique"—an approach to movement that emphasises an alert, responsive, and neutral body prepared to move from specific points of initiation in any direction. What one might contemplate is how a score-making system like Locus—and its associated instructions—and the evolution of a distinctive way of dancing are co-dependent. Brown's dancers have to hold onto a set of ideas (such as where each imaginary point is in space, original statement and translated sequence of numbers, and the movement instructions) and problem solve with them while moving to perform in the context of such a score-generating instrument.[6] As a "tool for information," according to Burrows, Locus captures physical intelligence in its drawn diagrammatic representations. This bears repeating: the physical intelligence of a dancer/choreographer can be captured and expressed in a drawing (or diagram or score). Another example of capturing physical intelligence is William Forsythe's CD-ROM *Improvisation Technologies: A Tool for the Analytical Dance Eye.* Motivated by a need to transmit quickly principles of improvisation he had developed in the nineteen-eighties, Forsythe turned to drawing as well. These drawings were made directly on top of a digital video image of Forsythe performing demonstrations of his principles for the camera. The result is a collection of nearly one hundred short demonstrations, most using dynamic drawings to annotate his movement paths and map out "spatial relationships in and around his body" (*2* p. 104).[7]

It is important to note that these procedures, these choreographic ideas, existed before the annotated videos that help to materialise them for viewers. And, like Brown, Forsythe's ideas played a role in the evolution of a distinctive way of moving. In his case, against the background of ballet, "It was easy to represent things this way—thinking in circles and lines and planes and points. That's not so unusual for ballet dancers, this system is basically a manipulation of their existing knowledge."[8] Forsythe refers to the Improvisation Technologies as a way of "taking mental note" while moving. This scaffolding for thinking while moving was first put in place by Forsythe with the dancers through practice, in the studio, and on the stage. Only later have these ideas been made visually accessible on the CD-ROM. These annotations draw the viewer's attention to something that is normally unseen in the studio and in performance. This type of drawing captures what the dancer might be thinking. A question to return to later: does this help the audience see other types of structure in the dancing?

This emphasis on "what the dancer is thinking" is picked up by the work of choreographer Wayne McGregor, who for nearly a decade has been engaged in a study of choreographic cognition in collaborative research with scientists.[9] They have shared in setting up empirical research,

Informations- und Abbildungsmittel sowie Inspirationsquelle, aus denen geschöpft wird, was zu sehen sein wird, dessen Form sich aber wesentlich von der endgültigen Aufführungsform unterscheiden kann."[4]

1 S. 104 zeigt das relativ bekannte Locus-Diagramm (1975), eins von mehreren choreografischen Systemen der amerikanischen Choreografin Trisha Brown. Es zeigt einen Kubus, in den 27 Punkte eingezeichnet sind. Jedem Punkt ist eine andere Zahl zugeordnet. Anhand einer Reihe von Übersetzungen schriftlicher autobiografischer Aufzeichnungen in die verschiedenen Zahlen und damit von Übertragungen auf die dazugehörigen Punkte entwickelte Trisha Brown ihre Choreografie. Der Tänzer konnte „durch die Punkte hindurch oder über sie hinweg springen, sie ansehen oder an den entsprechenden Stellen ihre Abfolge ändern, entweder Punkt für Punkt oder an Stellen, wo mehrere Punkte Gruppen bildeten".[5]

Trisha Brown gehört zu der kleinen Schar von Choreografen, die ganz eigene Bewegungen und Schrittkombinationen entwickelt haben. Ihr Stil wird vielfach als „release technique" (*release* = Freisetzung, Loslassen) bezeichnet und beschreibt eine Bewegungsart, die einen wachen, reaktionsschnellen und neutralen Körper in den Vordergrund rückt, der darauf vorbereitet ist, sich von spezifischen Ausgangspunkten aus in alle Richtungen zu bewegen. Man könnte darüber nachdenken, auf welche Weise ein Choreografieprogramm wie Locus (mit den dazugehörigen Ausführungsanweisungen) und die Entwicklung eines charakteristischen Tanzstils sich gegenseitig bedingen. Browns Tänzer müssen eine ganze „Ideenkette" im Kopf behalten (zum Beispiel die Stellen, an denen sich die imaginären Punkte im Raum befinden, den Wortlaut der Anweisungen, deren Übersetzung in Ziffern sowie die einstudierten Bewegungsabläufe und Schrittkombinationen). Desweiteren müssen sie, während sie diesen choreografischen Rahmen mit tänzerischen Bewegungen und Schritten füllen, etwaige auftretende Fehler ausgleichen.[6] Als Informationsmittel (Jonathan Burrows) fängt Locus die Intelligenz des Körpers in schematischen Darstellungen ein. Oder anders formuliert: Die inkorporale Intelligenz des Tänzers/Choreografen lässt sich in Zeichnungen, Diagrammen und/oder Texten darstellen und festhalten. Ein weiteres Beispiel hierfür ist die CD-ROM *Improvisation Technologies: A Tool for the Analytical Dance Eye* von William Forsythe. Um die Prinzipien der Improvisation, die er in den 1980er Jahren entwickelt hatte, rasch und verständlich zu vermitteln, begann Forsythe unter anderem auch Zeichnungen zu nutzen. Seine choreografischen Skizzen zeichnete er direkt auf digitale Videos, die ihn selbst bei der Ausführung seiner Prinzipien vor der Kamera zeigten. Daraus entstanden fast 100 kurze Demo-DVDs, von denen die meisten dynamische gezeichnete Anmerkungen zu Bewegungsverläufen enthalten und „räumliche Beziehungen in und um seinen Körper herum" aufzeichnen (*2* S. 104).[7]

Hier gilt es zu erwähnen, dass diese choreografischen Ideen bereits vor dem Aufkommen solcher mit Anmerkungen versehenen Videos existierten, mit deren Hilfe sie dem Zuschauer anschaulich vor Augen geführt werden. Wie bei Trisha Brown

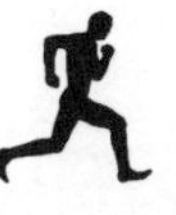

developing theoretical models, and applying results of the collaborative work in the studio when McGregor is giving the dancers complex tasks or instructions (sometimes similar to Brown's Locus) for generating movement material[10] (*3* p. 105). While the research work is still ongoing, McGregor and his dancers are now regularly augmenting this generation part of the creative process using a sort of "cognitive toolkit" that draws explicitly on insight from the collaborative research. Given the title, *Choreographic Thinking Tools,* this method currently focuses on the use and manipulation of internal imagery in the context of "tasking." One way of understanding imagery is to look again at the figure from Forsythe's *Improvisation Technologies* CD-ROM, where the annotation shows you what the dancer may be creating as a visual reference with their imagination. Most of the procedures in *Improvisation Technologies* involve our ability to manipulate visual imagery in space. The CD-ROM annotations draw the viewer's attention to the spatial-praxic focus of the dancers. Brown's Locus cube does something similar; it shows us the attention-focusing system, a primarily visual one, without the annotation. In both cases, they demonstrate the generative potential of structuring a mental space through thinking systems involving points, lines, and planes. *Choreographic Thinking Tools* extends the scaffolding for thinking while moving to include two other forms of imagery: auditory-verbal (sounds or voice in the head) and semantic. In all three forms, points in mental space need to be constantly updated as the focus of attention shifts.[11]

In the context of McGregor's work, unique properties of choreographic thinking are being exposed through collaborative work with scientists (*3* p. 105). The work does not seek to scientifically evaluate aesthetic judgment or validate artistic choices. It aims to uncover more about the kinds of intelligence involved in contemporary dance making and makes this information available to choreographers in a format that is useful. It draws from and contributes to evolving theories of embodied cognition, supporting various studies such as how gesture is recruited for creative problem solving in dance.[12] The work has also resulted in another type of drawing tool or sketching environment called the Choreographic Language Agent (CLA)[13] (*4, 5* p. 105). Formative to the development of the CLA has been a focused research into how computation and embodied practice can creatively intersect and includes a close collaboration with the artists of the OpenEnded Group who have worked extensively with other choreographers including Trisha Brown. The CLA is still in development, but the concept is as follows. With this tool, dancers first construct a 3-D drawing comprised of points, lines, and planes on the left side in the visual space. They then use the dropdown menus on the right side to select some aspect of their drawing, for example all points on the left side of the drawing. They then select an instruction to apply to them, for example rotate these points around their own axis. These two parts are assembled one after the other on the right screen and dragging the playback bar across them animates the drawing in the visual space. This sounds simple, but these assembled phrases

spielten auch Forsythes Videopartituren eine wichtige Rolle bei der Entwicklung seiner ganz eigenen, für ihn typischen tänzerischen Bewegungsformen auf der Basis des klassischen Balletts. „Es war einfach, alles auf diese Weise darzustellen und in Kreisen, Linien, Flächen und Punkten zu denken. Für Balletttänzer ist das nichts Ungewöhnliches, denn dieses System stellt im Grunde (nur) eine Manipulation ihres vorhandenen Wissens und Könnens dar."[8] Dieses „Einrüsten" des Denkens in der Bewegung hatte Forsythe zunächst bei Proben im Studio und auf der Bühne eingeübt. Erst später machte er die Methode mit Hilfe seiner CD-ROMs anschaulich zugänglich. Seine Anmerkungen auf den Videos lenken die Aufmerksamkeit des Zuschauers auf bestimmte Bewegungsaspekte, die normalerweise weder im Studio noch während der Aufführung gesehen werden. Diese Art Zeichnungen bilden ab, was der Tänzer beim Tanz denken könnte. Eine Frage, auf die ich später noch zurückkommen möchte, lautet: Hilft dies den Zuschauern, noch andere Strukturen in einem Tanzstück zu entdecken?

Die Betonung dessen, „was der Tänzer denkt", findet sich auch im Schaffen des Choreografen Wayne McGregor wieder, der sich seit fast einem Jahrzehnt in Zusammenarbeit mit verschiedenen Wissenschaftlern dem Thema der Wahrnehmung/des Erkennens choreografischer Strukturen widmet.[9] Das Team führte empirische Forschungsprojekte durch, entwickelte theoretische Modelle und wandte die Forschungsergebnisse bei der Probenarbeit im Studio an, wo McGregor seinen Tänzern und Tänzerinnen komplexe Aufgaben stellte oder Anweisungen gab (die gelegentlich Trisha Browns Locus ähnelten), um Bewegungsabläufe und Schrittkombinationen zu gestalten.[10] (3 S. 105) Das Forschungsprojekt ist noch nicht abgeschlossen und McGregor und seine Tanztruppe arbeiten ständig daran, diese schöpferische Arbeit fortzuführen und ihren Wissensfundus zu vergrößern, wobei sie eine Art kognitiven Werkzeugkasten nutzen, den McGregor *Choreographic Thinking Tools* nannte und in den er gezielt neue Einsichten und Erkenntnisse aus der gemeinsamen Forschungsarbeit einbezogen hat. Bei dieser Methode geht es derzeit vor allem um die Anwendung und Manipulation innerer Bilder im Rahmen choreografischer Aufgabenlösungen. Diese choreografische Bildsprache erschließt sich zum Beispiel dann, wenn man sich die Figur aus Forsythes CD-ROM *Improvisation Technologies* ... noch einmal anschaut: Die Anmerkung zeigt, welche Bewegungen der Tänzer im nächsten Moment vielleicht als visuellen Hinweis auf seine inneren Bilder ausführen wird. Die meisten in diesem Film gezeigten Bewegungsabläufe erfordern die Fähigkeit, mit einer visuellen Bildsprache im Raum zu spielen und die Bilder zu manipulieren. Die CD-ROM-Anmerkungen lenken die Aufmerksamkeit der Zuschauer auf die Konzentration der Tänzer und auf die räumliche Dimension ihrer Kunst. Trisha Browns *Locus-Kubus* bewirkt etwas Ähnliches. Er verdeutlicht, wie die Fokussierung der primär visuellen Aufmerksamkeit ohne die Anmerkungen funktioniert. Forsythe und Brown demonstrieren beide, welche „kinetische Zeugungskraft" in der Strukturierung eines gedachten Raums mit Hilfe

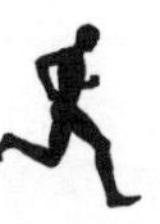

can be layered one on top of the other and produce surprising and complex animated drawings. Like the second type of score described by Burrows, the dancers take these as inspiration for movement generation into the studio space, returning to the CLA sketching environment to try out new combinations.

While both Forsythe's and Brown's dancers had to be holding sets of ideas in mind and problem solve with them while moving, the CLA moves parts of this process to its computer canvas as a page for working out choreographic ideas more interactively. Here, dancers can manipulate structural relationships that are both syntactic or language-like and visual-spatial; and they build further understanding of these manipulations by assimilating them into their movement generation in the studio. With its digital memory, the CLA uniquely documents aspects of their decision-making—making a part of their choreographic thinking process available for revisiting and examination.[14] The tools for information that have been discussed so far support choreographers and dancers in working creatively with choreographic ideas. As score generating systems, they offer themselves as objects of self-reflexive study, helping to increase the domain level expertise of the choreographer and dancer. But they are also available as study objects for other specialists interested in researching embodiment. The more of these objects of choreographic thinking that can be made available from different artists, the richer this research environment will become.[15]

How might these developments impact an audience that does not come to dance with such a specific research interest? If choreographic ideas and processes could be rendered productively tangible as has been discussed, could some of the same approaches be used to enhance an audience's experience of watching dance, specifically their ability to read and make sense of non-narrative choreographic forms? This question motivated Forsythe to develop another project, originally conceived as an "instructional DVD" that would again use digital video annotations to draw the viewer's attention to the forms of choreographic organisation in a finished dance titled *One Flat Thing, reproduced* (2000) (*6* p. 104). The following brief description by Norah Zuniga Shaw gives an impression of the piece: "Seventeen dancers fly, slide, reach, and twist their bodies within a grid of twenty steel tables. Seemingly on the edge of chaos their actions are controlled by a complex array of interdependencies that challenge and excite your sense of order as you watch. Time slips and slides between constant acceleration and sudden moments of active stillness, elements align and dissolve, dancers come and go, your eyes flicker in search of pattern, seeing and not seeing the changes that occur."[16] The project was developed over a period of four years in collaboration with researchers in both arts and science across the the campus at The Ohio State University, eventually launching on-line in April 2009 with the title *Synchronous Objects for One Flat Thing, reproduced*.[17] This extensive site makes a large amount of material available for exploration. My aim here is to briefly connect this project to the others already mentioned and speculate further on the

von Punkten, Linien und Flächen liegt. Forsythes *Choreographic Thinking Tools* erweitern den Rahmen, in dem sich choreografisches Denken bewegt, um zwei weitere metaphorische Systeme: Erstens das auditive und verbale (Töne oder Stimmen im Kopf) und zweitens das semantische. Bei allen drei Systemen müssen gedachte Punkte im gedachten Raum dem sich hin und her bewegenden Fokus der Aufmerksamkeit folgen und so ständig aktualisiert werden.[11] Im Rahmen von Wayne McGregors Forschungszusammenarbeit mit Wissenschaftlern werden spezifische Merkmale des choreografischen Denkens untersucht und sichtbar gemacht. (*3* S. 105) Damit will das Team keine wissenschaftlich fundierten ästhetischen Urteile formulieren oder künstlerische Entscheidungen bewerten, sondern neue Erkenntnisse über die Formen von Intelligenz gewinnen, die im modernen Tanz wirksam werden, und diese Informationen Choreografen in einem praktisch anwendbaren Format zur Verfügung stellen. Das Projekt baut auf Theorien zur Darstellung von Kognition auf, führt diese fort und untermauert diverse Untersuchungen, etwa zur Frage, auf welche Weise Gebärden zur Problemlösung im Tanz dienen können.[12] Aus diesem Forschungsprojekt ist ein weiteres digitales choreografisches Zeichentool, der sogenannte „Choreographic Language Agent" (CLA) hervorgegangen.[13] (*4, 5* S. 105) Maßgeblich für die Entwicklung war die Konzentration der For-

schung auf kreative Schnittpunkte von Computern und Körperpraxis, in enger Zusammenarbeit mit den Künstlern der OpenEnded Group, die vielfach mit anderen Choreografen, unter ihnen Thrisha Brown, zusammengearbeitet haben. Der CLA befindet sich noch in der Entwicklung, aber das Konzept lautet wie folgt: Die Tänzer erstellen zunächst auf der linken Seite der Bildschirmfläche eine 3-D-Zeichnung aus Punkten, Linien und Flächen. Dann wählen sie über das Auswahlmenü auf der rechten Seite einige Elemente ihrer Zeichnung aus, zum Beispiel alle Punkte auf der linken Hälfte der Bildfläche. Daraufhin aktivieren sie eine bestimmte Anweisung für diese Punkte, etwa dass diese sich alle um ihre eigene Achse drehen sollen. Diese beiden Anweisungen werden dann einer nach dem anderen auf der linken Seite der endgültigen Bildfläche zusammengefügt und animiert, indem man den Wiedergabebalken über die Zeichnung zieht. Das klingt einfach, aber die zusammengefügten Teile lassen sich auch übereinander legen, sodass komplexe und unerwartete Animationen entstehen. Wie bei dem von Jonathan Burrows beschriebenen Typus von Tanzpartitur nutzen die Tänzer diese Form als Inspirationsquelle für die Entwicklung von Bewegungen im Studio, wobei sie immer wieder in den virtuellen CLA-Raum zurückkehren, um neue Schrittkombinationen auszuprobieren.

Während die Tänzer von Forsythe und Brown jeweils einen ganzen Satz komplexer Konzepte und Anweisungen während einer Tanzaufführung im Kopf haben und ihre Bewegungen danach ausrichten mussten, überträgt der CLA diesen Denkprozess teilweise auf den Computerbildschirm, sodass die Tänzer in der Interaktion mit der 3-D-Tanzpartitur ihre Ideen entwickeln können. Dabei können sie strukturelle Beziehungen manipulieren (die Satzbildungen oder auch visuellen,

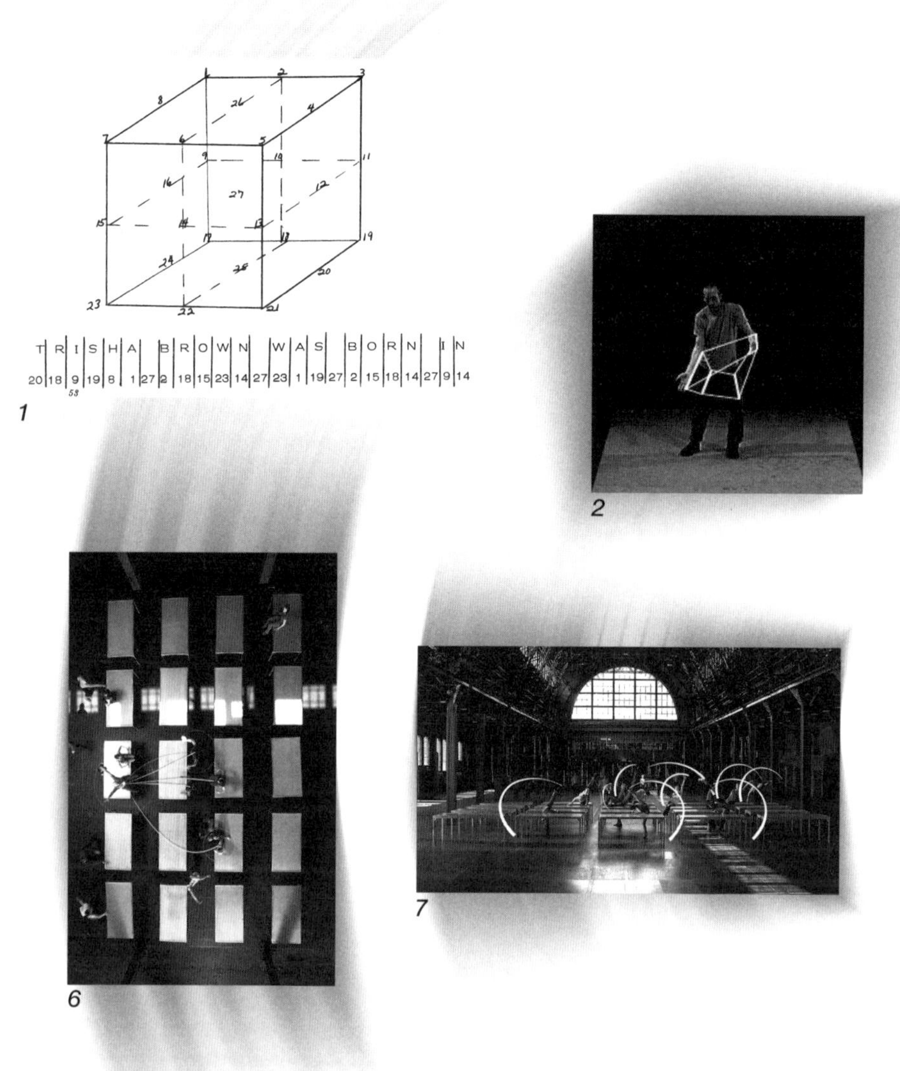

1 Trisha Brown: *Diagram for Locus,* 1975 — *2* Screenshots from William Forsythe's DVD *Improvisation Technologies: A Tool for the Analytical Dance Eye,* 1999 — *3* Wayne McGregor: *Random Dance,* University of California, San Diego, 2009 — *4, 5 Choreographic Language Agent,* left and right screens — *6 Cueing System,* still from annotated video illustrating the complex system of cueing in *One Flat Thing, reproduced,* 2000 — *7 Form Flow,* still from annotated video illustrating allignments, the way in which Forsythe designs relationships in space and time — *8 Counterpoint Tool,* interactive creative tool in which users can create their own visual counterpoint, reveal alignments in form and flow, and explore creating movement dependencies akin to cueing system in *One Flat Thing, reproduced.*

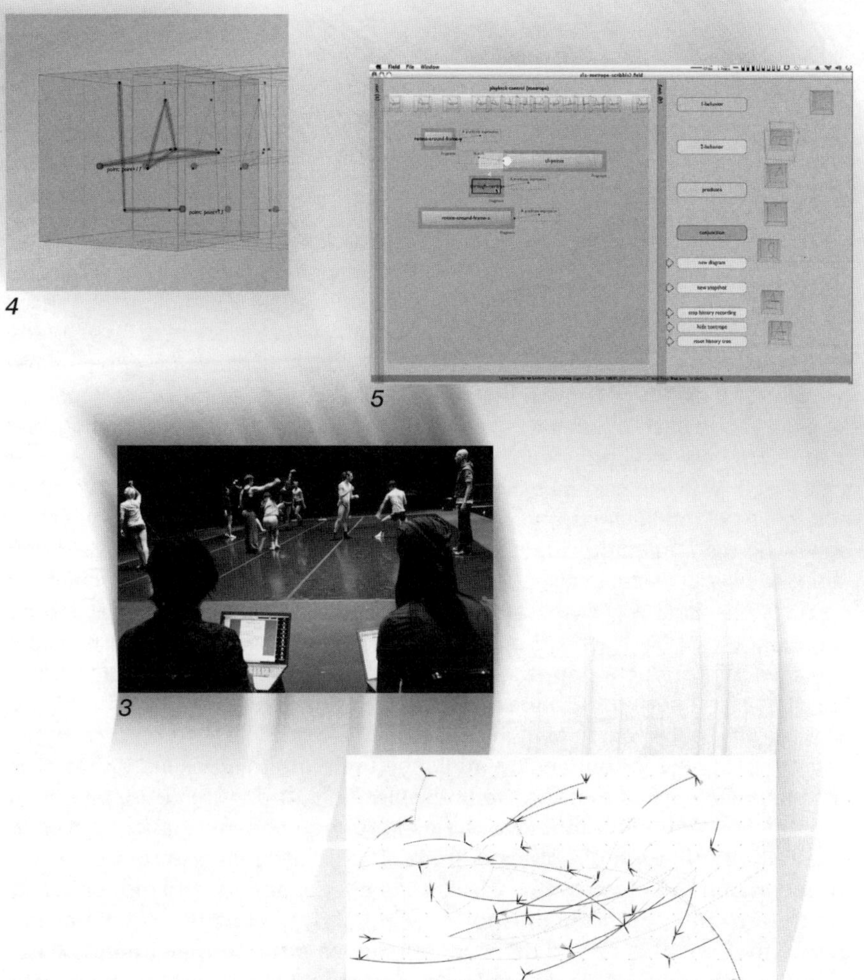

1 Trisha Brown: *Diagram für Locus*, 1975 — *2* Screenshots aus William Forsythe's DVD *Improvisation Technologies: A Tool for the Analytical Dance Eye*, 1999 — *3* Wayne McGregor: *Random Dance*, University of California, San Diego, 2009 — *4, 5* *Choreographic Language Agent*, linker und rechter Bildschirm — *6 Cueing System*, Standbild aus kommentiertem Video, das das komplexe System der Koordination in *One Flat Thing, reproduced* erläutert, 2000 — *7 Form Flow*, Standbild aus kommentiertem Video, das zeigt, wie Forsythe Beziehungen in Raum und Zeit entwirft. — *8 Counterpoint Tool*, interaktives kreatives Instrument, das es Nutzern ermöglicht, einen eigenen visuellen Kontrapunkt zu schaffen, Koordinierungen in Form und Bewegungsfluss zu entdecken und sich an der Erschaffung von Bewegungsabhängigkeiten nach dem Koordinationssystem von *One Flat Thing, reproduced* zu versuchen.

possibility of revealing and exploring aspects of physical intelligence in the context of expert dance practice. On the site, *One Flat Thing, reproduced* is described as an "ensemble dance that examines and reconfigures classical choreographic principles of counterpoint. (…)Three structural systems interact to create the counterpoint of the dance: movement material, cueing, and alignments."[18] Each of these structural systems is explained in more detail on the site. *6* and *7* show how the video annotations appear that show the cueing and alignments (*6, 7* p. 104). These lines drawn on top of the video make explicit selected inter-dancer relationships corresponding to that particular choreographic system. Thus, they are an indication of the focus of attention in the space at that particular moment. Whereas the *Improvisation Technologies* DVD draws the viewer's attention to what the dancer might be thinking with the body, *Synchronous Objects* foregrounds the overall distribution of attention that is facilitating coordinated decision-making. As has already been observed, scientists and philosophers are developing new theories of how the body shapes the mind, which will counter the prevailing view that physical intelligence is purely instinctive. We have already discussed how physical intelligence can be embedded in score generated tools. Now, observing the annotated videos of *One Flat Thing, reproduced,* we could contemplate how physical intelligence can be extended beyond the boundaries of a single individual.[19] However, this does not answer the question if audience experience can be enriched by such exposure to the workings of physical intelligence. For some non-researchers it might prove to be useful information, but is it enough to render visible what the dancer might be thinking while moving either alone or with the group?

Another proposal for enhancing audience understanding exists on the *Synchronous Objects* site in the Counterpoint Tool (*8* p. 105). This is a small interactive programme that lets one explore the concept of choreographic counterpoint through direct experience. The small clock-like forms can be moved in and out of unison by varying the shape, speed, and motion using the sliders. The Counterpoint Tool is a kind of dynamic interactive drawing device that enables one to discover an elusive structure, as contrapuntal interplay can easily slip out of balance. The question is: might working with it enhance one's ability to perceive this kind of coherence in any subsequent viewings of non-narrative dance, where the meaning and intelligence of the dance is grounded in such structures?

The aim of this essay has been to provide evidence to support the view that dance artists are in a unique position to shift prevailing attitudes toward physical intelligence as being a "lesser form of intellect confined to the bodily achievements."[20] This evidence has been shown in examples culled from the growing collection of choreographic resources being developed by research groups working in collaboration with contemporary choreographers. These efforts, if extended and multiplied, might help ensure that dance enters into a constitutive relationship with emerging conceptions of our intelligent thinking selves.

räumlichen Gestaltungen ähneln) und ihr Verständnis dieser Manipulationen vertiefen, indem sie diese in ihre choreografischen Entwicklungen im Studio integrieren. In seinem Datenspeicher dokumentiert der CLA auf einzigartige Weise bestimmte Aspekte ihrer tänzerischen Entscheidungsfindung und macht so den choreografischen Prozess für Überprüfungen und wiederholte Abrufe verfügbar.[14] Die hier beschriebenen Informations- und Instruktionsmittel unterstützen Choreografen und Tänzer bei der Ausarbeitung ihrer kreativen Ideen. Als Entwicklungs- und Gestaltungsmittel für Tanzpartituren bieten sie sich als selbstreflexive Studienobjekte an und erweitern die Kompetenzen von Choreografen und Tänzern. Sie können aber auch in anderen Fachdisziplinen mit dem Schwerpunkt auf der Verkörperlichung geistiger Phänomene als Forschungsobjekte dienen. Je mehr choreografisches Gedankengut in den oben beschriebenen Formen zur Verfügung steht, desto interessanter und ergiebiger wird dieses Forschungsfeld sein.[15]

Wie könnten diese Entwicklungen aber ein tanzbegeistertes Publikum beeinflussen, das gar kein wissenschaftliches Interesse für Tanz und Choreografie hat? Wenn choreografische Ideen und Prozesse so greifbar gemacht werden könnten, dass sie zur Wiederholung anregen, könnte man dann derlei Ansätze und Mittel nutzen, um eine Tanzaufführung als gesteigertes Erlebnis für die Zuschauer zu gestalten und ihnen zu einem tieferen Verständnis abstrakter, nicht erzählerischer Choreografien zu verhelfen?

Diese Frage veranlasste William Forsythe dazu, ein weiteres, ursprünglich als Lehr-DVD konzipiertes, choreografisches Instrument zu entwickeln, ebenfalls auf der Basis von schriftlichen Anmerkungen auf Computervideos, um Zuschauer auf die besonderen Formen choreografischer Organisation seines Tanzstücks *Synchronous Objects for One Flat Thing, reproduced* (2000) aufmerksam zu machen. (6 S. 104) Die folgende Kurzbeschreibung von Norah Zuniga Shaw vermittelt einen Eindruck von diesem Stück: „Siebzehn Tänzer (und Tänzerinnen) fliegen, gleiten, strecken die Arme aus und verdrehen ihre Körper auf einer mit zwanzig Stahltischen gerasterten Fläche. Ihre scheinbar chaotischen Bewegungen werden aber von einem komplexen Aufgebot wechselseitiger Abhängigkeiten gesteuert, die den Ordnungssinn des Zuschauers in Unordnung bringen. Das Tempo wechselt zwischen Beschleunigung und plötzlichem Stillstand; es werden Reihen gebildet und wieder aufgelöst; Tänzer kommen und gehen. Im Versuch, ein Muster zu erkennen, gehen die Blicke der Zuschauer hin und her und erfassen es bei all diesen schnellen Wechseln doch nicht."[16] Die Entwicklung dieses Tanzprojekts in Zusammenarbeit mit Angehörigen der geistes- wie naturwissenschaftlichen Fakultäten der Ohio State University nahm vier Jahre in Anspruch. Es wurde schließlich im April 2009 unter dem Titel *Synchronous Objects for One Flat Thing, reproduced* im Internet veröffentlicht.[17] Die umfangreiche Website hält zahlreiche Studienmaterialien bereit. Hier möchte ich dieses Projekt zu den bereits Erwähnten in Beziehung setzen und Überlegungen darüber anstellen, welche Möglichkeiten es gibt, weitere Aspekte

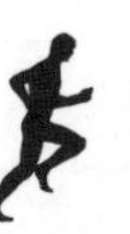

NOTES—[1] Because it was written for such a wide readership, one of my favorite essays on this topic is by the evolutionary biologist Stephen Jay Gould and is titled "The Brain of Brawn"; it was published in *The New York Times* 25 June 2000.—[2] For an overview of this area of research see: Robbins, P./Aydede, M.: "A Short Primer on Situated Cognition" in Robbins, Philip/Aydede, Murat (Eds.): *The Cambridge Handbook of Situated Cognition,* Cambridge 2008.—[3] See: Blackwell, A./deLahunta, S./McGregor, W.: "Transactables" in Allsopp, Ric/ Mount, Kevin: *Performance Research,* On The Page Issue, Vol. 9, No. 2. June 2004, 67–72.—[4] Burrows, Jonathan: *A Choreographer's Handbook,* London 2010, 141.—[5] Livet, Anne: *Contemporary Dance,* New York 1978, 54.—[6] See: deLahunta, S.: "Moving Ideas: Questions for the Dancing Mind", *ballettanz,* October 2005, 20–23.— [7] See: deLahunta, Scott/Rebecca Groves and Norah Zuniga Shaw: "Talking About Scores: William Forsythe's Vision for a New Form of Dance 'literature'" in: Gehm, Sabine, Husemann, Pirkko and von Wilcke, Katharina (eds): *Knowledge in Motion,* Bielefeld 2007, 91–100.—[8] Forsythe, W.: *Improvisation Technologies: A Tool for the Analytical Dance Eye,* Of the series: ZKM digital arts edition, Zentrum für Kunst und Medientechnologie, Karlsruhe 1999, 18.—[9] See: http://choreocog.net; see: http://www.randomdance.org/r_research.—[10] See: deLahunta, Scott/Barnard, Phil/McGregor, Wayne: "Augmenting Choreography: Insights and Inspiration from Science" in: Butterworth, Jo/Wildschut, Liesbeth (eds.): *Contemporary Choreography: A Critical Reader,* London 2009, 431–448.—[11] For more information about the imaging systems referred to, see the upcoming publication of "Points in mental space: an interdisciplinary study of imagery and tasks in movement innovation" (in submission). Co-authors May, J./Calvo-Merino, B./deLahunta, S./McGregor, W./Cusack, R./Owen, A./Veldsman, M./Ramponi, C./Barnard, P.: *Dance Research Journal* (electronic edition). In revision. Expected publication Summer 2011.—[12] See: Kirsh, D.: *Thinking With The Body,* The Annual Meeting of the Cognitive Science Society, (upcoming proceedings 2011).—[13] Developed as a Wayne McGregor | Random Dance / OpenEnded Group collaboration with Marc Downie, Nick Rothwell, CASSIEL; Luke Church & Alan Blackwell, Crucible/ Computer Laboratory, Cambridge University. Initial Project Funding from: Portland Green Cultural Projects.—[14] The part of this project still in development is that the dancers have to master this tool so that the time they spend figuring something out creatively is not spent learning how to use the tool. A CLA workshop is planned for early June 2011 with the dancers of WMRD.—[15] See Motion Bank http://theforsythecompany.com/ > motion bank—[16] See: deLahunta, Scott; Groves, Rebecca and Zuniga Shaw, Norah (ibid.).—[17] The co-creators with William Forsythe of *Synchronous Objects for One Flat Thing, reproduced,* (http://synchronousobjects.osu.edu) were Norah Zuniga Shaw, Assistant Professor and director of Dance and Technology, Department of Dance, The Ohio State University and Maria Palazzi, Director, Advanced Computing Center for the Arts and Design, The Ohio State University.—[18] "In OFTr counterpoint is defined as a field of action in which the intermittent and irregular coincidence of attributes between organisational elements produces an ordered interplay." (From a description on: http://synchronousobjects.osu.edu)—[19] See: Kirsh, D.: "Choreographic methods for creating novel, high quality dance" in: *Proceedings of the 29th Annual Conference of the Design and Semantics of Form and Movement.* Lucerne, Switzerland: Design and Semantics of Form and Movement, 2009, 188–195.—[20] Gould, ibid.

physischer Intelligenz im modernen Tanz sichtbar zu machen und zu untersuchen. Auf der Internetseite wird *Synchronous Objects for One Flat Thing, reproduced* als Ensembletanz beschrieben, „der klassische choreografische Kontrapunktprinzipien analysiert und neu konfiguriert. (...) Drei strukturierende Systeme wirken aufeinander ein, um den Kontrapunkt des Tanzes zu gestalten: Bewegungsmaterial, Einsatz auf Zeichen hin und Koordinierung."[18] Jedes dieser Struktursysteme wird auf der Website näher erläutert. Die Abbildungen 6 und 7 zeigen, wie die Anweisungen zum Tanz auf Einsatzzeichen hin sowie die Koordinierung oder Gruppierung auf dem Video erscheinen. (*6, 7* S. 104) Die in das Video eingezeichneten Linien entsprechen den Beziehungen zwischen einzelnen Tänzern/Tänzerinnen im Rahmen dieses speziellen Choreografiesystems und weisen somit auf den Punkt im Raum hin, der in diesem Moment den Fokus der Aufmerksamkeit bildet. Während die CD-ROM *Improvisation Technologies* (...) die Aufmerksamkeit des Betrachters darauf lenkt, welche Gedanken der Tänzer wohl gerade mit seinem Körper „ausspricht", stellt *Synchronous Objects* (...) die auf das Gesamtbild gerichtete Aufmerksamkeit in den Vordergrund, die die koordinierte tänzerische Entscheidungsfindung fördert.

Wie bereits erwähnt, entwickeln Neurobiologen und Philosophen derzeit neue Theorien zur Gestalt des Geistes, des Denkens durch den Körper, die der vorherrschenden Meinung widersprechen, physische Intelligenz sei ausschließlich instinktiv. Ich habe bereits erläutert, wie sich diese Theorien in choreografische Arbeitsmittel einarbeiten lassen, die aus Tanzpartituren entwickelt wurden. Nachdem wir nun die mit schriftlichen Anmerkungen versehenen Videos von *Synchronous Objects for One Flat Thing, reproduced* betrachtet haben, könnten wir uns überlegen, wie sich wohl die Intelligenz des Körpers über die Figur des jeweiligen Individuums hinaus fortsetzen ließe.[19] Damit ist aber noch nicht die Frage beantwortet, ob die Erklärung der inneren Struktur und Funktion physischer Intelligenz dem Zuschauer eines Tanzstücks größeren Genuss verschafft. Etliche Tanzbegeisterte ohne Forscherdrang könnten das als ganz hilfreiche Information empfinden, aber genügt es, die „Hintergedanken" des Tänzers sichtbar zu machen, während er sich entweder allein oder zusammen mit dem Ensemble bewegt? Der Abschnitt „Counterpoint Tool" (Kontrapunktinstrument, siehe *8* S. 105) auf der Internetseite über die „synchronen Objekte" schlägt noch eine andere Methode vor, mit der man dem Publikum zu einem besseren Verständnis der Choreografie verhelfen kann. Es handelt sich um ein kleines interaktives Programm, mit dem sich das Konzept des choreografischen Kontrapunkts direkt nachvollziehen lässt.Kleine Symbole, die ein bisschen wie Uhren aussehen, lassen sich in Einklang oder in Disharmonie bringen, indem man mit Hilfe von Schiebereglern ihre Form, Geschwindigkeit und ihren Bewegungsverlauf verändert. „Counterpoint Tool" ist somit eine Art dynamisch-interaktives Zeichengerät, mit dem man eine kurzlebige, flüchtige Struktur entdecken kann, da kontrapunktische Wechselspiele leicht „die Balance verlieren" können. Die Frage ist:

Würde unsere Wahrnehmung dieser Kohärenz bei jeder Vorführung eines abstrakten Tanzstücks, bei dem der Sinn- und Intelligenzgehalt der Choreografie auf derartigen Strukturen aufbaut, tatsächlich durch die Anwendung der „Counterpoint Tool"-Instruktionen gesteigert?
Mit diesem Essay wollte ich den Nachweis erbringen, dass Tanzkünstler in der einzigartig glücklichen Lage sind, die vorherrschende Meinung über die Beschaffenheit der Intelligenz des Körpers als einer „weniger wertvollen, auf körperliche Leistungen beschränkten Form des Intellekts"[20] zu widerlegen. Dieser Nachweis ist mit einer wachsenden Zahl choreografischer Arbeitsmittel belegt worden, die als Gemeinschaftsarbeiten von Wissenschaftlern unterschiedlicher Disziplinen und in Zusammenarbeit mit Choreografen entstanden sind. Wenn diese Bemühungen fortgesetzt und noch mehr solcher Materialien geschaffen werden, könnte das dazu beitragen, dass der moderne Tanz mit neuen Auffassungen von uns Menschen als intelligenten, denkenden Wesen eine kreative gestalterische Beziehung eingeht.

ANMERKUNGEN—[1] Weil er für eine breite Leserschaft geschrieben wurde, gehört „The Brain of Brawn" des Evolutionsbiologen Stephen Jay Gould zu meinen Lieblingsessays. *The New York Times* 25.06.2000.—[2] Robbins und Aydede geben hierzu einen Überblick in „A Short Primer on Situated Cognition". In: Philip Robbins/Murat Aydede (Hg.): *The Cambridge Handbook of Situated Cognition* Cambridge (GB) 2008.—[3] Vgl. Blackwell, A./deLahunta, Scott/McGregor, Wayne: „Transactables", in: Allsopp, Ric/Mount, Kevin (Hg.): *Performance Research, On The Page Issue*, Bd. 9, Nr. 2, Juni 2004, 67–72.—[4] Burrows, Jonathan: *A Choreographer's Handbook*, London 2010, 141.—[5] Livet, Anne: *Contemporary Dance*, New York 1978, 54.—[6] Vgl. deLahunta, Scott: „Moving Ideas: Questions for the Dancing Mind", in: *ballettanz*, Oktober 2005, 20–23.—[7] Vgl. deLahunta, Scott/Groves, Rebecca/Shaw, Norah Zuniga: „Talking About Scores: William Forsythe's Vision for a New Form of Dance 'literature'", in: Gehm, Sabine/Husemann, Pirkko/von Wilcke, Katharina (Hg.): *Knowledge in Motion*, Bielefeld 2007, 91–100.—[8] Forsythe, William: *Improvisation Technologies: A Tool for the Analytical Dance Eye.* Aus der Reihe „ZKM digital arts edition". Karlsruhe: Zentrum für Kunst und Medientechnologie 1999, 18.—[9] Vgl. http://choreocog.net; Vgl. http://www.randomdance.org/r_research.—[10] Vgl. deLahunta, Scott/Barnard, Phil/McGregor, Wayne: „Augmenting Choreography: Insights and Inspiration from Science", in: Butterworth, Jo/ Wildschut, Liesbeth: *Contemporary Choreography: A Critical Reader,* London 2009, 431–448.—[11] Weitere Informationen zu den erwähnten bildgebenden Verfahren in: Brown, T./May, J./Calvo-Merino, B./deLahunta, S./McGregor, W./Cusack, R./Owen, A./Veldsman, M./Ramponi, C./Barnard, P.: „Points in mental space: an interdisciplinary study of imagery and tasks in movement innovation" (zur Veröffentlichung in der Online-Ausgabe von *Dance Research Journal* eingereicht). Voraussichtliches Erscheinungsdatum: Sommer 2011.—[12] Vgl. Kirsh, D.: „Thinking With The Body." The Annual Meeting of the Cognitive Science Society. (Kongressbericht, in Vorbereitung, 2011)—[13] Projekt von Wayne McGregor | Random Dance/OpenEnded Group, mit Marc Downie, Nick Rothwell, CASSIEL, Luke Church & Alan Blackwell, Crucible/Computer Laboratory, Cambridge University. Erstfinanzierung durch Portland Green Cultural Projects.—

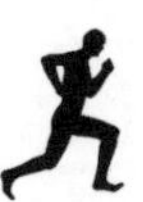

14 Die Realisierung des Projekts steht zum Teil insofern noch aus, als die Tänzer den Gebrauch dieses „Instruments" erlernen und so perfekt beherrschen müssen, dass sie damit keine Zeit verlieren, sondern sich der Entwicklung kreativer Ideen zu Schrittfolgen und Bewegungsabläufen widmen können. Ein CLA-Workshop mit den Tänzern von Random Dance soll Anfang Juni 2011 stattfinden.—**15** Vgl. Motion Bank http://theforsythecompany.com/ > motion bank—**16** Vgl. deLahunta, S., Rebecca Groves, Norah Zuniga Shaw: ebd. (Anm. 8).—**17** William Forsythe hat das Projekt *Synchronous Objects for One Flat Thing, reproduced* (http://synchronousobjects.osu.edu) mit Norah Zuniga Shaw (Assistenzprofessorin und Studienleiterin der Abteilung Tanz und Technologie des Department of Dance der Ohio State University) und Maria Palazzi (Leiterin des Advanced Computing Center for the Arts and Design der Ohio State University) durchgeführt.—**18** „In OFTr wird Kontrapunkt als Aktionsfeld definiert, in dem unregelmäßig und zufällig übereinstimmende Merkmale organisatorischer Elemente ein geordnetes Zusammenspiel erzeugen." (Aus einem Erläuterungstext auf: http://synchronousobjects.osu.edu).—**19** Vgl. Kirsh, D.: „Choreographic methods for creating novel, high quality dance", in: *Proceedings of the 29th Annual Conference of the Design and Semantics of Form and Movement.* Luzern, Schweiz: Design and Semantics of Form and Movement, 2009, 188–195.—**20** Jay Gould, ebd. (Anm. 1).

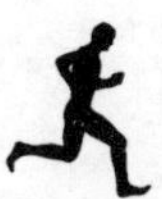

Inge Baxmann
The Form of Movement and Life.
Modern Ergonomics and Rhythmicising Life

Inge Baxmann **has been a professor at the Institute of Theatre Studies of the
University of Leipzig and Directeur d'etudes associé at the Maison des Sciences de l'Homme in Paris since 2001. She studied Romance languages and
literature. Post-doctoral lecturing qualification in cultural studies, 1997. Specialist research: symbolising and staging of the nation from the French Revolution to the present day, body studies, and the restructuring of knowledge
culture in the modern age. Publications include:** *Arbeit und Rhythmus. Lebensformen im Wandel* **(ed., 2009),** *Körperwissen als Kulturgeschichte. Die Archives Internationales de la Danse* **(ed., 2008).**

Inge Baxmann
Bewegungsform und Lebensform.
Moderne Arbeitswissenschaft und die Rhythmisierung des Lebens

Inge Baxmann ist seit 2001 Professorin am Institut für **Theaterwissenschaft**
der Universität Leipzig und Directeur d'Etudes associé an der **Maison des**
Sciences de l'Homme in Paris. Studium der **Romanistik und Literaturwissen-**
schaft. 1997 Habilitation in Kulturwissenschaften. **Forschungsschwerpunkte:**
Symbolisierung und Inszenierung der Nation zwischen **Französischer Revolu-**
tion und Gegenwart, Körperwissen und Umstrukturierung der **Wissenskultu-**
ren in der Moderne. Publikationen u. a.: ***Arbeit und Rhythmus. Lebensformen***
im Wandel (Hg., 2009), ***Körperwissen als Kulturgeschichte. Die Archives***
Internationales de la Danse (Hg., 2008).

MODERNITY AND THE SEARCH FOR FORM—From the turn of the twentieth century, technology and industrialisation were seen as symbolic of the dissolution of culture in "de-formed movement."[1] This was the phrase used by Rudolf Schwarz in his book *Wegweisung der Technik (Signposting By Technology)* in 1928, and in face of de-limitation and the destruction of roots he called upon people to remember that ultimately, tools are a "transformed life force."[2] On the one hand, movement is the key feature of modernity; on the other hand, it expresses fear of the de-limitations of the modern world and the search for a new form that combines movement and order.

The systems for the notation of movement that had been emerging in the natural sciences since the end of the nineteenth century aimed to fix the movement and fleeting quality of phenomena, to find a shape or a form for movement, and to visualise those things that remained hidden from the human senses: the basis for this was provided by film and its ability to accelerate motion, combine movements via montage or visualise whatever is imperceptible to the naked eye by using slow motion—that is, the smallest movements and structural patterns that only become discernible when extreme changes are made to temporal and dimensional relations. By means of modern media technology (photography and slow motion film), an order of movement invisible to the naked eye was revealed to an early forerunner of the notation of movement, physiologist Etienne Jules Marey, who transposed it into the "universal language" of graphic method: "A previously unknown world is revealed in this chaos."[3] (*9* p. 26)

ERGONOMIC BODY TECHNIQUES AND THE SYNCHRONISATION OF WORKING AND LIVING FORMS—In ergonomics, the purpose of notations of movement is to help acquaint management with the body techniques of the workers, to optimise these techniques, and thus to enable the workers to reincorporate the more effective work procedures. Fredrick Winslow Taylor was concerned with reducing superfluous movements: his "best possible way" in which to carry out a work activity was determined using film and photography. This was because those media could dissect complex working processes into micro-movements—that is, fragment them and reassemble them in a new way. The intention was for workers to later incorporate the new patterns of movement so that factory collectives could work according to a synchronised rhythm and thus more effectively.

Ergonomic scientists syntheticised body knowledge into a modern form of life, since the acceleration of the rhythm of movement and life they propagated aimed at a change in collective mentalities. The Taylorists' suggestion to suspend the discontinuity between the individual and the collective consisted of a mass culture that incorporated the individual into the beat of one great social machine. New forms of work and life were intended to overcome the dirt and noise of traditional industrial work and the stigma of the uneducated proletarian, physically crippled by monotonous labour.

DIE MODERNE UND DIE SUCHE NACH GESTALT—Technik und Industrialisierung galten seit der Jahrhundertwende als Sinnbild für die Auflösung der Kultur in „entstaltete Bewegung".[1] So formulierte es 1928 Rudolf Schwarz in seinem Buch *Wegweisung der Technik* und forderte, sich angesichts von Entgrenzung und Entwurzelung darauf zu besinnen, dass Werkzeug letztlich „transformierte Lebenskraft"[2] sei. Einerseits ist Bewegung das Kennzeichen der Moderne, andererseits ist sie Ausdruck der Angst vor der Entgrenzung der modernen Lebenswelt wie der Suche nach einer neuen Form, die Bewegung und Ordnung zusammenführt.

Die Bewegung und Flüchtigkeit von Phänomenen zu fixieren, für Bewegung eine Gestalt bzw. Form zu finden, sichtbar zu machen, was den menschlichen Sinnen verborgen bleibt, war das Ziel der Notationssysteme von Bewegung, wie sie seit Ende des 19. Jahrhunderts in den Naturwissenschaften entstanden: Grundlage dafür waren vor allem die Möglichkeiten des Films, Bewegung zu beschleunigen, über Montage zusammenzuführen oder mit Slow Motion sichtbar zu machen, was dem bloßen Auge nicht wahrnehmbar ist, nämlich kleinste Bewegungen und Strukturmuster, die nur durch extreme Veränderung der Zeit- und Größenverhältnisse erkennbar werden. Schon dem Vorläufer der Bewegungsnotation, dem Physiologen Etienne Jules Marey, enthüllte sich mittels moderner Medientechnologie (Fotografie und Filmzeitlupe) eine dem bloßen Auge nicht sichtbare Bewegungsordnung, die er in die „universelle Sprache" der grafischen Methode übertrug: „In diesem Chaos offenbart sich eine unbekannte Welt".[3] (9 S. 26)

KÖRPERTECHNIKEN DER ARBEIT UND DIE SYNCHRONISIERUNG VON ARBEITS- UND LEBENSFORMEN—In der Arbeitswissenschaft sollten Notationen von Bewegung dabei helfen, die Körpertechniken der Arbeiter in ein Wissen des Managements zu überführen, zu optimieren und den effektiveren Arbeitsablauf wieder von den Arbeitern inkorporieren zu lassen: Fredrick Winslow Taylor ging es um den Abbau überflüssiger Bewegungen: sein „best possible way", in der eine Arbeitshandlung zu vollziehen sei, wurde über Film und Fotografie ermittelt. Denn diese konnten komplexe Arbeitsvorgänge in Mikrobewegungen zerlegen, also fragmentieren und neu zusammensetzen. Die Arbeiter sollten diese neuen Bewegungsabläufe inkorporieren, so dass Fabrikkollektive, im Takt synchronisiert, effektiv arbeiten konnten.

Die Arbeitswissenschaftler synthetisierten das Körperwissen zugleich zur modernen Lebensform. Denn die von ihnen propagierte Beschleunigung von Bewegungs- und Lebensrhythmus zielte auf die Veränderung kollektiver Mentalitäten. Der Vorschlag der Tayloristen zur Lösung des Bruchs zwischen Individuum und Kollektiv bestand in einer Massenkultur, die den Einzelnen in die große soziale Maschine eintaktet. Neue Arbeits- und Lebensformen sollten den Schmutz und Lärm überkommener Industriearbeit und das Stigma des ungebildeten, durch einseitige Arbeit körperlich verkrüppelten Proleten überwinden.

The cultural model America seemed to anticipate such a "future of civilisation," a "technical dream," and journalist Heinrich Hauser expressed this in a report on his journey through America in 1926.[4] Hauser had his first confrontation with assembly-line work in one of the biggest harvester factories in the USA. "For the first time, I saw the moving conveyor belt. Its significance is not so much the technical aspect, perhaps. It is rather that it defines the rhythm, creating a gentle, irresistible pull throughout the entire factory and drawing people along with it. The work in the sheds is done with ease and no visible strain. For those used to loud factory workings, there is something almost conspiratorial about it."[5]

The assembly line developed a symbolic force for a new world shaped by technical rhythms. It ordered the workers' movements by rhythmicising them and so synchronised many individuals into a working collective. In the Ford works, Hauser discovered a social utopia that he believed was producing a new type of labourer.[6] He compared the assembly-line worker with a sportsman: "Often, the conveyor belts move at a surprising speed. The workers run along with their work, often facing backwards. The impression that emerges is almost sporting, rather like the boxer's 'foot-work.'"[7]

Technically oriented capitalist rationalisation, realised initially like islands in the factories themselves, was interpreted as appreciation of the producer. This sustained the hope for reconciliation between the classes in a fully organised, technology-based society. The plausible recipe was synchronisation of work and life in a society based on the model of industrial production. New experiences of movement and perception would eradicate the old contradiction between work and life in industrial activity that was suited to the worker, even playful. The machine was regarded as the model for the New Man, whose life—synchronised into its movements—would develop new dynamism. **Modernity signified massive restructuring of cultural techniques and collectives styles of perception, communication, and behaviour. Essentially, these were practised and habitualised by means of new styles of movement. The fields of training for such modern forms of life ranged from rhythmic gymnastics to expressive dance and nudism, from dodgem cars or big wheels at fairgrounds, to the habitualising of new styles of movement observed during cinema visits. The culture generated by industry prescribed movement, rhythm and a new tempo. The mechanical rhythm, the scientific organisation of work, and new, cosmopolitan ways of life changed the techniques of the body—not only in production and everyday office work but also in people's leisure time.**

In the great age of industrialisation, flexibility, permeability and attentiveness to situational change were already among the ideal characteristics of a new type of worker. Now the early twentieth century confronted people with a massive acceleration of perception, which encompassed the body and the human senses in a completely new way. Besides the conveyor belt and collective industrial work, modernity also brought new big-city transport technologies such as the tram and the automobile,

Das Kulturmodell Amerika erschien als Vorwegnahme einer solchen „Zukunft der Zivilisation", ein „technischer Traum", wie der Journalist Heinrich Hauser 1926 im Bericht über seine Reise durch Amerika formulierte.[4] Seine erste Konfrontation mit einer durch das Fließband bestimmten Arbeit erlebte Hauser in einer der größten Erntemaschinenfabriken der USA. „Zum ersten Mal sah ich das laufende Band. Seine Bedeutung liegt vielleicht gar nicht so sehr auf der technischen Seite. Es bestimmt vielmehr den Rhythmus, erzeugt einen sanften, unerbittlichen Zug durch die ganze Fabrik, der die Menschen mitreißt. Die Arbeit in den Hallen geschieht leicht, ohne sichtbare Anstrengung. Ist man an lärmende Betriebe gewöhnt, hat sie fast etwas Verschwörerisches."[5] Das Fließband entwickelte Symbolkraft für eine neue, durch technische Rhythmen geprägte Welt. Es ordnet die Bewegung der Arbeiter, indem es sie rhythmisiert, und synchronisiert so die Einzelnen zur Arbeitsgemeinschaft. Hauser entdeckte in den Ford-Werken eine Sozialutopie, die einen neuen Typus des Arbeiters hervorbringe.[6] Die Fließbandarbeiter verglich er mit Sportlern: „Die Transportbänder bewegen sich oft mit überraschender Geschwindigkeit. Die Arbeiter laufen bei der Arbeit mit, oft rückwärts gewandt. Es entsteht daraus ein fast sportlicher Eindruck, so etwas wie von der ‚Beinarbeit' eines Boxers."[7]

Die technisch orientierte kapitalistische Rationalisierung, vorerst inselhaft in der Fabrik realisiert, wurde als Wertschätzung der Produzenten interpretiert. Sie nährte die Hoffnung auf Klassenversöhnung in einer durchorganisierten, technisierten Gesellschaft. Das eingängige Rezept: eine Synchronisation von Arbeit und Leben in der Gesellschaft nach dem Vorbild der industriellen Produktion. Neue Bewegungs- und Wahrnehmungserfahrungen würden den alten Gegensatz von Arbeit und Leben in einer dem Menschen adäquaten, ja spielerischen industriellen Tätigkeit aufheben. Die Maschine galt als Vorbild für den Neuen Menschen, der – eingetaktet in ihre Bewegung – sein Leben dynamisiert.

Die Moderne bedeutete eine massive Umstrukturierung von Kulturtechniken und kollektiven Wahrnehmungs-, Kommunikations- und Verhaltensstilen. Diese wurden wesentlich über die neuen Bewegungsstile eingeübt und habitualisiert. Von der rhythmischen Gymnastik über Ausdruckstanz und Freikörperkultur, vom Autoskooter oder Riesenrad im Vergnügungspark bis zur Habitualisierung neuer Bewegungsstile durch ihr Betrachten beim Kinobesuch reichte das Trainingsfeld für die modernen Lebensformen. Die von der Industrie hervorgebrachte Kultur gab Bewegung, Rhythmus und ein neues Tempo vor. Der Maschinenrhythmus, die wissenschaftliche Arbeitsorganisation und neue, großstädtische Lebensweisen veränderten die Körpertechniken – nicht nur in Produktion und Büroalltag, sondern auch in der Freizeit.

Schon zur Zeit der großen Industrialisierung gehörten Flexibilität, Durchlässigkeit und die Aufmerksamkeit für Veränderungen von Situationen zum Ideal eines neuen Typus des Arbeitnehmers. Das frühe 20. Jahrhundert konfrontierte die Menschen nun mit einer massiven Beschleunigung der Wahrnehmung, die Körper und Sinne auf ganz neue Weise einbezog. Neben Fließband und kollektiver Industriearbeit

lifts or moving staircases, and new media such as film. Adaptation to constant movement, circulation, and a rapid reaction to situational changes became necessary for man to live (and survive).

According to Fritz Giese, ergonomic scientist and theoretician of dance and body culture, modern man had to learn to accept a loss of stable references and become capable of leading his life in a labile, temporary balance. Giese believed that he discerned a new "culture of motor functions" in contemporary big-city life in 1925, something that had been habitualised by the medium of film. Modern life called for "the capacity to adapt to situational changes."[8] This reevaluation of life was expressed in rhythm: "We can refer to all this—the prescription of man's tempo by machines and the other way around—as the motor activity of our age. And when we measure it against earlier epochs, we sense how our motor activity is based on different rhythms, sets a different beat to the predominant one even a hundred years ago. We have tempo—that is, our era is filled with intensified experiences, packed with work, tightly oriented towards an economy of utilisation in terms of our short lives. Lives that should not be regarded as pleasure but as work. This temporal motor activity shapes the face of the metropolis, of the new world."[9]

As an ergonomic scientist, he saw this as the expression of a new lifestyle. He believed there was a connection between "temporal motor activity" and the phenomenon of dancing girls who, as a mass body wearing the same dress and hairstyles, kicked up their legs in time to the beat.[10] The Tiller Girls or better still, the Taylor Girls were symptomatic of the possibility of measuring, standardising, and normalising living beings and of a new concept of the collective.[11] "The Tiller Girls and other girl troupes were dancing machines, albeit without military drill or lifeless obedience. The leading notion was not the compulsion to obedience but the technical and collective aspect of all technology."[12] Modern life demanded the "capacity to adapt to situational changes."[13] The reevaluation of life emerging in the modern age was expressed in rhythm: the perfectly synchronised movements of the revue girls (Taylor Girls) are not only captured on film, but simultaneously practised via this new perceptual apparatus. There is a systematic link between the notation of movement and models of modern life forms.

By contrast to Taylorism, psychotechnology in Germany, as developed primarily by Hugo Münsterberg and his pupil Fritz Giese, emphasised the autonomy of the living being, which does not become one with the machine: they maintained that the discontinuity—that is, the break–between man, machine, individual, and modern forms of life could not be abolished so easily. Ergonomic scientist Giese even considered that a successful link could be made between work and rhythm when it was oriented, not on a biological but on a mechanical rhythm—as in the factory. "(…) Working man must adjust to this tempo in his actions, in other words, he must fit in with the machine—that is modern production. But rhythm is a foundation, even in such assembly-line work. America in particular,

brachte die Moderne neue großstädtische Verkehrstechnologien wie Straßenbahn und Auto, Fahrstuhl oder Rolltreppe und neue Medien wie den Film hervor. Die Anpassung des Menschen an ständige Bewegung, Zirkulation und ein schnelles Reagieren auf Situationswechsel wurde (über-)lebensnotwendig.

Der moderne Mensch müsse lernen, den Verlust stabiler Referenzen zu verwinden und fähig sein, ein Leben im labilen und vorübergehenden Gleichgewicht zu führen, meinte Fritz Giese, Arbeitswissenschaftler und Theoretiker der Tanz- und Körperkultur. Im zeitgenössischen Großstadtleben glaubte er 1925 eine neue „Kultur der Motorik" zu erkennen, die das Medium Film habitualisiert hatte. Das moderne Leben erfordere die „Umstellungsfähigkeit auf Situationswechsel".[8] Im Rhythmus komme diese Umwertung des Lebens zum Ausdruck: „Wir können dies alles, diese Tempogebung von der Maschine zum Menschen und umgekehrt, die Motorik unserer Tage nennen. Und wenn wir sie an früheren Epochen messen, spüren wir, wie unsere Motorik andere Rhythmen, andere Takte bietet als noch die Zeit vor hundert Jahren. Wir haben Tempo, das heißt unsere Zeit ist intensiviert voller Erlebnisse, gepackt voll Arbeit, gespannt auf Ökonomie der Auswertung unseres kurzfristigen Lebens. Eines Lebens, das nicht ausgewertet sein soll als Vergnügen, sondern als Arbeit. Diese Zeitmotorik prägt das Gesicht der Großstadt, der neuen Welt."[9]

Der Arbeitswissenschaftler sah dies als Ausdruck eines neuen Lebensstils. Er stellte den Zusammenhang zwischen „Zeitmotorik" und dem Phänomen der Girls her, jener Massenkörper aus gleich gekleideten und frisierten Mädchen, die im Takt die Beine werfen.[10] Die Tiller- oder besser: Taylorgirls standen symptomatisch für die Möglichkeit der Vermessung, Standardisierung und Normierung des Lebendigen und für eine neue Vorstellung des Kollektiven.[11] „Die Tiller-Girls und andere Girltrupps waren Tanzmaschinen, ohne dabei militärischen Drill oder Kadavergehorsam zu besitzen. Nicht der Zwang des Gehorchens, sondern die Idee des Technischen und des Kollektiven aller Technik war der Leitgedanke."[12] Das moderne Leben erfordere die „Umstellungsfähigkeit auf Situationswechsel".[13] Im Rhythmus komme die Umwertung des Lebens, wie sie sich in der modernen Zeit vollziehe, zum Ausdruck: Die perfekt synchronisierten Bewegungen von Revuegirls (Taylorgirls) werden im Film nicht nur festgehalten, sondern durch dieses neue Wahrnehmungsdispositiv zugleich eingeübt. Es gibt einen systematischen Zusammenhang zwischen Bewegungsnotation und Modellen moderner Lebensformen.

Die Psychotechnik in Deutschland, wie sie vor allem von Hugo Münsterberg und seinem Schüler Fritz Giese entwickelt wurde, betonte im Gegensatz zum Taylorismus die Eigengesetzlichkeit des Lebendigen, das nicht in der Maschine aufgeht: Diskontinuität bzw. der Bruch zwischen Mensch, Maschine, Individuum und modernen Lebensformen lasse sich so nicht aufheben. Der Arbeitswissenschaftler Giese hielt eine gelungene Verbindung von Arbeit und Rhythmus selbst dann für möglich, wenn sie sich nicht am biologischen, sondern am Maschinenrhythmus

and especially model factories like the Ford works deliberately lend rhythm to the work flow."[14]

The difference between mechanical rhythm and human rhythm would continue to exist, but it would not necessarily constitute a contradiction. Reconciliation between the two would be possible, as long as the body techniques of industrial work and new perceptual forms were integrated as well. He saw the "royal road" of a new union between work and life in the interplay of body techniques rather than in isolated manual actions. While Taylorist motion analysis, for example, reduced the working man to separate mechanical actions, rhythm allowed the body and work to be synchronised. Giese elevated the "rhythmically trained hand at work" into a model for new forms of life.[15] Here, what was meant was not an isolated hand at work but the interplay of hands within a culture of work that represented a complex psychophysical activity.[16] Personal discovery of this rhythmic principle led to a sense of gratification in the worker.[17] This pleasurable synchronisation of perception and movement was a bodily technique not limited to the field of work; it entered into all areas of modern everyday life. Giese referred to insights concerning the link between work and rhythm already set out by Leipzig professor Karl Bücher towards the end of the nineteenth century.[18]

Karl Bücher's book *Arbeit und Rhythmus (Work and Rhythm)* first appeared in 1896. It developed into a publishing hit and went through six further editions by 1924.[19] In this extensive study, the national economist presented the thesis that dance, poetry, and music had developed from rhythmic workers' chants.[20] He drew the picture of a harmonic culture in which rhythm held together masses of people in collective work. He concluded that movement was the common denominator of all human activities and that rhythm was a socially unifying factor. Bücher maintained that "work was dance."

While American ergonomics adapted human movement to fit a mechanical beat, German ergonomic scientists like Fritz Giese emphasised the difference between beat (the regular repetition of one and the same thing) and rhythm (a similar and regular recurrence of the similar, which defines humanity and natural phenomena). Giese owed this insight to Karl Bücher, but also to Rudolf von Laban, a theoretician of expressive dance, choreographer, and industrial consultant. In the second decade of the twenthieth century he had founded a dance colony on Monte Verità in Ascona. Later he developed a notation of movement that was used to help rationalise English factories in the nineteen-forties. Laban's notation is still employed today: it is a system of recording movement used in choreography, which orders movements according to the categories of power-space-time. Laban started out from the assumption that a small number of tensions create the basis of all forms and movements. He viewed his dance notation as a universally valid terminology of movement, believing that it provided a descriptive form for things that could not be realised in words.[21] Laban wished to identify the concealed, shared, basic shape of

orientierte – wie in der Fabrik. „(...) Der arbeitende Mensch muss sich diesem Tempo in seinem Schaffen, muss sich also der Maschine anpassen; das ist moderne Fertigung. Aber auch in dieser Fließarbeit unterstützt der Rhythmus. Gerade Amerika und gerade Musterbetriebe wie die Fords rhythmisierten den Arbeitsfluß absichtlich."[14]

Der Unterschied zwischen dem Takt der Maschine und dem menschlichen Rhythmus bleibe bestehen, müsse jedoch nicht zwangsläufig ein Gegensatz sein. Eine Versöhnung beider sei unter der Voraussetzung möglich, dass man die Körpertechniken der Industriearbeit und neue Wahrnehmungsformen integriere. Statt in der Vereinzelung von Handgriffen sah er im Zusammenspiel von Körpertechniken den „Königsweg" einer neuen Verbindung von Arbeit und Leben.

Während beispielsweise die tayloristische Bewegungsanalyse den arbeitenden Menschen auf einzelne mechanische Handgriffe reduziere, ermögliche der Rhythmus eine Synchronisierung von Körper und Arbeit. Giese erhob die „rhythmisch geschulte Arbeitshand" zum Vorbild für neue Lebensformen.[15] Gemeint war nicht die isolierte Arbeitshand, sondern das Zusammenspiel der Hände innerhalb einer Arbeitskultur, die eine komplexe psychophysische Handlung darstelle.[16] Im Erlebnis dieses rhythmischen Prinzips entstehe eine den arbeitenden Menschen beglückende Erfahrung.[17] Diese lustvolle Synchronisierung von Wahrnehmung und Bewegung sei eine Körpertechnik, die sich nicht auf den Bereich der Arbeit beschränke, sondern in alle Bereiche des modernen Alltags eingehe. Giese verwies auf die Erkenntnisse über den Zusammenhang von Arbeit und Rhythmus, wie sie der Leipziger Professor Karl Bücher bereits gegen Ende des 19. Jahrhunderts entfaltet hatte.[18]

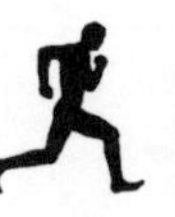

Das Buch *Arbeit und Rhythmus* von Karl Bücher war 1896 erstmals erschienen. Es wurde zu einem publizistischen Renner und hatte allein bis 1924 sechs Neuauflagen.[19] In seiner umfangreichen Studie entfaltete der Nationalökonom die These, Tanz, Dichtung und Musik hätten sich aus den rhythmischen Arbeitsgesängen entwickelt.[20] Er zeichnete das Bild einer harmonischen Kultur, in der der Rhythmus Menschenmassen bei der kollektiven Arbeit zusammengehalten habe. Bewegung, so das Ergebnis, sei der gemeinsame Nenner aller menschlichen Handlungen und der Rhythmus ein sozial vereinheitlichender Faktor. „Arbeiten ist Tanzen" behauptete Bücher.

Während die amerikanische Arbeitswissenschaft die menschliche Bewegung dem Takt der Maschine anpasste, betonten deutsche Arbeitswissenschaftler wie Fritz Giese den Unterschied zwischen Takt (als regelmäßige Wiederholung des Gleichen) und Rhythmus (die immer sich ähnelnde Rückkehr des Ähnlichen, wie sie den Menschen und die Naturerscheinungen bestimmt).

Diese Erkenntnis verdankte Giese nicht nur Karl Bücher, sondern auch Rudolf von Laban, Theoretiker des Ausdruckstanzes, Choreograf und Industrieberater. Er hatte in den 1910er Jahren auf dem Monte Verità in Ascona eine Tanzkolonie gegründet. Später entwickelte er eine Bewegungsnotation, die er in den 1940er Jahren zur Rationalisierung in englischen Fabriken verwendete. Labans noch heute

all movement by this means. Power represented the physical-mental impetus that preceded every human action and was expressed in rhythmic movement. The purpose of motion training was to exercise that power and maximise the workers' motivation. This pleasurable form of work promoted the worker's identification with his work and so eliminated the distinction between work and life. (*17* p. 37)

Laban claimed that the crystal (following the organic-based view of nature in Haeckel's work, for example) was the symbol of a new understanding of movement and space, connecting man and nature in a new way.[22] He constructed his "icosahedron" to illustrate the possible movements of the human body in space according to the model of the crystal. The analogy between the human body and natural forms based on universal laws of movement and tension firmly anchors mankind within nature. By this means, movement as a feature of modernity could be conveyed using the idea of returning to a universal order of nature, and it was possible to assuage fears of dissolution evoked by the experience of modernity. The shape of movement is a return to the original form.

The crystal creates a new, ordering pattern to defend against entropy and chaos: a "binding form." This connects movement, the key characteristic of modernity, to man's return to his origins, to union with nature and the cosmos. The analogy between crystal formation and living (also social) structures was widespread during that period. The crystal represented a symbol of integrity; it expressed a unity that evolved from movement and the complementarities of opposing tensions. Modern science's dissolution of the dichotomy of the subject/object and recognition of the mobility and perspective-bound nature of the observer standpoint led to a new understanding of unity. The epistemological focus of early twentieth-century biology or physics was an attempt to conceive the heterogeneous world as an entity in which contradictions produced harmonies. The principle of complementarities was part of the search for a new logic, which supposedly constituted the inner unity of the world. Movement and counter movement, transformation, complementarities, correspondences, and analogy were its categories.[23] The icosahedron or crystal, therefore, was the model of a mobile form, of the modern shape of movement. Like Rudolf von Laban, Fritz Giese also made reference to Raoul Francé, who brought together bios and technology by alluding to modern media technologies. Francé understood his work on plants as a pattern for modern forms of life. In his book *Die Pflanze als Erfinder (The Plant as an Inventor)* published in 1920, he pointed out analogies between the structure of plants and technical inventions. He saw his work as a life model with the purpose of reuniting mankind, technology, and nature. The idea of a fundamental unity of plants, animals, and man—which is based on shared organic structural principles—was visualised using micro- and x-ray photographs and by filmic slow motion, which could recognise growth processes that were inaccessible to the naked eye.

verwendete Notation ist ein Aufzeichnungssystem für Bewegung und Choreografie und ordnete Bewegungen nach den Kategorien Kraft-Raum-Zeit. Laban ging von der Annahme aus, dass ganz wenige Spannungen die Grundlage aller Formen und Bewegungen bilden. Laban verstand seine Tanznotation als universal gültige Bewegungsterminologie, sie biete eine Beschreibungsform für das, was in Worten nicht fassbar sei.[21] Laban wollte darüber die verborgene, gemeinsame Grundgestalt aller Bewegung erkennen. Die Kraft sei ein körperlich-geistiger Anstoß, der jeder menschlichen Handlung vorangeht und sich in rhythmischer Bewegung ausdrückt. Bewegungstraining trainiert diese Kraft und maximiert die Motivation der Arbeiter. Diese lustvolle Form der Arbeit fördert die Identifikation des Arbeiters mit seiner Tätigkeit und löst darüber die Trennung zwischen Arbeit und Leben auf. (*17* S. 37)

Laban erhob (im Anschluss an die organizistische Naturbetrachtung eines Haeckel) den Kristall zum Symbol eines neuen Bewegungs- und Raumverständnisses, das den Menschen auf neue Weise mit der Natur verbinde.[22] Er konstruierte seinen „Ikosaeder", der die Bewegungsmöglichkeiten des menschlichen Körpers im Raum veranschaulicht, nach dem Modell des Kristalls. Die Analogie zwischen menschlichem Körper und Naturformen über die universalen Bewegungs- und Spannungsgesetze verankert den Menschen in der Natur. Darüber ließ sich die Bewegung als Kennzeichen der Moderne mit der Vorstellung von der Rückkehr zu einer universalen Ordnung der Natur vermitteln und von der Erfahrung der Moderne evozierte Ängste vor Auflösung besänftigen. Die Gestalt der Bewegung ist die Rückkehr zur Urform.

Gegen Entropie und Chaos bilde der Kristall ein neues Ordnungsmuster, eine „bindende Form". Diese verknüpfe Bewegung, das Kennzeichen der Moderne, mit der Rückkehr zum Ursprung, zu einer Einheit mit Natur und Kosmos. Die Analogie zwischen der Kristallformation und lebenden (auch sozialen) Strukturen war in dieser Zeit weit verbreitet. Der Kristall bildete ein Ganzheitssymbol und war Ausdruck für eine Einheit, die aus der Bewegung und der Komplementarität entgegengesetzter Spannungen entsteht. Die Auflösung der Subjekt/Objekt-Dichotomie durch die modernen Wissenschaften, die Erkenntnis der Beweglichkeit und Perspektivengebundenheit des Beobachterstandpunkts führten zu einem neuen Verständnis von Einheit. Der epistemologische Fokus des frühen 20. Jahrhunderts in der Biologie oder der Physik lag in dem Versuch, eine heterogene Welt als Einheit zu konzipieren, in der Widersprüche Harmonien herstellen. Das Prinzip der Komplementarität war Teil der Suche nach einer neuen Logik, die die innere Einheit der Welt ausmachen sollte. Bewegung und Gegenbewegung, Umwandlung, Komplementarität, Korrespondenzen und Analogie bildeten ihre Kategorien.[23] Insofern war der Ikosaeder oder Kristall ein Modell für eine bewegte Form, für die moderne Gestalt der Bewegung. Fritz Giese verwies ebenso wie Rudolf von Laban auf Raoul Francé, der Bios und Technik durch den Verweis auf die modernen Medientechnologien zusammenführte. Francé verstand

Modern media technologies, therefore, not only reproduced but also constructed the evidence of a shared plan behind all life forms, ranging from plant to man, as a reality that could be experienced sensually. Means to this end were the still photo, slow motion, acceleration, micro-, and x-ray photographs. In interplay between new visualisation technologies like film and photography and the contemporary biosciences, in the early twentieth century the idea emerged of a quality shared by all life forms but concealed from human perception unless it was aided by technology.

In this way, the media motivated the concept of an inner unity among all life forms of differing dimensions, from the smallest single-cell creatures to mankind—an inner structure of the world that held together the micro- and the macrocosm.Raoul Francé summed this up using the model of biotechnology; he asserted that there was a structural equivalence between natural and technological forms. A new model thus evolved, which could be used to conceive movement and order as a unity: Raoul Francé saw order as the unity of complementary opposites. This constituted the inner structure of the living world on every level from micro to macro. The rhythms of living beings' movement could be visualised using photographic reduction or filmic deceleration/acceleration (e.g., plant growth). Comparison then made it possible to discern their shared construction plan.

It was a figure of modern desire to fix the fleeting and movement—the emblem of modernity—and lend shape to them in this way. This desire was realised in modern ergonomics via the notation of movement. The aim of new working techniques was to practise mental dispositions and types of behaviour at the same time, as these new body techniques not only encompassed a change in work practices, but also in forms of life. Before being captured by discourse and theorised, this fundamental change of knowledge cultures occurred in concealment—that is, initially and essentially in praxis and new practices. In Fordism, new links between work and forms of life already emerged through recourse to anthropotechnology, since the demands of the modern world called for a fresh configuration of the senses and an acceleration of the implementation of perceptions in action, not only in the field of industrial work. This was expressed not only in the ideal of the New Man but also in the image of the unstable individual. In that era already, the body techniques of knowledge were set within the context of internalising styles of work, communication, and behaviour, thus encompassing the entirety of life and its forms. These styles included mobility, flexibility, quickness, attention and constant readiness for action, as well as an internalised self-discipline, which even extended into the most private of spheres. The phantasm of control has always been inherent, therefore, in the dream of fixing movement in form.

seine Arbeit über Pflanzen als Vorbild für moderne Lebensformen. In seinem Buch *Die Pflanze als Erfinder* von 1920 verwies er auf die Analogien zwischen der Struktur von Pflanzen und technischen Erfindungen. Er verstand seine Arbeit als eine Lebenslehre, die Menschen, Technik und Natur wieder zusammenführen sollte. Die Idee einer fundamentalen Einheit von Pflanzen, Tieren und Menschen, denen gemeinsame organische Strukturprinzipien zugrunde liegen, wurde über die Mikro- und Röntgenfotografien und über die Zeitlupe im Film sichtbar, die dem bloßen Auge unzugängliche Wachstumsprozesse herausarbeiten konnten. Moderne Medientechnologien bildeten also nicht nur ab, sondern konstruierten die Evidenz eines gemeinsamen Plans aller Lebensformen von Pflanze bis Mensch als sinnlich erfahrbare Wirklichkeit. Mittel dafür waren: Standbild, Zeitlupe, Beschleunigung, Mikro- und Röntgenfotografie. Im Zusammenspiel zwischen neuen Visualisierungstechnologien wie Film und Fotografie und den zeitgenössischen Biowissenschaften entstand im frühen 20. Jahrhundert die Vorstellung von einer der menschlichen Wahrnehmung ohne technische Hilfsmittel verborgenen Gemeinsamkeit aller Lebensformen. Die Medien motivierten so die Vorstellung von einer inneren Einheit aller Lebensformen verschiedener Größenordnungen, von den kleinsten Zellentieren bis zum Menschen – einer inneren Struktur der Welt, die Mikro- und Makrokosmos zusammenhält. Raoul Francé fasste dies unter dem Modell der Biotechnik zusammen, er behauptete eine strukturelle Äquivalenz zwischen Naturformen und Formen der Technik. Damit entstand ein neues Modell, um Bewegung und Ordnung als Einheit zu denken: Raoul Francé sah Ordnung als eine Einheit komplementärer Gegensätze. Diese macht die innere Struktur der Lebenswelt auf allen Ebenen von klein bis groß aus. Bewegungsrhythmen der Lebewesen lassen sich über fotografische Verkleinerung oder filmische Verlangsamung/Beschleunigung (zum Beispiel Pflanzenwachstum) sichtbar machen. Ihr Vergleich lässt den gemeinsamen Bauplan erkennen.

Das Flüchtige zu fixieren und der Bewegung – dem Signum der Moderne – eine Gestalt geben, war eine Sehnsuchtsfigur der Moderne, das die moderne Arbeitswissenschaft mittels der Notation von Bewegung realisierte. Mit den neuen Arbeitstechniken wollte man zugleich mentale Dispositionen und Verhaltensstile einüben, denn diese neuen Körpertechniken des Wissens umfassten nicht nur die Veränderung der Arbeitspraktiken, sondern darüber hinaus der gesamten Lebensformen. Diese grundlegende Veränderung der Wissenskulturen vollzog sich im Verborgenen, das heißt erstmals und wesentlich in der Praxis und in neuen Praktiken, bevor sie diskursiv eingefangen und theoretisiert wurde. Schon im Fordismus entstanden neue Verbindungen von Arbeits- und Lebensformen über den Rekurs auf Körpertechniken, denn die Anforderungen der modernen Lebenswelt erforderten nicht nur im Bereich der industrialisierten Arbeit eine Neukonfiguration der Sinne und eine Beschleunigung der Umsetzung von Wahrnehmung in Handlung, wie sie sowohl im Ideal des Neuen Menschen wie auch des labilen Menschen zum Ausdruck kommt. Schon in dieser Zeit wurden die

NOTES—[1] Rudolf Schwarz therefore lamented in *Wegweisung der Technik,* 1928: "It is difficult to emphasise clearly the essence of what is happening here. Most of all, it becomes obvious that in the first moment the organic conditions are alread disintegrating and becoming nothing. In this way, the object falls from its developed context apparently into emptiness; in truth, however, it falls into the tight context of a series. Multiplication—although it is called reproduction—leads things and people into a strange, loveless sphere. It is as if they have been cut off from their roots." Schwarz, Rudolf: *Wegweisung der Technik,* Potsdam 1928, 41—42.—[2] Schwarz, Rudolf: *Wegweisung der Technik,* Potsdam 1928, 13.—[3] Not.Catalogue, 327—[4] His travel report appeared with the title *Feldwege nach Chicago* in 1926. Hauser, Heinrich: *Feldwege nach Chicago,* Berlin 1931.—[5] Hauser, ibid., 173.—[5] "There is a special type of Ford worker. There is something bright about the people, strongly conscious. They are more like chemists than labourers." Hauser, ibid., 231.—[6] Giese, Fritz: *Girlkultur. Vergleich zwischen deutschem und amerikanischem Rhythmusgefühl,* Munich 1925, 52.—[7] Giese, ibid., 28-29.—[8] Giese, ibid., 52.—[9] Giese, ibid., 28-29.—[10] Giese, ibid.—[11] Giese, ibid., 24.—[12] Giese, ibid.—[13] Giese, ibid., 25.—[14] Giese, ibid., 25.—[15] Giese, Fritz: *Psychologie der Arbeitshand,* Berlin/Vienna 1928, 1.—[16] Giese, ibid., 80ff—[17] Giese, ibid,191.—[18] "..das Verhältnis von Arbeit und Rhythmus. Hierauf hat zuerst Bücher hingewiesen. Arbeit wird unterstützt durch Rhythmus, rhythmische Bewegungen, rhythmische Zurufe usw." in: Giese, Fritz: *Girlkultur. Vergleich zwischen deutschem und amerikanischem Rhythmusgefühl,* Munich 1925, 24.—[19] Bücher, Karl: *Arbeit und Rhythmus,* Leipzig 1924, 334-335—[20] He found the material for his thesis not only among the "primitive peoples" (as they were still known at the time), but also among contemporary European farmers and artisans. Cf. Bücher, Karl: *Arbeit und Rhythmus,* Leipzig 1924, 340ff.—[21] "For the language of movement and dance expression consists only to a very small extent of conventional signs, replacing, as it were, words and phrases. The main bulk of movement and dance expression consists of motor elements, which can be freely combined to reveal something about the inner state of the moving person. Whether a person uses the language of movement for self-expression, liberation or enjoyment, or for the purpose of communicating with other people, is irrelevant to the present argument." in Laban, Rudolf von: *Principles of Dance and Movement Notation,* London 1956, 14. (trans.: Inge Baxmann).—[22] Cfl. Laban, Rudolf von: *Die Welt des Tänzers,* Stuttgart 1920, 59.—[23] : Meyer, Barbara Jane: *A Crystal of Patterns of Cognition of the Arts and Sciences through the Confluence of the Real and the Surreal in the Modern Age,* Ann Arbor/Michigan 1989, 173ff.

Körpertechniken des Wissens in den Kontext der Verinnerlichung von Arbeits-, Kommunikations- und Verhaltensstilen gestellt, die den gesamten Bereich der Lebensformen umfassen. Mobilität, Flexibilität, Schnelligkeit, Aufmerksamkeit und stete Handlungsbereitschaft sowie eine internalisierte Selbstdisziplinierung bis in die privatesten Bereiche gehörten dazu. Das Phantasma der Kontrolle gehörte so stets zum Traum, Bewegung in Gestalt festzustellen.

ANMERKUNGEN— [1] So beklagte Rudolf Schwarz 1928 in *Wegweisung der Technik:* „Es ist schwer, den Kern dessen, was da vorgeht, ganz klar herauszuheben. Am stärksten fällt auf, dass im ersten Augenblick schon die *organischen Bedingungen* zerreißen und zu nichts werden. Damit gerät das Ding aus seinen *gewachsenen* Beziehungen heraus und fällt scheinbar ins Leere, in Wahrheit aber in den straffen Verband seiner Serie. Vervielfältigung—und das heißt Reproduktion—bringt Dinge und Menschen in eine merkwürdige liebeleere Sphäre. Es ist, als würden sie von ihren Wurzeln abgeschnitten." Schwarz, Rudolf: *Wegweisung der Technik,* Potsdam 1928, 41-42.—[2] Schwarz, Rudolf: *Wegweisung der Technik,* Potsdam 1928, 13.—[3] Etienne Jules Marey zitiert nach Notation. Kalkül und Form in den Künsten. Katalog der Ausstellung hrsg. von Hubertus von Amelunxen u.a., Berlin 2008, 327—[4] Sein Reisebericht erschien 1926 unter dem Titel *Feldwege nach Chicago.* Hauser, Heinrich: *Feldwege nach Chicago,* Berlin 1931.—[5] Hauser, ebd., 173.—[6] „Es gibt einen Typ des Fordarbeiters. Die Menschen haben etwas Helles, stark Bewusstes. Sie gleichen mehr Chemikern als Arbeitern." Hauser, ebd., 231.—[7] Hauser, ebd., 231.—[8] Giese, Fritz: Girlkultur. *Vergleich zwischen deutschem und amerikanischem Rhythmusgefühl.* München 1925, 52—[9] Giese, ebd., 28-29.—[10] Giese, ebd.—[11] Giese, ebd., 24.—[12] Giese, ebd.—[13] Giese, ebd., 25.—[14] Giese, ebd., 25.—[15] Giese, Fritz: *Psychologie der Arbeitshand,* Berlin/Wien 1928, 1.—[16] Giese, ebd., 80ff.—[17] Giese, ebd., 191.—[18] „... das Verhältnis von Arbeit und Rhythmus. Hierauf hat zuerst Bücher hingewiesen. Arbeit wird unterstützt durch Rhythmus, rhythmische Bewegungen, rhythmische Zurufe usw." in: Giese, Fritz: *Girlkultur. Vergleich zwischen deutschem und amerikanischem Rhythmusgefühl,* München 1925, 24.—[19] Bücher, Karl: *Arbeit und Rhythmus,* Leipzig 1924, 334-335—[20] Das Material für diese These fand er nicht nur bei den „primitiven Völkern" (wie sie damals noch genannt wurden), sondern ebenso bei zeitgenössischen europäischen Bauern und Handwerkern. Vgl. Bücher, Karl: *Arbeit und Rhythmus,* Leipzig 1924, 340ff.—[21] „Denn die Sprache der Bewegung und des tänzerischen Ausdrucks besteht nur zu einem sehr geringen Teil aus konventionellen Zeichen, die Worte und Sätze ersetzen. Der größte Teil des Bewegungs- und tänzerischen Ausdrucks besteht aus motorischen Grundelementen, die frei kombiniert werden können, um etwas über den inneren Zustand der sich bewegenden Person zu offenbaren. Dabei ist es irrelevant, ob jemand die Sprache des Selbstausdrucks, der Befreiung oder der Freude benutzt oder um mit anderen zu kommunizieren." in Laban, Rudolf von: *Principles of Dance and Movement Notation,* London 1956, 14. (Übers.: Inge Baxmann).—[22] Vgl. Laban, Rudolf von: *Die Welt des Tänzers,* Stuttgart 1920, 59.—[23] Vgl. hierzu: Meyer, Barbara Jane: *A Crystal of Patterns of Cognition of the Arts and Sciences through the Confluence of the Real and the Surreal in the Modern Age,* Ann Arbor/Michigan 1989, 173ff.

Claus Pias has been professor of media theory and history at Leuphana University Lüneburg since 2010. Previously, he has held professorships—including in cognitive science and the philosophy of digital media—at the universities of Vienna, Essen, and Bochum. Study of electrical engineering, art history, German philology and philosophy in Aachen, Bonn, and Bochum. Fellow of the IFK Vienna, the IKKM Weimar, and the Wissenschaftskolleg zu Berlin. Publications include: *Abwehr. Modelle Strategien Medien* (ed., 2009), *Cybernetics – Kybernetik* (ed., 2004), *Herman Kahn – Szenarien für den Kalten Krieg* (ed., 2008), *ComputerSpielWelten* (2002).

Claus Pias
Die Lesbarkeit der Bewegung

Claus Pias ist seit 2010 Professor für Medientheorie und Mediengeschichte an der Leuphana Universität Lüneburg. Zuvor Professuren u. a. für Erkenntnistheorie und Philosophie der digitalen Medien an den Universitäten Wien, Essen und Bochum. Studium der Elektrotechnik, Kunstgeschichte, Germanistik und Philosophie in Aachen, Bonn und Bochum. Fellow des IFK Wien, des IKKM Weimar und des Wissenschaftskollegs zu Berlin. Publikationen u. a. *Abwehr. Modelle Strategien Medien* (Hg., 2009), *Cybernetics – Kybernetik* (Hg., 2004), *Herman Kahn – Szenarien für den Kalten Krieg* (Hg., 2008), *ComputerSpielWelten* (2002).

1—"The gesture spotting is a method that distinguishes meaningful gestures from unintentional movements. It is a prerequisite stage to gesture recognition and locates the start and end points of a gesture in an input sequence. Yet, this is an extremely difficult task due to both the multitude of possible gesture variations in spatiotemporal space and the co-articulation of successive gestures."[1]

The "figure of motion" prevails in every situation in which gestures can be made identifiable and interpretable. Gestures are units that—through whatever kind of observation—are separated, as spatial and temporal figures, from a background that is disregarded. Here, as shapes of movement, gestures fulfil a communicative purpose: isolation and identification allow gestures to take on a function—or to put it another way, to become operational. Using gestures, it is possible to perform an action, and not only between people, but above all between people and machines. Although the sphere of operational gestures has expanded considerably in recent years and now takes effect at the heart of our everyday lives, performance studies carried out in the humanities still pay very little attention to this field and prefer to devote themselves to the traditional domains of art, literature, music, and theatre.[2] The latest and most prominent examples of the boom in the gesticulative are surely the iPhone (2007) and the iPad (2010), which were delivered without instructions for their use in order to demonstrate that their functions could be understood instinctively, since they are operated by means of gestures. The remark that children succeed with this "spontaneously" where as it causes some problems for members of the older generation (who have already undergone "training as users") is commonplace, but it proves true every day, nonetheless. Intuitive ability is, after all, an effect of forgetting what has been learnt, which creates a strong illusion of evidentiality. As a result of this historicity, as we know, the ISO-Norm 9241 for software-ergonomics gives no stipulations for design but uses only the terms self-descriptive and conforming to expectations.

Gestures like maximising, minimising, pushing to one side, or turning—realised by the user's fingers on the screen—currently undermine the traditional hegemony of pressing keys, which has been interpreted as "the fundamental cultural technique of our age," as an "excess of button-pushing," or the embodiment of the principle of selectability.[3] And yet touchscreens, as Till Heilmann emphasises quite correctly, do not abolish the "key principle" from a technical viewpoint, they actually rather inflate it: our finger motion over a capacitive display simply triggers a large number of microscopic key pushes, the sum of which adds up to the shape of a movement, to just such a gesture. This gesture can be processed and operationalised as a sign. This inflation towards the high resolution of many invisible keys (which can then be subsumed in turn into the representation of a virtual typewriter keyboard) facilitates the technical integration of different types of gesture (mimetic, deictic, or arbitrary) and their flexible combination via an interface.[4] In technical terms we have keys; in the phenomenological sense, by contrast, we have gestures.

1–„The gesture spotting is a method that distinguishes meaningful gestures from unintentional movements. It is a prerequisite stage to gesture recognition and locates the start and end points of a gesture in an input sequence. Yet, this is an extremely difficult task due to both the multitude of possible gesture variations in spatiotemporal space and the co-articulation of successive gestures."[1]

Die „Gestalt der Bewegung" herrscht überall dort, wo Gesten identifizierbar und interpretierbar gemacht werden können. Gesten sind Einheiten, die – durch welche Art von Beobachtung auch immer – als räumliche und zeitliche Figuren von einem zu vernachlässigenden Grund getrennt werden. Dabei erfüllen Gesten als Gestalten der Bewegung einen kommunikativen Sinn: Isolation und Identifikation ermöglichen es, dass Gesten eine Funktion übernehmen – oder anders gesagt, dass sie operational werden. Mit Gesten lässt sich etwas machen, und zwar nicht nur unter Menschen, sondern vor allem auch unter Menschen und Maschinen.

Gleichwohl sich das Reich operationaler Gesten in den letzten Jahren erheblich erweitert hat und mittlerweile tief in unseren Alltag durchgreift, schenken die geisteswissenschaftlichen Performance Studies diesem Bereich kaum Aufmerksamkeit und widmen sich doch lieber den angestammten Domänen von Kunst, Literatur, Musik und Theater.[2] Das jüngste und prominenteste Beispiel für die Konjunktur des Gestischen sind sicherlich das iPhone (2007) und das iPad (2010), die ohne Anleitung zu ihrer Bedienung ausgeliefert wurden, um zu demonstrieren, dass diese sich von selbst versteht, weil sie ja durch Gesten geschieht. Die Feststellung, dass Kindern dies „spontan" gelinge, Angehörigen der älteren Generation (die bereits eine „Erziehung zum Benutzer" durchlaufen haben) jedoch gewisse Schwierigkeiten bereite, ist ein Gemeinplatz, der sich gleichwohl alltäglich bewahrheitet. Intuitivität ist eben ein Effekt des Vergessens von Gelerntem, der eine starke Illusion von Evidenz erzeugt. Aufgrund dieser Historizität gibt die ISO-Norm 9241 für Software-Ergonomie bekanntlich keine Gestaltungsanweisungen, sondern spricht nur von selbstbeschreibend und erwartungskonform.

Gesten wie vergrößern, verkleinern, beiseiteschieben oder drehen, die mit den Fingern auf dem Bildschirm ausgeführt werden, unterwandern derzeit die angestammte Hegemonie des Tastendrückens, die – in unterschiedlicher Weise – als „basale Kulturtechnik unserer Zeit", als „Exzess des Knopfdrucks" oder als Verkörperung des Prinzips der Wählbarkeit interpretiert wurde.[3] Dabei ist durch Touchscreens, wie Till Heilmann zu Recht betont, das „Prinzip Taste" aus technischer Sicht nicht abgeschafft, sondern vielmehr inflationiert: Der Fingerstrich über ein kapazitives Display löst einfach nur eine Vielzahl mikroskopischer Tastendrücke aus, deren Summe zur Gestalt einer Bewegung, zu einer Geste eben, verrechnet wird. Als Zeichen kann diese Geste verarbeitet und operationalisiert werden. Diese Inflation hin zu einer hohen Auflösung vieler unsichtbarer Tasten (die dann wiederum auch zur Darstellung einer virtuellen Schreibmaschinentastatur zusammengefasst werden können) ermöglicht, dass unterschiedliche Arten von

Equally important is the hugely expanded field of stationary computer games controlled by gestures, which—ranging from Bandai's Power Pad to Mattel's Power Glove or Amiga's Joyboard and to Sony's eyeToy or Move, Microsoft's Kinect or Nintendo's Wii—has a story of its own and involves a number of cross links to the worlds of art and work (the latter, in turn, have met with little interest in game studies).[5] Ian Bogost reminded us that playing on such interfaces—as opposed to the "intuitive quality" of the "liberated body" proclaimed by the sales strategies—is naturally based on highly artificial and instrumental gestures, which have to be learnt and practised initially.[6] Their significance is referred to as triggering or controlling, and computer gaming is an instantaneous test of their communicative success. Authors like Bart Simon therefore transpose the "actual" game to a form of *gestural excess*, which (from pleasure in the game and a desire for activity) produces a greater wealth of movements than is actually necessary for successful controlling.[7] This leads not only to a false assumption of heightened "realism" on the part of those who merely "observe in a participatory way" rather than playing themselves, but to all kinds of strange operational accidents as well.[8]

Theories from the field of engineering sometimes have the advantage that they can be proven via implementation.[9] The correct solution is the solution that works. This being the case, the passage quoted at the outset, taken from an essay on information science, defines the rather long-term philosophical and cultural questions about gesture and intentionality in a pragmatic way and for a restricted field only. For however complicated the details of implementation may be: control is successful when a movement is made correctly as a gesture and is also recognised as the correct gesture. Another working definition could be added: "A primary goal of gesture recognition research is to create a system which can identify specific human gestures and use them to convey information or for device control."[10] The first, longer part of this essay will be devoted to the question of successful controlling, to "device control" by means of historically changing "shapes of movement"—that is, to those acquired gestures necessary for the everyday use of computers that have now become embedded into the automatic regions of our body awareness. By contrast, my second, shorter section will direct attention to the aspect of "conveying information," that is, to the registration and emerging form of gestures with which the user does not "wish to say something," but which convey information about the user. In this sense, "gesture recognition" has a manipulative[11] aspect and one that serves identification. The manipulative side is relevant to those "meaningful gestures" that have to be produced voluntarily for successful interaction; by contrast, those serving identification form the basis of the "unintentional movements" that—in a reversal of attention—now make the user himself the object of examination. The purpose here is to recognise those patterns of movement that can be extrapolated into intentionalities. This means the concern is no longer gesticulative interaction with the computer, but the observation of gesticulative interaction via the computer, which is thus placed in the systematic position of a research tool.

Gesten (mimetisch, deiktisch, arbiträr) technisch integriert und über ein Interface flexibel kombiniert werden können.[4] Technisch haben wir Tasten, phänomenologisch dagegen Gesten.

Nicht minder bedeutsam ist der deutlich erweiterte Bereich von stationären, ebenfalls durch Gesten gesteuerten Computerspielen, der – von Bandais Power Pad über Mattels Power Glove oder Amigas Joyboard bis hin zu Sonys eyeToy bzw. Move, Microsofts Kinect oder Nintendos Wii – seine ganz eigene Geschichte hat und etliche Querverbindungen zur Kunst- und Arbeitswelt unterhält (letztere wiederum wurden von den Game Studies bislang nur wenig beachtet).[5] Ian Bogost hat daran erinnert, dass das Spielen an solchen Interfaces – entgegen der verkaufsstrategisch proklamierten „Intuitivität" eines „befreiten" Körpers – selbstverständlich auf höchst artifiziellen und instrumentellen Gesten basiert, die erst einmal trainiert werden müssen.[6] Deren Bedeutung heißt Auslösung oder Steuerung, und Computerspielen ist die instantane Überprüfung ihres Kommunikationserfolgs. Autoren wie Bart Simon verlegen daher das „eigentliche" Spiel in einen „gestischen Überschuss" *(gestural excess)*, der (aus Spielfreude und Bewegungslust) viel reichere Bewegungen produziert, als sie für die erfolgreiche Steuerung allein erforderlich wären.[7] Das führt nicht nur zur falschen Annahme eines gesteigerten „Realismus" von Seiten derer, die nur „teilnehmend beobachten" statt selbst zu spielen, sondern auch zu allerlei kuriosen Betriebsunfällen.[8]

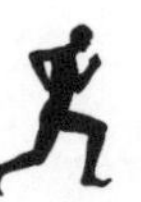

Nun haben ingenieurswissenschaftliche Theorien zuweilen den Vorzug, dass sie sich in der Implementierung erweisen.[9] Richtig ist, was funktioniert. Insofern definiert die eingangs zitierte Passage aus einem informatischen Aufsatz die philosophisch wie kulturhistorisch eher langlebigen Fragen nach Geste und Intentionalität auf pragmatische Weise und für einen eingeschränkten Bereich. Denn wie kompliziert die Details der Implementierung auch sein mögen: Steuerung gelingt, wenn eine Bewegung als Geste richtig gemacht und als solche richtig erkannt wurde. Dem wäre eine andere Arbeitsdefinition zur Seite zu stellen: „A primary goal of gesture recognition research is to create a system which can identify specific human gestures and use them to convey information or for device control."[10] Der erste, längere Teil dieses Aufsatzes wird sich der Frage der gelingenden Steuerung, der „device control" durch historisch wechselnde „Gestalten der Bewegung" widmen – jenen erlernten Gesten also, die der alltäglichen Computerbenutzung dienen und die mittlerweile in die Selbstverständlichkeit unseres Körperwissens abgesunken sind. Der zweite, kürzere Teil hingegen lenkt den Blick auf den Aspekt des „convey information", nämlich auf die Erfassung und Gestaltwerdung von Bewegungen, mit denen nicht der Benutzer „etwas sagen will", sondern die etwas über den Benutzer sagen. „Gesture recognition" hat in diesem Sinne eine manipulative[11] und eine erkennungsdienstliche Seite. Die manipulative betrifft die Figuren jener „meaningful gestures", die für gelingende Interaktion willentlich hervorgebracht werden müssen, die erkennungsdienstliche dagegen den Grund jener „unintentional movements",

2—It is well known that in the early days, interaction with computers was the exception rather than the rule. For a long time, the batch-modus—with its three stages of input, processing, and output—prevailed and user interventions during the course of the programme were taboo, unless the aim was to deal with problems. Interactivity as an operating modus that allows the user to control a calculating process during the programme first became common in connection with early warning systems and the Whirlwind computer. This had an interruption control *(interrupt)*, which could trigger regular jumps to subroutines that were able to assess in their turn the state of apparatus (modems via radar data) or people (users via on-screen input). Both were regarded to equal degrees as *devices*, to some extent as an environment that had to be periodically checked. And as the environment of early warning systems is an enemy environment, the first gesture was deictic: the purpose was to use a pen to mark and thus identify the enemy as such on the radar screen.

In the nineteen-sixties, people began to test possible civilian uses of the computer such as writing, art, or making music.[12] A classic of that time was the ergonomic evaluation of the mouse for the purpose of text editing.[13] In this context, it was not a matter of how text was produced (as the use of typewriter keyboards was already very familiar and had been optimised), but of effective selection and editing of text material that was being displayed on a screen. In an experimental set-up of radar screens, keyboard, and various pointing devices (mouse, lightpen, joystick, and the long-forgotten knee-control device), the authors used classic time and motion studies to measure how untrained staff efficiently marked passages of text, wasting as little time and energy as possible. Or to put it more graphically: "capturing the enemy reappeared as a mouse on an ordinary desk."[14] The remarkable aspect here is not only the continuity of ergonomic methodology since the nineteen-twenties. One should also note the decision (not specifically defined) to ignore longer-term motor learning processes, which might involve effort but prove equally worthwhile in the end. But the preference lay with the first contact and a steep learning curve, aiming to reach a certain level of control (literally) and so fulfil one's intentions as soon as possible.

3—In the meantime the mouse, particularly due to the increase in mobile terminals, belongs to a threatened species and has given way—after a Trackball and TrackPoint intermezzo—to smaller or larger touchpads, many of which now also work by processing gestures. These also date back to developments from the nineteen-sixties, back to the "axial age of computing," as Hans-Dieter Hellige once termed it. In the beginning, there were graphic tablets like the RAND Tablet developed at RAND Corporation in 1963/64. It was possible to write and draw on these using a pen[15] (*1* p. 140). However, this is only an apparent case of "remediation,"[16] that is, the simultaneous permeation and competition of old and new media, whereby the tablet as a "man-machine graphical communication

der – in einer Wendung des Blicks – nun selbst zum Untersuchungsgegenstand gemacht wird, um darin wiederum Bewegungsmuster zu erkennen, die sich auf Intentionalitäten hochrechnen lassen könnten. Damit geht es nicht mehr um gestische Interaktion mit dem Computer, sondern um die Beobachtung gestischer Interaktion durch den Computer, der damit in die systematische Position eines Forschungsinstruments rückt.

2—Die Interaktion mit Computern war in der Anfangszeit bekanntlich eher die Ausnahme als der Normalfall. Lange Zeit war der Batch-Modus mit seinem Dreischritt von Eingabe, Verarbeitung und Ausgabe vorherrschend, und Benutzereingriffe während des Programmablaufs waren tabu – es sei denn zur Beseitigung von Störungen. Interaktivität als Betriebsmodus, der die Steuerung eines Rechenprozesses durch die Benutzer während der Verarbeitung zulässt, wurde erstmals im Zusammenhang mit Frühwarnsystemen und dem Whirlwind-Rechner virulent. Dieser besaß eine Unterbrechungsleitung *(interrupt),* die regelmäßige Sprünge zu Subroutinen auslösen konnte, die wiederum den Zustand von Maschinen (Modems mit Radardaten) oder Menschen (Benutzer mit ihren Bildschirmeingaben) abfragen konnten. Beide galten gleichermaßen als *devices,* als Umwelt gewissermaßen, die es periodisch wahrzunehmen galt. Und da die Umwelt von Frühwarnsystemen eine feindliche ist, ist die erste Geste eine deiktische: Es galt, den Feind mit einem Stift auf dem Radarbildschirm als solchen zu markieren und zu identifizieren.

In den 1960er Jahren begann man die zivilen Einsatzmöglichkeiten des Computers wie Schreiben, Kunst oder Musikmachen zu erproben.[12] Ein Klassiker dieser Zeit ist die arbeitswissenschaftliche Evaluation der Maus zum Zwecke der Textverarbeitung.[13] Dabei geht es nicht etwa darum, wie man Text produziert (denn die Bedienung von Schreibmaschinentastaturen war allemal bekannt und optimiert), sondern um die effektive Auswahl und Bearbeitung von Text, der auf einem Bildschirm dargestellt wird. In einer Versuchsanordnung aus Radarbildschirm, Tastatur und verschiedenen Zeigegeräten (Maus, Lightpen, Joystick und die längst vergessene Kniesteuerung) vermessen die Autoren mit Hilfe klassischer Zeit- und Bewegungsstudien, wie ungelerntes Personal mit geringstmöglicher Verschwendung von Zeit und Energie „zielsicher" Textpassagen markiert. Oder, illustrativer formuliert: „Die Feindakquisition fand sich als Maus auf einem normalen Schreibtisch wieder."[14] Bemerkenswert daran ist nicht nur die Kontinuität arbeitswissenschaftlicher Methoden der 1920er. Festzuhalten ist auch die (nicht eigens thematisierte) Entscheidung, sich gar nicht erst auf längerfristige motorische Lernprozesse einzulassen, deren Aufwand sich am Ende vielleicht ebenfalls rechnen könnte. Die Präferenz liegt vielmehr auf dem Erstkontakt und einer steilen Lernkurve, die möglichst früh ein Plateau der zielführenden Beherrschung (im wortwörtlichen Sinne) erreichen soll.

device" adopts the acquired techniques of writing and drawing using pen and paper (the developers of the RAND-Tablet called it a "live pad of paper"). Just as Engelbart's text-editing was not a matter of writing texts, this was not a matter of handwriting and drawing, but rather of militarised applications such as the digitalisation of cartographic information or more efficient input for the projected programming environments of the era. "[To] 'write' in a natural manner," by contrast, is listed as one of the "more esoteric applications … for man-machine interaction" in the foreword to the RAND report. Following the thesis that intuitiveness is merely an evidential effect of having forgotten once learnt cultural techniques, it should be noted in this context that writing is actually no more natural than using a mouse but simply more familiar. Nevertheless, there were first experiments in the recognition of handwriting at the same time, although these did not work with graphic tablets but digitalised the tracks of movement produced by a so-called telautograph—a device to transpose handwriting dating from the late nineteenth century.[17] But the graphic tablets were seen as much more photogenic, especially if one blended out much of the technology and depicted no more than the user with pen and tablet in front of a screen, as all popular reports about the cybernetic workplaces of the future did at the time.

But the RAND developers were referring back (even in the name) to Ivan Sutherland's famous dissertation *Sketchpad: A Man-Machine Graphical Communication System,* which is quoted repeatedly as an ancestor to interactive media art[18] (2 p. 140). Sutherland's aim was to transform the lightpen used to pinpoint the enemy in early warning systems into a tool that could be used to make construction drawings. Optical and haptic work surfaces, which are separate in the case of the graphic tablet, become one in this case: the user draws directly onto the screen (assisted by a *chorded keyboard,* which will be explained in more detail below). It is true that Sutherland attached a short appendix to his work entitled "Artistic Drawing," and even considered the possibility of cartoon films, but the purpose of his undertaking also came within a framework delineated by ergonomic considerations of efficiency. The interactivity of Sketchpad was simply intended to optimise working processes in engineering.[19]

An example of the convergence of visual and haptic working surfaces—which the aesthetics of today's touchscreens have implemented by replacing vector with raster graphics—is Pierre Wellner's Digital Desk, which was created at the XEROX Europarc in 1990. By means of a video camera and projection, the user surface—for which the desktop metaphor with windows and icons was established by XEROX (and primarily Apple) in the nineteen-eighties—is folded back from the vertical plane of the screen onto the horizontal plane of the real desk[20] (*3* p. 140, *4* p.141). Here, a pen and the hand take over the role of the keyboard and mouse, which appears practicable—at least in the demonstration showing the use of a pocket calculator—because a virtual keyboard is projected onto the desk. But things become odder when paths of movement practised using the

3 — **Mittlerweile gehören Mäuse, insbesondere durch die Vermehrung mobiler Endgeräte, einer bedrohten Art an und sind – nach einem Trackball- und TrackPoint-Intermezzo – kleinen oder größeren Touchpads gewichen, von denen viele mittlerweile auch Gesten verarbeiten. Auch diese gehen auf Entwicklungen der 1960er Jahre zurück, auf jene „Achsenzeit des Computing", wie Hans-Dieter Hellige sie einmal genannt hat. Die Anfänge bilden Grafiktabletts wie das 1963/64 bei der RAND Corporation entwickelte RAND Tablet, auf dem man mit einem Stift zeichnen und schreiben konnte.[15] (1 S. 140) Nur scheinbar haben wir es jedoch mit einer „remediation"[16] zu tun, also einer Durchdringung und Konkurrenz alter und neuer Medien, bei der das Tablett als „Man-Machine Graphical Communication Device" an die erlernten Techniken des Schreibens und Zeichnens mit Stift und Papier („live pad of paper", wie die Entwickler des RAND Tablet es nennen) anschließt. So wie es bei Engelbarts Textverarbeitung nicht um das Schreiben von Texten ging, geht es auch hier nicht um Handschriften und Zeichnungen, sondern vielmehr um militärische Anwendungen wie die Digitalisierung kartografischer Informationen bzw. eine effizientere Eingabe für die seinerzeit projektierten grafischen Programmierumgebungen. „(To) ‚write' in a natural manner" dagegen wird im Vorwort des RAND-Reports noch als eine der „more esoteric applications (...) for man-machine interaction" aufgeführt. Dabei wäre, gemäß der These, dass Intuitivität nur ein Evidenzeffekt des Vergessens erlernter Kulturtechniken ist, anzumerken, dass Schreiben auch nicht natürlicher ist, als eine Maus zu benutzen, sondern eben nur vertrauter. Gleichwohl gab es zur selben Zeit auch erste Versuche der Handschriftenerkennung, die jedoch nicht mit Grafiktabletts arbeiteten, sondern dazu die Bewegungsspuren eines sogenannten Telautografen – ein Gerät zur Übertragung von Handschriften aus dem späten 19. Jahrhundert – digitalisierten.[17] Wesentlich fotogener nahmen sich aber die Grafiktabletts aus, vor allem wenn man weite Teile der Technik ausblendete und nur eine(n) Benutzer(in) mit Stift und Tablett vor einem Bildschirm abbildete, wie es in populären Berichten von kybernetisierten Arbeitsplätzen der Zukunft damals allerorts geschah.**

Dabei rekurrierten die RAND-Entwickler (schon im Titel) auf Ivan Sutherlands berühmte Dissertation *Sketchpad: A Man-Machine Graphical Communication System,* das immer wieder als Ahnherr interaktiver Medienkunst zitiert wird.[18] (2 S. 140) Sutherlands Ziel ist eine Transformation jenes Lightpens, mit dem auf Frühwarnsystemen der Feind selektiert wurde, in ein Werkzeug zur Anfertigung von Konstruktionszeichnungen. Optische und haptische Arbeitsfläche, die beim Grafiktablett entkoppelt sind, fallen hier zusammen: man zeichnet (ergänzt durch ein *chorded keyboard,* wovon gleich noch zu sprechen sein wird) direkt auf den Bildschirm. Zwar hatte Sutherland seiner Arbeit einen kurzen Anhang mit dem Titel „Artistic Drawing" beigelegt und sogar die Möglichkeit von Trickfilmen erwogen, doch lag der Sinn der Unternehmung ebenfalls in einem Rahmen, der durch arbeitswissenschaftliches Effizienzdenken abgesteckt war. Die Interaktivität des Sketchpad

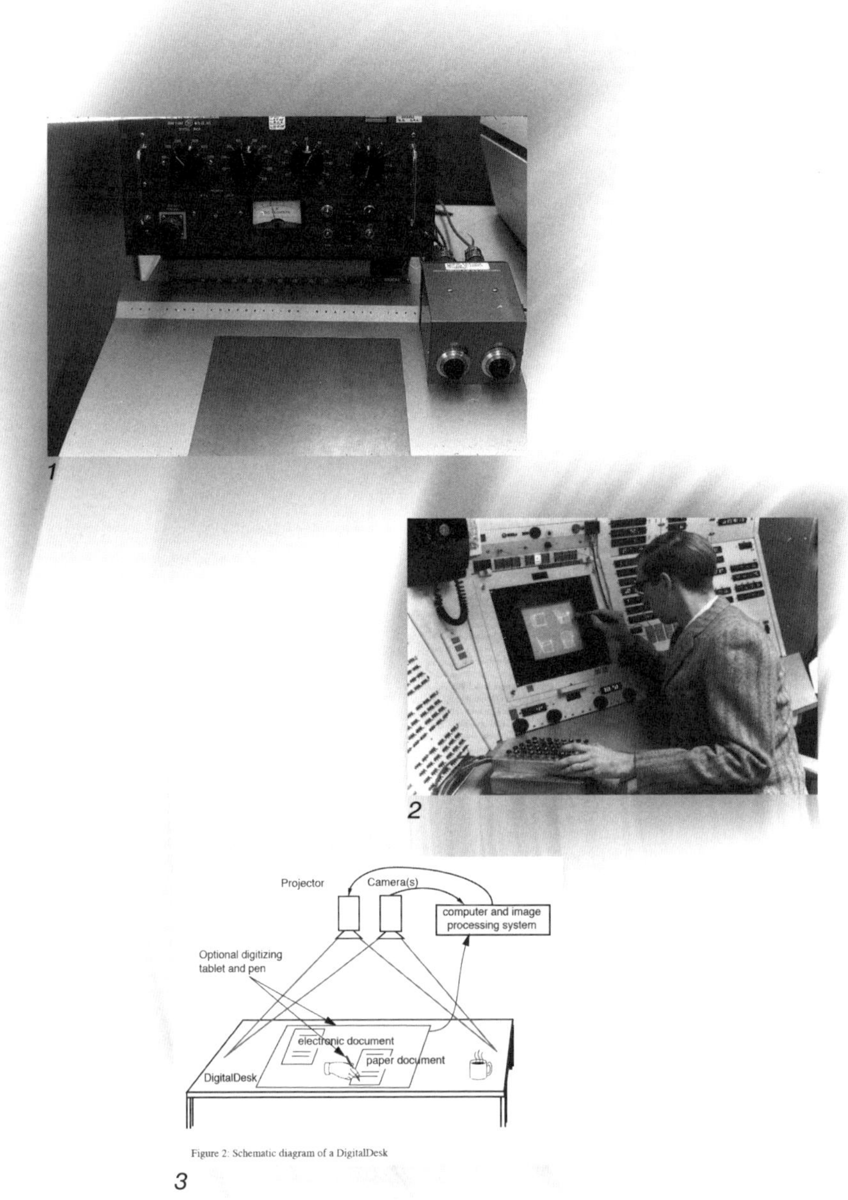

1 RAND Graphic Tablet, 1964 — *2* Ivan Sutherland's Sketchpad III, used by Timothy Johnson, 1963 — *3* Scheme of functions, Pierre Wellner's Digital Desk, 1991 — *4* Example application, table calculation using the Digital Desk, 1991 — *5* Advertising for Livermore's Typograph (1857) from Bill Buxton — *6* XEROX PARCTAB from Bill Buxton, 1992/93

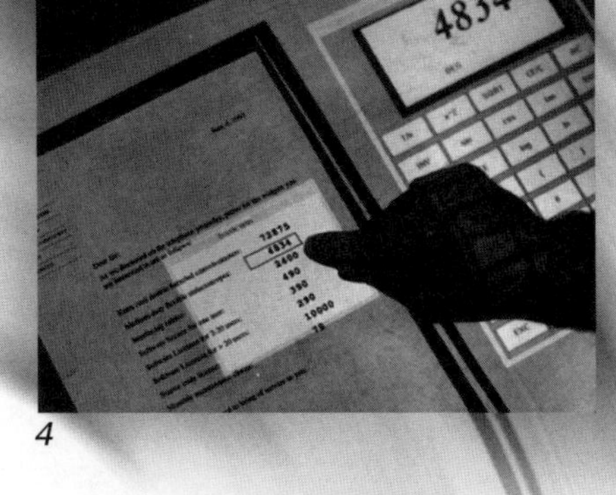

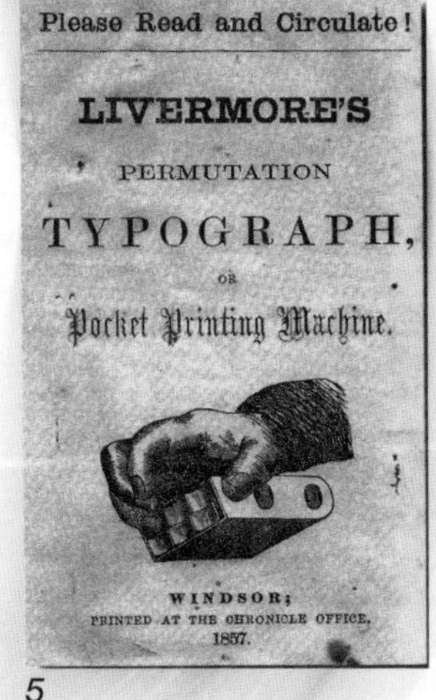

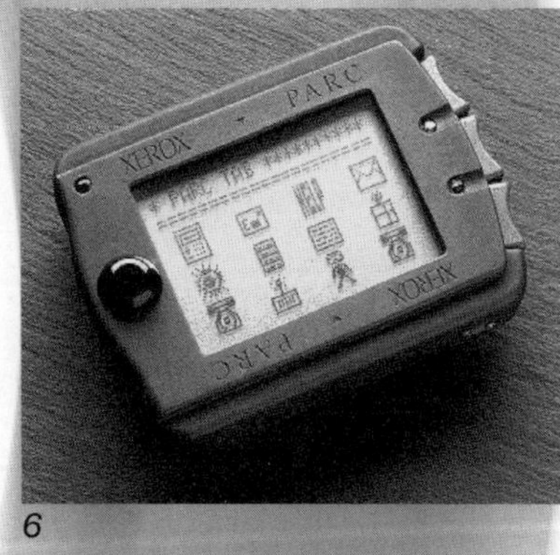

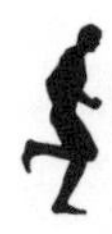

1 RAND-Grafiktablett, 1964 — 2 Ivan Sutherlands Sketchpad III, bedient von Timothy Johnson, 1963 —
3 Funktionsschema von Pierre Wellners Digital Desk, 1991 — 4 Beispielanwendung Tabellenkalku-
lation mit dem Digital Desk, 1991 — 5 Werbung für Livermore's Typograph (1857) nach Bill Buxton —
6 XEROX PARCTAB nach Bill Buxton, 1992/93

mouse, like clicking or "drag & drop," are now completed—immaterially like a grin without the Cheshire cat—using one's finger on the top of the desk.[21] Above all, the gestures that one has practised already with the mouse and now makes without it appear intuitive.[22] For the actual writing does not happen with a pen, exactly, but is still left to a solid keyboard, which first has to be extricated with considerable effort.

As in the case of Engelbart, in fact, here text editing does not mean writing, but editing or processing of texts. In the demonstration video, the scene headed "Taking Notes" begins with the sentence, "Oh, my deadline is tomorrow!" whereupon the fictive user shows how the "Digital Desk" helps him to assemble various quotations, bibliographical information, and images from other texts as quickly and efficiently as possible and to link them by adding a few new, filler sentences. And so he beats his deadline. Failing to fulfil the hopes of the nineteen-sixties, however, the technologies of the age of "automatic external symbol manipulation" (Engelbart) did not lead automatically to better ideas, but rather to accumulative styles of writing and thus to more pages (an experience readily made in everyday university life today). But the achievement of such a system lies mainly in the possibility of moving and recombining texts and images by means of specific hand movements, and filling the gaps between them as if in forms, meaning that it reverts directly to ergonomic studies of office work in the nineteen-twenties. Frank Gilbreth, for example, wrote of a rastered desk that he had designed:

"The purpose of the desktop divided into squares is to standardise movements, i.e., hand movements towards writing utensils such as pencil, ink, fountain pen, etc., which have their customary place. (...) The modern desk is (...) completely flat, with no kind of construction on it or small drawers to collect all kinds of possible and impossible objects, because it thus corresponds best to the work processes of modern administration practice today."[23]

The majority of office work, therefore, emerges as movement optimised with regard to energy and time, picking up and putting down standardised tools at standardised work places—something that led, as we know, to the utopia of the de-hierarchisation of work, according to which there would be no different training subjects in future, but only different repertoires of movement.[24] It seems that with the universal introduction of marking, clicking, and shifting we have come quite close to this ideal, albeit in an unexpected way.

4—As indicated several times, the illusion of intuitiveness—which emerged historically from an ergonomic concept of efficiency—is so dominant that it overshadows all other options. What about the option of not relying on motor activities that are learnt as quickly as possible (and can be applied rapidly as a result) but on those requiring longer practice, which cannot therefore be applied immediately but might be more effective in the long run? What about, in short, making the effort of adaptation into

sollte schlichtweg der Optimierung von Arbeitsabläufen im Ingenieurwesen dienen.[19]

Ein Beispiel für die Konvergenz von visueller und haptischer Arbeitsfläche, das durch die Umstellung von Vektor- in Rastergrafik die Ästhetik unserer heutigen Touchscreens implementieren konnte, gibt Pierre Wellners Digital Desk, der um 1990 am XEROX Europarc entstand. Dank Videokamera und Videoprojektion wird die Benutzeroberfläche, für die sich in den 1980ern durch XEROX (und vor allem durch Apple) die Schreibtischmetapher mit Fenstern und Icons eingebürgert hatte, aus der Vertikalen des Bildschirms in die Horizontale des realen Schreibtischs zurückgeklappt.[20] (*3* S. 140, *4* S. 141) Stift und Hand übernehmen dabei die Rolle von Tastatur und Maus, was zumindest in der Demonstration zur Benutzung eines Taschenrechners praktikabel erscheint, weil eine virtuelle Tastatur auf den Schreibtisch projiziert wird. Kurioser wird die Sache allemal, wenn an der Maus trainierte Bewegungsabläufe wie klicken oder „drag & drop" nun – immateriell wie ein Grinsen ohne Katze – mit dem Finger auf der Schreibtischplatte vollzogen werden.[21] Intuitiv erscheinen vor allem jene Gesten, die man schon mit der Maus geübt hat und nun einfach ohne sie macht.[22] Denn das Schreiben selbst geschieht gerade nicht durch einen Stift, sondern bleibt weiterhin einer realen, handfesten Tastatur überlassen, die erst mühsam hervorgekramt werden muss.

Wie bei Engelbart bedeutet Textverarbeitung nämlich nicht das Verfassen von Texten, sondern deren Bearbeitung. Im Demonstrationsvideo beginnt die Spielszene zur Vorführung von „Taking Notes" mit dem Satz „Oh, my deadline is tomorrow!", worauf der fiktive Benutzer vorführt, wie man nun dank des „Digital Desk" möglichst schnell und effektiv einige Zitate, Literaturangaben und Bilder aus anderen Texten zusammenklauben kann, um sie fristgerecht mit einigen neuen Füllsätzen zu verbinden. Anders als man in den 1960ern hoffte, führen die Technologien des Zeitalters der „automatic external symbol manipulation" (Engelbart) nicht automatisch zu besseren Ideen, sondern eher zu akkumulativen Schreibweisen und damit zu mehr Seiten (eine Erfahrung, die zu machen im heutigen universitären Alltag nicht schwerfällt). Dass aber die Leistung eines solchen Systems hauptsächlich darin liegt, Texte und Bilder durch bestimmte Handbewegungen zu verschieben, zu rekombinieren und Lücken zwischen ihnen wie in Formularen auszufüllen, führt direkt zurück auf arbeitswissenschaftliche Studien zur Büroarbeit in den 1920er Jahren. So schrieb etwa Frank Gilbreth über den von ihm entworfenen gerasterten Schreibtisch:

„Die in Quadrate eingeteilte Tischoberfläche dient zur Normalisierung der Bewegungen das heißt der Handgriffe nach den Schreibgeräten wie Bleistift, Tinte, Federhalter usw., die ihren Normplatz haben. (...) Der moderne Schreibtisch ist (...) vollkommen flach, ohne jeden Aufbau und ohne kleine Fächer zum Aufstapeln aller möglichen und unmöglichen Dinge, weil er so am besten mit den Arbeitsverfahren der heutigen neuzeitigen Verwaltungspraxis übereinstimmt."[23]

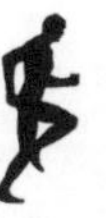

a productive focus rather than attempting to suspend it through evidence? The best example is given by musical instruments, whose use is only mastered with virtuosity following long practice. In the computer field, the corresponding devices are the so-called *chorded keyboards,* namely, reduced keyboards that allow differentiated input by means of key combinations pressed by several fingers.[25] Once learnt over a longer period of time they are highly effective, as everyone knows who swears by key combinations rather than mouse clicks in everyday computer use.

Such alternatives to the typewriter keyboard have been tested since the nineteenth century and have indeed been taken up once again in interface design, as in XEROX PARCtab, for example, an early hand-held device that was used with only three keys (like a trumpet with its three valves) (*5, 6* p. 141). The system by Engelbart mentioned above was already equipped with such a *chorded keyboard* that shared the work with the mouse, but is not examined in more detail as a rule—possibly because it might detract some of the glory of immediacy from "intuitive" *devices.* By contrast, the tradition of specialised keyboards has been maintained in the case of legal clerks and other *speech-to-text* reporters and their palantype or stenotype machines. It is possible to achieve 200 to 300 words per minute, including additional information such as "laughter" or "applause"—however, this is after practising for at least three years: a period that very few people would be willing to spend accustoming themselves to a new computer or new software. As a rule, people cannot afford to accept the flat learning curve of more complex physical knowledge.

The analogy to musical instruments and their use with several fingers (trumpet, piano, guitar, etc.) is not merely a superficial one; there are actual references in the history of computers. This is especially true of experimental music and its interface constructions for (often homemade) electronic instruments. The tablet experiments by Bill Buxton in the nineteen-eighties, for example, were not oriented on pen and mouse, that is to say, on writing and clicking, but on mixing desks and synthesisers.[26] Foils or pressed out stencils were placed on a "neutral" graphic tablet, defining separate areas of the pressure-sensitive base as buttons or push levers with which it was possible to regulate volume, frequency or oscillators, or to switch channels on and off. As this cannot take place only in succession and several things usually need to be organised at the same time, multitouch hardware (and corresponding software) is necessary.

This closes the circle, so to speak, to the current boom in multitouch displays and their gesture recognition, which have become mass market goods as a result of the iPhone. Perhaps, therefore, it is no coincidence that music apps were among the most-demanded of the first era. The boom in iPhone flutes, guitars, pianos, and other instruments[27] seems to be the outcome of that very constellation that should be described as the distinction between intuitiveness and virtuosity. Tasks in working life—like telephoning, mailing, arranging dates, etc.—need to be simple and quick to master without a handbook, for example, by clicking on

Der Hauptanteil von Büroarbeit erweist sich somit als energie- und zeit-optimierbare Bewegung zur Aufnahme und Ablage standardisierter Werkzeuge an normierten Plätzen – woraus bekanntlich die Utopie der beruflichen Enthierarchisierung entspringen konnte, derzufolge es in Zukunft keine verschiedenen Ausbildungsgegenstände mehr geben werde, sondern nur noch unterschiedliche Bewegungsrepertoires.[24] Diesem Ziel scheint die Universalisierung von Zeigen, Klicken und Schieben auf unvermutetem Wege doch recht nahegekommen zu sein.

4 — Wie mehrfach angedeutet, ist die Illusion der Intuitivität, die historisch einem arbeitswissenschaftlichen Effizienzdenken entsprang, so dominant, dass sie eine andere Option verschattet. Was nämlich wäre, wenn man nicht auf Motoriken setzte, die möglichst schnell erlernt (und damit rasch einsetzbar) sind, sondern auf solche, deren Einübung lange dauert, die dadurch nicht sofort einsetzbar sind, die aber auf lange Sicht vielleicht sogar effektiver sind? Was wäre, kurz gesagt, wenn man nicht versuchen würde, die Adaptionsleistung durch Evidenz verschwinden zu lassen, sondern sie stattdessen zum produktiven Zentrum macht? Das beste Beispiel dafür geben Musikinstrumente, deren Bedienung erst nach langer Übung virtuos beherrscht wird. Im Computerbereich entsprechen ihnen die sogenannten *chorded keyboards,* also reduzierte Tastaturen, die verschiedene Eingaben durch das Drücken von Tastenkombinationen mit mehreren Fingern erlauben.[25] Über lange Zeit erlernt, besitzen sie eine hohe Effektivität, wie alle wissen, die im Alltag auf Tastenkombinationen statt auf Mausklicks schwören. Solche Alternativen zur Schreibmaschinentastatur wurden seit dem 19. Jahrhundert erprobt und im Interfacedesign durchaus wieder aufgenommen, wie etwa im XEROX PARCtab, einem frühen Handheld, der über drei Tasten (wie eine Trompete über drei Klappen) bedient wurde. (*5, 6* S. 141) Auch das bereits erwähnte System von Engelbart war mit einem solchen *chorded keyboard* ausgestattet, das die Maus arbeitsteilig begleitete, auf das aber in der Regel nicht eingegangen wird – möglicherweise, weil es den „intuitiven" *devices* doch etwas vom Glanz der Unmittelbarkeit nehmen könnte. Erhalten hat sich die Tradition der spezialisierten Tastaturen hingegen bei Gerichtsschreibern und anderen *speech-to-text-*Reportern und ihren Palantype- bzw. Stenotypiermaschinen. Möglich sind dabei 200 bis 300 Wörter pro Minute inklusive Zusatzinformationen wie „Lachen" oder „Applaus" – allerdings erst nach einer Übungsdauer von mindestens drei Jahren: einem Zeitraum mithin, den man sich wohl kaum zur Gewöhnung an einen neuen Computer oder eine neue Software zu nehmen bereit wäre. Die flache Lernkurve eines komplexeren Körperwissens kann man sich in der Regel eben nicht leisten.

Die Analogie zu Musikinstrumenten und ihrer mehrfingrigen Bedienung (Trompete, Klavier, Gitarre usw.) ist keine bloß oberflächliche, sondern hat durchaus computerhistorische Bezüge. Dies gilt insbesondere für die experimentelle Musik und ihre Interfacekonstruktionen für (oft selbstgebaute) elektronische Instrumente. Die

icons and typing on virtual typewriters. In our so-called free time, by contrast, we prefer to make things—musical instruments, computer games, etc.—difficult and time consuming, burdening ourselves with complicated key combinations, training rapid reactions or performing precarious balancing acts using a gyro-sensor. Lack of resistance and the resistive are two sides of the same coin, whose attribution is cultural and therefore both contingent and historical.

Looking at the concepts of gesture responsive, multitouch interfaces like those already circulating a decade before the iPhone, it is possible to discern just how much the—arbitrarily definable—attribution of touch and movements relates to specific commands in the tradition of ergonomics from Gilbreth to Engelbart. While Wayne Westerman's definitive dissertation of 1999 discusses many technical problems regarding the recognition of touch and movement in detail and attempts to solve them, the purpose of the conceivable gestures (the meaning that should be attributed to them in the interaction) always seems self-evident and existent[28] (*7, 8* p. 150). Just as Frank Gilbreth once tabulated elementary gestures in the mechanised workplace in order to create chains of movements (selecting, grasping, letting go, etc.), now elementary gestures in the virtual work place lead to the creation of processes (*new file, cut, copy, paste,* etc.). And now completely different chains of movement in dance, gaming, or sport can also be assembled from them.

5—Finally, it is as well to recall that gestures—as the informational science definition at the outset indicated—not only serve to operate apparatus but also to ascertain information. This difference can be discerned in a positively emblematic way from two early PDAs, functional predecessors to today's Smartphones but without a telephone unit (*9* p. 150, *10* p. 151). Both devices use a pen for input and operation. For the Palm devices, the user needs to learn specific movements to input text, an artificial writing called "Graffiti," which was derived from XEROX' "Unistrokes."[29] A summary of this was frequently glued into the lid of the protective case just to be on the safe side. The Apple devices, the other way around, made it necessary for the computer to learn its user's handwriting, which one had to practise with the device—as clearly as possible and always in an identical manner.[30] Having mastered the movements of Palm writing, one could not only write quickly but also on every device one encountered. But even after good training and some disciplining of one's own handwriting, the Newton remained very slow and prone to mistakes, and above all, it was impossible to write on any other device as it would be accustomed to the handwriting of a different user. In other words, the Palm models its user through standardisation; gestures are recognised when they adhere to standard conditions (with a certain tolerance level). One can write successfully as soon as a prescribed movement is realised correctly. In contrast, the Newton models its user via recognition; gestures are recognised when they agree with previously made personal input (alias information). One can

**Tablet-Experimente von Bill Buxton aus den 1980ern beispielsweise ori-
entieren sich nicht an Stift und Maus, das heißt Schreiben und Klicken,
sondern an Mischpulten und Synthesizern.[26] Auf ein „neutrales" Grafiktablett werden dabei Folien oder ausgestanzte Masken aufgelegt, die
einzelne Areale der drucksensitiven Unterlage als Knöpfe oder Schiebe-
regler definieren, an denen Lautstärke, Frequenz oder Oszillatoren geregelt bzw. Kanäle ein- und ausgeschaltet werden können. Da dies nicht
ausschließlich nacheinander geschehen kann, sondern meist mehrere
Dinge gleichzeitig geregelt werden müssen, wird dafür Multitouch-Hard-
ware (und entsprechende Software) erforderlich.**
**Damit schließt sich gewissermaßen der Bogen zum gegenwärtigen Boom
der Multitouch-Displays und ihrer Gestenerkennung, die durch das iPhone
zu einer Ware für den Massenmarkt geworden sind. Vielleicht ist es daher
auch kein Zufall, dass ausgerechnet Musik-Apps zu den meistgefragten
Anwendungen der ersten Zeit gehörten. Der Boom an iPhone-Flöten,
-Gitarren, -Klavieren und anderen Instrumenten[27] scheint genau jener Kon-
stellation geschuldet, die als Differenz zwischen Intuitivität und Virtuosität
beschrieben werden sollte. Im Arbeitsleben müssen die Dinge – telefonieren,
mailen, Termine eintragen etc. – einfach und schnell zu beherrschen sein,
ohne Handbuch eben, durch Klicken auf Icons und durch Tippen auf virtuellen Schreibmaschinen. In der sogenannten Freizeit dagegen (macht man sich
die Dinge – Musikinstrumente, Computerspiele, etc. – lieber schwierig und
langwierig, bürdet sich vertrackte Tastenkombinationen auf, trainiert sich im
schnellen Reagieren oder übt seltsame Balanceakte mit dem Gyro-Sensor.
Widerstandslosigkeit und Widerständigkeit sind zwei Seiten derselben Medaille,
deren Zuweisung kulturell und damit ebenso kontingent wie historisch ist.**

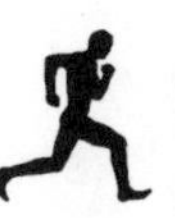

Schaut man auf die Konzepte gestischer Multitouch-Interfaces, wie sie bereits
ein Jahrzehnt vor dem iPhone kursierten, so lässt sich ablesen, wie sehr die –
willkürlich bestimmbare – Zuordnung von Berührungen und Bewegungen zu
bestimmten Kommandos in der Tradition der Arbeitswissenschaft von Gilbreth
bis Engelbart steht. Während etwa Wayne Westermans maßgebliche Dissertation von 1999 sehr viele technische Probleme der Berührungs- und Bewegungserkennung ausführlich diskutiert und zu lösen versucht, scheint der Sinn
der möglichen Gesten (die Bedeutung, die sie in der Interaktion bekommen sollen) immer schon selbstverständlich und vorgängig.[28] (7, 8 S. 150) So wie Frank
Gilbreth einst Elementargesten im mechanischen Arbeitsraum tabellierte, um
daraus Bewegungsketten zu bilden (wählen, greifen, loslassen usw.), sind es nun
Elementargesten im virtuellen Arbeitsraum, aus denen Prozesse gebildet werden
können (*new file, cut, copy, paste* usw.). Und auch diesmal können daraus ganz
andere Bewegungsketten in Tanz, Spiel oder Sport zusammengesetzt werden.

5—Zum Schluss gilt es zumindest daran zu erinnern, dass Gesten – wie in der informatischen Definition des Anfangs zu lesen stand – eben nicht nur der Steuerung von
Geräten, sondern auch der Informationserhebung dienen. Geradezu emblematisch

write successfully as soon as an individual movement is realised in a (more or less) identical way. In short, the Palm is a device conceived on the basis of ergonomics that standardises its user, whereas the Newton is a device conceived along the lines of intelligent recognition that individualises its user.

The huge field of computer-based analysis (and synthesis) of movement naturally goes much further than writing exercises on hand-held devices. In particular, applications in the domain of police records (as well as the film industry and dance) are a potentially rich source for cultural science concerned with questions of registering and systemising secret body knowledge. The computer-based approaches of *motion capturing* via light-points, which began in the nineteen-seventies, thus take over directly from the methods of ergonomics.[31] The first experiments were equally early, and included attempts to establish a person's gender from his or her way of walking, or to identify people from their individual gait.[32] This continues to the present day and is termed *remote biometrics,* that is, the registration of people's movements without touch, which is easy to manage by means of surveillance cameras, for example, and (in contrast to a fingerprint or an iris scan) does not require the person to stand still or even agree to the process. "What's really novel in this research," according to Thomas McKenna, project manager at the Office for Naval Research, "is that ... it's a new way of using surveillance that looks at activities, instead of looking for people."[33] Individuality is revealed in the temporality of movements and no longer in the pictorial quality of unchanging features. Typical fields of experiment are changes to a person's gait under a hidden burden (bomb?) or the unmasking of doubles through unconscious motor activities that dramatic training misses but everyday news images reveal.[34] Apologists of such methods hoping for subsidies now refer to a "human gait DNA," which promises to decipher one's individual style of walking as a non-deceptive identifying feature. The key notion is the idea (highly reminiscent of Lacan) of a motor subconscious that human perception misses, but can be data-accessed by computers and subsequently used for purposes of security or police records.

In this context, particularly interesting projects are those that connect this motor subconscious (more or less) detachedly to the future—that is, to questions of intentionality, such as a project based in Amsterdam with the evocative name CASSANDRA.[35] Its aim is the recognition of aggressive behaviour in public places (stations, bus stops, etc.) and early intervention. Those who move in a specific way (unknowingly) raise an alarm— which is ironically also a form of device control, although it occurs not via consciously learnt, artificial gestures, but via unconsciously acquired, artificial gestures that are then interpreted by the software as intentional (*11* p. 151). And this interpretation is certainly problematic: "We propose an architecture for capturing data and creating a test and evaluation system to monitor video sensors and tag aberrant human activities for immediate review by human monitors. A psychological perspective

lässt sich dieser Unterschied an zwei frühen PDAs ablesen, funktionalen Vorläufern heutiger Smartphones ohne Telefoneinheit. (*9* S. 150, *10* S. 151) Beide Geräte benutzen einen Stift zur Eingabe und Steuerung. Bei den Palm-Geräten muss der Benutzer zur Eingabe von Text bestimmte Bewegungen lernen, eine Kunstschrift namens „Graffiti", die sich von XEROX' „Unistrokes" ableitete[29] und deren Übersicht man sich zur Sicherheit gerne in den Deckel der Schutzhülle klebte. Bei den Apple-Geräten musste in umgekehrter Weise der Computer die Handschrift seines Benutzers lernen, die man – möglichst deutlich, jedenfalls aber immer mit sich selbst identisch – mit ihm trainieren musste.[30] Hatte man sich die Bewegungen der Palm-Schrift erst einmal zu eigen gemacht, war man nicht nur schnell beim Schreiben, sondern konnte es auch auf jedem beliebigen Gerät. Der Newton jedoch blieb, selbst nach gutem Training und einer gewissen Disziplinierung der eigenen Handschrift recht langsam und fehlerbehaftet, und man konnte vor allem auf keinem anderen Gerät schreiben, da dieses in der Regel schon an einen anderen Benutzer gewöhnt war. Mit anderen Worten: Der Palm modelliert seinen Benutzer durch Standardisierung; Gesten werden erkannt, wenn sie standardisierten Vorgaben (innerhalb gewisser Toleranzen) folgen. Schreiben gelingt, wenn und sobald eine Bewegungsvorschrift richtig ausgeführt wird. Der Newton hingegen modelliert seinen Benutzer durch Wiedererkennung; Gesten werden erkannt, wenn sie mit zuvor gemachten persönlichen Eingaben (alias Angaben) übereinstimmen. Schreiben gelingt, wenn und sobald eine individuelle Bewegung (mehr oder minder) identisch wiederholt wird. Kurz gesagt ist der Palm ein arbeitswissenschaftlich gedachtes Gerät, das seine Benutzer normalisiert, der Newton hingegen ein erkennungsdienstlich gedachtes Gerät, das seine Benutzer individuiert.

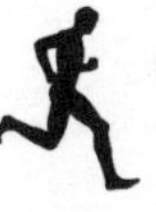

Selbstredend geht der riesige Bereich der computergestützten Analyse (und Synthese) von Bewegungen weit über Schreibübungen an Handhelds hinaus. Insbesondere die Domäne der erkennungsdienstlichen Anwendungen könnte (neben Filmindustrie und Tanz) eine reiche Quelle für eine Kulturwissenschaft sein, die sich mit Fragen des verborgenen Körperwissens, seiner Aufzeichnung und Systematisierung beschäftigt. Die computergestützten Ansätze des *motion capturing* durch Lichtpunkte, die in den 1970er Jahren begannen, knüpfen dabei direkt an die Methoden der Arbeitswissenschaft an.[31] Schon aus dieser Zeit stammen auch erste Versuche, etwa am Gang einer Person deren Geschlecht zu erkennen oder Personen anhand ihres individuellen Gangs zu identifizieren.[32] Dies hat sich bis heute unter dem Begriff *remote biometrics* fortgeschrieben, also der berührungsfreien Erfassung der Bewegungen von Personen, die sich etwa durch Überwachungskameras leicht bewerkstelligen lässt und die (anders als etwa ein Fingerabdruck oder ein Irisscan) weder ein Stillstehen noch eine Einwilligung der Person nötig macht. „What's really novel in this research", so Thomas McKenna, Projektmanager am Office for Naval Research, „is that (...) it's a new way of using surveillance that looks at activities, instead of looking for people."[33]

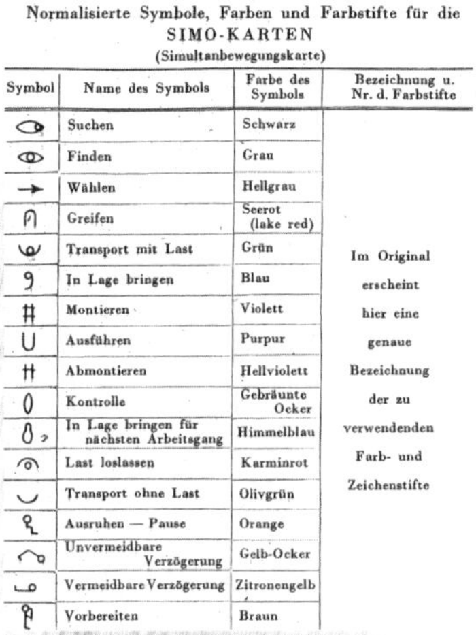

Normalisierte Symbole, Farben und Farbstifte für die
SIMO-KARTEN
(Simultanbewegungskarte)

Symbol	Name des Symbols	Farbe des Symbols	Bezeichnung u. Nr. d. Farbstifte
	Suchen	Schwarz	
	Finden	Grau	
	Wählen	Hellgrau	
	Greifen	Seerot (lake red)	
	Transport mit Last	Grün	Im Original
	In Lage bringen	Blau	erscheint
	Montieren	Violett	hier eine
	Ausführen	Purpur	genaue
	Abmontieren	Hellviolett	Bezeichnung
	Kontrolle	Gebräunte Ocker	der zu
	In Lage bringen für nächsten Arbeitsgang	Himmelblau	verwendenden
	Last loslassen	Karminrot	Farb- und
	Transport ohne Last	Olivgrün	Zeichenstifte
	Ausruhen — Pause	Orange	
	Unvermeidbare Verzögerung	Gelb-Ocker	
	Vermeidbare Verzögerung	Zitronengelb	
	Vorbereiten	Braun	

7

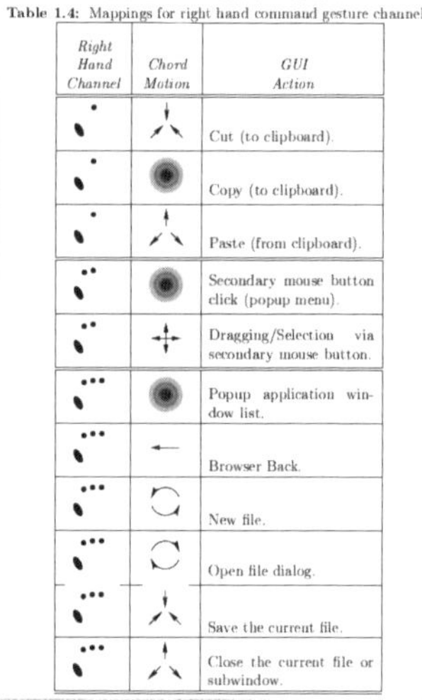

Table 1.4: Mappings for right hand command gesture channels.

Right Hand Channel	Chord Motion	GUI Action
		Cut (to clipboard).
		Copy (to clipboard).
		Paste (from clipboard).
		Secondary mouse button click (popup menu).
		Dragging/Selection via secondary mouse button.
		Popup application window list.
		Browser Back.
		New file.
		Open file dialog.
		Save the current file.
		Close the current file or subwindow.

8

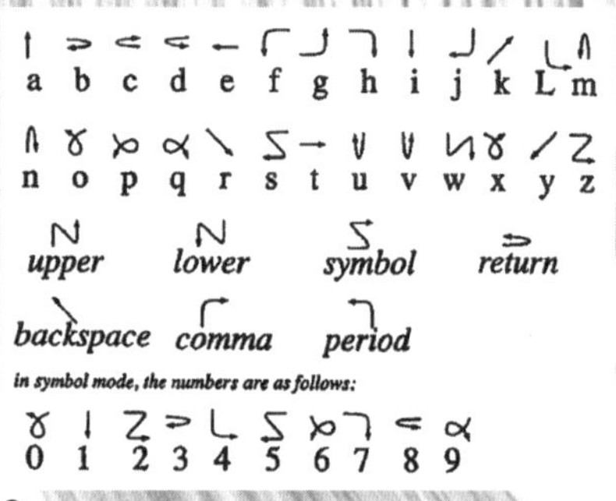

9

7 Therbligs of elementary movements from Frank and Lilian Gilbreth, 1924 — *8* Wayne Westerman: Elementary gestures for multitouch displays, 1999 — *9* XEROX "Unistrokes," model for the Palm "Graffiti" recognition, 1997 — *10* Apple's Message Pad Newton, 1993 — *11* Detection of aggression with CASSANDRA, 2007: calibrating the system to aggressive gestures with the help of actors — *12* Detection of aggression with CASSANDRA, 2007: measuring "aggression probability" with supplementary audio analysis

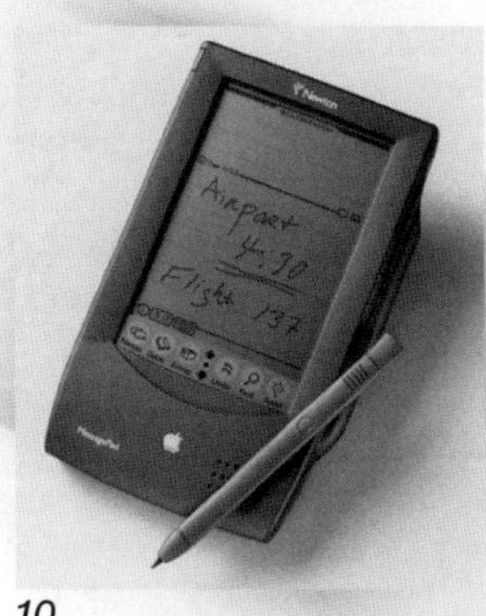

10

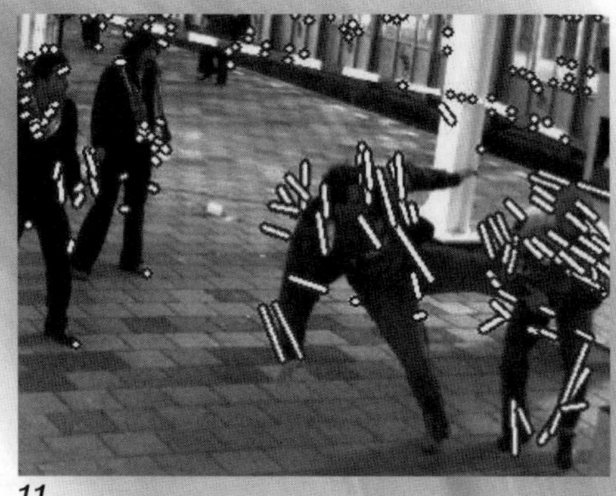

11

12

7 Therbligs von Elementarbewegungen nach Frank und Lilian Gilbreth, 1924 — **8** Wayne Wester-man: Elementargesten für Multitouch-Displays, 1999 — **9** XEROX „Unistrokes", Vorbild für die Palm-„Graffiti"-Erkennung, 1997 — **10** Apples Message-Pad Newton, 1993 — **11** Aggressionserkennung mit CASSANDRA, 2007: Kalibrierung des Systems auf aggressive Gesten mit Schauspielern — **12** Aggressionserkennung mit CASSANDRA, 2007: Messung der „Aggression Probability" mit er-gänzender Audioanalyse

provides the inspiration of depicting isolated human motion by point-light walker (PLW) displays, as they have been shown to be salient for recognition of action. Low level intent detection features are used to provide an initial evaluation of actionable behaviours. This relies on strong tracking algorithms that can function in an unstructured environment under a variety of environmental conditions. Critical to this is creating a description of 'suspicious behaviour' that can be used by the automated system."[36]

So the recognition of intention in suspicious behaviour requires a solid basis of description, a scheme of classification, and above all a calibration that distinguishes, for example, between the serious and the playful. In a delightful paradox, therefore, the CASSANDRA system is trained and calibrated by actors who act out (to the best of their knowledge and ability) aggressive gestures. Once again, life imitates art: actors perform a cultural repertoire of movements that finds its way into the computer as a "natural" repertoire. An actor acts out the patterns of movement of physical aggression to the computer as he imagines them, from (and by) which the computer is expected to recognise them accurately when they are no longer intended playfully but seriously—when they are "meant the way they seem." Here, Walter Benjamin's dictum that a gesture "is only falsifiable up to a point; and the more inconspicuous it is, the more habitually it is repeated, the more difficult it is to falsify"[37] comes to an unexpected conclusion (*12* p. 151).

Surely the issue would be more interesting in the opposite direction; that is, once the effects of gesture-controlled *surveillance* are embedded in the body. As we know to excess from the search machines of the World Wide Web, only things available to and legible by computer are found. One could therefore make the bold, reverse conclusion that in future the only recognisable things will be those moving in a manner detectable by machines. Since there have been ideas on the recognition of car thieves' movement in underground garages,[38] as a car thief one should perhaps consider body training that makes one unrecognisable as such and thus invisible. And in the future perhaps victims of rape in underground garages should learn to move like victims so that the automated security perceives them as such. Computer games are training fields for machine legible movements that are regarded nonetheless as "free" (or at least as liberating by comparison to the joystick and gamepad). In this context, the difference between skill (e.g., skittles) and significance (e.g., aggression) made by Ian Bogost with respect to gestures, for instance,[39] might be subject to irritation or even fully deconstructed. PlayStation Move and eyeToy, Nintendo Wii or Microsoft Kinect practise good motor behaviour in the "eyes" of the viewer (alias the surveillance camera)—the latter even using the seductive slogan "you are the controller."

"Performance research" as it is called in theatre studies, might not be the only field to find a rich source of material here; not insistent on the peculiarity of "physical co-presence," but calling for methodical self-

Individualität offenbart sich in der Zeitlichkeit von Bewegungen und nicht mehr in der Bildlichkeit unveränderlicher Merkmale. Typische Experimentierfelder sind etwa die Veränderung des Gangs unter einer versteckten Last (Bombe?) oder die Entlarvung von Doppelgängern durch unbewusste Motoriken, die dem Schauspieltraining entgehen und aus alltäglichen Nachrichtenbildern gewonnen werden könnten.[34] Auf Fördergelder spekulierende Apologeten solcher Verfahren sprechen mittlerweile gar von einer „Human Gait DNA", die den individuellen Gang als untrügliches Identifizierungsmerkmal zu entziffern verspricht. Die leitende Vorstellung bildet die (geradezu Lacan'sche) Idee eines motorischen Unbewussten, das der menschlichen Wahrnehmung verschlossen ist, von Computern aber datenmäßig erschlossen und erkennungsdienstlich benutzt werden kann.

Besonders interessant scheinen hier Unternehmungen, die dieses motorische Unbewusste (mehr oder minder) unbekümmert mit der Zukunft, das heißt mit Fragen der Intentionalität kurzschließen, wie etwa ein in Amsterdam beheimatetes Projekt mit dem sprechenden Namen CASSANDRA.[35] Dessen Ziel ist die Erkennung von aggressivem Verhalten im öffentlichen Raum (Bahnhöfe, Bushaltestellen usw.) und frühzeitige Intervention. Wer sich auf eine bestimmte Weise bewegt, schlägt (ohne es zu wissen) Alarm – was auf ironische Weise auch eine Form von Gerätesteuerung ist, die allerdings gerade nicht durch bewusst erlernte, künstliche Gesten geleistet wird, sondern sich durch unbewusst erlernte, künstliche und von der Software dann als intentional gedeutete Gesten ereignet. (*11* S. 151) Und diese Deutung ist allemal problematisch:

„We propose an architecture for capturing data and creating a test and evaluation system to monitor video sensors and tag aberrant human activities for immediate review by human monitors. A psychological perspective provides the inspiration of depicting isolated human motion by point-light walker (PLW) displays, as they have been shown to be salient for recognition of action. Low level intent detection features are used to provide an initial evaluation of actionable behaviors. This relies on strong tracking algorithms that can function in an unstructured environment under a variety of environmental conditions. Critical to this is creating a description of ‚suspicious behavior' that can be used by the automated system."[36]

Die Intentionalitäts-Erkennung verdächtigen Verhaltens braucht also eine robuste Beschreibungsbasis, ein Klassifikationsschema und vor allem eine Kalibrierung, die etwa zwischen Ernst und Spiel unterscheidet. In einer wunderbaren Paradoxie wird das CASSANDRA-System daher durch Schauspieler trainiert und kalibriert, die ihm (nach bestem Wissen und Gewissen) aggressive Gesten vorspielen. Wieder einmal ahmt das Leben die Kunst nach: Schauspieler führen ein kulturelles Repertoire von Bewegungen auf, das seinen Weg als „natürliches" Repertoire in den Rechner findet. Man spielt dem Rechner vor, wie man sich die Bewegungsmuster körperlicher Aggression vorstellt, worauf (und woran) dieser dann

reflection by forms of machine-based "performance research." This is perhaps valid for the cultural sciences in general: such informational processes and models might be of interest to their approaches to body history. Projects like CASSANDRA are themselves a form of analysis of cultural patterns of movement, or more pointedly: they are research on body knowledge beyond the customary sphere of research in the humanities. The ergonomics of the nineteen-twenties certainly had some (utopian) awareness of the fact that they were not only analysing movements but also implementing a kind of comprehensive design of mentality, by shaping patterns of movement at the same time. The informational gesture spotting systems of today (whether in interface design or in surveillance) do something similar, but one asks oneself whether it makes things any better that they no longer know what they are doing.

NOTES—[1] Jung, Keechul: "Recognition-Based Gesture Spotting in Video Games," in: Kang, Hyun/Lee, Chang Woo (eds.): *Pattern Recognition Letters,* 2004, 1701–1714.—[2] Cf. Most recently Wulf, Christoph/Fischer-Lichte, Erika (eds.): *Gesten: Inszenierung, Aufführung, Praxis,* Munich 2010.—[3] Heilmann,Till: "Digitalität als Taktilität. McLuhan, der Computer und die Taste," in: *Zeitschrift für Medienwissenschaft,* 2/2010, 131–140; Bickenbach, Matthias: "Knopfdruck und Auswahl," in: LiLi, 117, 2000, 9–32; Engell, Lorenz: "Tasten, Wählen, Denken," in: Münker, S./Roesler, A./Sandbothe, M. (eds.): *Medienphilosophie: Beiträge zur Klärung eines Begriffs.* Frankfurt am Main 2003, 53–77; "Leider fehlt das Tastendrücken." Based on: Flusser, Vilém: *Kompendium Gesten. Versuch einer Phänomenologie,.* Düsseldorf 1991.—[4] Cf. the distinction made by Nespoulous, J.L./Perron P./Roch Lecours A.: *The Biological Foundations of Gestures: Motor and Semiotic Aspects,* Hillsdale 1986; and Kendon, Adam: *Gesture, Visible Action as Utterance,.* Cambridge 2004.—[5] Cf. for example Behrenshausen, Bryan G.: "Toward a (Kin)aesthetic of Video Gaming: The Case of Dance Dance Revolution," in: *Games and Culture,* 2–4/2007, 335–354; Crogan, Patrick: "The Nintendo Wii, Virtualisation And Gestural Analogics," in: *Culture Machine,* 11/2010, 82–101; Giddings, Seth/Kennedy, Helen W.: "Incremental Speed Increases Excitement: Bodies, Space, Movement and Televisual Change," in: *The Journal of Television and New Media,* 11.3.2010, Swalwell, M.: "Movement and Kinaesthetic Responsiveness: A Neglected Pleasure", in: Swalwell, M./Wilson, J. (eds.): The Pleasures of Computer Gaming: Essays on Cultural History, Theory and Aesthetics, Jefferson 2008, 72–93.—[6] Bogost, Ian: *Persuasive Games: Gestures as Meaning.* At http://www.gamasutra.com/view/feature/4064/persuasive_games_gestures_as_.php?print=1 (last access: 5.2.2011).—[7] Simon, Bart (3.2009): *Wii are Out of Control: Bodies, Game Screens and the Production of Gestural Excess.* At http://ssrn.com/abstract=1354043 (last access 5.2.2011).—[8] At http://kinectionlost.com (last access 5.2.2011).—[9] Pias, Claus: "Maschinen—Sprachen" in: Bäumler, T./Bühler, B./Rieger, S. (eds.): *Nicht Fisch—nicht Fleisch. Ordnungssysteme und ihre Störfälle.* Zurich/Berlin 2011, 187–208.—[10] Fisher, Robert B.: *Compendium of Computer Vision.* At http://homepages.inf.ed.ac.uk/rbf/CVonline/ (last access 5.2.2011).—[11] In the sense of Pflüger, Jörg: "Konversation, Manipulation, Delegation. Zur Ideengeschichte der Interaktivität," in: Hellige, H.D. (ed.): *Geschichten der Informatik. Visionen, Paradigmen, Leitmotive.* Berlin 2004, 367–408.—[12] A survey of the history of interaction is given by Hellige, Hans Dieter: "Krisen- und Innovationsphasen in der Mensch-Computer-Interaktion," in: Hellige (ed.): *Mensch-Computer-Interface. Zur Geschichte und*

in Zukunft treffsicher erkennen soll, wenn sie nicht mehr spielerisch, sondern ernst und „so gemeint" sind. Walter Benjamins Diktum, dass die Geste „nur in gewissem Grade verfälschbar [ist], und zwar je unauffälliger und gewohnheitsmäßiger sie ist"[37], findet hier ein unerwartetes Ende. (*12* S. 151)

Interessanter würde die Sache sicherlich in umgekehrter Richtung, sobald sich nämlich die Effekte von gestengetriebener *surveillance* in die Körper eingraben. Denn wie von den Suchmaschinen des WWW sattsam bekannt, wird nur das gefunden, was auch maschinenlesbar vorliegt. Man könnte daher den Umkehrschluss wagen, dass zukünftig auch nur erkannt werden wird, was sich maschinenerkennbar bewegt. Seit es Überlegungen zur Bewegungserkennung von Autoknackern in Tiefgaragen gibt,[38] sollte man als Autoknacker ein Körpertraining erwägen, das einen nicht mehr als solchen erkennbar und damit unsichtbar macht. Und vielleicht müssen zukünftig auch Vergewaltigungsopfer in Tiefgaragen lernen, sich opfermäßig zu bewegen, um von der automatisierten Security als solche wahrgenommen zu werden. Trainingsfelder der maschinenlesbaren und dennoch als „frei" (oder zumindest im Vergleich zu Joystick und Gamepad als befreiend) empfundenen Bewegung sind dabei Computerspiele. Der Unterschied von Fertigkeit (zum Beispiel Kegeln) und Bedeutung (zum Beispiel Aggression), wie ihn etwa auch Ian Bogost für Gesten macht,[39] könnte hier eine Irritation oder gar Dekonstruktion erfahren. PlayStation Move und eyeToy, Nintendo Wii oder Microsoft Kinect üben bewegungsmäßiges Wohlverhalten in den „Augen" des Beobachters (alias Überwachungskamera) ein – letztere gar mit dem verführerischen Slogan „you are the controller".

Nicht nur die „Aufführungsforschung", wie es in der Theaterwissenschaft heißt, könnte hier ein reiches Material vorfinden, das eben nicht auf der Besonderheit „leiblicher Kopräsenz" insistiert, sondern durch Formen maschineller „Aufführungsforschung" zur methodischen Selbstreflexion herausgefordert wird. Dies gilt vielleicht für die Kulturwissenschaft im allgemeinen, für deren Formen der Körpergeschichtsschreibung solche informatischen Verfahren und Modelle von einigem Interesse sein könnten. Projekte wie das hier exemplarisch erwähnte CASSANDRA sind selbst eine Form der Analyse kultureller Bewegungsmuster – oder zugespitzter gesagt: Sie sind Forschungen zum Körperwissen jenseits der geisteswissenschaftlichen Forschung. Die Arbeitswissenschaft der 1920er Jahre hatte sehr wohl ein (utopisches) Bewusstsein davon, dass sie nicht nur Bewegungen analysiert, sondern durch die Gestaltung von Bewegungsmustern zugleich eine Art umfassendes Mentalitätsdesign leistet. Die informatischen Gestenerkennungssysteme von heute (sei es nun im Interfacedesign oder in der Überwachung) leisten ähnliches, aber man fragt sich, ob die Sache dadurch besser wird, dass sie nicht mehr wissen, was sie tun.

Zukunft der Computerbedienung. Bielefeld 2008, 11–92.—[13] English, William K./Engelbart, Douglas C./Berman, Melvyn L.: "Display Selection Techniques for Text Manipulation," in: *IEEE Transactions on Human Factors in Electronics,* HFE- 8(1), 03/1967, 5–15.—[14] Roch, Axel: "Die Maus. Von der elektronischen zur taktischen Feuerleitung," in: *LAB. Jahrbuch für Künste und Apparate.* 1996, 167.—[15] Davis, M.R./Ellis, T.O.: "The RAND Tablet: A Man-Machine Graphical Communication Device," in: *RAND RM-4122-ARPA.* Santa Monica, August 1964.—[16] Bolter, Jay David/Grusin, Richard: *Remediation. Understanding New Media.* Cambridge, MA. 2000.—[17] Mermelstein, Paul/Eyden, Murray: "A System for Automatic Recognition of Handwritten Words," in: *Proceedings of the Fall Joint Computer Conference.* San Francisco, 27–29 October 1964, 333–342.—[18] Sutherland, Ivan: *Sketchpad: A Man-Machine Graphical Communication System.* Technical Report No. 296, Lincoln Laboratory, MIT, 30. January 1963; cf. on Sutherland, recently Margarethe Pratschke: *Windows als Tableau. Zur Bildgeschichte grafischer Benutzeroberflächen.* Diss. HU Berlin 2011, 14–28.—[19] First interest in the designing movement of the hand came at the end of the nineteen-sixties in the highly utopian experiments of the "Architecture Machine Group" around Nicholas Negroponte at MIT. Cf. Weckherlin, Gernot: "Architekturmaschinen und wissenschaftliches Entwerfen," and Pias, Claus: "Jenseits des Werkzeugs" in: Gethmann, D./Hauser, S. (eds.): *Kulturtechnik Entwerfen.* Bielefeld 2009, 203–226, 269–286.—[20] Wellner, Pierre: "Interacting with Paper on a Digital Desk," in: *Communications of the ACM,* 36/1993, 87–96. The somewhat later counterpart at XEROX PARC was called "Active Desk." The stimulus came from the development of *electronic whiteboards,* i.e., interactive boards which were used for experiments as from the nineteen-seventies. They worked with video (re)projections in circa 1990. The desks turn these boards onto the horizontal plane, as it were. One ought not to forget Apple's *science fiction* of the speech-controlled *Knowledge Navigator* at that time, e.g., at http://www.youtube.com/watch?v=bwP4vBgHixI (last access 5.2.2011).—[21] The demo-video can be found at: http://www.youtube.com/watch?v=S8lCetZ_57g (last access 5.2.2011).—[22] This idea is being continued to the present day: Mistry, Pranav/Maes, P.: "Mouseless: A Computer Mouse as Small as Invisible," in: CHI2011, Vancouver 2011 at http://www.pranavmistry.com/projects/mouseless/ (last access 5.2.2011).—[23] Gilbreth, Frank B.: *Bewegungsstudien. Vorschläge zur Steigerung der Leistungsfähigkeit des Arbeiters.* Berlin 1921, 37.—[24] So that differentiated (and differentiating) working clothes could also be abandoned in favour of general "sportswear" (ibid., 48).—[25] A comprehensive survey is given by Buxton, Bill: *Sketching User Experiences: Getting the Design Right and the Right Design.* San Francisco 2007; Buxton: "A Touching Story: A Personal Perspective on the History of Touch Interfaces Past and Future," in: *SID Symposium Digest of Technical Papers,* 41/1 (2010), 444–448; as well as his extensive collection of material: "Human Input to Computer Systems: Theories, Techniques and Technology" at http://www.billbuxton.com/inputManuscript.html (last access 5.2.2011).—[26] Cf. Buxton, William/Hill, Ralph/Rowley, Peter: "Issues and Techniques in Touch-Sensitive Tablet Input," in: *Computer Graphics (Proceedings of SIGGRAPH '85),* 19/3 (1985), 215–223.—[27] One well worth seeing is the Ocarina concert at http://www.youtube.com/watch?v=kfrONZjakRY (latest access 5.2.2011).—[28] Westerman, Wayne (1999): *Hand Tracking, Finger Identification, And Chordic Manipulation On A Multi-Touch Surface.* Diss., University of Delaware.—[29] Want, Roy/Schilit, Bill/N., Norman/I Adams et al.: "The PARCtab Ubiquitous Computing Experiment," in: Imielinski, T./Korth, H.F. (eds.): *Mobile Computing.* Boston/Dordrecht 1996, 45–102 (Patent Submission 1995).—[30] Cf. Pias, Claus: "Digitale Sekretäre: 1968, 1978, 1998," in: Siegert B./ Vogl J. (eds.): *Europa. Kultur der Sekretäre,* Zurich/Berlin 2003, 235–251.—[31] Johansson, G.: "Visual Perception of Biological Motion and a Model for its Analysis," in: Perception & Psychophysics, 14/1973, 201–211.—[32] Kozlowski, L.T./Cutting, J.E.: "Recognizing the Sex of a Walker

ANMERKUNGEN—[1] Jung, Keechul: „Recognition-Based Gesture Spotting in Video Games", in: Kang, Hyun/Lee, Chang Woo (Hg.): *Pattern Recognition Letters,* 2004, 1701–1714.—[2] Vgl. zuletzt Wulf, Christoph/Fischer-Lichte, Erika (Hg.): *Gesten: Inszenierung, Aufführung, Praxis,* München 2010.—[3] Heilmann, Till: „Digitalität als Taktilität. McLuhan, der Computer und die Taste", in: *Zeitschrift für Medienwissenschaft,* 2/2010, 131–140; Bickenbach, Matthias: „Knopfdruck und Auswahl", in: *LiLi,* 117, 2000, 9–32; Engell, Lorenz: „Tasten, Wählen, Denken" in: Münker, S./Roesler, A./Sandbothe, M. (Hg.): *Medienphilosophie: Beiträge zur Klärung eines Begriffs,* Frankfurt am Main 2003, 53–77; „Leider fehlt das Tastendrücken" in: Flusser, Vilém: *Kompendium Gesten. Versuch einer Phänomenologie,* Düsseldorf 1991.—[4] Vgl. die Unterscheidung von Nespoulous, J.L./Perron, P./Roch Lecours, A.: *The Biological Foundations of Gestures: Motor and Semiotic Aspects,* Hillsdale 1986; und Kendon, Adam: *Gesture, Visible Action as Utterance.* Cambridge 2004.—[5] Vgl. zum Beispiel Behrenshausen, Bryan G.: „Toward a (Kin)aesthetic of Video Gaming: The Case of Dance Dance Revolution", in: *Games and Culture,* 2–4/2007, 335–354; Crogan, Patrick: „The Nintendo Wii, Virtualisation And Gestural Analogics", in: *Culture Machine,* 11/2010, 82–101; Giddings, Seth/Kennedy, Helen W.: „Incremental Speed Increases Excitement: Bodies, Space, Movement and Televisual Change", in: *The Journal of Television and New Media,* 11.3.2010; Swalwell, M.: „Movement and Kinaesthetic Responsiveness: A Neglected Pleasure", in: Swalwell, M./Wilson, J. (Hg.): *The Pleasures of Computer Gaming: Essays on Cultural History, Theory and Aesthetics,* Jefferson, NC 2008, 72-93.—[6] Bogost, Ian: „Persuasive Games: Gestures as Meaning", auf http://www.gamasutra.com/view/feature/4064/persuasive_games_gestures_as_. php?print=1 (letzter Zugriff: 5.2.2011).—[7] Simon, Bart (3.2009): „Wii are Out of Control: Bodies, Game Screens and the Production of Gestural Excess", auf http://ssrn.com/abstract=1354043 (letzter Zugriff: 5.2.2011)—[8] Auf http://kinectionlost.com (letzter Zugriff: 5.2.2011).—[9] Pias, Claus: „Maschinen – Sprachen", in: Bäumler, T./Bühler, B./Rieger, S. (Hg.): *Nicht Fisch – nicht Fleisch. Ordnungssysteme und ihre Störfälle,* Zürich/Berlin 2011, 187-208.—[10] Fisher, Robert B.: „Compendium of Computer Vision", auf http://homepages.inf.ed.ac.uk/rbf/CVonline/ (letzter Zugriff: 5.2.2011).—[11] Im Sinne von Pflüger, Jörg: „Konversation, Manipulation, Delegation. Zur Ideengeschichte der Interaktivität", in: Hellige, H.D. (Hg.): *Geschichten der Informatik. Visionen, Paradigmen, Leitmotive,* Berlin 2004, 367–408.—[12] Einen Überblick zur Geschichte der Interaktion gibt Hellige, Hans Dieter: „Krisen- und Innovationsphasen in der Mensch-Computer-Interaktion", in: ders. (Hg.): *Mensch-Computer-Interface. Zur Geschichte und Zukunft der Computerbedienung,* Bielefeld 2008, 11–92.—[13] English, William K./Engelbart, Douglas C./Berman, Melvyn L.: „Display Selection Techniques for Text Manipulation", in: *IEEE Transactions on Human Factors in Electronics,* HFE- 8(1), 03/1967, 5–15.—[14] Roch, Axel: „Die Maus. Von der elektronischen zur taktischen Feuerleitung" in: *LAB. Jahrbuch für Künste und Apparate,* 1996, 167.—[15] Davis, M.R./Ellis, T.O.: „The RAND Tablet: A Man-Machine Graphical Communication Device", *in RAND RM-4122-ARPA.* Santa Monica, August 1964.—[16] Bolter, Jay David/Grusin, Richard: *Remediation. Understanding New Media,* Cambridge, Mass. 2000.—[17] Mermelstein, Paul/Eyden, Murray: „A System for Automatic Recognition of Handwritten Words", in: *Proceedings of the Fall Joint Computer Conference,* San Francisco, 27.–29. Oktober 1964, 333–342.—[18] Sutherland, Ivan: *Sketchpad: A Man-Machine Graphical Communication System,* Technical Report No. 296, Lincoln Laboratory, MIT, 30. Januar 1963.; vgl. zu Sutherland jüngst Pratschke, Margarethe: *Windows als Tableau. Zur Bildgeschichte grafischer Benutzeroberflächen,* Diss. HU Berlin 2011, 14–28.—[19] Um die entwerfende Bewegung der Hand ging es erst Ende der 1960er in den utopisch aufgeladenen Experimenten der „Architecture Machine Group" des MIT um Nicholas Negroponte. Vgl. Weckherlin, Gernot: „Architekturmaschinen und wissenschaftliches Entwerfen", sowie Pias, Claus: „Jenseits des Werkzeugs", in Gethmann, D./

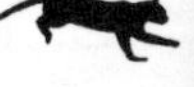

from a Dynamic Point-Light Display," in: *Perception & Psychophysics,* 21/1977, 575–580; Cutting, J.E./ Kozlowski, L.T.: "Recognizing Friends by Their Walk: Gait Perception Without Familiarity Cues," in: *Bulletin of the Psychonomic Society,* 9/1977, 353–356.—[33] "Gait-Recognition Biometric Technology to Help Soldiers Manning Checkpoints," in: *Homeland Security Newswire,* 5 November 2009.—[34] Nixon, Mark/Tan,Tieniu/Chellappa, Rama: *Human Identification Based on Gait,* New York 2005; Meyer, Iris: "Erkennung von micro-expressions," a lecture given at *HyperKult 17: Ordnungen des Wissens,* 3-4 July 2008, at http://weblab.uni-lueneburg.de/kulturinformatik/hyperkult/archiv/hk_17/imeyer.mp4 (last access 5.2.2011).—[35] Zajdel, W./Krijnders, J.D./Andringa, T./Gavrila, D.M.: "CASSANDRA: Audio-Video Sensor Fusion for Aggression Detection" in: *IEEE Conference on Advanced Video and Signal Based Surveillance,* London 2007, 200–205.—[36] Cohen, Charles J./Scott, Katherine A./Huber, Marcus J. et al. : "Behavior Recognition Architecture for Surveillance Applications," in: *37th IEEE Applied Imagery Pattern Recognition Workshop,* Washington 2008, 1–8.—[37] Benjamin, Walter: Gesammelte Schriften, ed. by Tiedemann, R./Schweppenhäuser, H. Frankfurt/Main 1971–1989, Vol. II, 521.—[38] Gavrila, D.M.: "The Visual Analysis of Human Movement: A Survey," in: *Computer Vision and Image Understanding,* 73/1 (1999), 82–98, here 83.—[39] Cf. Note 7.

Hauser, S. (Hg.): *Kulturtechnik Entwerfen,* Bielefeld 2009, 203–226, 269–286.—[20] Wellner, Pierre: „Interacting With Paper on a Digital Desk", in: *Communications of the ACM,* 36 (1993), 87–96. Das etwas spätere Gegenstück am XEROX PARC hieß „Active Desk". Die Anregung kam aus der Entwicklung von *electronic whiteboards,* also interaktiven Tafeln, mit denen seit den 1970ern experimentiert wurde und die um 1990 mit Video(rück)projektion arbeiteten. Die *desks* drehen die Tafel gewissermaßen in die Horizontale. Nicht zu vergessen ist Apples *science fiction* des sprachgesteuerten *Knowledge Navigator* zu dieser Zeit, zum Beispiel auf http://www.youtube.com/watch?v–bwP4vBgHixl (letzter Zugriff 5.2.2011).—[21] Das Demo-Video findet sich unter: http://www.youtube.com/watch?v–S8lCetZ_57g (letzter Zugriff 5.2.2011).—[22] Diese Idee schreibt sich übrigens bis heute fort: Mistry, Pranav/Maes, P.: „Mouseless: A Computer Mouse as Small as Invisble", in: CHI2011, Vancouver 2011 auf http://www.pranavmistry.com/projects/mouseless/ (letzter Zugriff 5.2.2011).—[23] Gilbreth, Frank B.: *Bewegungsstudien. Vorschläge zur Steigerung der Leistungsfähigkeit des Arbeiters,* Berlin 1921, 37.—[24] Sodass auch die differierende (und differenzierende) Berufskleidung zugunsten allgemeiner „Sportanzüge" abgeschafft werden könne (ebd., 48).—[25] Die umfassendste Übersicht gibt Buxton, Bill: *Sketching User Experiences: Getting the Design Right and the Right Design,* San Francisco 2007; ders.: „A Touching Story: A Personal Perspective on the History of Touch Interfaces Past and Future", in: *SID Symposium Digest of Technical Papers,* 41/1 (2010), 444–448; sowie seine reiche Materialsammlung: „Human Input to Computer Systems: Theories, Techniques and Technology", auf http://www.billbuxton.com/inputManuscript.html (letzter Zugriff 5.2.2011).—[26] Vgl. Buxton, William/Hill, Ralph/Rowley, Peter: „Issues and Techniques in Touch-Sensitive Tablet Input", in: *Computer Graphics (Proceedings of SIGGRAPH '85),* 19/3 (1985), 215–223.—[27] Besonders sehenswert ist das Ocarina-Konzert auf http://www.youtube.com/watch?v–kfrONZjakRY (letzter Zugriff 5.2.2011).—[28] Westerman, Wayne: *Hand Tracking, Finger Identification, And Chordic Manipulation On A Multi-Touch Surface,* Diss., University of Delaware 1999.—[29] Want, Roy/Schilit, Bill/ Norman, N./Adams, I. (u.a.): „The PARCtab Ubiquitous Computing Experiment", in: Imielinski, T./Korth, H.F. (Hg.): *Mobile Computing,* Boston/Dordrecht 1996, 45–102 (Patenteinreichung 1995).—[30] Vgl. Pias, Claus: „Digitale Sekretäre: 1968, 1978, 1998", in: Siegert B./ Vogl J. (Hg.): *Europa. Kultur der Sekretäre,* Zürich/Berlin 2003, 235-251—[31] Johansson, G.: „Visual Perception of Biological Motion and a Model for its Analysis", in: *Perception & Psychophysics,* 14 (1973), 201–211.—[32] Kozlowski, L.T./Cutting, J.E.: „Recognizing the Sex of a Walker From a Dynamic Point-Light Display", in: *Perception & Psychophysics,* 21 (1977), 575–580; Cutting, J.E./ Kozlowski, L.T.: „Recognizing Friends by Their Walk: Gait Perception Without Familiarity Cues", in: *Bulletin of the Psychonomic Society,* 9 (1977), 353–356.—[33] „Gait-Recognition Biometric Technology to Help Soldiers Manning Checkpoints", in: *Homeland Security Newswire,* 5. November 2009.—[34] Nixon, Mark/Tan,Tieniu/Chellappa, Rama: *Human Identification Based on Gait,* New York 2005; Meyer, Iris: „Erkennung von ‚micro-expressions'", Vortrag bei *HyperKult 17: Ordnungen des Wissens,* 3.-4. Juli 2008, auf http://weblab.uni-lueneburg.de/kulturinformatik/hyperkult/archiv/hk_17/imeyer.mp4 (letzter Zugriff 5.2.2011).—[35] Zajdel, W./Krijnders, J.D./Andringa, T./Gavrila, D.M.: „CASSANDRA: Audio-Video Sensor Fusion for Aggression Detection", in: *IEEE Conference on Advanced Video and Signal Based Surveillance,* London 2007, 200–205.—[36] Cohen, Charles J./Scott, Katherine A./ Huber, Marcus J. u.a. : „Behavior Recognition Architecture for Surveillance Applications", in: *37th IEEE Applied Imagery Pattern Recognition Workshop,* Washington 2008, 1-8.—[37] Benjamin, Walter: *Gesammelte Schriften,* hrsg. von Tiedemann, R./Schweppenhäuser, H., Frankfurt/Main 1971–1989, Bd. II, 521.—[38] Gavrila, D.M.: „The Visual Analysis of Human Movement: A Survey", in: *Computer Vision and Image Understanding,* 73/1 (1999), 82–98, hier 83.—[39] Vgl. Anm. 7

Stephan Rammler
The Reinvention of Mobility. The Politics of Mobility as World Design

Stephan Rammler has been professor of "Transportation Design & Social Sciences" at the HBK Brunswick since 2002, having set up the college's specialist diploma subject and master's degree course of the same name. In 2007 he was a founding director of the ITD (Institute for Transportation Design). His specialist fields include mobility and futurology research, transport, energy and innovation policies, questions of cultural transformation, and sustainable environmental and social politics. In 2009 he was commissioned to set up a specialist field of research into "Cultural Transformation Processes" at the HBK Brunswick.

Stephan Rammler
Die Neuerfindung der Mobilität. Mobilitätspolitik als Weltdesign

Stephan Rammler ist seit 2002 Professor für **Transportation Design & Social** Sciences an der HBK Braunschweig und baute dort den gleichnamigen Dip- lomstudienschwerpunkt und Masterstudiengang auf. **Seit 2007 ist er Grün-** dungsdirektor des ITD. **Seine Arbeitsschwerpunkte sind die Mobilitäts- und** Zukunftsforschung, Verkehrs-, Energie- und Innovationspolitik, **Fragen kultu-** reller Transformation und zukunftsfähiger **Umwelt- und Gesellschaftspolitik.** Seit 2009 ist er beauftragt, einen Forschungsschwerpunkt „kulturelle Trans- formationsprozesse" an der HBK Braunschweig aufzubauen.

Mobility and modernity determine each other reciprocally: one is quite inconceivable without the other. This relation may be described as an "affinity between modern social development and growth in mobility." This means reciprocal permeation and development with respect to the emergence and spread of modern society and the permanently growing opportunities and demands for mobility, as well as their implementation in a dynamic, rising transport capacity. Continually progressing social differentiation and economic division of labour creates traffic, which enables the spatiotemporal integration of spheres of activity and the economy which are becoming ever more differentiated. The other way around, traffic and the opportunities for mobility it provides are what facilitate new differentiations and thus a modernisation of society and further division of labour. This connection is valid to equal degrees with respect to both human and goods traffic. To put it bluntly, traffic is what holds together the modern world while simultaneously driving it apart.[1]

The automobile plays a special role as a spatiotemporal, integrating mechanism of the permanently advancing processes of individualisation, flexibilisation, and pluralisation. The further the individualisation, temporal equalisation, and de-timing of spatiotemporal paths progresses, the more our choice of transport is dependent on its power to enable autonomy and flexibility. To put it another way: the more *self-mobility* a means of transport allows, the more attractive it becomes to the user. This is the essential reason for the success of the motor car, besides a growth in prosperity, an increase in freedom, and the symbolic-expressive aspects of identity creation, differentiation, and social integration.

Spatial and temporal structures with an affinity to the motor car evolved as a consequence of this reciprocal impact between modernisation and motorisation, and within these structures, the realisation of modern societies' promise of freedom and prosperity became tied more and more closely to the use of the car and its infrastructural and institutional preconditions. Here, it is not only a matter of the expansion of freedoms associated with the (auto-) mobile, but above all of forming overall cultural dependencies on (auto-) mobility or, to be more exact, of automobility as a social model from which a range of differing lifestyles and orientations of meaning have developed. Now, automobility as a sociocultural system is permanently *bequeathed:* as the structured quality of the material and institutional contexts of activity, as the dressing and impregnating of automobile-related, subjective concepts of activity, key images, lifestyles, and habits. This link between the structural and the active dimensions of mobility behaviour explains the enormous stability of automobile lifestyles.[2]

One might say that we live in a *constructed* world. By investigating his own inner and outer nature, man has shaped and fixed his environment. In this way every stone used in building, every metre of asphalt, every ton of steel tracks, every port, airfield, station, every production plant and settlement has become a datum of future development. Transport economist Voigt coined the term "anteludial effects" to describe the

Mobilität und Moderne bedingen sich gegenseitig. Das eine ist ohne das andere nicht denkbar. Man kann dieses Verhältnis als „Wahlverwandtschaft zwischen moderner Gesellschaftsentwicklung und Mobilitätswachstum" bezeichnen. Gemeint ist die gegenseitige Durchdringung und Beförderung bei der Entstehung und Ausbreitung der modernen Gesellschaft und der stetigen Steigerung von Mobilitätschancen und -anforderungen sowie ihre Umsetzung in eine dynamisch steigende Verkehrsleistung. Die immer weitergehende soziale Differenzierung und ökonomische Arbeitsteilung erzeugt Verkehr, der die raumzeitliche Integration der sich ausdifferenzierenden Handlungs- und Wirtschaftssphären ermöglicht. Umgekehrt sind es der Verkehr und die durch ihn eingeräumten Mobilitätschancen, die weitere Ausdifferenzierungen und damit gesellschaftliche Modernisierung und Arbeitsteilung erst ermöglichen. Dieser Zusammenhang gilt für Personen- wie Güterverkehr gleichermaßen. Zugespitzt ist Verkehr also das, was die moderne Welt zusammenhält und zugleich auseinander treibt.[1]

Das Auto spielt eine besondere Rolle als raumzeitliche Integrationsmaschine der immer weiter voranschreitenden Individualisierungs-, Flexibilisierungs- und Pluralisierungsprozesse. Je stärker die Vereinzelung, zeitliche Entzerrung und Enttaktung von Raum-Zeit-Pfaden fortschreitet, desto mehr wird das Maß der Ermöglichung von Autonomie und Flexibilität auch für die Verkehrsmittelwahl zu einem zentralen Entscheidungskriterium. Anders formuliert: Je mehr *Selbstbeweglichkeit* ein Verkehrsmittel ermöglicht, desto attraktiver wird es für 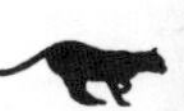 den Nutzer. Dies ist neben Wohlstandswachstum, Freizeitzuwachs und den symbolisch-expressiven Aspekten der Identitätsstiftung, Distinktion und Sozialintegration der wesentliche Grund für den Erfolg des Autos.

Als Folge dieser Wechselwirkung von Modernisierung und Motorisierung entstanden autoaffine Raum- und Zeitstrukturen, in denen die Verwirklichung der Freiheits- und Wohlstandsversprechen moderner Gesellschaften immer enger an die Nutzung des Autos und dessen infrastrukturelle und institutionelle Voraussetzungen gekoppelt wurden. Es geht dabei nicht nur um die Ausweitung (auto-)mobiler Freiheiten, sondern vor allem um die Ausprägung gesamtkultureller Abhängigkeiten von der (Auto-)Mobilität, eben um die Automobilität als Gesellschaftsmodell, aus dem sich eine Vielfalt von Lebensstilen und Sinnorientierungen entwickelt hat. Automobilität als soziokulturelles System wird nun immer weiter *vererbt*: als Strukturiertheit der materiellen und institutionellen Handlungskontexte, als Zurichtung und Imprägnierung der automobilbezogenen subjektiven Handlungskonzepte, Leitbilder, Lebensstile und Gewohnheiten. Diese Kopplung der Struktur- und Handlungsdimension des Mobilitätsverhaltens ist die Erklärung für die enorme Stabilität automobiler Lebensstile.[2]

Man kann sagen: Wir leben in einer *gemachten* Welt. In Auseinandersetzung mit seiner inneren und äußeren Natur hat der Mensch seine Umwelt geprägt und festgeschrieben. Jeder verbaute Stein, Meter Asphalt, jede Tonne Schienenstahl, jeder Hafen, Flugplatz, Bahnhof, jede Produktionsanlage und Siedlung werden damit

impact of transport systems on design, which is caused by fixing "which may perhaps have been justified in its time, but—in case of any possible or actual improvement to transport values—has had the impact of binding or a counter force against the developmental trend of the basic structure since then."[3] A transport system, once in place, therefore, cannot be removed again without immense difficulty. The same applies to the mental dispositions of modern man. Every action, every thought, every constantly stimulating emotion contributes to the creation of mental patterns, and the more often these are implemented, thought and felt, and the more generations have been socialised in this particular sense, the more stable and resistant they become to any efforts for change. Actions become habits and habits become institutions, which may be more steadfast than any steel infrastructures. In this way, beginnings have great power over the future. This applies always and everywhere—to changes in the structure of mobility as well. Usually, transport sciences have concerned themselves with the visible structures: engineers as the object of their design efforts, economists as the subject of their calculations, researchers in transport politics as the subject of control considerations. Only the social sciences have begun—with the concepts of structure, habit, and routine among their theoretical ballast—to include mental shaping and disposition in their explanation of the structure of modern mobility.[4] Those who wish to implement transport policies today, therefore, need to face up to the momentous fact that we are imprisoned not only within our material infrastructures, but also within our social institutions and subjective habits.

As a logical next step, the present outcome might be concentration on creating a sustainable development of mobility. However, the renewed question is, do we know everything we need to know in order to design mobility successfully? For although we can see mobility's historic derivation and explain why its development will follow a stable path under *ceteris paribus* conditions, we still have problems looking into the future. The future has never been less transparent than now. Besides fundamental limitations when analysing the future, this is because the future we are entering now appears highly contingent. It is more difficult to grasp than the future was even one or two decades ago. In this situation, the previous concepts explaining mobility could rapidly become unusable because the social frame of reference that determined them via reciprocal effects—their *affinitive* opposite—has been exhausted and outlived itself. The probability of this becoming reality increases from day to day.

We have reached the end of mobility as we know it. Fossil-driven passage through space is a historic episode that is now coming to an end. The combined cultural model of mass automobile motorisation and suburban forms of living is heading towards a dead-end as well.

But the demand for mobility is growing, and the world's fleet of private cars will have almost doubled by 2030. This means that combustion and emissions could have more than doubled by 2050.[5] Researchers predict that we are heading for the worst climate change scenario if these

zum Datum zukünftiger Entwicklung. Der Verkehrsökonom Voigt[3] prägte den Begriff der „Anteludialeffekte" für die Gestaltungswirkungen von Verkehrssystemen, die durch Festlegungen hervorgerufen wurden, „die seinerzeit vielleicht berechtigt gewesen sein mögen, sich aber seitdem bei möglicher oder tatsächlicher Verbesserung der Verkehrswertigkeit als Fessel oder Gegenkraft gegen die Tendenz der Entwicklung der Grundstruktur auswirken". Ein Verkehrssystem, das einmal existiert, kann also nicht ohne Weiteres wieder beseitigt werden. Gleiches gilt für die mentalen Dispositionen des modernen Menschen. Jede Handlung, jeder Gedanke, jede stetig erregende Emotion trägt zur Ausprägung mentaler Muster bei und diese werden umso stabiler und resistenter gegen Veränderungsbemühungen, je häufiger sie getätigt, gedacht und empfunden und je mehr Generationen in ihrem Sinne sozialisiert wurden. Handlungen werden zu Gewohnheiten und Gewohnheiten zu Institutionen, die beharrungsmächtiger sein können als stählerne Infrastrukturen. So haben die Anfänge große Macht über die Zukunft. Das gilt immer und überall, auch für Veränderungen der Mobilitätskultur. Meist haben sich die Verkehrswissenschaften mit den sichtbaren Strukturen beschäftigt: Die Ingenieure als Gegenstand ihrer Gestaltungsbemühungen, die Ökonomen als Gegenstand ihrer Berechnungen, die Verkehrspolitikforschung als Gegenstand ihrer Steuerungsüberlegungen. Erst die Sozialwissenschaften haben begonnen – die Konzepte von Struktur, Habitus und Routine im theoretischen Gepäck –, mentale Prägungen und Dispositionen in ihre Erklärung der modernen Mobilitätskultur einzubeziehen.[4] Wer nun also Verkehrspolitik betreiben will, wird sich mit der folgenreichen Tatsache konfrontiert sehen, dass wir nicht nur im Käfig unserer materiellen Infrastrukturen, sondern auch unserer sozialen Institutionen und subjektiven Gewohnheiten leben.

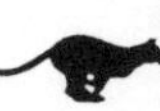

Als folgerichtiger Schritt ergäbe sich nun die Konzentration auf die Frage der Gestaltung einer nachhaltigen Mobilitätsentwicklung. Doch sei erneut gefragt, ob wir alles wissen, um Mobilität gestalten zu können. Denn: Wir können Mobilität historisch herleiten und erklären, warum ihre Entwicklung unter *ceteris paribus* Bedingungen einem stabilen Entwicklungspfad folgen wird, doch haben wir Probleme beim Blick in die Zukunft. Nie war Zukunft weniger transparent. Das liegt neben prinzipiellen Grenzen der Zukunftsanalyse daran, dass sich die Zukunft, in die wir hineingehen, höchst kontingent darstellt. Sie ist schwerer zu fassen, als Zukunft noch vor ein oder zwei Jahrzehnten zu erfassen war. In dieser Situation könnten die bisherigen Erklärungskonzepte zur Mobilität schnell genau deswegen unbrauchbar werden, weil der sie wechselwirksam bestimmende gesellschaftliche Referenzrahmen, ihr wahlverwandtschaftliches Gegenüber, sich erschöpft und selbst überlebt. Die Wahrscheinlichkeit, dass dieser Fall eintritt, wird von Tag zu Tag größer.

Wir sind am Ende der uns bekannten Mobilität. Die fossil befeuerte Raumüberwindung ist eine historische Episode, die gerade zu Ende geht. Auch das kombinierte

trends continue. But this problem could cause a reduced sense of urgency towards a much more dangerous development: in fact, the finite nature of fossil resources should be the main issue in the current discussion on mobility, since it presents an incomparably greater crisis potential than climate change in the short to mid term. Although the two are closely linked, the provision of energy is the fateful question of the twenty-first-century. Tackling it means tackling the key to many other problems and indeed remaining capable of action at all—in the climate question as well. In 2007 58 per cent of the worldwide demand for crude oil was created by the sphere of transport. This means that there is intense competition for crude oil in this sector, in road transport in particular. Today wars are not least waged to keep the transport sector alive as the vital motor behind our societies.[6] This fossil mobility with its ecological and geopolitical consequences increases the risk of global destabilisation to a horrendous extent. It means that mobility design that saves resources also represents a key parameter in defence against the dangers to security that result from our dependence on crude oil.

The majority of the world's population lives in urban regions. Future population growth will also be concentrated in urban areas. Cities are laboratories of modernisation; they are both a forum and medium of modern ways of life, gigantic wheels of interlocking systems that regulate housing, work, consumption, and mobility. That means that the future of mobility will be decided in the city of the future.[7] We should not underestimate the rotten state of our urban service infrastructures. They need to be modernised, and capital will also be required to build up new infrastructures for regenerative energy. User-specific solutions, also with respect to the ageing of the population, will have to be sought in the field of *universal design,* that is, in the design of mobility systems to span all age groups. Demographic change also brings a change in settlement patterns, which heightens the difficult matter of possible financing for public transport infrastructures.

The interim conclusion may be formulated quite simply: a growing number of people, who are getting older and older, live in an increasingly restricted space, consuming more and more resources and thereby creating more and more emissions. While the overtaxing of its ecological systems is leading the earth towards irreversible damage, the limits of geopolitical and cultural tenability are being reached due to competition for resources and a de-levelling of social situations brought about by the unequal distribution of wealth and mortal risks. In this way, such rapid dynamics of transformation are evolving that the world—viewed in a simple, empirical way— will no longer be the world we know in the foreseeable future. In other words, we find ourselves in a period of transition to the "world survival society." The "world risk society," according to Ulrich Beck,[8] is defined by risks produced by this society itself. Going further than this definition, I would define the "world survival society" as the final worsening of modernisation's reflexive consequences to raise the question of mankind's survival. The transition comes about when risks turn into

Kulturmodell von automobiler Massenmotorisierung und suburbaner Lebensform steckt in einer Sackgasse.

Doch: Der Mobilitätsbedarf wächst, die weltweite Pkw-Flotte wird sich bis 2030 fast verdoppeln. Damit könnten sich Verbrauch und Emissionen bis 2050 mehr als verdoppeln.[5] Forscher sagen voraus, dass wir uns auf das schlimmste Szenario des Klimawandels zubewegen, wenn sich diese Trends fortsetzen. Dennoch könnte angesichts dieses Problems der Sinn für die Dringlichkeit einer weitaus gefährlicheren Entwicklung verloren gehen: Die Endlichkeit fossiler Ressourcen sollte deswegen das Hauptthema in der gegenwärtigen Mobilitätsdiskussion sein, weil sie kurz- und mittelfristig ein ungleich größeres Krisenpotenzial aufweist als der Klimawandel. Gleichwohl beides eng verknüpft ist, ist die Energieversorgung die Schicksalsfrage des 21. Jahrhunderts. Sie anzugehen bedeutet, den Schlüssel zu vielen anderen Problemen anzupacken und überhaupt handlungsfähig zu bleiben, auch in der Klimafrage. 2007 wurden 58 Prozent des weltweiten Erdölbedarfs vom Transportbereich erzeugt. Damit ist dieser Sektor und besonders der Straßentransport Triebkraft intensiver Konkurrenz um Erdöl. Kriege werden heute auch darum geführt, den Transportsektor als Lebensmotor unserer Gesellschaften am Leben zu halten.[6] Diese fossile Mobilität mit ihren ökologischen und geopolitischen Folgen befördert das Risiko globaler Destabilisierungen ungeheuren Ausmaßes. Damit stellt die Ressourcen sparende Gestaltung von Mobilität auch im Bereich der Abwehr der sicherheitspolitischen Gefahren der Erdölabhängigkeit eine zentrale Stellschraube dar. 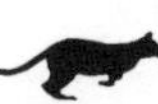

Der größere Anteil der Weltbevölkerung lebt in urbanen Regionen. Auch das kommende Bevölkerungswachstum konzentriert sich in den Stadtregionen. Städte sind Modernisierungslaboratorien, sind Forum und Medium moderner Lebensweise, gigantische Räderwerke ineinandergreifender Systeme zur Regulierung von Wohnen, Arbeiten, Konsum und Mobilität. Das heißt, dass die Zukunft der Mobilität in der Stadt der Zukunft entschieden wird.[7] Nicht unterschätzen sollten wir den maroden Zustand der urbanen Versorgungsinfrastrukturen. Sie müssen modernisiert werden. Auch wird Kapital benötigt, um neue Infrastrukturen für die regenerative Energie aufzubauen. Nutzerspezifische Antworten auch hinsichtlich einer zunehmenden Alterung der Bevölkerung werden im Bereich des *Universal Design,* also der altersgruppenübergreifenden Gestaltung von Mobilitätssystemen zu suchen sein. Demografischer Wandel bringt zudem die Veränderung der Siedlungsmuster mit sich, was die Frage der Finanzierbarkeit von öffentlichen Verkehrsinfrastrukturen verschärft.

Das Zwischenfazit können wir auf eine einfache Formel bringen: Immer mehr Menschen, die immer älter werden, leben auf immer engerem Raum, verbrauchen immer mehr Rohstoffe und erzeugen dabei immer mehr Emissionen. Während die Überbeanspruchung der ökologischen Systeme die Erde in den Bereich irreversibler Schäden bringt, werden durch Ressourcenkonkurrenz und Entnivellierung sozialer Lagen durch ungleiche Reichtumsverteilung und ungleiche Verteilung von

concrete dangers, and this is the case right now. In this situation, in many respects, we should be raising the system question in a radical way and a priori, orienting all our actions as from now on our capabilities for the future.[9] This starts out from the assumption that changing the system to create a society with a tenable future is possible and that every development from now on should be oriented on this prime aim. It is based on the assumption that society can learn, implement concerted action, make technology available in good time, and on the precondition that the *switching points* of irreversible eco-systemic changes are not yet behind us. This self-determined, systematic cultural transformation is the opposite to the potentially chaotic dynamics of transformation that will ensue if we do not act. Its aim is the creation of a desirable state. And that, according to Herbert Simon,[10] is the precise and comprehensive definition of design: it is a matter of designing a new global culture of survival, a design that overcomes modernity, a world design as the design of survival into a post-modern epoch, whatever it may be called.

In face of this situation, our current political ideas resemble maintenance measures on the Titanic rather than a change in course that would take us past the iceberg. This can also be said of mobility politics. The technologically brilliant but sometimes conceptually unimaginative mobility industry faces the challenge of developing completely new concepts of mobility, but finds itself caught in the path dependence of our mobility culture, just like traffic policies and the transport sciences. We should abandon the essential lie embraced by critical discourse on mobility that it is possible to make substantial changes within the presently valid path of development. All concepts to optimise, direct, fluidize, and shift traffic cannot escape the fact that we are on the wrong path completely as long as we continue to operate within the current, purely growth-oriented social model.

The design of mobility has always been an implicit matter of social politics and has even been conceived that way explicitly on occasion. Mobility policy is a key issue of cultural transformation towards a society with a sustainable future. To date, we have wanted to make mobility tenable for the future by turning a few screws, whereas it is actually a matter of fully reconstructing the overall machinery of mobility. The incremental logic of previous transport and business policies is understandable granted that the challenges of the future field of mobility policy must face the aspect of steadfastness in their sphere of origin, i.e., within the cultural model of the mobility machine. Policies to expand on spheres of possibility are easier to legitimise and implement in principle than policies that hit those affected on established expectation levels and dependency structures. In face of this situation, *naive* appeals targeting behaviour patterns are simply no option. The decisive question is, how can we succeed in countermanding the narrative of modern mobility which promises freedom and self-mobility by providing a new promising narrative and making this into the foundation of consistent, attractive planning and political visions of tenable mobility for the future?

Lebensrisiken die Grenzen der geopolitischen und kulturellen Tragfähigkeit erreicht. Damit entsteht eine so rasante Transformationsdynamik, dass die Welt – schlicht empirisch betrachtet – in absehbarer Zeit nicht mehr so sein wird, wie wir sie kennen. Wir befinden uns mit anderen Worten im Übergang zur Weltüberlebensgesellschaft. Die Weltrisikogesellschaft ist nach Ulrich Beck[8] durch von dieser Gesellschaft selbst produzierte Risiken definiert. In Überschreitung dieser Definition würde ich die Weltüberlebensgesellschaft durch den Akt der finalen Zuspitzung der reflexiven Modernisierungsfolgen auf die Überlebensfrage der Menschheit definieren. Der Übergang findet statt, wenn Risiken in konkrete Gefahren umschlagen, wie es gerade der Fall ist. In dieser Situation müssten wir in vielerlei Hinsicht die Systemfrage radikal stellen und ab sofort alle unsere Handlungen an einem Zukunftsfähigkeits-Apriori ausrichten.[9] Es geht davon aus, dass der Systemwechsel hin zu einer zukunftsfähigen Gesellschaftsform machbar ist und dass sich jede weitere Entwicklung an diesem obersten Ziel auszurichten hat. Es basiert auf der Annahme von sozialer Lernfähigkeit, konzertiertem Handeln, rechtzeitiger Verfügbarkeit von Technologie und der Voraussetzung, dass die *Schalterpunkte* irreversibler ökosystemischer Veränderungen nicht hinter uns liegen. Diese selbst gewählte und zielgerichtete kulturelle Transformation ist das Gegenteil der potenziell chaotischen Transformationsdynamik, die sich im Falle von Nicht-Handeln einstellen würde. Sie hat die Erzeugung eines gewünschten Zustands zum Ziel. Und genau das ist nach Herbert Simon[10] die umfassende 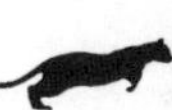 **Definition von Design: Es geht um das Design einer neuen globalen Kultur des Überlebens, um ein Design, das die Moderne überwindet, um Weltdesign als Überlebensdesign hin zu einer nachmodernen, wie auch immer dann zu benennenden Epoche.**

Angesichts dieser Lage gleichen unsere politischen Konzepte eher Wartungsmaßnahmen auf der Titanic als der Kursänderung, die uns am Eisberg vorbeibringt. Das gilt auch für die Mobilitätspolitik. Die technologisch brillante, aber konzeptionell mitunter fantasielose Mobilitätsindustrie ist mit der Entwicklung völlig neuer Mobilitätskonzepte gefordert, sieht sich aber in der Pfadabhängigkeit unserer Mobilitätskultur ebenso gefangen wie die Verkehrspolitik und die Verkehrswissenschaften. Wir sollten aufräumen mit der Lebenslüge der kritischen Mobilitätsdiskurse, wir könnten innerhalb des geltenden Entwicklungspfades etwas substanziell ändern. Alle Optimierungs-, Lenkungs-, Verflüssigungs- und Verlagerungskonzepte für den Verkehr kommen nicht an der Tatsache vorbei, dass wir gänzlich auf dem falschen Pfad sind, solange wir uns innerhalb des geltenden, rein wachstumsorientierten Gesellschaftsmodells bewegen.

Die Gestaltung von Mobilität war implizit immer schon Gesellschaftspolitik und wurde manchmal auch explizit so gedacht. Mobilitätspolitik ist ein Dreh- und Angelpunkt der kulturellen Transformation hin zu einer zukunftsfähigen Gesellschaft. Bislang wollen wir Mobilität zukunftsfähig machen, indem wir an Schrauben drehen, während es darauf ankommt, die gesamte Mobilitätsmaschine neu zu konstruieren.

Our imaginative powers are well ahead of mobility policies: rather than incremental, unsystematic policies motivated by power politics, in the design of mobility we need impulses to stimulate the power of imagination. We lack images, positive visions and stories of a new culture of mobility. What is missing is the inner map of a continent to which we are drawn because its promises are more attractive than our present-day experience. The kind of inner image that was so vital to the "America travellers of the mind"[11] before they set out in search of a better life in the new world. The pull of such guiding images and narratives of a better world and its functioning reality, motivating and concentrating our strengths, are the only things that will help to generate the "sense of possibility" (Robert Musil)—i.e., the comprehensive consensus and innovative mentality throughout society—that we need in order to be open to far-reaching changes and to support corresponding policies. The difficulties of change begin at the limits of the conceivable. They begin with the necessity to imagine the new and first free oneself from mental habits. This initial step is necessary before we can change the way we act. Such *narrative politics of mobility* cannot be left to isolated visionaries; they need to emerge from a collective, decentralised, and networked innovatory logic, which should be organised and fed into political processes and public debates via new channels.

Contemplation of the future field of mobility provides indications of which design areas will be most important and which design strategies should be employed. Criteria of judgement are the speed and extent of the ecological and social relief to be expected, the force of innovation, range, and depth of the overall system, and finally the power to shape culture, in other words, the possible contribution to the reinvention of our modern civilisation. This will not make the classic systemising of fields of action, strategies, and measures in transport politics obsolete: however, they will be evaluated using different logics of innovation; the previously part-systemic, incremental logics of innovation—oriented on technical carrier systems and the processes and optimising of organisational control—will be opposed by the ideal of a mobility policy with ambitions for the whole of society. Corresponding to the paradigmatic character of mobility, this approach must enquire systematically and with disciplinary openness about the changes that need triggering in other fields of design in order to arrive at changes in the practice of mobility. On the other hand, it is necessary to ask what changes in the practice of mobility, in an incubatory sense, could lead in their turn to sustainable changes in other part-systems.

The triad of innovation encompassing the—ideally—closely tuned design of products, processes, and systems realises this matrix with a view to defining levels of action, protagonists, and target parameters like user-friendliness, universal design, reduction of energy and resource consumption, lack of harm to the environment, health, and society, etc.

Product innovation begins with individual means of transport or transport carriers. Here, it is possible that the functionality of the apparatus

Die inkrementelle Logik der bisherigen Verkehrs- und Unternehmenspolitik ist verständlich angesichts der Tatsache, dass die Herausforderungen des Zukunftsraums der Mobilitätspolitik mit dem Beharrungsmoment ihres Herkunftsraums, eben des Kulturmodells der Mobilitätsmaschine konfrontiert sind. Politiken zur Erweiterung von Möglichkeitsräumen sind prinzipiell einfacher zu legitimieren und umzusetzen als Politiken, die bei den Betroffenen auf etablierte Erwartungsniveaus und Abhängigkeitsstrukturen treffen. Angesichts dieser Lage verbieten sich alle *naiven* Verhaltensappelle. Entscheidend ist die Frage, wie es gelingen kann, der Freiheit und Selbstbeweglichkeit versprechenden Erzählung moderner Mobilität ein neues, verheißungsvolles Narrativ entgegenzusetzen und zur Grundlage konsistenter und attraktiver Planungs- und Politikvisionen zukunftsfähiger Mobilität zu machen.

Die Macht unserer Fantasie geht der Mobilitätspolitik voraus: Viel mehr als inkrementelle, unsystematische und machtpolitisch motivierte Politiken brauchen wir bei der Gestaltung von Mobilität Impulse für die Macht unserer Fantasie. Uns fehlen Bilder, positive Visionen und Geschichten einer neuen Mobilitätskultur. Es fehlt die innere Landkarte eines Kontinents, zu dem wir uns hingezogen fühlen, weil seine Versprechen attraktiver sind als das Erleben der Gegenwart. So ein inneres Bild, wie es in den „Amerikafahrern des Kopfes"[11] lebendig war, bevor sie aufbrachen, um in der neuen Welt ein besseres Leben zu finden. Erst die Sogwirkung dieser leitenden, Kräfte bündelnden und motivierenden Bilder und Erzählungen der funktionierenden Wirklichkeit einer besseren Welt werden helfen, den „Möglichkeitssinn" (Robert Musil) – im Sinne eines übergreifenden Konsenses und einer gesellschaftsweiten Innovationsmentalität – entstehen zu lassen, den wir brauchen, um uns auf tiefe Veränderungen einzulassen und die entsprechenden Politiken mitzutragen. Die Schwierigkeiten von Wandel beginnen an der Grenze der Vorstellbarkeit. Sie beginnen bei der Notwendigkeit, das Neue zu denken und sich aus Gewohnheiten zunächst mental zu befreien. Erst diesem Schritt werden veränderte Handlungsweisen folgen können. Eine solche *narrative Mobilitätspolitik* kann nicht Aufgabe einzelner Visionäre sein, sondern muss einer kollektiven, dezentralen und vernetzten Innovationslogik entspringen, die es zu organisieren und über neue Kanäle in politische Prozesse und öffentliche Debatten einzuspeisen gilt.

Aus der Betrachtung des Zukunftsraums der Mobilität ergeben sich Hinweise, welche Gestaltungsfelder im Vordergrund stehen und welche Gestaltungsstrategien zum Einsatz kommen sollten. Beurteilungskriterien sind die erwartbare Geschwindigkeit und Größenordnung ökologischer und sozialer Entlastungseffekte, die gesamtsystemische Innovationsstärke, Reichweite und Tiefgängigkeit und schließlich die kulturelle Prägekraft, also der Beitrag zur Neuerfindung unserer modernen Zivilisation. Die klassischen Systematisierungen von verkehrspolitischen Handlungsfeldern, Strategien und Maßnahmen sind damit zwar nicht obsolet, werden aber aus einer anderen Innovationslogik heraus bewertet: Der bislang

or systems of apparatuses used to implement transportation processes will not be changed, and that only the character of the product will be modified in order to realise one or several of the abovementioned aims. Product innovations ought to begin during the planning and production process, for instance when it comes to the question of design oriented on the reusability of components; this optimises usage, and sensible subsequent use should be taken into account from the beginning (for example, reutilisation and re-reutilisation). The combustion engine's incremental increase in efficiency is part of this strategy, as well as the development of new forms of impulsion for all traffic (e-car, H2-car, Transrapid) and even entirely new technological concepts (Segway, RailCab). Product innovations are usually based on technical inventions. On the other hand, the innovative achievement may be oriented towards a combination of existing technologies, a new standard (size, weight), or a new type of usage. Product innovations should always aim at an increase in product efficiency, i.e., at fulfilling a function while deploying fewer resources or expanding product function with the same, or ideally with reduced consumption of resources. Innovations in usage begin with the operation of means of transport. Here, it is a matter of how the given demands of mobility can be satisfied without employing new products, or satisfying them with a different use of given products, or with a new concept for the framework conditions of use. The innovative impulse in this case refers to at least a (re-)organisation of active procedures with given products in a given environment. This can occur with or without corresponding product innovations. Politically, the great pragmatic significance of innovations in use results from the situation described above; the fact that the world has developed as a rigid sociotechnical system. **The world of objects is firmly cast in steel and concrete, just as man's world has become fixed in steadfast usage and behaviour routines. A change towards the target criteria of sustainability must come to terms with this basic condition. Usually, there is neither the money nor the political will necessary to take the step towards a large-scale conversion of products or the system. On the contrary, often the solution probably lies with the perspective of much more efficient use of existing products and infrastructures. This strategy is characterised by a low level of technological intervention. It is a strategy of clever social handling of the world as it currently exists, since its potentials in all fields of requirement have not yet been exhausted, by any means. Classic innovations of use are "sharing concepts" with different forms and ranges of effectiveness. Generally speaking, sharing means of transport aims to fulfil needs as comprehensively as possible with the lowest possible deployment of resources.**

Our mobile way of life is centred on the car. Bearing in mind the impact of automobility on the exploitation of resources and global warming, and the economic and social significance of the car and mineral oil industries, the modernisation of automobility and its energy systemic, infrastructural and socio-functional fields is one of the key factors of an ecological industrial

teilsystemischen – auf technische Trägersysteme, organisatorische Verlaufssteuerung und -optimierung ausgerichteten – inkrementellen Innovationslogik wird das Ideal einer auch gesamtgesellschaftlich ambitionierten Mobilitätspolitik entgegengesetzt. Dem paradigmatischen Charakter der Mobilität entsprechend muss dieser Ansatz systematisch und in disziplinärer Offenheit danach fragen, welche Veränderungen in anderen Gestaltungsfeldern angestoßen werden müssten, um zu Veränderungen in der Mobilitätspraxis zu kommen. Andererseits ist zu fragen, welche Veränderungen der Mobilitätspraxis im inkubatorischen Sinne wiederum zu nachhaltigen Veränderungen in anderen Teilsystemen führen könnten.

Die Innovationstrias einer idealerweise eng aufeinander abgestimmten Gestaltung von Produkten, Abläufen und Systemen realisiert diese Matrix mit Blick auf definierte Handlungsebenen, Akteure und Zielparameter wie Nutzerfreundlichkeit, Universal Design, Verringerung des Energie- und Ressourcenverbrauchs, der Umwelt-, Gesundheits- und Sozialverträglichkeit etc.

Produktinnovation setzt bei einzelnen Verkehrsmitteln bzw. Verkehrsträgern an. Dabei wird die Funktionalität der für die Abwicklung von Verkehrsabläufen eingesetzten Geräte oder Gerätesysteme gegebenenfalls nicht verändert, sondern nur die Produktausprägung modifiziert, um eines oder mehrere der oben genannten Ziele zu realisieren. Produktinnovationen sollten während des Planungs- und Produktionsprozesses ansetzen, etwa bei der Frage einer an Wiederverwertbarkeit von Komponenten orientierten Gestaltung, sie optimieren den Gebrauchsprozess und sollten eine sinnvolle Nachnutzung von Beginn an mit in den Blick nehmen (zum Beispiel Zweit- und Drittverwertung). Die inkrementelle Effizienzsteigerung des Verbrennungsmotors gehört ebenso zu dieser Strategie wie die Entwicklung neuer Antriebskonzepte für alle Verkehrsträger (E-Auto, H_2-Auto, Transrapid) bis hin zu ganz neuen technologischen Konzepten (Segway, RailCab). Produktinnovationen basieren meist auf technischen Inventionen. Andererseits kann die Innovationsleistung auf die Kombination vorhandener Technologien, auf einen neuen Standard (Größe, Gewicht) oder eine neue Nutzungsform hin ausgerichtet werden. Produktinnovationen sollten immer auf die Erhöhung der Produkteffizienz zielen, also die Erfüllung einer Funktion mit geringerem Ressourceneinsatz bzw. die Darstellung erweiterter Produktfunktion bei gleichbleibendem, im Idealfalle verringertem Ressourcenaufwand. Nutzungsinnovationen setzen beim Betrieb von Verkehrsmitteln an. Es geht hier darum, wie gegebene Bedürfnisse der Mobilität befriedigt werden können, ohne dafür neue Produkte einzusetzen bzw. wie sie durch einen anderen Einsatz der gegebenen Produkte bzw. der Gestaltung ihrer Nutzungsrahmenbedingungen befriedigt werden. Der Innovationsimpuls bezieht sich hier also mindestens auf die (Neu-)Organisation von Handlungsabläufen mit gegebenen Produkten in einem gegebenen Umfeld. Dieses kann mit oder ohne korrespondierende Produktinnovationen stattfinden. Die große politikpragmatische Bedeutung von Nutzungsinnovationen resultiert aus der oben beschriebenen Situation,

policy in modern societies today. If we succeed in transformation here, we will also succeed in every other area of demand and industry. Against this background, I assume that the classic form of automobility familiar to us today, in a double sense—as a cultural model of mass motorisation and as a technological path of development—has, indeed must have reached the end if we apply the criteria of tenability for the future: the form of automobility that is so familiar to us, i.e., private possession of a vehicle with a combustion motor, sufficient loading and transport capacity, moderate costs and a large operating range, cannot possibly be implemented universally, even if we did arrive at an efficiency level of one litre per 100 kilometres. The electro-car is equally impossible to universalise, as long as it tries to follow in the footsteps of the combustion vehicle as its functional equivalent in the sense of *conversion design.* If we really take the current state of affairs seriously, the only way towards enduring, sustainable mobility is via the de-individualisation of private mobility and goods logistics on the basis of fully regenerative energy in the mid term: a massive re-evaluation of collective transport carriers and the redevelopment of our economic and settlement structures. Automobility means no more than self-mobility, and up until now self-mobility—for us as modern human-beings—has been encoded as private motor vehicles operating on a fossil energy basis, available to all. As outlined above, this notion has been deeply inscribed into our infrastructures of housing, economy and production. But it is possible to realise the function of self-mobility in another way—not as a single technological artefact, but as the output of smooth-running interaction between components of a system. Rather than moving through the world inside an artefact in order to get from A to B, in the spirit of this design philosophy, I would be moved within the world by means of a system in order to get from A to B. In this sense, therefore, the automobility of the future is indeed a largely *automobile-free future.* It is the self-mobile movement of people and goods on the basis of de-individualising urban traffic, founded in turn on a modern, highly developed collective transport system and in combination with innovative strategies of use for what might be called micro-mobility, i.e., individual transport carriers lower in standard than today's dominant image of the private motor vehicle. At the core, the design of mobility is a transformation policy. If redevelopment is successful in this hub of modern societies, it will succeed in every field of demand and functions. Truly tenable mobility for the future, in the long term, is avoided mobility–meaning that it is essentially a question of our lifestyles and levels of requirements, and ultimately of our notion of prosperity.

dass die Welt sich als rigides sozio-technisches System entwickelt hat. Die Dingwelt ist so fest in Stahl und Beton gegossen, wie die Menschwelt sich in beharrlichen Nutzungs- und Verhaltensroutinen fixiert hat. Eine Veränderung in Richtung der Zielkriterien der Nachhaltigkeit muss sich mit dieser Grundbedingung arrangieren. Meist ist weder Geld noch politischer Wille vorhanden, die notwendig wären, den Schritt zu groß angelegten Produkt- oder Systemkonversionen zu machen. Im Gegenteil liegt die Lösung wohl oft in der Perspektive der sehr viel effizienteren Nutzung von Produkten und Infrastrukturen. Diese Strategie zeichnet sich durch eine geringe technologische Eingriffstiefe aus. Es ist eine Strategie des klugen sozialen Umgangs mit der aktuell jeweils vorgefundenen Welt, deren Potenziale in allen Bedürfnisfeldern bei weitem noch nicht ausgeschöpft sind. Klassische Nutzungsinnovationen sind „Sharing-Konzepte" unterschiedlichster Ausprägung und Reichweite. Allgemein gesprochen hat das Teilen von Verkehrsmitteln das Ziel, eine möglichst umfassende Bedürfnisbefriedigung mit einem möglichst geringen Aufwand an Ressourcen zu realisieren.

Im Zentrum unserer mobilen Lebensweise steht das Auto. Mit Blick auf den Beitrag der Automobilität zum Ressourcenverbrauch und zur Klimaerwärmung und die ökonomische und gesellschaftliche Bedeutung der Automobil- und Mineralölbranche ist die Modernisierung der Automobilität und ihrer energiesystemischen, verkehrsinfrastrukturellen und sozialen Funktionsräume heute einer der Dreh- und Angelpunkte ökologischer Industriepolitik in modernen Gesellschaften. Gelingt die Transformation hier, so gelingt sie auch in allen anderen Bedürfnisfeldern und Wirtschaftsbereichen. Vor diesem Hintergrund gehe ich davon aus, dass die klassische, uns bekannte Automobilität heute im doppelten Sinne – als kulturelles Modell der Massenmotorisierung und als technologischer Entwicklungspfad – am Ende ist, ja sein muss, wenn wir die Kriterien der Zukunftsfähigkeit anlegen: Die uns so vertraute Automobilität, also der Privatbesitz eines Fahrzeugs mit Verbrennungsmotor, hinreichender Lade- und Transportkapazität, moderaten Kosten und einer großen Reichweite ist in keiner Weise global verallgemeinerungsfähig, selbst wenn wir irgendwann bei einer Effizienz von einem Liter pro 100 Kilometer landen könnten. Ebenso wenig verallgemeinerungsfähig ist das Elektroauto, wenn es dem Verbrennungs-Pkw im Sinne des *Conversion Design* funktional äquivalent nachzueifern versucht. Wenn wir die Lage der Dinge wirklich ernst nehmen, führt der einzige Weg zu einer dauerhaft nachhaltigen Mobilität nur über die Ent-Individualisierung der Privatmobilität und der Güterlogistik auf Basis einer mittelfristig vollkommen regenerativen Energiebasis, der massiven Aufwertung der kollektiven Verkehrsträger und des Umbaus unserer Wirtschafts- und Siedlungsstrukturen. Automobilität bedeutet ins Deutsche übersetzt schlicht Selbstbeweglichkeit. Für uns moderne Menschen ist Selbstbeweglichkeit bislang als massenhaft verfügbarer Privat-Pkw auf fossiler energetischer Basis codiert und wie beschrieben in unsere Siedlungs-, Wirtschafts- und Produktionsinfrastrukturen tief eingeschrieben.

NOTES—[1] Cf. Rammler, Stephan: *Mobilität in der Moderne – Geschichte und Theorie der Verkehrs-soziologie,* Berlin 2001. Und Ders.: „So unvermeidlich wie die Käuzchen in Athen – Anmerkungen zur Soziologie des Automobils.", in IVP-Schriften, Technische Universität Berlin, Institut für Land- und Seeverkehr, Fachgebiet Integrierte Verkehrsplanung. Berlin 2003.—[2] Cf. Rammler 2003.—[3] Voigt, Fritz: "Verkehr und Industrialisierung" in: *Zeitschrift für die gesamte Staatswissenschaft,* Nr. 109/1953, 199ff.—[4] Cf. Franke, Sassa: *Car Sharing: Vom Ökoprojekt zur Dienstleistung,* Berlin 2001.—[5] Internationale Energie-Agentur (IEA): *World Energy Outlook 2007,* Paris 2007.—[6] At a conservative estimate, the USA spent 600 billion dollars to keep up its military presence in the Gulf region between 1991 and 2003 alone. This does not take into account the direct cost of the two Gulf wars.—[7] Cf. Schöller-Schwedes, Oliver/Rammler, Stephan: *Mobile Cities. Dynamiken weltweiter Stadt- und Verkehrsentwicklung,* Münster 2008—[8] Beck, Ulrich: *Risikogesellschaft. Auf dem Weg in eine andere Moderne,* Frankfurt a. M.: 1986.—[9] Rammler, Stephan Ders.: "Das Ende der Moderne zwischen Apokalypse und Utopie. Gedanken zur kulturellen Transformation in der Weltüberlebensgesellschaft", in: *Lerchen_feld,* Magazin der Hochschule für Bildende Künste Hamburg, Nr. 05/2010, 19–24.—[10] Simon, Herbert: *Die Wissenschaften vom Künstlichen,* Berlin 1990.—[11] Burckhart, Martin: *Metamorphosen von Raum und Zeit. Eine Geschichte der Wahrnehmung,* Frankfurt/Main u.a.: 1997, 158.

Die Funktion der Selbstbeweglichkeit könnte aber auch anders realisiert sein. Eben nicht als technologisches Einzelartefakt, sondern als Output des reibungslosen Zusammenspiels von Komponenten eines Systems. Statt mich in einem Artefakt durch eine Welt zu bewegen, um von A nach B zu kommen, werde ich also im Sinne dieser Designphilosophie durch ein System in der Welt bewegt, um von A nach B zu kommen. Die Automobilität der Zukunft ist in diesem Sinne also tatsächlich eine weitgehend *autofreie Zukunft.* Sie ist selbstbewegliche Mobilität von Menschen und Gütern auf Grundlage der Ent-Individualisierung des städtischen Verkehrs auf der Basis eines modernen, hoch entwickelten Kollektivverkehrs und einer Verknüpfung mit innovativen Nutzungsstrategien für das, was man Mikromobilität nennen könnte, also individuelle Verkehrsträger unterhalb des Niveaus des heutigen Fahrzeugleitbildes. Mobilitätsgestaltung ist im Kern Transformationspolitik. Gelingt der Umbau in diesem Herzstück moderner Gesellschaften, gelingt er in allen ihren Bedürfnis- und Funktionsbereichen. Wirklich zukunftsfähige Mobilität ist langfristig letztlich nur vermiedene Mobilität und damit im Kern eine Frage nach unseren Lebensstilen und Bedürfnisniveaus, letztlich nach unserem Wohlstandskonzept.

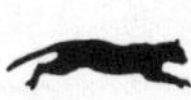

ANMERKUNGEN—1 Vgl. Rammler, Stephan: *Mobilität in der Moderne – Geschichte und Theorie der Verkehrssoziologie,* Berlin 2001. Und Ders.: "So unvermeidlich wie die Käuzchen in Athen – Anmerkungen zur Soziologie des Automobils," in *IVP-Schriften,* Technische Universität Berlin, Institut für Land- und Seeverkehr, Fachgebiet Integrierte Verkehrsplanung. Berlin 2003.— **2** Vgl. Rammler 2003.— **3** Voigt, Fritz: „Verkehr und Industrialisierung" in: *Zeitschrift für die gesamte Staatswissenschaft,* Nr. 109/1953, 199ff.— **4** Vgl. Franke, Sassa: *Car Sharing: Vom Ökoprojekt zur Dienstleistung,* Berlin 2001.— **5** Internationale Energie-Agentur (IEA): *World Energy Outlook 2007,* Paris 2007.— **6** Konservativ geschätzt hat die USA zwischen 1991 bis 2003 allein für die Aufrechterhaltung militärischer Präsenz in der Golfregion 600 Milliarden Dollar aufgewendet. Die unmittelbaren Kosten der beiden Golfkriege sind nicht berücksichtigt.— **7** Vgl. Schöller-Schwedes, Oliver/Rammler, Stephan: *Mobile Cities. Dynamiken weltweiter Stadt- und Verkehrsentwicklung,* Münster 2008— **8** Beck, Ulrich: *Risikogesellschaft. Auf dem Weg in eine andere Moderne,* Frankfurt/Main: 1986.— **9** Rammler, Stephan: „Das Ende der Moderne zwischen Apokalypse und Utopie. Gedanken zur kulturellen Transformation in der Weltüberlebensgesellschaft", in: *Lerchen_feld,* Magazin der Hochschule für Bildende Künste Hamburg, Nr. 05/2010, 19–24.— **10** Simon, Herbert: *Die Wissenschaften vom Künstlichen,* Berlin 1990.— **11** Burckhart, Martin: *Metamorphosen von Raum und Zeit. Eine Geschichte der Wahrnehmung,* Frankfurt/Main u.a. 1997, 158.

Christophe Girot **has been professor at the Chair of Landscape Architecture of the ETH Zurich since 2001.** Subjects of research: modern history, theory **and topological methods** in landscape design, new media in the analysis and **perception of landscape.** His office, Atelier Girot, places an emphasis on sus**tainable topology** and design in large-scale landscape architecture. Publica**tions include:** *Cadrages II Blicklandschaften. Landschaft in Bewegung | Land**scapevideo. Landscape in Movement* (ed., 2010), *Grandes paisajes de **Europa** (ed., 2009), *Landscape Architecture in Mutation* (ed., 2005).

Christophe Girot
Landschaft in Bewegung

Christophe Girot ist seit 2001 Professor am Lehrstuhl für Landschaftsarchitektur an der ETH Zürich. Forschungsthemen: Moderne Geschichte, Theorie und topologische Methoden im Landschaftsentwurf, neue Medien in der Landschaftsanalyse und -wahrnehmung. Sein Büro Atelier Girot legt den Schwerpunkt auf nachhaltige Topologie und Entwurf in der großmaßstäblichen Landschaftsarchitektur. Publikationen u. a. *Cadrages II Blicklandschaften. Landschaft in Bewegung | Landscapevideo. Landscape in Movement* (Hg., 2010), *Grandes paisajes de Europa* (Hg., 2009), *Landscape Architecture in Mutation* (Hg., 2005).

The reality of landscape vision has become quite blurry today; in an age where images have dematerialised and atomised into minute particles of information, the question becomes really a matter of definition. The substantive value of our gaze on landscapes has changed considerably through this process of dematerialisation of the gaze, and it is not necessarily what a society looks at in a field of pixels, but rather what it ignores in the blackness of a screen's background that actually matters. A selective perceptual attrition has taken effect in our highly mobile society and has had determinant consequences on the fieldwork we undertake, and on the perception we convey in landscape architecture. This explains only in part, why a landscape can no longer be considered as a spatial entity per se, but rather as a multipolar environmental coagulum without any particular perceptual focus. Landscape, as a direct consequence of this perceptual evolution, is in danger of disintegrating into a form of background noise upon which other more significant events can be played, focused upon, and displayed.

One of the most striking examples of such visual disembodiment has come to us lately through so-called laser point cloud photography adapted in recent years for the purpose of landscape studies at the ETH LMVL[1] (1 p. 188). The exquisite filigreed imagery resulting from highly precise terrestrial laser scans are visually quite stunning. Point cloud imagery is generated by countless swarming white pixels suspended against a virtual black background. These pixels flock together almost magnetically to form a diaphanous landscape image of extraordinary beauty and precision. Each pixel contained in every image is valued as a separately positioned entity, triangulated and suspended to a battery of satellites in the sky. In other words a pixel standing next to another in one of those point cloud photographs does, regardless of the depth of field, hold an entirely different geographic position and coding than the other. Although visual neighbours, they can be as distant as several hundred metres from one another in computational geographic reality. To explain this matter further, point cloud photographs taken in and around the same location can subsequently be merged electronically to fuse into a highly precise, geographically positioned virtual 3-D model containing an extraordinary level of topological detail about the site.

The stunning beauty of these negative images developed in the point cloud process, reminds one of the extraordinarily subtle nuances found on old nineteenth-century monochromatic aquatints. But the main difference between these old prints and a point cloud model is that the swarm of points that form the model image can actually be visited and travelled through in all possible scales and directions of motion. This possibility of real time movement within a virtual 3-D landscape model has had immediate repercussions on the landscape design process, which has become much more interactive and immersive. But, despite the intrinsic refinement of this extraordinary kind of electronic landscape embroidery, the fascination that emanates from a point cloud picture and model cannot define the totality of a landscape environment; far from it,

Die Wirklichkeit unserer Landschaftsbetrachtung ist heute recht diffus geworden. In einer Zeit, in der Bilder von ihrer materiellen Grundlage losgelöst und in winzigste Informationspartikel aufgelöst worden sind, wird der Begriff Landschaft zu einer Frage der Definition. Der substanzielle Wert unserer Vor- und Darstellung von Landschaften hat sich durch diesen Loslösungs- und Auflösungsprozess, durch die Entmaterialisierung des Bildes, grundlegend verändert. Es ist nicht mehr von Belang, was wir auf einer Fläche voller Pixel ins Auge fassen, wichtig ist vielmehr, was für uns unsichtbar im Dunkel hinter der Bildschirmfläche geschieht. In unserer hochmobilen Gesellschaft vollzieht sich seit einiger Zeit ein selektiver Schwund der Wahrnehmung, der sich auf die von uns durchgeführte Feldforschung auswirkt und ebenso auf die Erkenntnisse, die wir in der Landschaftsarchitektur vermitteln. Das erklärt zum Teil, warum eine Landschaft nicht länger als räumliche Einheit betrachtet werden kann, sondern uns vielmehr zu einem multipolaren Gemenge aus Umwelteindrücken gerinnt, bei dem die Aufmerksamkeit auf keinen bestimmten Fixpunkt mehr gerichtet ist. Die unmittelbare Konsequenz aus dieser sich verändernden Wahrnehmung ist die Gefahr, dass Landschaft zu einer Art untergeordneter Hintergrundkulisse herabgestuft wird, vor der andere, bedeutendere Ereignisse inszeniert, wahrgenommen und eingeblendet werden.

Ein Extrembeispiel für diese Entkörperlichung des Sichtbaren stellt die sogenannte lasergenerierte Punktwolken-Fotografie dar, die in den letzten Jahren für die Landschaftsstudien am LMVL[1] der ETH Zürich eingeführt wurde. 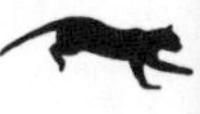 (*1* S. 188) Die vorzüglichen Bilder, die ein hochpräziser terrestrischer Laserscanner liefert, zeigen kleinste Details und sind sehr eindrucksvoll. Punktwolkenbilder werden von unzähligen weißen Pixeln erzeugt, die vor einem virtuellen schwarzen Hintergrund wimmeln. Die Pixel bilden dichte Cluster, als würden sie magnetisch voneinander angezogen, und erzeugen transparente Landschaftsbilder von außergewöhnlicher Schönheit und Genauigkeit. Jedes Pixel in den unterschiedlichen Bildern wird als separat positionierte Einheit gewertet, in einem Netz trigonometrischer Punkte angeordnet und mit Hilfe einer Vielzahl von GPS-Satelliten am Himmel „aufgehängt". Anders gesagt: Auf einem Punktwolkenscan hat jedes Pixel ungeachtet der Bildtiefe eine andere geografische Position und wird anders kodiert als jedes weitere, direkt daneben liegende Pixel. Obwohl sie im Bild unmittelbar benachbart erscheinen, können sie in der rechnerisch erfassten Geografie bis zu mehrere Hundert Meter voneinander entfernt sein. Punktwolkenbilder, die am selben Ort oder in unmittelbarer Nähe gescannt werden, lassen sich anschließend elektronisch zu einem noch präziseren, GPS-codierten virtuellen 3D-Landschaftsmodell zusammenfügen, das eine erstaunlich große Anzahl exakter topologischer Details des betreffenden Ortes darstellt.

Die faszinierende Schönheit der Negative, die das terrestrische Laserscanning liefert, erinnert an die ungewöhnlich feinen Nuancen monochromer Aquatintaradierungen des 19. Jahrhunderts. Der Hauptunterschied zwischen den alten Grafiken

the point cloud image betrays, in essence, a tremendous act of visual reduction with a strong propensity to neutralise and objectify the content of the gaze in order to make it better quantifiable. The white spot that inhabits each pixel in a point cloud photograph is qualitatively neutral, not to say neutered, for it only retains quantitative information about a given geographic position. In other words, in this representation, the rest of the content is gone and the pixel cloud only delivers crucial binary instructions about one specific position in the physical world. What about the significance of the black space that surrounds each white pixel point? Does the unsung gap in-between the pixels have meaning any longer? A point cloud image, in order to function, must remain absolutely objective to be of any use in advanced terrain surveying techniques. In this process, all landscape nuances about the quality of the light and air, the hues and atmospheric depth situated between the pixel point and the viewer have been ignored and left aside for technical reasons.

Advanced laser scanner technology using point clouds has also led, amongst other things, to the engineering and implementation of an extraordinary high-speed rail line cutting straight across the Alps. The AlpTransit company has succeeded in building the longest tunnel in the world under the Gotthard Pass in Switzerland thanks to such precision technology, creating a subterranean metaworld that has reduced the traditional landscape view of the Alps to almost nothing. More than two-thirds of the high-speed journey is effectively done underground on stretches that range up to seventy kilometres in pitch darkness through the rock. This takes us one step beyond the original remarks of Paul Virilio written in the late twentieth century, about our changing perception though velocity, in the sense that we have now reached an absolute value.[2] Entering the obscurity of these new tunnels, the traveller joins an immaterial blackness similar to that found in the background of a point cloud pixel screen. Both black realms lack the proper perceptual depth and definition. This condition no longer has the poetry of interstellar darkness, where even the most infinite cue of light shimmers gracefully on the back of our retina evoking heaven's mysteries. This is only the utter and finite darkness of a man-made cave, albeit dressed in the proper technical attire for high speed displacement. This tunnel is a place where landscape perception completely ceases to exist in the normal sense of the word and where fundamental human notions such as recognition and location are dismissed altogether. It is interesting to note that the complete erasure of alpine topography through the tunnel comes together with the complete erasure of landscape toponymy. In other words, passengers will traverse a nameless space for the sake of velocity; and the naming of all the places out of sight will matter no longer. This also means that the images of the landscapes that are missed can also be transformed into virtual myths. Most high-speed passengers riding through the seamless tunnel will probably revert to an artificially supported vision carried on some backlit screen, to gaze at things during the entire journey into blackness.

und einem Punktwolkenmodell besteht aber darin, dass man jeden der einzelnen Wolkenpunkte, aus denen sich der Scan zusammensetzt, ansteuern, aufsuchen und durchfahren kann, und zwar in alle Richtungen und in jedem erdenklichen Maßstab. Die Möglichkeit, die Augen in Echtzeit durch eine virtuelle dreidimensionale Landschaft schweifen zu lassen, hat dazu geführt, dass die landschaftsarchitektonische Entwurfsarbeit wesentlich interaktiver und umfassender geworden ist. Und dennoch, trotz der Raffinesse dieser faszinierenden elektronischen „Landschaftsstickerei": Ein Punktwolkenfoto oder -modell ist weit davon entfernt, eine Landschaft mit all ihren Facetten voll zu erfassen, weil es im Wesentlichen eine erhebliche Reduktion unserer Sehfähigkeit darstellt und stark dazu neigt, Gesehenes auszublenden und zu vergegenständlichen, um dadurch ein besser messbares Ergebnis liefern zu können. Der weiße Fleck jedes Pixels auf einem Punktwolkenscan ist in qualitativer Hinsicht sozusagen „geschlechtslos", um nicht zu sagen „kastriert", denn er registriert ausschließlich quantitative Informationen über eine bestimmte geografische Position. Mit anderen Worten: In dieser Darstellung ist der weitere Inhalt verschwunden und die Pixelwolke liefert nur die wesentlichen binären Instruktionen zu einer ganz bestimmten Position in der realen Welt. Was bedeutet aber der schwarze Raum um jeden weißen Pixelpunkt? Ist diese unbesetzte Lücke zwischen den Pixeln überhaupt noch von Bedeutung? Ein Punktwolkenbild muss absolut objektiv sein (wenn es bei hoch entwickelten Landvermessungstechniken eine Rolle spielen soll) und ignoriert aus technischen Gründen alle qualitativen Facetten einer Landschaft – das Licht und die Luft, die Farben und die atmosphärische Dichte, die den Raum zwischen Pixelabbild und Betrachter der Landschaft füllen.

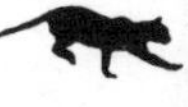

Die fortgeschrittene und auf Punktwolken basierende Laserscanner-Technologie machte es unter anderem überhaupt erst möglich, eine Bahntrasse für Hochgeschwindigkeitszüge quer durch die Schweizer Berge zu entwerfen und auch zu bauen. Dem AlpTransit-Unternehmen gelang es dank derartiger Präzisionstechniken, den längsten Tunnel der Welt unterhalb des Gotthard-Passes zu realisieren und eine unterirdische Metawelt zu schaffen, die das bisherige Erlebnis des Alpenpanoramas auf ein kaum vorhandenes Minimum reduziert hat. Die Hochgeschwindigkeitstrasse verläuft zu über zwei Dritteln in Form von bis zu 70 Kilometer langen, stockfinsteren Tunneln durch das Felsgestein der Alpen. Mit dieser rasenden Reise durch dunkle Tunnel verändert sich unsere visuelle Wahrnehmung noch drastischer als von Paul Virilio beschrieben[2]: Die Kombination von Hochgeschwindigkeit und Dunkelheit ist nicht mehr zu überbieten. Bei der Einfahrt in die Dunkelheit der Tunnelröhren verschwindet der Reisende in einer immateriellen Schwärze, die stark derjenigen ähnelt, die sich im Pixel-Hintergrund der Punktwolken befindet. Beiden Sphären der Dunkelheit fehlt eine angemessene perzeptorische Tiefe und ein klarer Umriss. Diese Finsternis entbehrt der Poesie einer sternenklaren Nacht, in der noch der schwächste Lichtschimmer auf bezaubernde Weise die Mysterien des Himmels auf unsere Netzhaut projiziert. Es ist die absolute,

But this will only be a pale substitute for all the foregone alpine scenery left out of sight. If you add to this the vertiginous speed of displacement operated through the solid mass of the Alps, you quickly realise that we have reached the absolute limits of spatial cognition or any palpable landscape reality for that matter.

The new Gotthard tunnel is a monument to twenty-first-century, speed-induced, visual attrition, and this will probably have far reaching consequences on our perception of the world. In some respects, the tunnel has become the cenotaph of established landscape perception, and our long-standing tradition of journeying and territorial observation. The paragon of such visual attrition can be found in the underground Skymetro shuttle that runs between the Midfield Terminal and the Main Building at Zurich Airport. It is there, in the unlikely location of an underground track crossing the runways, that the patent absence of landscape is compensated by the sublime message of a virtual "TunnelMovie" projection.[3] All arriving and departing passengers catch a brief glimpse of a spectral animation along the tunnel walls, featuring either the Matterhorn or a full-fledged blond Heidi standing and smiling in a sunny alpine meadow amidst the sounds of cow bells and yodels as she waves a kiss goodbye. This is the moment when all harried passengers show a sign of relief and smile at each other knowingly, for they have unexpectedly shared thirty seconds of a genuine Swiss landscape myth inside the rambling darkness of an unlikely shuttle tunnel. The spectral sequencing of images in this tunnel animation rushes by with faint diaphanous colours interspersed by countless black intervals that deliver a choppy flipbook-like quality to the short show. The choppy visual effect of the "TunnelMovie" further helps confer a subliminal quality to the message. The antiquated spectral vision used in the animation seems like it could have been done by a disciple of Etienne-Jules Marey over a century ago. It is interesting to note that the archaic visual mode in which the "Tunnel Heidi" is conveyed somehow augments its credibility and reception on the part of the public. In an act of operative cultural metonymy, the "TunnelMovie" glosses over a genuine spirit of tradition, on the albeit rather banal and vulgar world of an airport underground. This leads us back to the cardinal postulate defined by Roland Barthes, in which he says that whatever the condition, each epoch creates its own mythologies, based on notions borrowed from the past that are then transformed into the contemporary realm we dwell in.[4] One could well imagine, in this respect, the new tunnel under the Gotthard Pass, being installed similarly with delightful "TunnelMovie" animations of alpine myths in the near future (2 p. 188). The high-speed journey through the darkness of the entire mountain range would last only a matter of minutes, but that would probably be enough to communicate a substantial dose of alpine landscape myth ersatz to travellers. The thirst for such visual palliatives in a world of rapid motion, shows to what extent our vision has become detached, not to say dislocated from the ambient landscape reality. This could be also said about the countless sound walls being erected across the Swiss territory to enclose both roads and

endliche Dunkelheit einer von Menschen ausgeschachteten Höhle, ausgestattet mit der nötigen Technik für pfeilschnelle Fortbewegung. In diesen Tunneln ist die Landschaftsbetrachtung aufgehoben; grundlegende menschliche Erlebnisse wie der Anblick und das Wiedererkennen einer Gegend bleiben dem Reisenden verwehrt. Interessanterweise fällt die vollständige Auslöschung der ursprünglichen Alpentopografie durch die Tunnel mit der totalen Vernichtung der Landschaftstoponymie, also der Wissenschaft der Landschaftsnamensgebung, zusammen. Mit anderen Worten: Die Reisenden durchfahren um der Schnelligkeit willen einen namenlosen Ort, die Bezeichnungen aller aus dem Blick geratenen Orte werden bedeutungslos. Somit werden die im Tunnel nicht mehr möglichen Ausblicke in virtuelle Landschaftsmythen verwandelt. Die meisten Reisenden werden auf der rasenden Fahrt durch den dunklen Tunnel wahrscheinlich auf von Bildschirmen künstlich erzeugte Bilder starren, die aber nur kümmerlichen Ersatz für den zuvor gebotenen Anblick der Alpen sind. Wenn dann noch die schwindelerregende Geschwindigkeit der Fortbewegung durch die massiven Felsberge der Alpen hinzukommt, spürt man schnell, dass der Mensch hier die äußersten Grenzen seiner räumlichen Wahrnehmungsfähigkeit erreicht hat und darüber hinaus auch das Ende jeder nachvollziehbaren landschaftlichen Wirklichkeit.

Der neue Gotthard-Tunnel setzt dem 21. Jahrhundert ein von Geschwindigkeitsrausch und visuellem Verlust geprägtes Denkmal, das wahrscheinlich weitreichende Auswirkungen auf unsere Wahrnehmung der Welt haben wird. 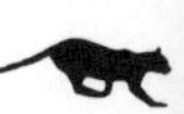 In mancherlei Hinsicht ist diese Bahntunnelstrecke zum Kenotaph gewohnter Landschaftsschau, herkömmlicher Formen des Reisens und der Betrachtung von Landschaft und Natur geworden.

Nirgendwo aber wird die Aussicht so gründlich ausgelöscht wie im unterirdischen Skymetro-Shuttle zwischen dem Mittel- und dem Hauptterminal des Züricher Flughafens. An diesem unmöglichen unterirdischen Ort – ein Bahntunnel, der unter den Landebahnen hindurchführt – soll das Manko der versperrten Aussicht durch die virtuellen Landschaftsbilder eines „TunnelMovies"[3] kompensiert werden. Allen ankommenden und abfliegenden Passagieren wird eine gespenstische Vorführung auf den Tunnelwänden geboten, ein kurzer Überblick über die Landschaften der Schweiz, komplett mit Matterhorn und einer blonden Heidi, die fröhlich lächelnd im Sonnenlicht auf einer Almwiese steht und untermalt von Kuhglockengeläut und Gejodel allen Shuttlepassagieren ein Küsschen zuwirft. Das ist der Moment, in dem die gestressten Passagiere sich erleichtert und wissend anlächeln, weil sie zu ihrer Überraschung in der Dunkelheit eines unwirklichen Shuttletunnels 30 Sekunden lang an einem echten Schweizer Landschaftsmythos teilhatten. Die Bildabfolge dieser Tunnelanimation rauscht in transparenten Farben geisterhaft an einem vorbei, unterbrochen von unzähligen schwarzen Feldern „die den kurzen „TunnelMovie" wie ein Daumenkino wirken lassen. Diese visuelle Zerstückelung verleiht der Bewegtbild-Botschaft zusätzlich eine unterschwellige Bedeutungsebene. Die antiquierte, geisterhafte Darstellung könnte

rails into secluded acoustic corridors completely detached from the landscapes they traverse. The effects of visual reduction in rapid transit, will most certainly have a growing impact on the deepening perceptual negation of landscapes. It may well be, that animations such as "TunnelMovie" could become widespread as last resort to the mythical embodiment of landscapes. The animations yield at best a surrogate point of view, albeit one to be remembered in a global world that would otherwise implacably continue to transpierce our landscapes into oblivion. Gilles Deleuze hinted at such an experiential necessity in his work on empiricism and subjectivity.[5]

The convergence of terrestrial laser scanner technology together with the introduction of high speed trains cutting into the Alps led ironically to the elaboration of a new form of hyperrealist "nature," meant to regenerate massive heaps of excavation material produced as a direct consequence of the new tunnel constructions (*3* p. 189). In terms of classification, this mode of landscape intervention clearly addresses nature of a fourth kind, which is highly transformative and bears no resemblance to past genres whether they be wilderness, agriculture, or garden. The man-made plantations are conceived on top of an artificial topology made out of an industrial substrate resulting from tunnel excavations (*4* p. 189). Both the chemical reaction of the shredded bedrock as well its specific physical and mechanical properties signify that the heap can only foster a completely different kind of "mutant" vegetation with respect to the surroundings. But programmatic exigencies proposed that the massive heap of material be dressed up naturally in the most conventional manner. In other words, this new genre of nature was not allowed to emancipate itself completely from the imprint of the past. The implementation of these heaps reached an unprecedented level of accuracy and definition thanks, more particularly, to advances in precision point cloud surveying (*5* p. 188). However, the image that was actually sought after by authorities was unreal, and rather one of a primeval setting belonging to some foregone age. The problem was that the image to be portrayed could not match that reality, neither the situation nor the site conditions made it easy to "idealise" the project (*6* p. 188). The decision-making process behind the approval of these artificial heaps in the Alps was such that it justified its demands irrespective of the constraints at hand (*7* p. 189). The landscape architect was asked to conform the design of the mound to a register of traditionalist alpine imagery. Advanced techniques of landscape visualising and modelling were used in this instance not so much to test possible variations about the future, but rather to replicate an image of traditional landscape authenticity pending approval. The example that follows shows to what extent the form of the heap did not necessarily express the function and technical exigencies of the project itself, but rather complied to a preconceived idea of nature that seldom matched the physical reality of the site.

It is precisely the displacement between a particular landscape vision and its ambient reality that is of particular interest in the case of the

ebenso gut von einem Schüler Etienne-Jules Mareys stammen und somit vor über hundert Jahren entstanden sein. Interessanterweise gelingt es durch den Einsatz dieses archaisch anmutenden künstlerischen Stilmittels, die Glaubwürdigkeit der „Tunnel-Heidi" und deren Akzeptanz durch das Publikum zu erhöhen. In einem Akt des operativen Kulturtransfers beschwört der „TunnelMovie" den echten Geist der Tradition in der eher banalen Alltagswelt unterirdischer Flughafenanlagen.

Das führt uns zurück zum zentralen Postulat von Roland Barthes, demzufolge jede Epoche ungeachtet der jeweils herrschenden Verhältnisse ihre eigenen Mythen kreiert, und zwar auf der Basis überlieferter Vorstellungen, die dem gegenwärtigen Zeitgeist angepasst werden.[4] Gut vorstellbar, dass der neue Gotthard-Tunnel demnächst mit ähnlich entzückenden „TunnelMovie"-Animationen alpiner Mythen ausgestattet wird. (2 S. 188) Die rasende unterirdische Fahrt durch das gesamte Gebirgsmassiv wird zwar nur wenige Minuten dauern, dennoch wäre dies lange genug, um den Reisenden eine ordentliche Dosis mythologischer Alpenersatzlandschaft einzuflößen. Die Sehnsucht nach derartigen visuellen Beruhigungsmitteln in einer Welt, in der sich alles immer schneller bewegt, zeigt uns, wie weit sich das traditionelle Landschaftsbild in unseren Köpfen bereits von der realen Landschaft losgelöst und entfernt hat. Das Gleiche ließe sich auch von den zahlreichen Lärmschutzwänden überall in der Schweiz behaupten, die Autobahnen und Eisenbahnstrecken umschließen und abgeriegelte „Lärmkorridore" bilden, die vollkommen von der Landschaft losgelöst sind. Diese Einschränkungen des menschlichen Sehfelds und der Fernsicht bei schnellen Fahrten werden mit Sicherheit unsere Wahrnehmung der Landschaft zunehmend negativ beeinflussen. Es ist gut möglich, dass Animationen wie der „TunnelMovie" als Ultima Ratio einer verklärenden Darstellung realer Landschaften weite Verbreitung finden werden. Die Animationen könnten im äußersten Fall als erinnerungswürdige „Ersatz-Ansichten" in einer globalisierten Welt dienen, in der unsere Landschaften unerbittlich weiter durchlöchert werden, bis ihr ursprünglicher Zustand völlig in Vergessenheit geraten sein wird. In seinem Werk über Empirie und Subjektivität hat Gilles Deleuze die Notwendigkeit einer solchen Erfahrung angedeutet.[5]

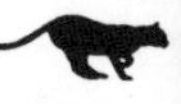

Die Konvergenz terrestrischer Laserscannertechnik mit der Einführung von Hochgeschwindigkeitsbahntrassen, die das Alpenmassiv durchschneiden, hat ironischerweise zum Entstehen einer neuen Form „hyperrealistischer Natur" geführt, dazu gedacht, massive Berge von Abraummaterial zu renaturieren, die während des Gotthard-Tunnelbaus aufgehäuft wurden. (3 S. 189) Nach den Kriterien der Klassifizierung stellt dieser Eingriff in die Natur eine neue, vierte Art der Landschaftsgestaltung dar, die keine Ähnlichkeiten mehr mit den früheren Formen wie Wildnis, Landwirtschaft oder Gartenanlage aufweist. Die von Menschenhand angelegten Pflanzungen und Schonungen entstehen somit auf einer Topologie, die aus einem industriellen Substrat (dem Tunnelabraum) künstlich geformt wurde. (4 S. 189) Aufgrund der chemischen Reaktionen sowie der spezifischen physikalischen

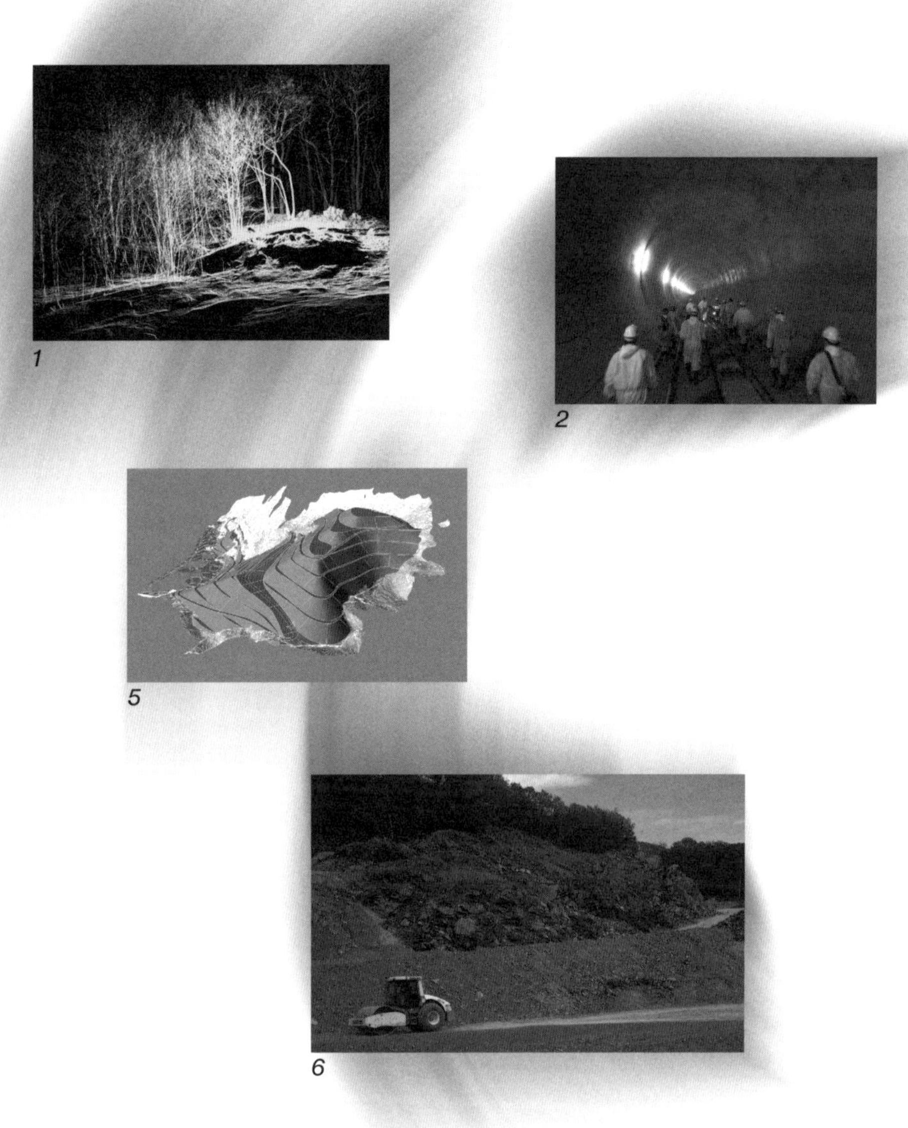

1 Point cloud picture of the Sigirino site — 2 New Gotthard Tunnel, AlpTransit AG — 3 Sigirino site — 4 3-D virtual site model of Sigirino based on point clouds — 5 3-D virtual project model of Sigirino mound — 6 Compaction of the Sigirino heap in layers — 7 Vegetation test strips on the slopes of the Sigirino mound — 8 3-D virtual rendering of the Sigirino mound — 9 Landscape detail of the Sigirino mound

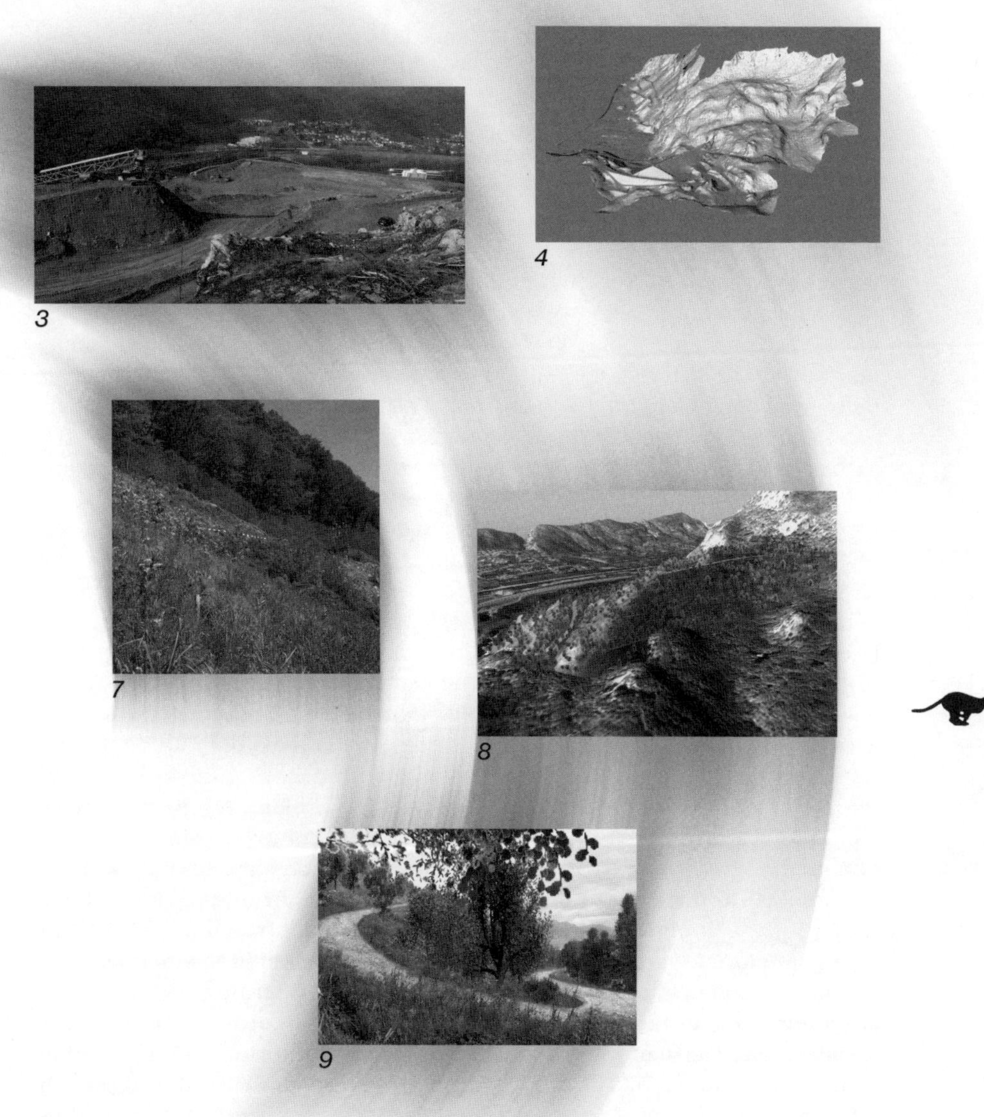

1 Punktwolkenbild des Sigirino-Geländes — *2* Neuer Gotthard-Tunnel, AlpTransit Gotthard AG — *3* Sigirino-Gelände — *4* Virtuelles, auf Punktwolken basierendes 3-D-Modell des Sigirino-Geländes — *5* Virtuelles 3-D-Projektmodell der Sigirino-Abraumhalde — *6* Aufteilung der Sigirino-Halde in Schichten — *7* Versuchsweise Bepflanzung auf den Hängen des Sigirino-Bergs — *8* Virtuelles 3-D-Rendering des Sigirino-Bergs — *9* Landschaftsdetail des Sigirino-Bergs

Sigirino excavation heap. Advanced techniques of landscape simulation imbedded in a 3-D GIS point cloud base were not even possible ten years ago, but, ironically, they have become absolutely necessary today—strongly influencing the role of the designer through a process of strict decisional feedback loops. The terrestrial laser scanner with its point cloud technology delivered a very detailed level of information about the site at Sigirino, and was able to provide a precise response to terrain conditions, enabling the 3.5 million cubic metres of excavation material to be modulated according to expected aesthetic criteria, while respecting extreme site constraints (*8* p. 189). Thus, the same instrumentation used to obtain maximum accuracy in determining the trajectory of the AlpTransit Sotto-Cenere tunnel section was also used with great precision to define the spirited implementation of all its residual rubble. The technology was not only used to survey differential settlement on the heap, it also allowed the repeated testing of the projected form of the mound against the overall Vedeggio River Valley site. The topological shaping of the mound with its curved slopes, terraces, and paths was clearly defined by authorities, and it was interesting to note that the particular aesthetics recommended by Swiss Federal agencies and environmental organisations regarding the Sigirino Mound referred unequivocally to aesthetic criteria on natural beauty established by William Hogarth in the late eighteenth century. In this case, the landscape designer was part of a discussion defining the specific aesthetics of this nature of a fourth kind derived directly from extreme site conditions, but was asked instead to facilitate the implementation of a preestablished image of nature. The engineering programme implied a variety of topological constraints ranging from maximum slope inclinations to regular runoff management around the perimeter of the heap. Regardless of the topological complexity of the project, the designer was asked to integrate curves in the mound topography in order to make it appear more "natural" (*9* p. 189). It would have been simpler and far more economical to build the mound with parallel straight-edged height lines rather than with convoluted ones, but this would not have obeyed the precepts of nature that this artificial landscape was expected to embody.

The actual elaboration of the form of the heap at Sigirino, with its convoluted lines was in fact quite other than "natural." In order to trace these curves at each level of the mound, and to facilitate the step-by-step buildup of the 300 layers constituting its complete 150-metre-tall body, each 0.5-metre-thick compaction layer had to plot out its perimeter precisely with geographic bearings in the X,Y, and Z axes, informing a battery of satellite guided excavators on how to follow its form. This is where the point cloud technology, with its extraordinary topological precision, became the vital instrument of contemporary natural aesthetics. The plotting of the curved slopes would otherwise not have been possible for lack of sufficient bearings. Simpler forms and geometries would have been much easier, less costly to build and may not have required such a high-tech guidance system to confect each and every layer. The irony is,

und mechanischen Eigenschaften des zu Schotter gebrochenen Felsge-
steins kann dort also nur eine ganz andere Vegetation als die ursprüngliche gedeihen. Aber die programmatischen Vorgaben erforderten, dass
die massive Abraumhalde auf konventionelle Weise ganz natürlich
bepflanzt würde. In anderen Worten: Diese neue Gattung der Natur
durfte sich nicht vollständig von früheren Formen emanzipieren. Die
Modellierung der Abraumhalde zu einem grünen Hügel erreichte eine
noch nie dagewesene formale Genauigkeit und Klarheit, insbesondere
dank der Erfassung des Gebiets mittels Punktwolken. (5 S. 188) Das von
den Behörden gewünschte Erscheinungsbild war streng genommen
unwirklich und entsprach einer urzeitlichen, längst verschwundenen Sze-
nerie. Das Problem war, dass durch die Umgestaltung niemals eine
ursprüngliche Naturlandschaft wiederhergestellt werden konnte. (6 S. 188)
Weder die Lage noch die Bedingungen auf dem Gelände eigneten sich für
das idealisierende Projekt. Im Genehmigungsverfahren für diesen künstlichen grünen Hügel in den Alpen wurden aber die behördlichen Wünsche
und Entscheidungen ohne Rücksicht auf die Gegebenheiten des Geländes
und der Lage gerechtfertigt und durchgesetzt. (7 S. 189) Der Landschaftsarchitekt wurde aufgefordert, seinen Entwurf dem traditionellen Erscheinungsbild der Alpenlandschaft anzupassen. Hochmoderne Techniken zur Land-
schaftsvisualisierung und -modellierung wurden hier angewandt – nicht so
sehr, um mögliche Alternativen zu testen, sondern um die Genehmigung für
die Gestaltung einer Landschaft zu erwirken, die wie eine Reproduktion wirkt.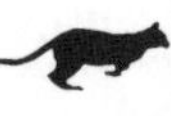
Das folgende Beispiel zeigt, dass die Form der bepflanzten Abraumhalde
nicht unbedingt Zweck und technische Schwierigkeiten des Projekts aus-
drückten, sondern sich nach einer vorgegebenen Naturauffassung richteten,
die nur an wenigen Stellen der physischen Realität des Geländes entsprach.
Genau diese Diskrepanz zwischen einer bestimmten Vorstellung von Landschaft und realer Umgebung ist im Fall der Sigirino-Abraumhalde interessant.
Modernste Techniken der Landschaftssimulation mit Hilfe von 3D-GIS-Punkt-
wolkenscans gab es vor zehn Jahren noch gar nicht, während sie ironischerweise bereits heute absolut unverzichtbar geworden sind und großen Einfluss
auf den Designer ausüben, weil er seine gestalterischen Entscheidungen ständig eng mit den Behörden abstimmen und genehmigen lassen muss. Der terrestrische Laserscanner mit Punktwolken-Darstellungstechnik lieferte sehr detaillierte Informationen über das Gelände bei Sigirino und ermöglichte dadurch eine
Modellierung der 3,5 Millionen Kubikmeter Abraum, unter Berücksichtigung der
gewünschten ästhetischen Kriterien und extremen Einschränkungen, die das
Gelände erforderte. (8 S. 189) So wurde dasselbe Instrumentarium, das beim
Bau des Cenero-Basistunnels den Streckenverlauf absolut präzise festgelegt
hatte, schließlich auch für die Umwandlung der Abraumhalde in eine neue Land-
schaftsformation genutzt. Mit dieser Technik wurde nicht nur die ungleichmäßige
Setzung der Halde vermessen, sie ermöglichte auch immer wieder den Abgleich
der entworfenen Form mit der Topologie des Vedeggiotals. Die Modellierung der

that the symbolic idea of nature conveyed by the convoluted shape of the mound, actually required far more artifice and technology to come into being. That a virtual image of nature be so dependent on technology to convey its form, can question the validity of the aesthetic premise. It would be difficult for that matter to argue that the jagged Sotto Cenere mountain range along the entire Vedeggio River valley in Ticino has anything curvilinear to show. Therefore, in this case, it is the very reductive and a priori notion that an expression of nature is necessarily curved, which imposed itself on a context where this simply was not the rule. The dependency on a highly technological procedure to obtain the more "natural" definition of a project conformed to an arbitrary preconception that is quite symptomatic of our times. Nature has become so scientific, technological, and dogmatic today, that there is actually little room left for etudes or improvisation in matters of landscape design of such scale and engineering complexity. There is a risk when designs of such scale comply solely to the image of an ecology foretold, where the entire scale and physical presence of the industrial operation is negated and controlled by "natural" artifice. In this sense, it is interesting to look for an aesthetic treatise in landscape architecture that could explain the present condition. The last to date is probably an early text by James Corner, which consecrates the definitive globalisation of nature and its landscapes to the reign of ecology.[6]

During the various phases of approval at Sigirino, several attempts were made at shaping the heap in a simpler more geometric forms. But, it was not until the mound's topography actually matched an idea of restorative nature expected by the authorities, that the project finally gained approval. The same can be said about the art and manner in which the vegetation was expected to be planted on the mound, where tree alignments on the slopes were banned, delivering an image of natural integration that would somehow compensate for all the damage entailed during the tunnel project. The discipline of landscape design was severely compromised in this project, when an unprecedented kind of "hyperrealist" gestalt of ecological nature came into being on the heap. Here again point cloud technology combined with electronic tree implantations helped produce 3-D models that gave an extraordinary illusion of landscape reality, actually years before it could ever exist. Whether the imagery produced corresponds to any plausible reality in the future was less important than the stylistic branding of nature that was being addressed. In other words, the image of nature projected on the Sigirino mound to this day remains as virtual as the "TunnelMovie" image of Heidi.

It is, therefore, quite arguable whether the complete erasure of landscape vision in a tunnel palliated by a movie is actually worse than the site implementation of an illusory nature trying to be real. Both cases deal with the illusion of nature that underlines a definitive loss of originality as a direct or indirect consequence of velocity.

Halde mit geschwungenen Hängen, Terrassen und Fußwegen war amtlich festgelegt worden. Dabei bezogen sich die gestalterischen Empfehlungen der zuständigen Schweizer Behörden und mehrerer Umweltorganisationen für die Sigirino-Aufschüttung interessanterweise eindeutig auf die ästhetischen Kriterien für eine schöne Natur, die William Hogarth Ende des 18. Jahrhunderts aufgestellt hat. In diesem Fall war der Landschaftsarchitekt nicht einer von mehreren in einem Team, das die spezifische Ästhetik dieser „Natur der vierten Art" als direkte Folge der extrem schwierigen Geländebeschaffenheit diskutierte, sondern er bekam die kategorische Anweisung, die Reproduktion eines bereits feststehenden Naturbilds zu ermöglichen. Die Ingenieure mussten verschiedene topologische Zwänge berücksichtigen: von maximalen Hangneigungen bis hin zur Drainage rund um den unteren Abschnitt der renaturierten Abraumhalde. Ohne Rücksicht auf die topologische Komplexität des Projekts wurde der Landschaftsarchitekt angewiesen, die Hänge geschwungen zu gestalten, um den grünen Hügel natürlicher wirken zu lassen. (9 S. 189) Es wäre einfacher und wesentlich billiger gewesen, ihn mit geraden, parallel verlaufenden statt mäandernden Höhenlinien zu modellieren, das hätte aber den Vorstellungen von der Art Natur widersprochen, die diese künstliche Landschaft verkörpern sollte.

Die fertig modellierte Form des Sigirino-Schotterbergs mit seinen geschwungenen Höhenlinien sieht allerdings keineswegs natürlich aus. Um die kurvigen Höhenlinien auf jeder Ebene der Halde anzulegen und den sukzessiven 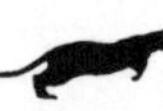 Aufbau der 300 Schichten des insgesamt 150 Meter hohen Hügels zu ermöglichen, mussten die Umrisse jeder 0,5 Meter dicken Schicht mit höchster Präzision berechnet werden. Daher wurden die Bagger per Satellit gesteuert, damit die geplante Form eingehalten werden konnte. Dabei wurde die Punktwolkentechnik mit ihrer extremen topologischen Präzision zum entscheidenden Instrument einer zeitgenössischen Naturästhetik. Die Gestaltung der geschwungenen Hänge wäre ohne geografische Funkpeilung gar nicht möglich gewesen. Der Bau einfacherer Formen und Geometrien hätte kostengünstiger und mit weniger Aufwand realisiert werden können, man hätte kein derart hochtechnisches Leitsystem für die Ausführung jedes Arbeitsschrittes benötigt. Die Ironie liegt darin, dass die Umsetzung der Vorstellung einer natürlich geschwungenen Hügelformation einen wesentlich größeren technischen Aufwand erforderte. Dass diese Übertragung eines virtuellen Naturbilds in greifbare Realität dermaßen von industrieller Technik abhängig ist, stellt die Gültigkeit des ästhetischen Vorbilds in Frage. Man kann auch nicht behaupten, dass die zerklüftete Cenero-Gebirgskette entlang des Tessiner Vedeggiotals an irgendeiner Stelle sanft geschwungen wäre. Hier greift also das Apriori-Konzept, das Natürlichkeit mit dem Gegenteil von Geradlinigkeit gleichsetzt, zu kurz und ist einem Kontext aufgezwungen worden, in dem die Eigenschaft „geschwungen" gar keine regelmäßige Erscheinung ist. Die Tatsache, dass die Herstellung einer „natürlicheren" Form, die ohne Rücksicht auf den Kontext festgelegt wurde, dermaßen von hoch technischen

Both examples address a strong mythical base, that of a return to the alpine arcadia of our forefathers. It is precisely the temporal illusion of reality based on the premise of a return to some "truer" form of nature that raises a deep epochal question for us. We are now completely detached from the notion of place, and even the precepts of a change in landscape perception due to rapid motion developed ten years ago need to be thoroughly reexamined. In a world of rapid motion, landscapes become increasingly victim of their own immutable position. Do we now accept only nurturing the human gaze with myths projected on black matter, thus foregoing landscape's inherent poetic reality?

NOTES—[1] The *Landscape Modeling and Visualising Laboratory* (LMVL) at the ETH is an interdepartmental unit funded by the Swiss National Foundation equipped with an eighteen-station *render farm* and an advanced terrestrial 3-D laser scanner capable of gathering highly precise geographic information at any location on the territory.—[2] Virilio, Paul: "L'entrevue," in: *Un Paysage d'Èvènements,* Paris 1996.—[3] The TunnelMovie installation in the Skymetro at Zürich airport was was realised by the Habegger company in 2008. It is actually viewed by six million passengers every year.—[4] Barthes, Roland: *le mythe, aujourd'hui,* in: Mythologies., Paris 1957, 193.—[5] Deleuze, Gilles: *Empirism et Subjectivité,* Paris 1998.—[6] Corner, James: "Representation and Landscape," in: Swaffield, S. (ed.): *Theory in Landscape Architecture,* Philadelphia 2002, 147–148.—[7] Girot, Christophe: "Movism," in: *Cadrages I, le Regard Actif.* GTA Verlag, ETH Zurich 2002.

Verfahren abhängt, ist symptomatisch für unsere Zeit. Unser Umgang mit der Natur ist heute so wissenschaftlich, technisch und dogmatisch geprägt, dass im Bereich von derart umfangreichen und komplexen Landschaftsgestaltungen tatsächlich wenig Raum für Versuche oder Improvisation bleibt. Bei Raumplanungen dieser Größenordnung, die allein dem in den Köpfen der Planer entwickelten Naturmodell folgen, ist es riskant, den Umfang und die physische Präsenz des technisch-indust-riellen Umsetzungsverfahrens zu negieren und von „natürlicher Künstlich-keit" bestimmen zu lassen. Deshalb sind Abhandlungen zur Ästhetik der Landschaftsarchitektur von Interesse, die die gegenwärtige Situation erklären könnten. Das Neueste zu diesem Thema ist wahrscheinlich ein Essay von James Corner, der die endgültige Globalisierung der Welt und ihrer natürlichen Landschaften der Herrschaft der Ökologie unterordnet.[6]

Im Laufe der verschiedenen Genehmigungsverfahren für das Sigirino-Pro-jekt wurden mehrere Versuche unternommen, der Halde eine einfachere, geometrischere Form zu geben. Die Baugenehmigung wurde schließlich aber erst für die Form erteilt, die den behördlichen Vorstellungen von einer wiederhergestellten Natur entsprach. Das gleiche gilt auch für die Gestal-tung der Bepflanzung des Schotterbergs. Es war zum Beispiel nicht erlaubt, an den Hängen Baumreihen zu pflanzen, denn der neue Berg sollte wie natürlich entstanden und bewachsen erscheinen und so den Umweltscha-den scheinbar ausgleichen, den der Tunnelbau angerichtet hatte. Die land-schaftsarchitektonische Fachkompetenz wurde bei diesem Projekt massiv ignoriert, sodass auf dem Hügel eine Art „hyperrealistische Natur" geschaffen wurde, die ihresgleichen sucht. Auch hier wurden mit Hilfe der Punktwolken-technik digitale 3D-Simulationen von Baumpflanzungen erstellt, die außeror-dentlich real wirkten und die Bäume sogar in ihrem erst viele Jahre später zu erwartenden ausgewachsenen Stadium zeigten. Es war nicht so wichtig, ob die Bilder einem tatsächlichen künftigen Entwicklungsstand der Landschaft entsprachen. Wichtiger war die stilistische Markenbildung des gestalteten Landschaftsraums. Demnach ist das auf die Abraumhalde bei Sigirino proji-zierte Naturbild bis heute ebenso virtuell geblieben wie das Heidi-Bild im Shut-tle-Tunnel des Züricher Flughafens.

Man kann darüber streiten, ob ein Naturfilm als besänftigender Ersatz für die Auslöschung der Landschaftsbetrachtung in einem Tunnel schlimmer ist als die Schaffung einer Ersatzlandschaft, die natürlich zu sein versucht. In beiden Fällen haben wir es mit einer Illusion von Natur zu tun, die definitiv einen Verlust an Authentizität verkörpert – eine Folge, ob direkt oder indirekt, des Baus schnel-ler Verkehrsmittel.

Beide Beispiele haben eine stark mythische Basis: die Sehnsucht nach der Rück-kehr in das alpine Arkadien unserer Vorväter. Genau diese illusorische Vorstellung von Realität auf der Grundlage einer Rückkehr zu einer „echteren" Natur wirft eine Frage von epochaler Bedeutung auf. Wir haben uns jetzt völlig von der Bedeutung einer Lokalität als unverwechselbarem, unauswechselbarem Ort gelöst; selbst die

vor zehn Jahren verfassten Erläuterungen zu einer veränderten Wahrnehmungsweise von Landschaft bei immer schnellerer Fortbewegung müssen erneut einer gründlichen Überprüfung unterzogen werden.[7] In einer mobilen Welt hoher Geschwindigkeiten werden Landschaften zunehmend das Opfer ihrer eigenen Unbeweglichkeit. Doch sind wir wirklich bereit, auf die Poesie der realen Landschaft zu verzichten und unseren Blick nur noch an auf schwarzen Hintergrund projizierten Mythen zu laben?

ANMERKUNGEN—[1] LMVL: Das *Landscape Modeling and Visualising Laboratory* an der ETH Zürich ist eine interdisziplinäre Abteilung, die von der Schweizer Nationalstiftung „Pro Helvetia" finanziert wird und mit einer 18 Stationen umfassenden *render farm* sowie einem hochentwickelten 3D-Laser-Scanner für Landschaftsaufnahmen ausgestattet ist. Mit diesem Scanner lassen sich hochaufgelöste Bilder und geografische Informationen von jedem Standort eines untersuchten Gebiets aufnehmen.—[2] Virilio, Paul: „L'entrevue", in: ders. *Un paysage d'évènements,* Paris 1996 (deutsche Ausg.: *Ereignislandschaft.* München/Wien 1998).—[3] Das „TunnelMovie"-System in der Skymetro am Flughafen Zürich wurde 2008 von der Firma Habegger installiert. Pro Jahr sehen es sechs Millionen Flugpassagiere.—[4] Barthes, Roland: *Le mythe, aujourd'hui, 193* Paris 1957 [deutsche Ausg.: *Mythen des Alltags.* Frankfurt 1964; 2003; Berlin 2010 (Übersetzung: Horst Brühmann)]—[5] Deleuze, Gilles: *Empirisme et subjectivité,* Paris 1998.—[6] Corner, James: „Representation and Landscape", in: S. Swaffield (Hg.): *Theory in Landscape Architecture,* Philadelphia 2002, 147f.—[7] Vgl. Girot, Christophe: „Movism", in: *Cadrages I, le Regard Actif,* Zürich 2002.

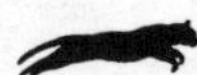

Michael Schumacher has been a professor of design and construction at the University of Hanover since 2007. In 1988 he founded the office **schneider+schumacher** in Frankfurt, which has realised numerous awarded buildings since then. Study at the TU Kaiserslautern and the Städelschule in Frankfurt/Main, where he subsequently taught. Chairman of the BDA Hessen for many years and a member of the municipal building council of the City of Frankfurt. Publication: *MOVE. Dynamic Components and Elements in Architecture* (ed., 2010)

Adeline Seidel has been a scientific assistant at the Weißenhof Institute of the State Academy of Fine Arts Stuttgart since 2010 and at the Chair of Urban Design, Department of Architecture at the TU Darmstadt since 2006. Prior to this, she worked with *urban drift* Berlin for the exhibition *Talking Cities* at **ENTRY 2006** Zeche Zollverein and in various architectural and planning offices in Germany and Switzerland. She is co-founder and editor of the magazine **GENERALIST** – *Magazin für Architektur.*

Michael Schumacher
Die Poesie der Bewegung in der Architektur
Interview

Michael Schumacher ist seit 2007 Professor für **Entwerfen und Konstruieren an**
der Universität Hannover. 1988 gründete er das **Büro schneider+schumacher**
in Frankfurt, das zahlreiche ausgezeichnete Bauten realisierte. **Studium an**
der TU Kaiserslautern und an der Städelschule in **Frankfurt/Main, an der er**
auch später lehrte. Langjähriger Vorsitzender des **BDA Hessen und Mitglied**
im Städtebaubeirat der Stadt Frankfurt. Publikation: *MOVE, Bewegliche Kom-*
ponenten und Bauteile in der Architektur (Hg., 2010).

Adeline Seidel ist seit 2010 wissenschaftliche **Mitarbeiterin am Weißenhof-**
Institut an der Staatlichen Akademie der Bildenden **Künste Stuttgart und seit**
2006 am Lehrstuhl für Entwerfen & Siedlungsentwicklung, **Fachbereich Archi-**
tektur der TU Darmstadt. Zuvor Mitarbeit bei *urban drift* **Berlin für die Aus-**
stellung *Talking Cities* auf der *ENTRY 2006* Zeche Zollverein **und in verschie-**
denen Architektur- und Planungsbüros in Deutschland und der Schweiz. **Sie ist**
Mitbegründerin und Herausgeberin von *GENERALIST - Magazin für Architektur.*

Adeline Seidel: When, where, and how does "motion" play a part in architecture, **and what influence does it have on its form?**

Michael Schumacher: Although architecture is immobile by nature, motion plays a large part. Expressed in overall categories, one could say that motion is employed either to change the function of architecture, to protect it, or to improve its energy use. Buildings always contain mobile components for functional reasons, and these often represent a precondition to their sustainability. Examples can be found in every building: doors or stadium roofs are either open or closed, and windows have sun-protection slats—all these are subject to the logics of function, construction, and of course aesthetics. So, motion always needs to be understood in the context of architectural, aesthetic, and constructive issues. **Things that are mobile—like all things—are characterised by specific forms. But here the definition of form is more complex than in the case of static objects, since the form changes as a result of the movement. In architecture, it is often a matter of functional and aesthetic control over three states: closed, open, and moving in-between. The wonderful Switch Pitch balls by Chuck Hoberman handle motion with reference to form. In its initial state, the ball is divided in a seemingly complex way into two colours, one of which is dominant. If the ball is moved, by throwing it up into the air, for instance, it changes colour (*1* p. 204). Due to a complex inverse motion, the coloured areas inside change places with those outside. The interim state is not ball-shaped; it is more like a star. It is possible at that stage to see into the construction. The form is an essential function of the motion, and it could not be any other way. Although ultimately the form and motion are quite simple, they appear complicated and incomprehensible to us. That is the source of their magic. Transferred to a banal construction component like a door, this means that it fits perfectly into the door frame in its closed state. When being opened, it often stands in space somehow or other and as a rule it cannot find an "attractive" opening position. It is almost as if the door is waiting to be closed again in order to find a "good" position.**

AS: What types of "motion" in past architecture should be mentioned—and where do we stand today? Is it possible to discern a development over the last 100 years?

MS: It is possible to derive all motion from the basic categories of turning and pushing, or combinations of the two—and this will always be the case. Industrialisation and systematic material research undertaken more often during recent decades, as well as greater precision in the making of building components have made more complex sequences of motion possible, sometimes with quite astonishing effects. Think of the wonderful opening mechanisms by Santiago Calatrava, for example: walls that move with a wave-like motion, and roofs that open up. One fine example is his design for a garage door at the company headquarters of Ernsting in Coesfeld-Lette, which is subdivided into many jointed parts (*2* p. 204, *3, 4* p. 205). Today, it is possible that we stand on a threshold where

Adeline Seidel: Wann, wo und wie spielt „Bewegung" in Architektur eine Rolle und welchen Einfluss hat sie auf ihre Gestalt?

Michael Schumacher: Obwohl die Architektur ihrem Wesen nach immobil ist, spielt Bewegung eine große Rolle. In großen Kategorien betrachtet kann man sagen, dass Bewegung entweder dazu dient, Architektur in ihrer Funktion zu verändern, sie zu schützen oder energetisch zu verbessern. Gebäude beinhalten aus funktionalen Gründen immer auch bewegliche Teile, die oftmals eine Voraussetzung ihrer Dauerhaftigkeit darstellen. Beispiele finden sich in jedem Gebäude: Türen oder Dächer von Stadien sind entweder offen oder zu, Fenster besitzen Sonnenschutzlamellen – all das unterliegt der Logik von Funktion, Konstruktion und auch von Ästhetik. Die Beweglichkeit ist also immer im Zusammenhang mit Fragen der Architektur, der Ästhetik und der Konstruktion zu verstehen. Bewegliche Dinge sind wie alle Dinge durch spezifische Formen charakterisiert. Die Definition der Form ist jedoch komplexer als bei statischen Gegenständen, da sich die Form durch die Bewegung verändert. Es geht in der Architektur häufig um die funktionale und gestalterische Kontrolle von drei Zuständen: geschlossen, offen und bewegt dazwischen. Die wunderbaren Spielbälle von Chuck Hoberman gehen in Bezug auf die Form mit Bewegung um. Im Ausgangszustand eins zeigt sich eine scheinbar kompliziert gegliederte Kugel in zwei Farben, von denen eine dominant ist. Bewegt man die Kugel, etwa indem man sie in die Luft wirft, wechselt die Kugel die Farbe. (1 S. 204) Durch eine komplexe inverse Bewegung tauschen sich die innenliegenden Farbflächen gegen die außenliegenden aus. Der Zwischenzustand zeigt keine Kugel, sondern eher eine Art Stern. Jetzt kann man in die Konstruktion hineinblicken. Die Form ist eine zwingende Funktion der Bewegung, die nicht anders sein könnte. Obwohl Form und Bewegung am Ende einfach sind, erscheinen sie uns kompliziert und unbegreiflich. Darin liegt ihre Magie. Übertragen auf ein banales Bauteil wie eine Tür bedeutet dies: In geschlossenem Zustand passt sie perfekt in die Zarge. Beim Öffnen steht sie häufig irgendwie im Raum und findet in der Regel auch keine „schöne" Öffnungsposition. In gewisser Weise wartet die Tür darauf wieder geschlossen zu werden, um eine „gute" Position zu finden.

AS: Welche Arten der „Bewegung" in der Architektur waren in der Vergangenheit nennenswert – wo stehen wir heute? Kann man eine Entwicklung der letzten 100 Jahre aufzeigen?

MS: Alle Bewegungen lassen sich auf die Grundkategorien Drehen, Schieben oder eine Kombination von beiden zurückführen, daran wird sich auch niemals etwas ändern. Durch die Industrialisierung und die verstärkt in den letzten Jahrzehnten betriebene systematische Materialforschung sowie die höhere Präzision in der Ausführung von Bauteilen wurden komplexere Bewegungsabläufe mit zum Teil verblüffenden Effekten möglich. Denken Sie zum Beispiel an die wunderbaren Öffnungsmechanismen von Santiago Calatrava: Wände, die sich wellenförmig bewegen, Dächer, die sich

fragmentary biochemical motions within building components (for example in the space between insulating planes of glass) disclose new possibilities for development. It is not the mechanical optimising of a function that creates attractive motion but a conscious accentuation, a slight exaggeration. This has nothing to do with higher construction costs: on the contrary, it is all about using motion to increase the utility value of structures and therefore their sustainability (e.g., by means of closable stadium roofs) or to improve the energy balance. The systematic development of new materials in industry will increase the potential for moveable components in architecture.

AS: **In James Bond or science fiction films, the architecture is often staged through motion. The control desk revolves in the engine room, for example, rooms continue into secret corridors and previously invisible doors open to reveal a concealed space. But what possibilities does moveable architecture offer in everyday life? And what opportunities do mobile elements create in architecture?**

MS: Now, you have brought up a topic that interests me greatly. Because besides the practical aspects of motion that we employ every day when we open or shut a door, it is also decisively important to me as an architect how and in what way we do so, and what forms of expression are associated with it. Motion is always expression as well—like in dance, for example. That's why we use the phrase "the poetry of motion in architecture." Today, new possible ways of staging motion are available as a result of better materials, greater precision and computer-driven machines. Let me cite two practical examples from our own work: the façade of the Westhafen-Tower (5, 6 p. 204) in Frankfurt/Main consists of triangular window elements that open or close automatically, operated by luminance, wind, and rain sensors; they regulate the climate inside the tower in a comparable way to a bird's feathers. Or what about the "eyes" or rather the skylights in the extension to the Städel Museum in Frankfurt/Main being constructed at present? They control the brightness of the museum space according to the external light conditions, in a similar way to our own eyes. Our aim should be to utilise the available possibilities in order to design a richer, more poetic architecture with respect to motion, which is only one aspect among many. There is no set of instructions, no perfect recipe for this. It is similar to dance; architects need to be quite clear about the relevant problems of motion and work out a solution which is as attractive and elegant as possible.[1]

AS: **What typologies and mechanisms of motion can be found in architecture? How do these mechanisms influence a space or a building in detail?**

MS: Typologically, everything is a matter of turning and pushing. The question of how these mechanisms influence a space or a building is extremely complicated. That is why extreme care in design is vital, as both the requisite mechanisms and the

öffnen. **Ein besonderes Beispiel ist sein in zahlreiche Gelenke aufgeglie-
dertes Garagentor für den Ernsting's-Firmensitz in Coesfeld-Lette.** (*2* S. 204,
3, 4 S. 205) **Heute stehen wir möglicherweise an der Schwelle, an der kleintei-
lige biochemische Bewegungen innerhalb von Bauteilen (wie etwa dem Zwi-**
schenraum von Isolierglasscheiben) neue Entwicklungsmöglichkeiten aufzeigen.
Schöne Bewegung ist kein mechanisches Optimum einer Funktion, sondern eine
bewusste Betonung, eine kleine Übertreibung. Das hat nichts mit höheren Bau-
kosten zu tun, umgekehrt geht es ja gerade darum, den Nutzwert von Häusern
und dadurch ihre Nachhaltigkeit durch Bewegung zu erhöhen (etwa durch ver-
schließbare Stadiondächer) oder die Energiebilanz zu verbessern. Die systematische Entwicklung von neuen Materialien in der Industrie wird das Potenzial für
bewegliche Komponenten in der Architektur erhöhen.

AS: In James-Bond- oder Science-Fiction-Filmen **wird die dort gezeigte Archi-**
tektur oft durch Bewegung inszeniert. **So drehen sich Schaltzentralen in den**
Maschinenraum, **Räume fahren in einen geheimen Gang und zuvor unsichtbare**
Türen öffnen sich zu einem verborgenen Raum. **Welche Möglichkeiten bietet**
aber eine bewegliche Architektur in unserem Alltag? **Und welche Möglichkeiten**
bieten sich für die Architektur durch bewegliche Elemente?
MS: **Hier sprechen Sie ein Thema an, das mich im Kern interessiert. Denn
neben den praktischen Aspekten der Bewegung, die wir jeden Tag nutzen,
wenn wir eine Türe öffnen oder schließen, ist es für mich als Architekt
von entscheidender Bedeutung, wie und in welcher Art wir das tun und was
damit an Ausdrucksformen verbunden ist. Bewegung ist immer auch Ausdruck, wie etwa beim Tanzen. Wir benutzen deshalb den Terminus „die Poesie der Bewegung in der Architektur". Durch bessere Materialien, höhere
Präzision und computergesteuerte Maschinen bieten sich neue Möglichkeiten der Inszenierung von Bewegung. Ich nenne zwei praktische Beispiele aus
unserer Arbeit: Die Fassade des Westhafen-Towers** (*5, 6* S. 204) **in Frankfurt/
Main besteht aus dreieckigen Fensterelementen, die sich automatisch gesteuert durch Helligkeits-, Wind- und Regensensoren öffnen oder schließen und vergleichbar mit einem Vogelgefieder das Klima innerhalb des Turmes regeln. Oder
die „Augen", vielmehr die Oberlichter bei der gerade im Bau befindlichen Erweiterung des Städel Museums in Frankfurt/Main, die die Helligkeit des Museumsrau-
mes je nach äußeren Lichtverhältnissen ähnlich unseren eigenen Augen steuern.**
Ziel sollte es sein, die Möglichkeiten zu nutzen, die Architektur auch in Bezug auf
den Aspekt Bewegung, der ja nur einer von vielen ist, reicher und poetischer zu
gestalten. Eine Anleitung, ein Rezept dafür gibt es nicht. Es ist wie beim Tanz;
Architekten müssen sich über die jeweiligen Probleme der Bewegung klar sein und
dafür eine möglichst reizvolle und elegante Lösung erarbeiten.[1]

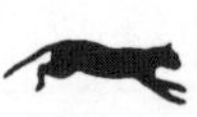

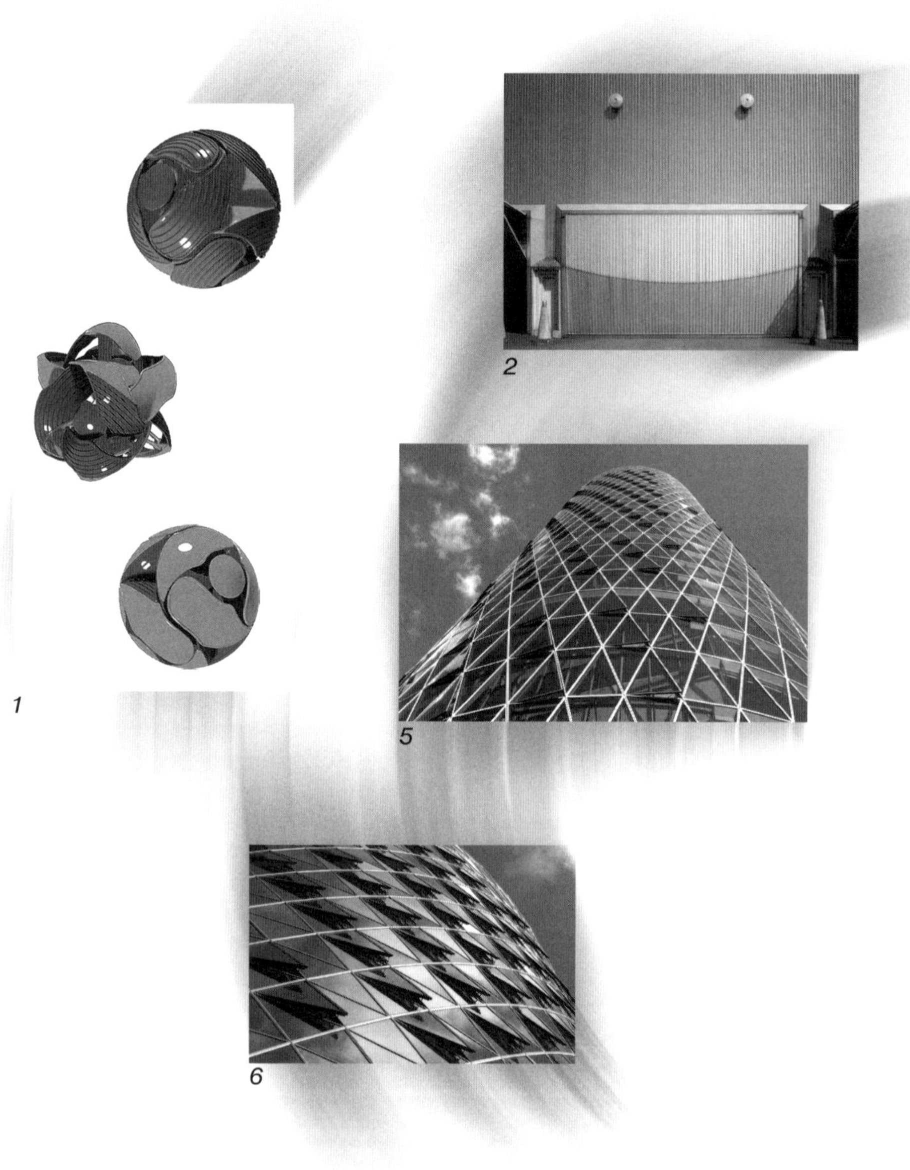

1 Chuck Hoberman: Switch Pitch, 2004 — *2, 3, 4* Bruno Reichlin, Fabio Reinhardt and Santiago Calatrava: façade design and gates to Ernsting's distribution centre in Coesfeld-Lette, 1983/84 — *5, 6* schneider+schumacher: façade of the Westhafen-Tower in Frankfurt/Main — *7, 8* CargoLifter hangar

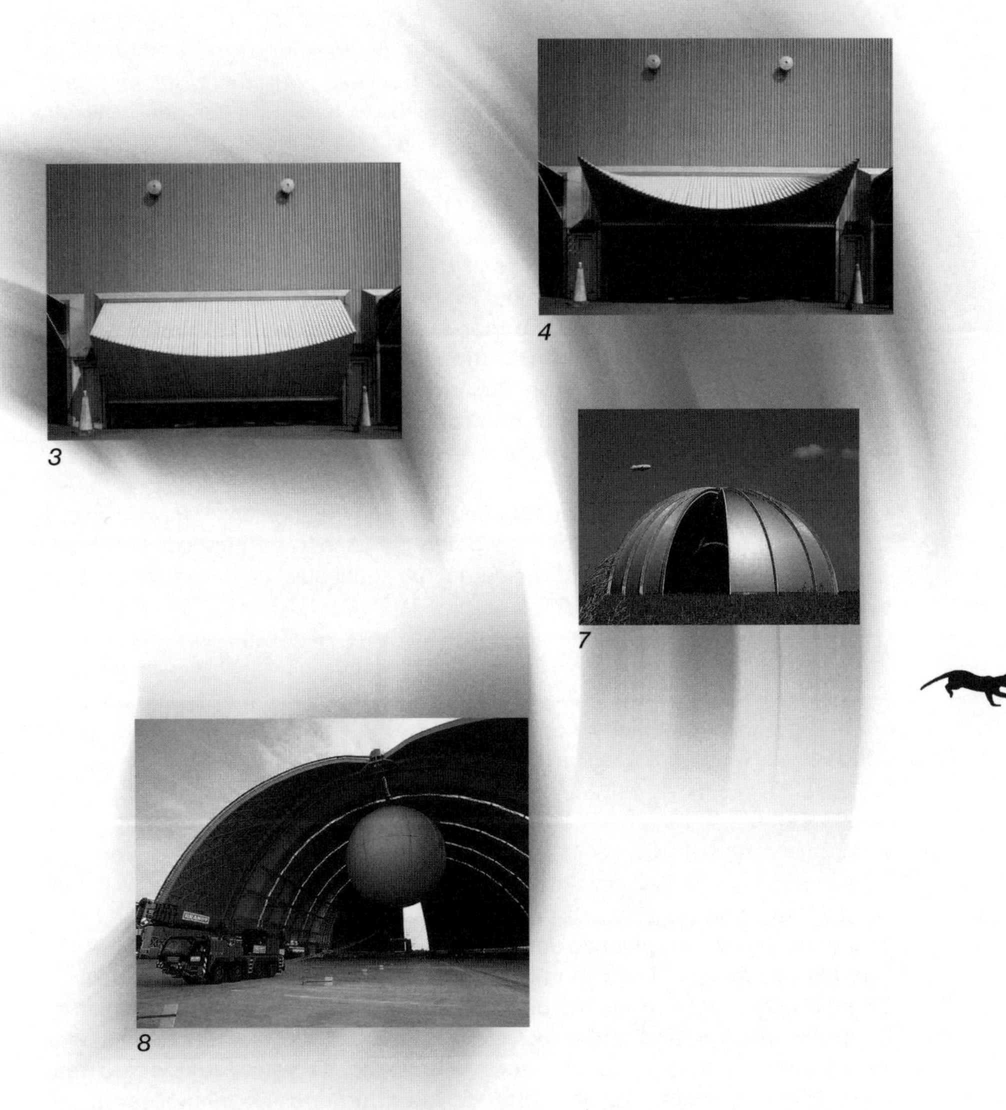

1 Chuck Hoberman: Switch Pitch, 2004 — **2, 3, 4** Bruno Reichlin, Fabio Reinhardt und Santiago Calatrava: Fassadengestaltung und Tore des Ernsting's-Vertriebscenter in Coesfeld-Lette, 1983/84 — **5, 6** schneider+schumacher: Fassade Westhafen-Tower in Frankfurt/Main — **7, 8** CargoLifter Werfthalle

associated noises and securing measures influence a space to a massive extent. In the car industry, for example, the days are long gone in which the sound only ensued from the geometry of the exhaust manifold and the vibrations it produced. Now the sound is refined as long as the form. Sound designers investigate the sound while the engine is idling, in phases of acceleration and at top speed. In the building business, by contrast to car manufacturing, little attention has been paid to the sound as yet. **The sound made by servomotors moving to open a window is pure chance, and so it tends to be rather unpleasant as a rule. The thin profiles of the façade vibrate and transport the amplified sound of the motors almost everywhere. Generally, there will be signals as well: so that no one gets trapped, closing movements in architecture are often accompanied by penetrating warning noises, which may thoroughly spoil one's pleasure in the movement. Sound is an immanent accompaniment to motion, and its dramaturgical potential must be used in order to accentuate the beauty of the motion rather than destroy it.**

AS: **How do "typologies" of motion (manual and mechanical) behave subject to the design of their possible movements and the size of building components? And what concrete influence do individual building components have on the design of architecture?**
MS: A fly functions in a different way to an elephant and so its appearance is very different, too. The size and mass of building components is decisive with respect to their movement and the associated expressive possibilities. A heavy door can only be moved slowly by hand or mechanically. Therefore, the impression given will be one of mass and gravity. The designers of science-fiction films know how to utilise this in a clever way, although in the process they often conjure up ridiculous creatures or computer-generated machines that could not exist in the real world governed by the laws of volume. One structural example of the design influence that individual building components can have on architecture is the CargoLifter hangar south of Berlin. It is a huge shed conceived as an arch construction with two gigantic domed gateways at the head ends. (*7, 8* p. 205) The decisive means of design in the case of this hangar—which no longer fulfils its original function—is the opening mechanism of those gates. There is no further design, and this effect is often used as a vehicle of advertising. **Within our own work, in this context I recall a conservatory that we built in 1995: it was a classic terraced house situation and the client wanted a conservatory with a framework of steel profiles. Two wings of the door create a glass wall onto the garden. The chief attraction: as protection from overheating, the glass roof opens on the horizontal plane with the aid of a hinge on the upper mounting. This also means that in summer the veranda can be turned into a roofed-in terrace.**

AS: Welche Typologien und Mechanismen der Bewegung gibt es in der Architektur? Wie beeinflussen diese Mechanismen im Einzelnen den Raum und das Gebäude?

MS: Typologisch läuft alles auf ein Drehen und Schieben hinaus. Das Thema, wie die Mechanismen den Raum und das Gebäude beeinflussen, ist ausgesprochen vielschichtig. Deshalb bedarf es äußerster Sorgfalt bei der Gestaltung, denn sowohl die erforderlichen Mechanismen als auch die damit verbundenen Geräusche und Sicherungsmaßnahmen beeinflussen massiv den Raum. Die Zeiten in der Autoindustrie sind vorbei, in denen sich der Klang (oder „Sound") nur aus der Geometrie des Auspuffkrümmers und den dadurch hervorgerufenen Schwingungen ergab. Am Klang wird genauso lange gefeilt wie an der Form. Sounddesigner untersuchen den Klang im Leerlauf, in den Beschleunigungsphasen und bei Höchstgeschwindigkeit. In der Baubranche wird dem Klang anders als bei den Autobauern bisher wenig Aufmerksamkeit geschenkt. Wie es klingt, wenn sich die Stellmotoren bewegen, die das Fenster öffnen, ist purer Zufall, deshalb klingt es in der Regel auch eher unangenehm. Die dünnen Fassadenprofile schwingen gut und transportieren den Schall der kleinen Motoren verstärkt überall hin. Dazu kommen in der Regel die Töne: Damit sich niemand klemmt, sind Schließbewegungen in der Architektur häufig von penetranten Warntönen begleitet, die die Freude an der Bewegung gründlich vergällen können. Der Klang ist ein immanenter Begleiter der Bewegung, dessen dramaturgisches Potenzial es zu nutzen gilt, um die Schönheit der Bewegung hervorzuheben und nicht zu zerstören.

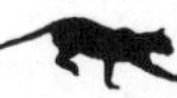

AS: Wie verhalten sich Bewegungs-„Typologien" (manuell und mechanisch) in Abhängigkeit zu der Gestaltung ihrer Bewegungsmöglichkeiten und zur Größe der Bauteile? Und welchen konkreten Gestaltungseinfluss haben die einzelnen Bauteile auf die Architektur?

MS: Eine Fliege funktioniert anders und sieht deshalb auch anders aus als ein Elefant. Die Größe und Masse von Bauteilen spielt für die Bewegung und für die damit verbundenen Ausdrucksmöglichkeiten eine entscheidende Rolle. Eine schwere Tür lässt sich von Hand oder auch mechanisch nur langsam bewegen. Sie wirkt deshalb massiv und gravitätisch. Die Designer von Science–Fiction-Filmen wissen das geschickt einzusetzen, obwohl sie dabei oft lächerliche, mit dem Computer generierte Kreaturen oder Maschinen entstehen lassen, die aufgrund von Massegesetzen in der realen Welt gar nicht existieren könnten. Ein gebautes Beispiel für den Gestaltungseinfluss einzelner Bauteile auf die Architektur ist die CargoLifter Werfthalle südlich von Berlin. Eine riesige Halle, die als Bogenkonstruktion konzipiert ist und die über zwei gigantische Kuppeltore an den beiden Kopfenden verfügt. (7, 8 S. 205) Bei dieser Halle, die nicht mehr ihre ursprüngliche Funktion erfüllt, ist das alles entscheidende Gestaltungsmittel der Öffnungsmechanismus dieser Tore. Mehr Gestaltung gibt es nicht – und dieser Effekt wird gerne auch als Werbeträger genutzt. In unserer eigenen Arbeit denke ich dabei

AS: **What tasks does this create for the architect, who becomes a designer of motion?**

MS: I see architects as people who suggest worlds to others (smaller worlds or bigger ones in urban development): worlds that are worth living in, enduring, and beautiful. Because the motion of building components (or even of entire houses) is part of this, they need to be all-rounders who know what they are doing with respect to the possibilities and problems of motion. As in other areas of planning, it is conceivable that experts may emerge e.g., façade planners as separate service providers offering complex information about mechanisms or motors. This field of work would demand fundamental knowledge of physics and engineering, as well as comprehensive awareness of the products for pushing and turning available on the market, in order to move building components of different weights. Knowledge of architecture would also be essential, of course. I could imagine a specialist Master's degree in this subject, creating a link between architecture, mechanical engineering, and industry.

AS: **Wherever there are movable elements, the danger of constructive-technical problems developing in precisely this place increases rapidly. What constructive aspects must be taken into account during planning?**

MS: That's true. Realising motion in architecture is very demanding technically. We need to weigh very carefully whether and just how mobile building components are employed. Our publication work led us to many examples of buildings that can be transformed in a fascinating way. In the process, we also became aware of the amount of know-how and care necessary to work out solutions that function well. These solutions need to be related to the age of each building, as well. When motion succeeds, it is a lasting source of pleasure.

AS: **To what extent does planning work change for architects when they deploy moving elements? And what altered or expanded usages result?**

MS: Think of a venue for events—a large hall that is being made to change its size according to the size of the audience expected. That means for the architect, in addition to the mechanical problems that need solving, he cannot lose sight of the spatial issues, either. What does the room look like when it is small, what is it like when it's big? How long will the change last? What else needs to change so that the space comes across as convincing in both or several stages?

AS: **What demands on architecture can be defined by the design of motion?**

MS: The same ones as ever: architecture should be lasting and beautiful.

an einen Wintergarten, den wir 1995 realisiert haben: Eine klassische Reihenhaus-Situation und der Bauherr wünschte sich einen Wintergarten, dessen Konstruktion aus Stahlprofilen bestehen sollte. Zwei Türflügel bilden eine Glaswand zum Garten. Der besondere Clou: Das gläserne Dach, das sich zum Schutz vor Überhitzung mit Hilfe eines Gelenks an der oberen Aufhängung bis zur Horizontalen öffnen kann, wodurch der Wintergarten im Sommer zur überdachten Terrasse wird.

AS: **Welche Aufgaben entstehen daraus für den Architekten, der somit auch** zum Gestalter von Bewegung wird?

MS: **Architekten sind für mich Menschen, die für ihre Mitmenschen Welten vorschlagen (kleinere oder im Städtebau größere). Welten, die lebenswert, dauerhaft und schön sind. Da die Bewegung von Bauteilen (oder auch von ganzen Häusern) dazu gehört, müssen sie sich als Allrounder mit den Möglichkeiten und den Problemen von Bewegung auskennen. Es ist wie in anderen Bereichen des Planens vorstellbar, dass sich Experten herausbilden, wie etwa Fassadenplaner, die die komplexen Informationen zu Mechanismen oder Motoren als eigenständige Dienstleistung anbieten. Der Aufgabenbereich würde fundamentale physikalische Ingenieurkenntnisse erfordern, ebenso wie den Überblick über die am Markt vorhandenen Produkte zum Schieben und Drehen, um Bauteile unterschiedlicher Gewichtsklassen zu bewegen. Zudem wären Kenntnisse der Architektur grundlegend. Zu dieser Thematik ließe sich ein spezieller Master denken, der das Verbindungsglied zwischen Architektur, Maschinenbau und Industrie darstellt.** 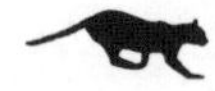

AS: **Sobald es bewegliche Elemente gibt, ist die Gefahr, dass genau an dieser** Stelle bautechnische Probleme auftreten, besonders hoch. **Welche konstruktiven** Aspekte gilt es bei der Planung zu beachten?

MS: **Das ist wahr. Bewegung in der Architektur zu verwirklichen, ist technisch anspruchsvoll. Es muss sorgsam abgewogen werden, ob und wie bewegliche Bauteile eingesetzt werden. Durch die Publikationsarbeit haben wir sehr viele Beispiele gefunden, die faszinierende wandelbare Bauten zeigen. Deutlich wurde dabei auch, welches Know-how und welche Gründlichkeit erforderlich sind, um Lösungen zu erarbeiten, die auf das Lebensalter von Gebäuden bezogen gut funktionieren. Wenn Bewegung gelingt, ist sie ein dauerhafter Quell der Freude.**

AS: **Inwiefern ändert sich durch den Einsatz von beweglichen Elementen die** Planung für den Architekten? **Welche Nutzungsänderungen bzw. -erweiterun**gen ergeben sich daraus?

MS: **Denken Sie sich einen Veranstaltungsraum, eine große Halle, die ihre Größe abhängig von den erwarteten Zuschauern ändern soll. Für den Architekten bedeutet das, neben den mechanischen Problemen, die zu lösen sind, auch die räumlichen nicht aus den Augen zu verlieren. Wie wirkt der Raum klein, wie wirkt er groß? Wie lange dauert die Veränderung? Was muss sich sonst verän**dern, damit der Raum in beiden oder mehreren Stadien überzeugen kann?

NOTE—[1] In the context of a research project on this topic, Michael Schumacher published: Schumacher, Michael/Schäffer, Oliver/Vogt, Michael-Marcus: *MOVE - Dynamic Components and Elements in Architecture,* Basel 2010.

AS: Welche Ansprüche an Architektur können durch eine Gestaltung von Bewegung definiert werden?

MS: Dieselben wie immer in der Architektur: Sie sollte dauerhaft und schön sein.

ANMERKUNG— [1] Im Zusammenhang mit einem Forschungsprojekt zu dem Thema „Bewegung in der Architektur" wurde das folgende Buch veröffentlicht: Schumacher, Michael/Schäffer, Oliver/ Vogt, Michael-Marcus: *MOVE - Architektur in Bewegung. Dynamische Komponenten und Bauteile.* Basel 2010.

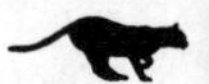

Chris Bangle
Strategise Emotion. Considering Car Design
Interview

Chris Bangle is an automobile designer. After working for Opel AG and Fiat, **in 1992 he became designer-in -chief for the BMW Group and created an international sensation with his visionary design** *GINA,* **an experimental roadster with a flexible external chassis.** After pushing car design language to its **limits for twenty-eight years, Bangle announced his departure from the auto industry on February 3, 2009.** He is pursuing his own design-related endeavours **from his studio in Italy,** focusing on new ideas and cutting-edge innovation.
www.chrisbangleassociates.com

Chris Bangle
Strategise Emotion. Überlegungen zum Autodesign
Interview

Chris Bangle ist Automobildesigner. Nach Tätigkeiten für die Opel AG und Fiat wurde er 1992 Designchef bei der BMW Group und sorgte mit dem visionären Entwurf *GINA*, einem experimentellen Roadster mit flexibler Karosserieaußenhaut, international für Furore. Nachdem er über 28 Jahre lang die Grenzen der Ausdrucksmöglichkeiten im Autodesign ausgelotet hat, gab Bangle am 3. Februar 2009 seinen Rückzug aus der Autoindustrie bekannt. Er entwickelt nun von seinem Studio in Italien aus seine eigenen Designideen weiter, mit dem Fokus auf neue Konzepte und Innovationen.
www.chrisbangleassociates.com

Annett Zinsmeister: The car industry has to consider the shape of movement **and the design of movement in many respects. As an automobile designer for different manufacturers like Opel (Vauxhall) and Fiat, and chief designer at BMW you have been involved in this issue with great success.** Your automo**bile designs and pioneering concepts have triggered considerable attention and international acclaim. What basic parameters and special qualities char**acterise a high-quality design in the car industry?

Chris Bangle: I will have to introduce a new term for your audience, that of the "car designer." "Car design" is not the same as "automobile design," or "automobile design;" The latter is an assemblage of real-world objective problem solving while the former is the configuration of a complex set of culturally specific, highly subjective meanings into a physical statement described by geometries, colours, textures, materials, etc. (*1* p. 220). In short, automobile design makes an object that will provide transportation, car design moves you … in your heart. As they say, the way to a man's wallet is through his heart; but of course it must be a functional set of meanings the customer buys. If said customer doesn't get the banal service of transportation as promised by his car, his brain will overrule his heart and the emotional construct—the design—will be deemed a failure. **The real-world physics of an object hurtling through the countryside at break-neck speeds require that it perform well aerodynamically and this good per-formance should be reflected in its aesthetics. Thus there are wonderful moments of overlap between the two worlds. Unfortunately, one set of car design meanings was formed when the physics were poorly understood; we have "aerodynamic looks" that have been with us for seventy years, which are in fact counterproductive. Additionally, there are designs that function phenomenally well aerodynamically but are so disturbing aesthetically that they are functionally pariahs (*2* p. 220).**

The quality of car design is measured in how well it manages this tight-rope-walk of satisfying the immutable laws of physics and the innumera-ble idiosyncrasies of the customer mindset. Furthermore, the "virtual artist"—the brand—has its own needs that must be met for it to grow and prosper, often defining the playing field for creativity in a manner that the only way forward is to regurgitate as "new" all that has come before.

AZ: **What aspects lead to consideration of the design of movement playing a central or secondary role in the car industry?** What are the consequences **for design?**

CB: "Movement/motion" plays a big role in automotive design. What else is there to think about? How a car parks? How to keep if from scratching? How the radio works? How long the guarantee lasts? These are all correct and important questions to someone—usually an engineer—but not so vital to those you normally think about as car designers - the exterior and interior designers. Consider my answer above and the decisions and priorities that must be made to maintain that precarious balance between rational and emotional requirements. Let

Annett Zinsmeister: Die Automobilbranche muss sich in vielerlei **Hinsicht mit** der Frage nach der Gestalt der Bewegung und der **Gestaltung von Bewegung** auseinandersetzen. Als Automobildesigner für unterschiedliche **Hersteller** wie beispielsweise Opel, Fiat und als **Chefdesigner für BMW hast Du dich** sehr erfolgreich mit dem Thema beschäftigt. **Deine Automobilentwürfe und** zukunftsweisenden Konzepte haben international **große Aufmerksamkeit und** Anerkennung erhalten. Welche **grundsätzlichen Parameter und besonderen** Kriterien zeichnen ein qualitätvolles Design in der **Automobilbranche aus?**

Chris Bangle: Für Deine Leser muss ich einen neuen Begriff einführen, den des „Autodesigners". „Autodesign" ist nicht dasselbe wie „Automobilentwurf" oder „Automobildesign". Letzteres entspricht einer Montage objektiver Lösungen für konkrete Probleme, Ersteres hingegen bedeutet die Zusammenfügung eines komplexen Baukastens kulturspezifischer, absolut subjektiver Interpretationen eines physischen Gebildes, das sich in Geometrien, Farben, Texturen, Materialien usw. beschreiben lässt. (*1* S. 220) Kurz gesagt, Automobildesign bringt ein Objekt hervor, das einen von A nach B transportiert, während Autodesign einen ebenso im Innersten bewegt. Bekanntlich führt der Weg zur Brieftasche eines Mannes durch sein Herz; ein Auto aber muss natürlich auch funktionalen Ansprüchen genügen. Wenn der Wagen, den der Kunde sich anschaffen will, ihm nicht die versprochene Transportfunktion bietet, wird sein Kopf sein Herz überstimmen, sodass er das emotionale Konstrukt – das Design – für misslungen halten wird. Da die Physik erfordert, dass ein mit rasender Geschwindigkeit durch die Landschaft sausendes Objekt aerodynamisch geformt ist und da derlei gutes aerodynamisches Verhalten zugleich ästhetische Überlegungen widerspiegeln sollte, gibt es fantastische Überschneidungen zwischen beiden Welten. Leider entstand bereits ein Gestaltungskanon, als die Autobauer noch nicht viel über Aerodynamik wussten. Es kursieren zum Beispiel noch heute „aerodynamische Stromlinienformen", die vor 70 Jahren entworfen wurden und tatsächlich gar nicht aerodynamisch sind. Außerdem gibt es Autos, deren aerodynamisches Design fantastisch funktioniert, die aber ästhetisch so wenig ansprechend sind, dass man sie als funktional fragwürdig bezeichnen könnte. (*2* S. 220)

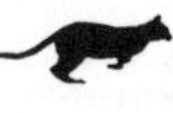

Die Designqualität eines Autos misst sich daran, wie gut der Designer die Gratwanderung zwischen der Berücksichtigung unwiderlegbarer physikalischer Gesetze einerseits und der Befriedigung des unergründlichen Eigensinns der Kunden andererseits bewältigt hat. Darüber hinaus hat die „virtuelle Künstlerin" – nämlich die Automarke – ihre eigenen Bedürfnisse, die erfüllt werden müssen, damit sie wachsen und gedeihen kann. Häufig definiert die Marke das Spielfeld für die Kreativität des Designers auf eine Art und Weise, dass der einzige Weg nach vorne darin besteht, alles vorher Dagewesene noch einmal durchzukauen, wieder von sich zu geben und als neu zu deklarieren.

us assume that the meaning of Schutzverkleidung (rub strips) changes and suddenly becomes passé for a luxury car. Is it any wonder, then, that no rational argument for their use as protection can keep them in the design?

AZ: "GINA Vision," the design of a flexible chassis, obviously takes up the **shape of movement in a more complex way.** In place of a rigid chassis form, **you and your team have** developed the concept of a flexible and therefore **mobile shell. The form** is no longer fixed but elastic, offering the possibility of **complex and flowing movements.** GINA is a car that is not merely a functional **object but one which** develops a positively sensual performance. In this way, **entirely new possibilities** emerge in the design of movement with reference **to the automobile.**

CB: I agree with you completely. In fact, GINA is beyond being just an interesting car: It is the embodiment of a new design philosophy that has already had many practitioners but perhaps no iconic symbol as yet. GINA is more than a "car made out of cloth," but even if that were all, it would still be impressive (*3* p. 221, *4* p. 220). For the curious, the cloth skin is really many different stretch fabrics—some with BMW proprietary materials – pulled over the aluminium space frame of the BMW Z8. All the safety protection is in this chassis; the skin performs weather protection, aerodynamic and aesthetic functions. It is about as susceptible to vandalism as a normal cabrio cloth top, but can be completely reskinned in a few hours by one person. Even while kept secret, GINA had great influence on attitudes about form and processes for material handling within BMW. Its name officially means "Geometry and form In 'N' Adaptations," but as I said it has come to mean more than a concept car: it is a philosophy of design. The fundamental aspects of this approach are in themselves not new, but in combination create a different landscape for Design.
The critical features of this GINA Design Philosophy are: 1. *Context over Dogma*—Context-specific solutions take precedence over preconceived notions of how things must be. 2. *No fixed tools* or "fixed" anything, for that matter. Fixed tools have a high investment because they only do one job. Afterwards, they are recycled or discarded. Robotic metal-forming is not fixed because it can be reprogrammed to do many jobs. In the case of a cloth skin for a car, the sewing machines creating it are incredibly flexible; not many tools can be making cars one day and blue jeans the next! 3. *Materials do the talking*—Allowing the natural shaping contours of a material to guide the final form means giving up some control. In the case of GINA, the wrinkles inside the doors are a very nice detail; at the same time the elastic skin "hangs" in perfect surfaces from just a few support splines. This natural effect of spline ridges pushing through the elastic material was one of the many characteristics of GINA that was emulated in normal cars. 4. *Emotion*—The secret to appeal of new methods and materials is in their ability to arouse passions in the observer and user. GINA looks for these effects first, then seeks other "functional justifications." More than "sculpture as surface;" with a wink GINA allowed "gesture as surface" to become meaningful. 5. *Celebrate the humanistic*—

AZ: Bei welchen Aspekten spielen Überlegungen zu einer **Gestaltung von** Bewegung in der Automobilindustrie eine zentrale oder auch **nebensächliche** Rolle? Was bedeutet dies für das Design?

CB: **In der Automobilindustrie spielt Bewegung beim Autodesign eine große Rolle. Worüber sollte man sonst nachdenken? Wie ein Auto einparkt? Wie man Kratzer im Lack vermeidet? Wie das Radio funktioniert? Wie lang die Garantiezeit ist? Das sind für einige Leute – meist die Ingenieure – alles korrekte und wichtige Fragen, aber nicht so wichtig für die Kunden, für die ein Autodesigner normalerweise derjenige ist, der die Karosserie und den Innenraum gestaltet.** Man bedenke meine Antwort auf Deine erste Frage und welche Entscheidungen getroffen und welche Prioritäten gesetzt werden müssen, um diese labile Balance zwischen rationalen und emotionalen Ansprüchen zu erreichen. Ist es da noch verwunderlich, dass – wenn etwa die Schutzverkleidung plötzlich als passé für einen Luxuswagen angesehen wird – kein rationales Argument ihre Weiterverwendung als Schutz- und Designelement durchsetzen kann?

AZ: „GINA Vision", der Entwurf einer flexiblen Karosserie, **greift das Thema der** Gestalt der Bewegung in einer deutlich **komplexeren Art und Weise auf. Anstelle** einer starren Karosserieform hast **Du mit deinem Team das Konzept zu einer flexiblen** und somit beweglichen Hülle **entwickelt. Die Form ist nicht mehr fixiert,** sondern elastisch und bietet die **Möglichkeit von komplexen und fließenden** Bewegungen. GINA ist ein Auto, **das nicht rein funktionales Objekt ist, sondern** eine geradezu sinnliche Performance **entwickelt. Damit entstehen ganz neue** Möglichkeiten in der Gestaltung von **Bewegung in Bezug auf das Automobil.**

CB: **Ja, das sehe ich genauso. Tatsächlich ist GINA viel mehr als nur ein interessantes Auto, es ist die Verkörperung einer neuen Designphilosophie, zu der es zwar schon einige praktische Ansätze gab, die es aber bislang zu keinem ikonischen Ausdruck gebracht haben. GINA ist mehr als ein „Auto aus Stoff", aber auch wenn es nur das wäre, würde es beeindrucken. (3 S. 221, 4 S. 220) Wen es interessiert: Die Bespannung des Aluminiumrahmens für den BMW Z8 besteht aus verschiedenen Stretchtextilien, darunter einige von BMW entwickelte Materialien. Diese Karosserie erfüllt sämtliche Sicherheitserfordernisse: Die textile Form schützt vor Regen, ist aerodynamisch und sieht gut aus. Sie ist nicht anfälliger gegen Vandalismus als ein normales Cabrioverdeck, lässt sich aber innerhalb weniger Stunden von einem Kfz-Techniker komplett ersetzen. Schon während der geheim gehaltenen Entwicklungsphase veränderte GINA die allgemeine Einstellung zu Formen und Verfahren der Materialverarbeitung bei BMW. Der Name steht für „Geometrie und Funktion in n-facher Ausprägung", aber wie gesagt: mittlerweile bezeichnet GINA nicht nur ein Konzeptfahrzeug, sondern eine ganze Designphilosophie. Die grundlegenden Aspekte dieses Ansatzes sind nicht neu, zusammen genommen aber öffnen sie den Weg in neue Designwelten.**

Automatised efficiencies and the high cost of fixed tooling have worked to create the efficiency of a "global sameness" to objects of production.
The nature of non-fixed tooling in GINA gives us a new chance to put the "human back in the loop." The relationship between man and machine can become more flexible, perhaps allowing new cultural DNA to enter the manufacturing processes. The GINA Philosophy is applicable to all types of design where the production of objects is the focus, and makes a good metaphorical reference for the other design projects as well.[1]

AZ: GINA Vision—as the name suggests—embodies a design oriented towards **the future. The future of mobility is a question that designers have to face up to as well …**
CB: Actually you could argue that GINA is "past-timeframe oriented design," because it still deals with the car as a single object, probably purchasable or at least given over to a single owner, reliant on a (admittedly new, courageous, and variable) sculptural gesture as its communication medium. Why is this particularly "future-oriented"? The fact that GINA resonates with young people[2] is **all well and good but this particular rendition does not as yet address some of their needs. If we envision the car as being primarily a shared object that is perhaps only a part-time transportation device, there will certainly be more communication with its exterior than shape alone can manage.**

AZ: **Today more than ever, isn't there a need for visions that can be implemented in the midterm? How do you see the corresponding bridging technology in the car industry, and** what corresponding challenges will design face?
CB: "Vision" … well, as the saying goes, "If you have a problem with the 'Visions' then you should see a doctor!" Of course vision is always needed to guide the courageous development of a culture or a company, but that does not mean that the popularly accepted definition of what constitutes such a vision appeals to you or me. Brand value, shareholder value, production efficiencies, local content … they are all interest groups that insist on their own version of the vision. To you or me, the idea of stimulating and inspiring design that is innovative and provocative might be the desirable vision for a car company to have, but with the enormous upfront costs involved the conservative instincts of management are hard to counter. This **makes it even harder on design to bring innovation into their work, but nevertheless we should all encourage it. The alternative—a slow decay into derivative banality—is too easy to succumb to and almost impossible to break free from, particularly in times where the need to respond for external pressures (fuel economy, shifting business model, etc.) is great.**

Die entscheidenden Kriterien der GINA-Designphilosophie sind: 1. *Kontext vor Dogma.* Kontextspezifische Lösungen haben Vorrang vor vorgefassten Meinungen darüber, wie die Dinge sein sollten. 2. *Keine festgelegten Werkzeuge* oder ähnlich „Fixiertes". Nicht umfunktionierte Werkzeuge erfordern hohe Investitionen, weil sie nur eine einzige Aufgabe erfüllen. Danach werden sie entweder recycelt oder entsorgt. Industrieroboter, mit denen Bleche geformt werden, sind dagegen in diesem Sinne nicht „fixiert", weil sie sich für verschiedene Aufgaben programmieren lassen. Auch die Industrienähmaschinen, mit denen die Textilkarosserien genäht werden, sind unglaublich flexibel - es gibt sicher nicht viele Maschinen, mit denen man heute Autos und morgen Jeans herstellen könnte! 3. *Materialien sprechen lassen.* Wenn man als Designer den materialbedingten formgebenden Konturen erlaubt, die Formgestaltung zu steuern, gibt man einen Teil der eigenen Kontrollgewalt ab. Im Fall von GINA sind die Knitterfalten auf der Innenseite der Türen ein schönes Detail. Gleichzeitig hängt die elastische Haut vollkommen faltenlos über nur einigen wenigen Keilrippen. Die plastische Wirkung dieser Rippen, die sich natürlich unter dem Stoff abmalen, gehört zu den vielen Designdetails von GINA, die später für normale Metallkarosserien nachgeahmt wurden. 4. *Emotion.* Der geheimnisvolle Reiz neuer Methoden und Materialien liegt in ihrer Fähigkeit, Begeisterung beim Beobachter und Anwender zu erwecken. GINAs Designer bemühten sich in erster Linie darum, diese Wirkung zu erzielen, und erst in zweiter Linie um funktionelle Justierungen. GINA begnügte sich nicht damit, eine „plastische Oberfläche" zu sein, sondern verlieh – sozusagen mit einem Augenzwinkern – , der „Oberfläche als Geste" Bedeutung. 5. *Das Menschliche feiern.* Die automatisierte Hochleistungsfähigkeit und die hohen Kosten fester Produktionsanlagen haben dazu geführt, dass alle möglichen Produkte heute höchst effizient in globaler Gleichförmigkeit erzeugt werden.

Die Art der flexiblen Werkzeuge, mit denen GINA gefertigt wurde, eröffnet eine neue Chance, den Menschen wieder mit einzubeziehen. Die Beziehung zwischen Mensch und Maschine kann wieder flexibler werden und dann vielleicht ermöglichen, dass Herstellungsprozesse mit einer neuen kulturellen DNA angereichert werden. Die GINA-Philosophie lässt sich auf alle Arten von Produktdesign übertragen und stellt einen guten metaphorischen Bezugspunkt für andere Designprodukte dar.[1]

AZ: „GINA Vision" verkörpert – wie der Name vermuten lässt – ein zukunftsorientiertes Design. Die Zukunft der Mobilität ist eine Frage, der sich auch Designer stellen müssen …

CB: Ja, man könnte tatsächlich sagen, dass das Design von GINA nicht von zeitlichen Vorgaben abhängig ist, weil hier das Auto immer noch ein Einzelobjekt darstellt, das wahrscheinlich verkaufbar ist oder jedenfalls einem einzigen Besitzer übergeben wird und sich auf eine (zugegebenermaßen neue, mutige und variable) skulpturale Geste als Kommunikationsmedium verlässt. Warum sollte das aber besonders zukunftsorientiert sein? Die Tatsache, dass GINA junge Leute anspricht, ist gut und schön, aber dieses spezielle

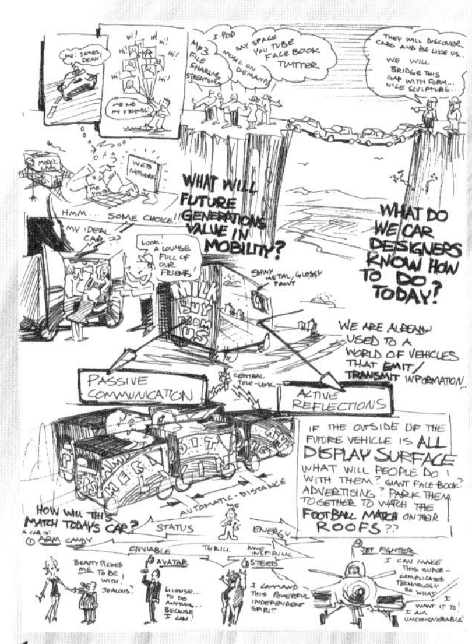

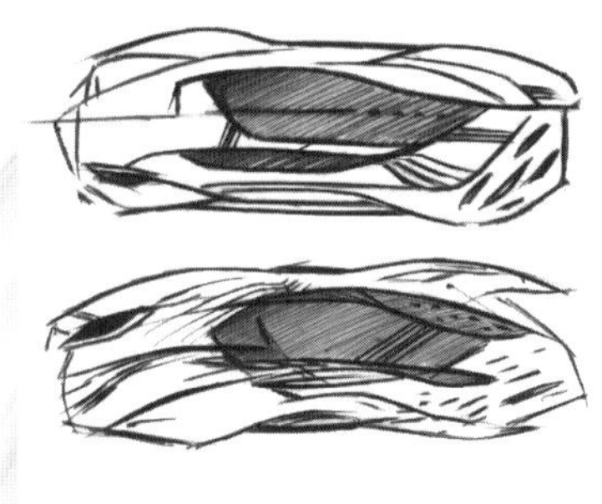

1

2

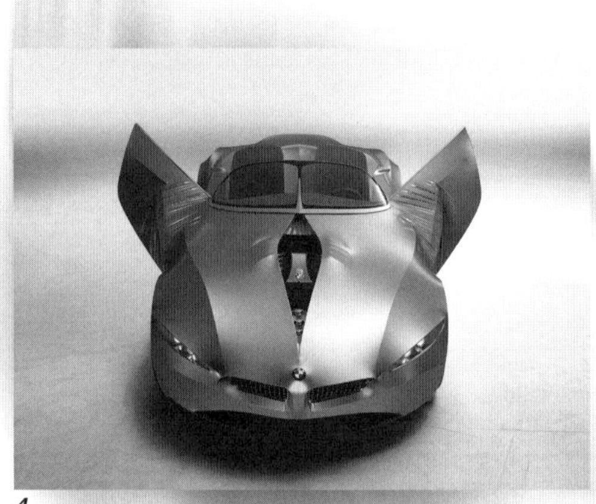

4

1 Detail of my sketch for PEM 2050 for an Australian magazine — 2 Engin Tulay's two unique top views. An energy of assymetry and a gesture of attack. "Aero issues?" OK, issues, but solvable — 3, 4 The GINA ConceptCar. The sexiness of fabric is in its ability to reveal without showing, imply without answering — 5 My concept sketch of the *Cvar* of 2050. The *Car-Avatar* part helps us all day long and combines with the part *Mobility* and *Enviroment* when you need to move — 6 Future Cvar (Car) Designer at work. He creates a gesture and the models all take on the pose. Will people buy new *Cvar*-Gestures like they do ringtones today?

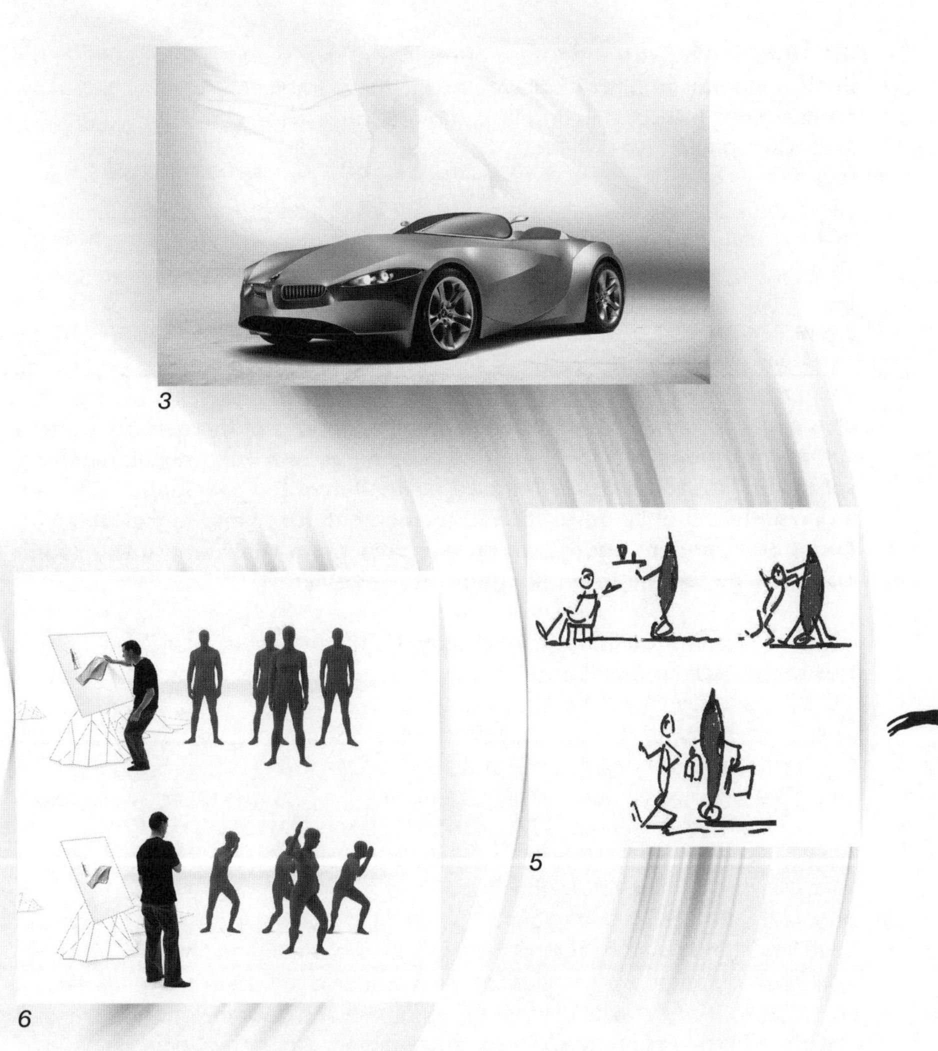

1 Meine Zeichnung zu PEM 2050 (Ausschnitt) für ein australisches Magazin — *2* Zwei Aufsichten von Engin Tulay: Energie der Asymmetrie und eine Angriffsgeste. „Probleme mit der Aerodynamik? Die bekommen wir schon gelöst." — *3, 4* GINA ConceptCar. Der Stoff wirkt sexy, denn er enthüllt, ohne zu zeigen, er macht Andeutungen, anstatt Antworten zu geben — *5* Meine Konzeptzeichnung des *Cvar* von 2050. Das *Auto-Avatar*-Element hilft uns über den Tag und ergänzt sich automatisch mit den Elementen *Mobilität* und Umfeld, wenn *Bewegung* erforderlich ist — *6* Ein Auto-(Avatar)-Designer der Zukunft bei der Arbeit. Er erschafft eine Geste und alle Avatare übernehmen die Pose. Werden die Leute neue *Cvar*-Gesten kaufen wie heute Klingeltöne?

AZ: How do you see the future of the car and what does this mean for the design of auto-mobility? Will we need to leave traditional ideas behind in the foreseeable future, thinking in completely new directions in the long term? And if so, in what ways?

CB: Yes, but it is not so simple. What will be the critical acceptance factors of the car of the future? "Physicality on demand"? That it conforms to the ideal of the "objects that promote sharing"? That it serves as "intelligent social glue"? That it allows us to live "longer" by living "slower" because they do "more" so we can do "less"? These are just a few of the observations that came out of my work with the MIT students in the *PiNk!* project a few years ago.[2] *PiNk!* highlighted the emergence of sharing as a basis for all future product functions, and we examined the challenges of car sharing and mass electric vehicle use. We were also eager to convert the powerful emotive factors of the car today into a viable contributor to the economic, ecological, and cultural sustainability solutions. This requires an entire re-evaluation of the car. Today's cars are a constellation of "nice-to-have" moving sculptures and regrettable sustainability consequences, which has cost them their link to the young customers that the previous generation enjoyed.

AZ: What further deliberations resulted from that type of analysis in the context of the *PiNk!* project? How, and in what form did they evolve?

CB: In a performance-neutral shared-vehicle environment of 2050, we predicted a dire need to readdress the common paradigm of the future, in order to keep personal emotional mobility from becoming irrelevant. We did this by first defining Personal Emotional Mobility as requiring three components; *Mobility, Environment,* and a characteristic we described as *"Car-Avatar"* (5, 6 p. 221). The first two elements might be found in an elevator (auto … mobile?) or a taxi, but it is the last one that makes a car a reflection of the owner and a link to enviable cohort groups. (*Mobility+Car-Avatar* alone might be … a motorcycle?). Next we separated the three into stand-alone components, capable of self-reintegration and assembly, as well as autonomous function. *Mobility* became self-driving, wheel-battery units that would be available to everyone for hire and seek their own recharging stations where the tires would also be controlled, etc. (eliminating the need to run power into every parking place in the world and keeping today's gas stations in a valuable service role). This does not reduce their battery's capability for ePower storage and resell, but keeps the investment in the hands of centralised commercial players instead of burdening the everyman. The *Environment* could be a simple ubiquitous safety box, perhaps even foldable for compact storage, again to be used on demand. The interiors would be spartan (ItalDesign's BIGA was an inspiration to us) but the flat exteriors could be solid digital display surfaces. This would bring a new business model into play, be it pay-by-advertising or pay-for-communication privileges. Some went as far as to suggest the boxes be homeless shelters when not in mobile use.
The key to our holistic solution was the concept of a new interpretation of the

Modell erfüllt immer noch nicht einige ihrer Bedürfnisse, etwa nach einem gemein-
schaftlich und nur temporär genutzten Fahrzeug, das auf jeden Fall nach außen
kommunikativer wirkt, als es einer Form allein möglich wäre.

AZ: **Sind nicht heute mehr denn je Visionen gefragt, deren Umsetzung mittel-**
fristig realisierbar ist? **Wie könnte die entsprechende Brückentechnologie in**
der Automobilbranche aussehen und vor welchen Herausforderungen steht
dementsprechend das Design?
CB: **„Visionen" – nun ja, wie es heißt: „Wer Visionen hat, sollte zum Arzt
gehen." Natürlich ist für die mutige Entwicklung einer Kultur oder Firma
immer eine Vision nötig, aber das heißt noch lange nicht, dass die allgemein akzeptierte Definition einer solchen Vision Dir oder mir gefällt. Mar-
kenwert, *shareholder value,* Produktionseffizienz, Standortvorteil – das sind
alles Interessen, deren Vertreter auf ihre eigene Version der jeweiligen Vision
pochen. Für Dich oder mich wäre die Vorstellung eines stimulierenden, inspi-
rierenden Designs, das noch dazu innovativ und provokant ist, vielleicht eine
wünschenswerte Vision, die ein Autohersteller haben sollte. Bei den enormen
Entwicklungskosten im Vorfeld sind aber die konservativen Instinkte des
Managements schwer zu überwinden. Das macht es den Designern zwar noch
schwerer, innovativ zu sein, aber trotzdem sollten wir alle sie dazu ermutigen.
Die Alternative wäre die schleichende Rückkehr zur derivativen Banalität, der
man nur allzu leicht nachgibt und von der man sich kaum befreien kann, besonders nicht in Zeiten, in denen Designer schon aus äußeren Gründen (Energiever-
knappung, andere Geschäftsmodelle etc.) unter großem Druck stehen, immer wieder Neues, Anderes schaffen zu müssen.**

AZ: Wie siehst Du die Zukunft des Automobils bzw. **des Autos und was bedeu-**
tet dies für das Design von Auto-Mobilität? **Müssen wir uns in absehbarer Zeit**
von herkömmlichen Vorstellungen verabschieden und langfristig **in ganz andere**
Richtungen denken? Und wenn ja, in welche?
CB: **Ja, aber das ist alles nicht so einfach. Welche entscheidenden Ak-
zeptanzfaktoren muss das Auto der Zukunft besitzen? Gestaltwerdung
„on demand"? Dass es den Idealen eines Gebrauchsgegenstands entspricht, der sich für eine gemeinschaftliche Nutzung anbietet? Dass es
als intelligenter „sozialer Kitt" dient? Dass es uns ermöglicht, länger, weil
„langsamer" zu leben, indem es mehr leistet, damit wir weniger tun müssen? Das sind nur einige der Fragen, die bei dem Studienprojekt *PiNk!*
aufkamen, das ich vor einigen Jahren mit Studenten durchgeführt habe.**[2]
**Besonders *PiNk!* gab Aufschluss über das zunehmend beliebte Carsharing
als Basis für alle zukünftigen Produktfunktionen, und wir untersuchten die
Herausforderungen, vor die uns einerseits das Carsharing und andererseits
der Massengebrauch von Elektroautos stellen. Außerdem wollten wir die heute
herrschende emotionale Kraft des Autos zu einem entscheidenden Faktor für
ökonomisch, ökologisch und kulturell nachhaltige Lösungen umfunktionieren.**

emotional connection to the car, the *Car-Avatar.* These would be highly complex, mechatronic-transforming machines formed as sculptural art-objects that would perform many functions of real service in the future (notice we consciously avoided the term Robot). The challenge of creating such complex machines will be an inspiration to today's culture of mechanical engineering expertise, which the electric car in and of itself has little need for. In our vision of tomorrow, when you tell your *Car-Avatar,* "Go get the car," it would literally assemble itself from roving components, two-, four-, or six-wheel-battery units as needed. The personalisation of the ubiquitous *Environment* would be part of the *Car-Avatar's* onboard toolset; useful when making the seat on the train or the bus attractive as one's personal seat. Perhaps the *Car-Avatar* would ride along outside the *Environment,* showing itself off just as a finely sculpted car does today. One of the car's critical advantages over almost every other form of personal mobility is your ability to set your own pace. This feature is what separates them from horses (all horses walk about at the same pace, they don't run far), foot, train, bus, and plane travel. Even the most expensive ticket on an airplane only gets you through the waiting lines faster. In a completely tele-linked future we looked for non-regressive, pay-as-you-drive schemes that would tax those in a hurry but allow them to set their own pace, and distribute the proceeds to their slower drivers as a reward.[3]

AZ: **Mobility researchers see the future of tenable mobility**–that is, mobility on **the "basis of completely regenerative energy in the mid term"**—in the de-indi**vidualisation of private mobility and goods logistics.** They see the future of auto**mobility as a largely "car-free" future.**[4] What is your response to this assessment? *CB:* No single system can offer all things to all people, the only question is if the amount of participants willing to purchase/invest or otherwise pay-for-use are sufficient to keep the game running. Often, you hear cars being compared to horses; once the prime mobility method and now reduced to hobby and race use. But the comparison does not take into account that making a car is considerably more investment-intensive than breeding horses. Once the critical mass is lost, then the industry and know-how behind the products collapses. Anyone can make a "car" with the performance and complexity of a Model T, but it takes billions of Euros and hundreds of thousands of people to make a modern car industry tick. However, if you compare the development curves of the Chinese and Indian markets to those of the West, it appears that they will continue to supply us with cars after those in Europe have long switched to their busses and trams. In areas with large distances are still traversed daily, the subsidies that the governments will dole out to keep those constituents happy will ensure they have their pickups and SUVs to get them around all year long ... I am sure you will hear the argument that the "indigenous lifestyle of the suburbanite" is at least as valid to maintain as that of the natives of the rainforest.

Dazu mussten wir völlig neu überlegen, was ein Auto eigentlich ist oder sein soll. Heute ist es eine wünschenswerte, aber nicht unbedingt notwendige bewegliche Skulptur – mit verheerender Umwelt- und Energiebilanz. Dieser Mangel an Nachhaltigkeit hat die junge Generation dem Auto entfremdet.

AZ: **Welche weiterführenden Überlegungen haben sich aus derlei Analysen** im Rahmen des *PiNk!*-Projektes ergeben? Und welche Gestalt haben sie angenommen?

CB: Für das leistungsneutrale Gemeinschaftsauto des Jahres 2050 prognostizierten wir die dringende Notwendigkeit, das überkommene Zukunftsparadigma neu zu formulieren, um zu verhindern, dass der emotionale Faktor der Mobilität irrelevant wird. Hierfür definierten wir zunächst die Persönliche emotionale Mobilität, die aus drei Komponenten bestehen muss: *Mobilität, Umfeld* und einer besonderen Funktion, die wir *Auto-Avatar* (5, 6 S. 221) nannten. Die ersten beiden Elemente findet man auch in einem Aufzug oder einem Taxi, das dritte hingegen macht das Auto zu einer Projektion seines Besitzers und zu einem Bindeglied zwischen konkurrierenden Altersgenossen. (Lediglich *Mobilität* plus *Auto-Avatar* wäre vielleicht … ein Motorrad?) Als nächstes trennten wir die drei Komponenten voneinander und machten sie zu selbstständigen Elementen, die in der Lage waren, sich selbst zu re-integrieren, zusammenzusetzen und autonom zu funktionieren. Aus *Mobilität* wurden selbstständig fahrende, mit Akku betriebene Mietfahrzeuge, die ihre eigenen Aufladestationen ansteuern, wo auch ihre Reifen etc. kontrolliert werden. So kann man darauf verzichten, jeden Parkplatz auf der Welt mit Stromanschlüssen auszustatten, und Tankstellen bleiben als wichtige Dienstleistungsunternehmen erhalten. Zudem wird weder die elektrische Speicherkapazität der Akkus reduziert noch deren Wiederverkäuflichkeit beeinträchtigt, und die Investition bleibt in der Hand zentralisierter kommerzieller Akteure, statt die Allgemeinheit finanziell zu belasten. Das *Umfeld* – der „automobile Hohlkörper" – könnte eine simple „Sicherheitskiste" sein, vielleicht sogar eine zusammenklappbare für platzsparendes Parken. Die Innenräume wären spartanisch ausgestattet (der BIGA von ItalDesign war dabei für uns eine Inspiration), aber die ebenen Außenflächen könnten als massive Bildschirme ausgebildet werden. Dadurch käme ein neues Geschäftsmodell ins Spiel – die Finanzierung der Autokosten entweder durch Werbung oder durch das Angebot des Internetzugangs gegen Nutzungsgebühren. Jemand schlug sogar vor, die Kistenautos, wenn sie nachts nicht als fahrbarer Untersatz gebraucht werden, als Nachtasyle für Obdachlose zu nutzen.

Der Schlüssel zu unserer holistischen Lösung war die Neuinterpretation der emotionalen Beziehung des Autobesitzers zu seinem Wagen, die wir *Auto-Avatar* nannten. Ein *Auto-Avatar* wäre eine hochkomplexe, mechatronisch wandelbare und wie eine Skulptur künstlerisch geformte Maschine, die aber in Zukunft zahlreiche konkrete Dienstleistungen erbringen würde. (Den Begriff

More interesting to me is where the shift in car design will happen ... will it still be preoccupied with making brand statements in metal, or will the computer game world take over all of its capabilities and the only exciting new "drives" you will have in the future will be in your simulators?

***AZ:* How would you describe your own personal handling of the topic, the *Figure of Motion?* What are the most important, biggest and most interesting challenges you face with respect to the design of movement and mobility?**
CB: Klaus Kapitza, the long time head of BMW ZT Design Studio, once said what I wish I had said: "I am interested in everything that moves." I would add, "and that moves you emotionally as well." I am learning a lot about how people react to design and to art outside of the auto industry, and some of the lessons reflect well upon the principles of emotional movement practised by car design. Not everything we have done as car designers is bad, and in fact we have built an enviable body of work that architects and product designers have tried to emulate. It is my personal goal to keep this culture of car design vibrantly alive, not by supplication but by challenging the dogmas on which it is founded. **This is the greatest test, if a culture has the courage to ask the questions by which it will be defined, and if it has the balls to walk the talk of the answers. "Leaders take you where you don't want to go," is a quote I have heard attributed to Gertrude Stein, but in this industry leaders are not easy to find unless you have got to where anyone can claim comfort. Our stand will be one of basic humanism and humanity; if any group of skilled enthusiasts can resist the tide of time and technology and keep a role for their creative input a valued one.**

NOTES—[1] http://www.chrisbangleassociates.com/ GINA—[2] See also on YouTube: "Chris Bangle TEDx Munich *GINA meets PiNk!*"—[3] http://www.chrisbangleassociates.com/ Personal emotional mobility 2050—[4] See also the contribution by Stephan Rammler: *The Reinvention of Mobility. The Politics of Mobility as World Design,* 160-176

Roboter haben wir bewusst vermieden.) Die Entwicklung derart komplexer Maschinen ist eine Herausforderung und wird für die heutige Maschinenbaukultur eine Quelle der Inspiration werden, während das Elektroauto eine solche Quelle kaum nötig hat. Wenn Du in unserer Zukunftsvision Deinem Auto-Avatar sagst: „Hol' das Auto!", würde er es buchstäblich aus „herumstreunenden" Komponenten zusammensetzen, je nach Bedarf aus zwei-, vier- oder sechsrädrigen akkubetriebenen Einheiten. Die Innenausstattung und Apparaturen im Auto-Avatar würden es ermöglichen, das ubiquitäre *Umfeld* so individuell umzubauen, dass es im Zug oder Bus als persönlicher Sitz dienen kann. Vielleicht könnte der *Auto-Avatar* sogar das Umfeld eskortieren, statt darin zu sitzen, und sich als ebenso raffiniert geformt zeigen wie ein heutiges schön modelliertes Auto. Ein entscheidender Vorteil des Autos gegenüber fast jeder anderen Form von Fortbewegungsmitteln ist die Tatsache, dass man damit das eigene Reisetempo bestimmen kann. Das unterscheidet es von der Fortbewegung zu Pferd (Pferde laufen ungefähr gleich schnell und schaffen nur bestimmte Tagesdistanzen), zu Fuß, im Zug, Bus oder Flugzeug. Selbst ein Flugticket 1. Klasse verschafft einem ja nur einen kleinen Zeitvorteil in den Warteschlangen am Flughafen. Für eine komplett televernetzte Zukunft suchten wir nach nicht-regressiven Modellen für Autofahrten nach einer Art „Pay-as-you-drive"-Schema, die zwar denjenigen, die es eilig haben, Gebühren auferlegen, aber auch erlauben, das eigene Tempo selbst zu bestimmen. Die Gewinne würden dann als Belohnung unter den langsameren Fahrern aufgeteilt.[3]

AZ: Für die Mobilitätsforschung liegt die Zukunft einer vertretbaren Mobilität, das heißt einer Mobilität, die auf einer mittelfristig vollkommen regenerativen Energieform basiert, in der Ent-Individualisierung der Privatmobilität und Güterlogistik. Sie sehen die Zukunft der Automobilität in einer weitgehend autofreien Zukunft.[4] Was sagst Du zu dieser Einschätzung?
CB: Es gibt kein System, das allen Menschen alles bieten kann. Die Frage ist nur, ob die Zahl derjenigen, die bereit sind, etwas zu kaufen, in etwas zu investieren oder für eine Leistung zu zahlen, groß genug ist, um die Gesamtwirtschaft am Laufen zu halten. Oft werden Autos mit Pferden verglichen, dem früheren Hauptverkehrsmittel, das heute nur noch in der Freizeit oder im Pferdesport genutzt wird. Der Vergleich lässt aber die Tatsache außer Acht, dass die Autoindustrie wesentlich höhere Investitionen erfordert als die Pferdezucht. Wenn erst einmal die kritische Masse dahin ist, bricht die Autoindustrie zusammen und das Knowhow hinter dem Produkt geht verloren. Jeder mit den nötigen Kenntnissen und Mitteln könnte ein Auto bauen, das in Leistung und Komplexität einem Model T entspricht, aber es erfordert Milliarden Euro und viele Hunderttausend Arbeitskräfte, um eine moderne Autoindustrie auf Dauer erfolgreich zu betreiben. Wenn man allerdings die Entwicklungskurven des chinesischen und des indischen Automarkts mit ihren westlichen Entsprechungen vergleicht, muss man vermuten, dass China und Indien uns noch mit Autos beliefern werden, nachdem wir in

Europa längst auf Busse und Straßenbahnen umgestiegen sind. Gegenden, in denen viele Menschen immer noch täglich lange Arbeitswege zurücklegen müssen, wird die Regierung auch weiterhin mit Zuschüssen versorgen, um ihre Wähler zufrieden zu stellen, sodass diese auch weiterhin das ganze Jahr über mit ihren Pickups und Geländewagen herumfahren werden. Ich bin sicher, dass man irgendwann den „traditionellen Lebensstil des Vorstädters" als mindestens ebenso erhaltenswert ansehen wird wie den der Eingeborenen im tropischen Regenwald. Für mich wäre es aber interessanter zu wissen, in welchem Bereich sich das Autodesign verändern wird. Werden sich Autodesigner immer noch darauf konzentrieren, Markenstatements aus Metall abzuliefern, oder wird die Computerindustrie ihnen etwa alle ihre Kenntnisse und Kompetenzen abnehmen, sodass dann die einzigen spannenden neuen Fahrerlebnisse schließlich nur noch die im Fahrsimulator sind?

AZ: Wie würdest Du deinen persönlichen Umgang mit dem Thema "Gestalt der Bewegung" beschreiben? Was sind für Dich die wichtigsten, größten, interessantesten Herausforderungen hinsichtlich der Gestaltung von Bewegung und von Mobilität?

CB: Klaus Kapitza, der langjährige Leiter der ZT-Designabteilung von BMW, hat einmal etwas gesagt, was ich selbst gerne gesagt hätte: „Ich interessiere mich für alles, was sich bewegt." Ich würde hinzufügen: „Und für alles, was einen auch emotional bewegt". Ich lerne viel darüber, wie Menschen außerhalb der Automobilindustrie auf Design und Kunst reagieren und habe aufschlussreiche Erkenntnisse gewonnen über die Grundlagen für „emotionale Bewegung", die im Autodesign zur Anwendung kommen. Nicht alles, was wir Autodesigner zustande gebracht haben, ist schlecht. Genau genommen haben wir ein beneidenswertes Gesamtwerk geschaffen, das Architekten und Produktdesigner nachzuahmen versucht haben. Mein persönliches Ziel ist es, die Kultur des Autodesigns am Leben zu halten, nicht durch blinde Verehrung, sondern indem ich die Dogmen in Frage stelle, auf denen sie sich gründet. Das ist der größte Test: ob Kulturschaffende den Mut haben, die Fragen zu stellen, durch die sich Kultur definiert, und ob sie dann auch den Mumm haben, auf die Antworten Taten folgen zu lassen. Gertrude Stein soll sinngemäß einmal gesagt haben, dass Anführer einen dahin führen, wo man gar nicht hin will, aber in diesem Industriezweig sind Anführer nicht leicht zu finden, es sei denn, man will sowieso dorthin, wo jedermann Komfort und Bequemlichkeit beanspruchen kann. Wir treten für grundlegende Menschlichkeit und für die Menschheit ein. Wenn irgendeine Gruppe enthusiastischer Fachleute gegen den Strom der Zeit und Technik schwimmen und noch einen Platz für ihren kreativen Beitrag freihalten kann, wird das ein wertvoller Standpunkt sein.

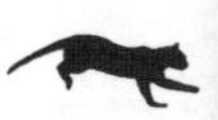

ANMERKUNGEN—[1] http://www.chrisbangleassociates.com GINA—[2] Vgl. YouTube: Chris Bangle TEDx, München: „GINA meets PiNk!"—[3] http://www.chrisbangleassociates.com/ Personal emotional mobility 2050 (zuletzt gesehen: 29.05.2011)—[4] siehe hierzu der Beitrag von Stephan Rammler: *Die Neuerfindung der Mobilität. Mobilitätspolitik als Weltdesign*, 161–177.

ACKNOWLEDGMENT—The basis of this publication was the symposium "The Figure of Motion" held by the Weißenhof-Institute, which took place at the State Academy of Fine Arts in December 2010 and met with a very positive response. In 1980, the Weißenhof-Institute was founded and since then it has developed into an institution promoting discourse between different disciplines, an interdisciplinary platform realising diverse events and publications. It is programmatically representative, therefore, of the art academy's special character as a place uniting art, design, architecture and science under one roof and its potential for wide-reaching cooperation, which is also mirrored by this publication.

At this point I would like to thank Adrian Riemann, Marian Rupp, and Fabian Schewe for their innovative graphic design, giving motion and typography a totally new appearance with the help of a self-developed software and for handling the publication until it went to press, as well as my colleague Prof. Uli Cluss for the good collaboration in supervision.

We took the subject *The Figure of Motion* to heart, planning this volume and preparing it for printing within only a few months. This great achievement only proved possible due to the great commitment of all those involved. Above all, my sincere gratitude is due to the authors, who transformed their lecture notes into texts ready for printing in only a few weeks. Thanks also go to those at JOVIS Verlag Berlin for their highly professional collaboration, especially to Philipp Sperrle for his editing and all people involved on behalf of the publisher. We are grateful to Lucinda Rennison and Annette Wiethüchter for their quickly done, professional translations. I owe a special, personal debt of gratitude to Adeline Seidel for her committed coordination of the project from the symposium to the presentation of this publication.

Annett Zinsmeister, Stuttgart/Berlin 2011

DANKSAGUNG—Das vom Weißenhof-Institut veranstaltete Symposium „Gestalt der Bewegung", das im Dezember 2010 an der Staatlichen Akademie der Bildenden Künste stattgefunden hat und sich großer positiver Resonanz erfreute, bot die Grundlage für die vorliegende Publikation. Das Weißenhof-Institut wurde 1980 gegründet und hat sich seither zu einer Institution entwickelt, die als interdisziplinäre Plattform den Diskurs zwischen unterschiedlichen Disziplinen mit Veranstaltungen und Publikationen befördert. Es steht programmatisch für die Besonderheit der Kunstakademie, Kunst, Design, Architektur und Wissenschaft unter einem Dach zu vereinen und für das Potenzial vielseitiger Kooperationen, welches auch diese Publikation widerspiegelt.

An dieser Stelle möchte ich Adrian Riemann, Marian Rupp und Fabian Schewe herzlich danken für die überaus innovative grafische Gestaltung des Buches, das Bewegung und Schrift mittels eines eigens geschriebenen Programmes in einer völlig neuen Gestalt in Erscheinung treten lässt. Dank gilt ihnen auch für die Bearbeitung der Publikation bis zur Drucklegung sowie meinem Kollegen Prof. Uli Cluss für die gute Zusammenarbeit in der gemeinsamen Betreuung.

Wir haben uns das Thema *Gestalt der Bewegung* zu Herzen genommen und den vorliegenden Band in nur wenigen Monaten gestaltet und zur Druckreife geführt. Diese besondere Leistung konnte nur dank dem großen Engagement aller Beteiligten zustande kommen. Mein herzlicher Dank gilt allen Autoren, die in nur wenigen Wochen ihr Vortragsmanuskript in einen druckfertigen Text verwandelten. Dem JOVIS Verlag Berlin sei gedankt für die professionelle Kooperation, Philipp Sperrle für das Lektorat sowie allen Beteiligten seitens des Verlages. Lucinda Rennison und Annette Wiethüchter danken wir für die zügige und professionelle Übersetzung. Ein besonderer und persönlicher Dank gilt Adeline Seidel für ihre engagierte und hervorragende Projektkoordination von der Veranstaltung bis hin zur vorliegenden Publikation.

Annett Zinsmeister, Stuttgart/Berlin 2011

PICTURE CREDITS—*Figure of Motion: 1* in Zöllner, Frank: Leonardo da Vinci, Sämtliche Gemälde und Zeichnungen. Taschen 2003 *2* in Richard, Ralph: The life and works of John Weaver: An account of his life, writings and theatrical productions, with an annotated reprint of his complete publications. Princeton Book Company 1985 *3* ©1893 Eadweard Muybridge (14699Y U.S. Copyright Office) (expired) *4* http://en.wikipedia.org/wiki/File:The_Horse_in_Motion.jpg *5* in Marey, E.J.: La méthode graphique. Paris 1878, 281 *6 middle and right* http://en.wikisource.org/wiki/Popular_Science_Monthly/Volume_6/November_1874/Human_Locomotion *7* from E-J. Marey: Le Mouvement. Paris 1894 *8 left* from Musée Marey, Beaune *8 middle and left* http://www.ctie.monash.edu.au/hargrave/marey.html *9* http://www.ctie.monash.edu.au/hargrave/marey.html *10 left* http://de.wikipedia.org/wiki/Eadweard_Muybridge *10 right* http://en.wikipedia.org/wiki/Nude_Descending_a_Staircase,_No._2 *11* http://www.rolf-lauter.com *12* http://www.collezioni-f.it/balla.html *14* http://www.e-flux.com/journal/view/219 *16* Theatermuseum München *17* http://ludersocke.blog.de/2009/04/29/theater-film-tanz-gegenseitige-beeinflussung-reform-6029484/ *18* Zentrum für Kunst und Medientechnologie, Deutsches Tanzarchiv Köln, Stiftung Kultur, 1994/1999—*Mobile and Stabile: 1* http://kaufmann-mercantile.com/images/alexander-calder-mobile.jpg *2* photographer: Csaba Petrik von http://www.midcenturia.com/2011/01/alexander-calders-man-sculpture.html *3* © Kunsthaus Zürich, Vereinigung Züricher Kunstfreunde, in: Beyeler Museum AG (ed.): Giacometti. Ostfildern 2009 *4* in Wilhelm Lehmbruck Museum der Stadt Duisburg (ed.), Naum Gabo. o.O., o.J. *5* © The Museum of Modern Art, New York; photographer: Imaging Studio Staff, The Museum of Modern Art, New York, in: Barry Bergdoll/Terence Riley (ed.): Mies in Berlin. Ludwig Mies van der Rohe. Die Berliner Jahre. Munich 2002 *6* © The Museum of Modern Art, New York; photographer: Kay Fingerle, in: Barry Bergdoll/Terence Riley (ed.): Mies in Berlin. Ludwig Mies van der Rohe. Die Berliner Jahre. Munich 2002 *7-8* photographer: Anriet Denis, in: Jean-Francois Gonthier (Hg.): Le Corbusier vivant. Paris 1999 *9-10* photographer: Christian Richters, in: N.N., "Möbius Haus. Van Berkel und Bos" in: Arch+ 146 (1999)/April. *11* graphic: Ben van Berkel/Caroline Bos: Christian Marquart: "Oben geht es um die Marke, unten um die Wurst. Rundgang durch das neue Mercedes-Benz-Museum Stuttgart" in: Bauwelt 97 (2006) *12* in Christian Marquart: "Oben geht es um die Marke, unten um die Wurst. Rundgang durch das neue Mercedes-Benz-Museum Stuttgart", in: Bauwelt 97 (2006), photographer: Christian Richters *13* in: Kunstmuseum Wolfsburg (ed.): James Turrell. The Wolfsburg Project. Ostfildern 2009, Photographer: Zooey Braun *14* in Arch+ 200 (2010), photographer: Hisao Suzuki—*Dynamismo of Post-Industry: 1* http://en.wikipedia.org *2* 2.bp.blogspot.com *3* www.kultur-online.net *4* in Dinkla, Söke (ed.): Jenny Holzer. Die Macht des Wortes. / I Can't Tell You. Ostfildern 2006, photographer: Attilio Maranzano *5* in: Dinkla, Söke (Hg.): PubliCity: Constructing the Truth. Kunst im öffentlichen Raum. Nürnberg 2006, photographer: Rainer Schlautmann/Stadt Duisburg *6-7* in: Dinkla, Söke/Janssen, Karl (ed.): Ruhrlights: Twilight Zone 2010. Ostfildern 2010, photographer: Werner Hannappel/RUHR.2010 *8* Simulation: Heike Mutter and Ulrich Genth/Stadt Duisburg *9* photographer: Daan de Haan—*Traces and Artefacts of Physical Intelligence: 1* in Livet, Anne: Contemporary Dance. New York 1978 *2* Chris Ziegler (designer's screenshot) *3* photographer: Adriene Hughes *4-5* The left and right screens of the Choreographic Language Agent, Screenshot *6-8* Synchronous Objects Project, The Ohio State University and The Forsythe Company—*The Legibility of Movement: 2* www.wizspace.co *3-4* www.billbuxton.com *6* nano.xerox.com *7* www.hanksville.org *10* www.reghardware.com *11-12* http://www.gavrila.net/avss2007_cassandra.pdf—*Landscape in Motion: 1* © LVML/ETH & Atelier Girot *2* © Ilmar Hurxkxens Atelier Girot *3-5* © Atelier Girot *6-7* © Christophe Girot Atelier Girot *8-9* © Atelier Girot —*The Poetry of Motion in Architecture: 1* © www.hoberman.com *2-4* © Santiago Calatrava Archives *5-6* © Jörg Hempel *7-8* Quelle: www.cargolifter.com—*Strategise Emotion. Considering Car Design: 1-2* © Chris Bangle Associates S.r.l. *3-4* © BMW AG *5-6* © Chris Bangle Associates S.r.l.

ABBILDUNGSVERZEICHNIS—*Gestalt der Bewegung: 1* aus Zöllner, Frank: Leonardo da Vinci, Sämtliche Gemälde und Zeichnungen. Taschen 2003 *2* aus Quelle: Richard, Ralph: The life and works of John Weaver: An account of his life, writings and theatrical productions, with an annotated reprint of his complete publications. Princeton Book Company 1985 *3* ©1893 Eadweard Muybridge (14699Y U.S. Copyright Office) (expired) *4* http://en.wikipedia.org/wiki/File:The_Horse_in_Motion.jpg *5* Quelle: Marey, E.J.: La méthode graphique. Paris 1878, 281 *6 Mitte und rechts* http://en.wikisource.org/wiki/Popular_Science_Monthly/Volume_6/November_1874/Human_Locomotion *7* Quelle: in: E-J.Marey: Le Mouvement. Paris 1894 *8 links* von Musée Marey, Beaune *8 Mitte und links* http://www.ctie.monash.edu.au/hargrave/marey.html *9* http://www.ctie.monash.edu.au/hargrave/marey.html *10 links* http://de.wikipedia.org/wiki/Eadweard_Muybridge *10 rechts* http://en.wikipedia.org/wiki/Nude_Descending_a_Staircase,_No._2 *11* http://www.rolf-lauter.com *12* http://www.collezioni-f.it/balla.html *14* http://www.e-flux.com/journal/view/219 *16* Theatermuseum München *17* http://ludersocke.blog.de/2009/04/29/theater-film-tanz-gegenseitige-beeinflussung-reform-6029484/ *18* Zentrum für Kunst und Medientechnologie, Deutsches Tanzarchiv Köln, Stiftung Kultur, 1994/1999.—***Mobile und Stabile: 1*** http://kaufmann-mercantile.com/images/alexander-calder-mobile.jpg *2* Fotograf: Csaba Petrik von http://www.midcenturia.com/2011/01/alexander-calders-man-sculpture.html *3* © Kunsthaus Zürich, Vereinigung Züricher Kunstfreunde, aus: Beyeler Museum AG (Hg.): Giacometti. Ostfildern 2009 *4* aus Wilhelm Lehmbruck Museum der Stadt Duisburg (Hg.), Naum Gabo, o.O., o.J. *5* © The Museum of Modern Art, New York Fotograf: Imaging Studio Staff, The Museum of Modern Art, New York, aus: Barry Bergdoll/Terence Riley (Hg.): Mies in Berlin. Ludwig Mies van der Rohe. Die Berliner Jahre. München 2002 *6* © The Museum of Modern Art, New York, Fotograf: Kay Fingerle, aus: Barry Bergdoll/Terence Riley (Hg.): Mies in Berlin. Ludwig Mies van der Rohe. Die Berliner Jahre. München 2002 *7-8* aus Jean-Francois Gonthier (Hg.): Le Corbusier vivant. Paris 1999, Fotograf: Anriet Denis *9-10* Fotograf: Christian Richters in: N.N., „Möbius Haus. Van Berkel und Bos" in: Arch+ 146 (1999)/April. *11* Grafik: Ben van Berkel/Caroline Bos: Christian Marquart: „Oben geht es um die Marke, unten um die Wurst. Rundgang durch das neue Mercedes-Benz-Museum Stuttgart", in: Bauwelt 97 (2006) *12* Fotograf: Christian Richters, aus: Christian Marquart: „Oben geht es um die Marke, unten um die Wurst. Rundgang durch das neue Mercedes-Benz-Museum Stuttgart", in: Bauwelt 97 (2006). *13* aus Kunstmuseum Wolfsburg (Hg): James Turrell. The Wolfsburg Project. Ostfildern 2009, Fotografin: Zooey Braun *14* aus Arch+ 200 (2010), Fotograf: Hisao Suzuki—***Dynamismo der Postindustrie: 1*** http://en.wikipedia.org *2* 2.bp.blogspot.com *3* www.kultur-online.net *4* aus Dinkla, Söke (Hg.): Jenny Holzer. Die Macht des Wortes. / I Can´t Tell You. Ostfildern 2006, Fotograf: Attilio Maranzano *5* aus Dinkla, Söke (Hg.): PubliCity: Constructing the Truth. Kunst im öffentlichen Raum. Nürnberg 2006, Fotograf: Rainer Schlautmann/Stadt Duisburg *6* aus Dinkla, Söke/Janssen, Karl u.a. (Hg.): Ruhrlights: Twilight Zone 2010. Ostfildern 2010, Fotograf: Werner Hannappel/RUHR.2010 *7* aus Dinkla, Söke/Janssen, Karl u.a. (Hg.): Ruhrlights: Twilight Zone 2010. Ostfildern 2010, Fotograf Werner Hannappel/RUHR.2010 *8* Simulation von Heike Mutter und Ulrich Genth/Stadt Duisburg *9* Fotograf Daan de Haan—***Spuren und Artefakte physischer Intelligenz: 1*** Livet, Anne: Contemporary Dance. New York 1978 *2* Bild: Chris Ziegler (Screenshot des Designers) *3* Fotograf: Adriene Hughes *4-5* Das linke und rechte Programmfenster der Software Choreographic Language Agent, Screenshot *6-8* Synchronous Objects Projekt, The Ohio State University and The Forsythe Company—***Die Lesbarkeit der Bewegung: 2*** www.wizspace.co *3-4* www.billbuxton.com *6* nano.xerox.com *7* www.hanksville.org *10* www.reghardware.com *11-12* http://www.gavrila.net/avss2007_cassandra.pdf—***Landschaft in Bewegung: 1*** ©LVML/ETH&Atelier Girot *2* © Ilmar Hurxkxens Atelier Girot *3-5* © Atelier Girot *6-7* © Christophe Girot Atelier Girot *8-9* © Atelier Girot—***Poesie der Bewegung in Architektur: 1*** © www.hoberman.com *2-4* © Santiago Calatrava Archives *5-6* © Jörg Hempel, Fotograf *7-8* Quelle: www.cargolifter.com—***Strategise Emotion. Überlegungen zum Autodesign: 1-2*** © Chris Bangle Associates S.r.l. *3-4* © BMW AG *5-6* © Chris Bangle Associates S.r.l.

© 2011 by jovis Verlag GmbH

Texts by kind permission of the authors.

Pictures by kind permission of the photographers/holders of the picture rights.

All rights reserved.

CONCEPT AND EDITING: **Annett Zinsmeister, Adeline Seidel**

TRANSLATION: **Lucinda Rennison (German–English), Ann**ette Wiethüchter (English–German)

DESIGN AND SETTING: **Adrian Riemann, Marian Rupp, Fabian Schewe** *www.soleils.org*

PRINTING AND BINDING: **fgb. freiburger graphische betriebe**

Bibliographic information published by the Deutsche Nationalbibliothek

The Deutsche Nationalbibliothek lists this publication in the Deutsche Nationalbibliografie; detailed bibliographic data are available on the Internet at *http://dnb.d-nb.de*

Weißenhof-Institut

Staatliche Akademie der Bildenden Künste Stuttgart

Am Weißenhof 1

D-70191 Stuttgart

www.weissenhof-institut.abk-stuttgart.de

jovis Verlag GmbH

Kurfürstenstraße 15/16

10785 Berlin

www.jovis.de

ISBN 978-3-86859-110-1

© 2011 by jovis Verlag GmbH

Das Copyright für die Texte liegt bei den Autoren.

Das Copyright für die Abbildungen liegt bei den Fotografen/Inhabern der Bildrechte.

Alle Rechte vorbehalten.

KONZEPT UND REDAKTION: Annett Zinsmeister, Adeline Seidel
ÜBERSETZUNG: Lucinda Rennison (Deutsch–Englisch), **Ann**ette Wiethüchter (Englisch–Deutsch)
GESTALTUNG UND SATZ: Adrian Riemann, Marian Rupp, Fabian Schewe ➤ *www.soleils.org*
DRUCK UND BINDUNG: fgb. freiburger graphische betriebe

Bibliografische Information der Deutschen Nationalbibliothek
Die Deutsche Nationalbibliothek verzeichnet diese Publikation in der Deutschen Nationalbibliografie;
detaillierte bibliografische Daten sind im Internet über *http://dnb.d-nb.de abrufbar.*

Weißenhof-Institut
Staatliche Akademie der Bildenden Künste Stuttgart
Am Weißenhof 1
D-70191 Stuttgart
www.weissenhof-institut.abk-stuttgart.de

jovis Verlag GmbH
Kurfürstenstraße 15/16
10785 Berlin
www.jovis.de

ISBN 978-3-86859-110-1